PERMANENT INCOME, WEALTH, AND CONSUMPTION

Thomas Mayer

PERMANENT INCOME, WEALTH, AND CONSUMPTION: A Critique of the Permanent Income Theory, the Life-Cycle Hypothesis, and Related Theories

Berkeley   Los Angeles   London

University of California Press

University of California Press
Berkeley and Los Angeles, California
University of California Press, Ltd.
London, England
Copyright © 1972, by
The Regents of the University of California
ISBN: 0-520-02103-7
Library of Congress Catalog Card Number: 71-170721
Printed in the United States of America

To Dorothy

Contents

List of Tables

One of the standard issues in empirical economics in recent years has been the testing of the permanent income theory and the life cycle hypothesis. A vast number of empirical tests of these theories have been published. Unfortunately, these empirical tests did not suffice to clarify the issue. In fact, their very large number combined with the disagreements in their results probably means that the whole subject is as much "up in the air" as it was in the late 1950's. Even an economist who makes a strenuous effort to keep up with empirical macro-economics is unlikely to have read most of these tests, and of those he has read there are probably many which he has not had time to evaluate adequately. As a result of this there is much confusion in the theory of the consumption function. The plethora of conflicting empirical evidence is such that an economist can decide on the basis of personal likes and dislikes whether he wants to accept or reject these "new theories" of the consumption function, and he can then find numerous empirical tests which will support and justify his chosen point of view. This is, of course, the opposite of the way things should be; empirical tests should limit the opinions which people may justifiably hold.

One of the things I have therefore tried to do in this book is to examine carefully the previous empirical tests of the permanent income theory, the life cycle hypothesis, and related theories. I have been concerned not with describing the theories, but rather with evaluating them, and with distilling from this large body of literature a series of confirmed propositions. This has been a challenge because so many tests reach conflicting conclusions. I have therefore tried to see whether it is possible to explain away this apparent conflict and to show that the valid empirical evidence supports with a unified voice certain propositions. The fact that this has been a feasible task suggests that the current status of empirical economics is not as bad as it seems. Although there is much apparent conflict in the evidence cited by various economists, it has been possible, at least in this one case, to eliminate the conflict.

The key to obtaining agreement between the various tests is to notice that most of those tests which are favorable to the permanent income theory and related theories do not even attempt to show that such a theory is *fully* valid. Instead, they show that there is a *tendency* in the direction predicted by this theory. Conversely, those tests which claim to refute the life cycle hypothesis or the permanent income theory do so by showing that these theories are not *fully* valid. The obvious way to synthesize these tests is therefore by saying that these "new theories" of the consumption function are *partially* valid. Such an intermediate position, which for want of a better name I have called the "standard income theory," sounds wishy-washy. To make it a serious contender it has to be quantified.

I have therefore undertaken a series of new tests which are concerned primarily with quantifying this standard income theory. These tests, which make up approximately half the book, are based primarily on household budget data rather than on time series data. In undertaking these tests I have focused on tests based on data sources which have not previously been used in this discussion. Lacking the tools of sophisticated econometricians I have generally used very simple techniques. This book is not for anyone whose main interest is in discovering new econometric techniques.

It gives me great pleasure to acknowledge the large debts I have accumulated to many people and organizations in the years I have worked on this book. I am greatly indebted to those who supplied me with unpublished data: Dr. Heiniger of the (Swiss) Bundesamt für Industrie, Gewerbe und Arbeit; M. Perrot of the Institut National de la Statistique et Etudes Economiques; Mrs. Dorothy Projector, Board of Governors, Federal Reserve System; and Mrs. Reddies and Dr. Martin of the (West German) Statistisches Bundesamt, the Institute of Economics and Statistics of Oxford University, and the Survey Research Center of the University of Michigan.

I am also greatly indebted for that necessary ingredient of empirical research, generous financing, to the National Science Foundation, which has shown great patience with continually postponed completion dates; to the American Philosophical Society, whose kind help allowed me to microfilm and process data used in Chapters 13 and 14; and to the Faculty Research Fund of the University of California, Davis. The University of California computer centers at Davis and at Berkeley kindly provided some free time.

Thomas Cargill, Michael Landsberger, Toshiyuki Mizoguchi, and Julian Simon have read much, or all, of the manuscript, and I am deeply indebted to them for their helpful comments. In addition, I received very helpful comments on earlier versions of certain chapters from W. P. Strassmann (Chapters 1, 10, and 16), Andrzej Brzeski, Allan Meltzer, Richard Peterson, Ramachandra Ramanathan, J. Ernest Tanner and Hal Varian (Chapter 13), Margaret Gordon and Albert Fishlow (Chapter 10), and James Holmes, Jacob Mincer, and Margaret Reid (Chapter 15). None of them are, of course, responsible for remaining errors.

I have been greatly aided by a large group of very capable and devoted research assistants and programmers. Over the years they have included James Brundy, Kelvin Calandri, Geoffrey Carliner, Roozbeh Chubak, Noel Luke, Adil Kanaan, John Lee, Hal Varian (who has contributed Appendix II), and Abdolhossain Zahedani. In addition, Alan Cohn, Dennis Fanucchi, Andrea Harzell, Sukhamay Kundu, Lulu Lin, Anthony Mutsear, Richard Piper, Allan Shapiro, David Vanderford, and Gary Walton assiduously calculated seemingly endless columns of figures. Moreover, dealing as I am with much foreign language material, I am indebted to a whole host of translators. I am also grateful to Mr. Gene Tanke for his careful and patient editorial work.

Chapter 10 appeared, in an earlier version, in the *American Economic Review,* and Chapter 13 in the *Journal of Money, Credit, and Banking.* I am indebted to both for permission to reprint this material. I would also like to record my debt to Princeton University Press for granting permission to quote Milton Friedman's *A Theory of the Consumption Function* numerous times.

Mrs. Mildred Schumway has very ably kept the books on my research grants and related matters. I am indebted to Mrs. Shirley Kelly for typing with great efficiency a manuscript so messy that toward the end, even I could hardly make sense out of it, and to Mrs. Marguerite Crown for retyping seemingly endless revisions.

T. M.

Part One
PRELIMINARIES

INTRODUCTION

This Part consists of two chapters which set the stage for what follows. The first of these chapters discusses the scope of this book as well as some necessary definitions. Chapter 2 provides a brief summary of the theories to be tested. Although some of them, such as Friedman's permanent income theory and the Modigliani-Brumberg-Ando life cycle hypothesis are well known, others, for example, the Pennsylvania School's normal income theory, or the Ball-Drake model are less widely known. Since the focus of this book is on empirical testing rather than on theoretical development, I have confined myself to a brief description of the theories.

One

INTRODUCTION

The theory of the consumption function was changed radically in the mid-1950s with the emergence of "the new theories" of the consumption function—that is, the permanent income theory, the life cycle hypothesis, and related theories.[1] Since then there has grown up a substantial body of literature testing and evaluating these theories. But there is still great disagreement about their validity because nobody has taken the trouble to go through these tests systematically, separating valid from invalid tests, and seeing precisely what the valid tests really show.

In this book I shall attempt to synthesize the results of previously published tests to see if one can explain away the disagreement between those test results which claim to confirm the theory and those which claim to disconfirm it. I shall also present new tests. The purpose of these new tests is to confirm the results which emerged in previous tests and also to make as specific as I can the synthesis which allows one to reconcile the results of previous tests.

In brief, I will try to show that *all* the valid evidence on the new theories of the consumption function—the evidence from previously published tests as well as from the new tests presented here—is consistent with a theory which is intermediate between the more traditional approach to the consumption function and the new theories. Such an intermediate approach accepts the proposition that consumption depends on income of several years and that the marginal propensity to consume is greater for permanent than for transitory income. However, it does not support the claims of the new theories that consumption is proportional to permanent income and that it is independent of transitory income. Nor does it accept the very long lag in the consumption function which supporters of the new theories think they have found. Such

1. The term "new theories" was used in his review article by Michael Farrell ("The New Theories of the Consumption Function," *Economic Journal*, Vol. LXIX, December 1959, pp. 678–96) and has been used by others since then.

an intermediate position may sound vague and "wishy-washy." But in many of the new tests presented below I am more specific and show that the lag in the consumption function is only about half as long as Friedman claims, and that the marginal propensity to consume *permanent* income is somewhat closer to the marginal propensity to consume *measured* income than it is to the permanent income theory's estimate. Thus while my estimates lie in between those of the new theories and the traditional theories, they lie somewhat closer to those of the traditional theories.[2]

To establish such results one must examine *all* the previous tests of the "new theories." There is an unfortunate tendency in economics to disregard this step. Someone presenting a new theory simply runs some tests, and if his theory is confirmed by these tests he treats it as generally validated, despite the fact others have previously confirmed rival theories. Such a way of working is only natural. It is usually much more pleasant to work out one's own tests than to examine carefully other people's work. And it is natural, too, to give much more credence to one's own findings than to other people's. But understandable as it may be, such a procedure is far removed from the standard scientific canon.[3] In the physical sciences such an approach is simply not permitted; if an experimenter obtains results which differ from those obtained by others, he will not expect his theory to be accepted unless he can either show an outright fault in previous experiments or show that his experiment is clearly superior to the previous ones. Yet in economics we persist in piling test upon test in the quaint belief that one's own test—being one's own—obviously deserves more credence than those tests previously published by others.

The outcome of such an egocentric approach is obvious. Old results do not die, nor do they fade away; they are just buried in an outpouring of new research. The result is confusion. There are a vast number of unevaluated tests in the literature, some supporting the permanent income theory, and some rejecting it. This provides an unfortunate amount of freedom; an economist can decide on very casual grounds whether or not he accepts the permanent income theory, and can then buttress his choice by pointing to a set of tests which support his view, whatever it happens to be. This situation is illustrated by the almost scandalous way in which the profession has treated Friedman's tests of the perma-

2. These results are subject to the qualification—discussed below—that I am defining consumption to include the purchase of consumer durables, rather than their use.

3. Lest it be assumed that I claim any moral superiority on this score, I hasten to add that in previous work I have been just as guilty of this practice as others have been.

nent income theory. When Friedman presented his theory, he provided some sixteen tests which confirmed it. Yet economists writing on the permanent income theory have, for the most part, ignored these tests. They have presented new tests and have assumed that if these new tests disconfirm the permanent income theory then the theory is invalidated—even though Friedman's many tests, which they have no reason to reject, confirm it.

At first glance such a procedure may seem justified. It is an old bromide that it takes just one unfavorable piece of evidence ("fact") to disconfirm a theory regardless of how well the theory has performed on other tests. This is an inadequate description of how scientists actually work,[4] and furthermore it is not applicable in a situation where there are only two possibilities—for example, either consumption is proportional to permanent income or it is not. For instance, one of the pieces of evidence used by Friedman is his demonstration that if the permanent income elasticity of consumption were actually less than unity, then we would find a tendency for the distribution of income to become more unequal over time. And since we do not observe such a tendency, the income elasticity of consumption cannot be less than unity.[5] Suppose now that someone undertakes a new test which shows that the income elasticity of consumption is less than unity. This new test alone does not permit us to reject the proposition that the permanent income elasticity of consumption is equal to unity, for the rival proposition that it is less than unity is disconfirmed by Friedman's test. Clearly, this conflict of evidence can be resolved only by critically examining both pieces of evidence.

Moreover, there is another point. The new theories of the consumption function, as well as the traditional theories, are paradigms for which their supporters have provided much empirical evidence. Thus, when a supporter of one of these paradigms is confronted with a new test which claims to contradict his paradigm, he is often ready to reject the new test without much ado because he has the evidence of so many other tests to support his view. Hence, new tests of the permanent income theory or of the life cycle hypothesis are not likely to change many opinions among those already committed. The way to settle the dispute is not merely to undertake new tests, but also to examine critically the evidence previously provided by the supporters and the critics of the new theories.

I have therefore devoted about half of this book to examining previ-

4. See Thomas Kuhn, *The Structure of Scientific Revolutions* (Chicago, University of Chicago Press, 1962).
5. I am using this test only as an illustration of my point; its actual validity is discussed below.

ous tests. In doing so, I have been concerned with evaluating these tests rather than with describing them. Since most of them can be found in readily available sources, there is little purpose in describing them in detail. I tried to provide just enough of a description so that the reader can follow my evaluation.

Such an evaluation of the previous literature must be comprehensive. To examine only a few tests is not sufficient because any test which is omitted may be just the one which provides strong confirmation or disconfirmation of the permanent income theory or a related theory. I therefore intended to cover all the existing tests, but I have not quite succeeded in this. For one thing, I have not been able to locate copies of some unpublished tests. In addition, I had to pass up some Japanese tests because of the language problem. Third, I have not dealt with consumption functions fitted to foreign time series except those which had special relevance for the wealth theories or had been fitted to a cross-section of countries. My lack of familiarity with foreign data would have made any attempt to evaluate all foreign functions very time-consuming. Finally, I am sure that I have inadvertently overlooked some tests. Hence, if the reader notices that I have omitted a certain test, he should interpret this not as an unfavorable reflection on the validity of this test, but rather as a reflection on my own research.[6]

Even so, there are many tests to be covered—many more than I thought there were when I started on this book. Some readers may find this long journey through so many tests tedious. In part for this reason, I have provided at the end of Chapters 3–6 summary tables which list the tests, classify them as valid or invalid, and give a brief indication of what they show. Any reader wishing to skip some of the discussion of these tests, and willing to take my judgment on faith, can simply turn to these tables.

After evaluating the existing tests I present my own tests. I have tried to undertake as varied a set of tests as I could. I very much doubt that it is possible to resolve the debate by any single "crucial experiment." Definitive tests are rare—perhaps even nonexistent—in economics, and it is highly unlikely that as complex an issue as the validity of the permanent income theory could be settled by any single test. Nearly every test one can think of suffers from some weakness, and even if the test procedure is above criticism, one can always criticize—and usually with considerable justification—the underlying data.[7] Hence, the best way of

---

6. Two as yet unpublished manuscripts reached me too late for inclusion. They are A. S. Deaton, "Wealth Effects on Consumption in a Modified Life-Cycle Model," and W. H. Somermeyer and K. van de Rotte, "A Macro-savings Function for the Netherlands, 1949–1966."

7. For example, when confronted with a test using Israeli data which contradict the proportionality hypothesis, Friedman did not abandon this

proceeding is to undertake many tests. If one runs a number of tests and finds that they all agree, then one can accept the result of these tests even if each of them suffers from some different defect. To set this forth more formally, consider a test of the proposition that $A > B$. Suppose that this test does suffer from some defect, but that this defect is not very great. If this test shows that, in fact, $A > B$ then there are two possibilities; either this proposition is true or else the result obtained is due to the defect in the test. Suppose that before looking at this test one assigns an a priori probability of, say 80 percent to $A < B$, and that one assigns an a priori probability of 25 percent to the proposition that the defect of the test is large enough to lead to the wrong result. In this case, when confronted with such a test which shows $A > B$, it is rational to reject the test and to continue to believe that $A < B$. But suppose that there are five such tests and that they each suffer from quite different defects. If all of these five tests, though admittedly defective, agree in showing that $A > B$, then it is rational to reject the hypothesis that $A < B$ even though none of the tests individually would make one do so. This is really nothing new; all it means is that circumstantial evidence can be convincing if there is enough of it.

It may be useful at this point to outline what is to follow. Chapter 2 provides a summary of the various theories to be tested. Chapter 3 starts the evaluation of previous tests with a detailed discussion of the various tests presented by Milton Friedman in his *A Theory of the Consumption Function*. The following three chapters deal with the tests of the permanent income theory undertaken by others. Part III (Chapters 7–9) then deals with numerous consumption functions which have been fitted to aggregate time series. Chapters 7 and 8 subject many of these consumption functions to a simple naïve model test. Chapter 9 then takes the survivors of the naïve model test and examines how they rank when used in a projection test. In addition, Chapter 9 gives the results of using different methods of regressing consumption on income. Part IV (Chapters 10–12) presents a series of tests using as permanent income proxies, occupation, race, and location. The final part then consists of three chapters using budget study data in other tests plus a summary chapter. Chapter 13 deals with a small sample of households for whom income and consumption data are available for five years. Chapter 14 uses a handful of budgets which cover a longer time span.

---

hypothesis but suggested that he would do so only if this test would yield the same result when applied to other data. ("Note on Nissan Liviatan's Paper," in Carl Christ (ed.), *Measurement in Economics; Studies in Mathematical Economics and Econometrics in Honor of Yehuda Grunfeld* (Stanford, Stanford University Press, 1963) p. 63. Similarly, in my discussion below I am rejecting one test, a test which does not fit any known theory of the consumption function, on the grounds that the data are bad.

Chapter 15 then uses data on the net worth of households to test the proportionality hypothesis. The final chapter provides a summary of the results. Appendix I then describes an unsuccessful test. But before proceeding with this material, problems of method and definition must be discussed.

One of the most radical claims of the permanent income theory and of the life cycle hypothesis is that consumption is proportional to permanent income—that is, that the permanent income elasticity of consumption is equal to unity. Although this is the most fascinating hypothesis of the new theories—and one which I have tried to test in numerous ways—it is by no means clear that this hypothesis is really testable with presently available techniques. The only way to test this hypothesis is to compare households with different permanent incomes either at one moment of time (cross-section tests) or over time (time series tests). Such comparisons assume that one can isolate the effects of differences in permanent income. But many other factors, apart from permanent income differences, can affect consumption; and if some of these factors are correlated with permanent income then there is the danger of obtaining a spurious correlation between permanent income and the propensity to consume.

This type of problem is, of course, a frequent one in economics and the way to guard against it is to include such factors as separate variables in the regression, or at least to look at them and see the direction of the bias they introduce. Unfortunately, the necessary data are frequently not available. The variable which is probably the most troublesome in this way is the tastes factor. If differences in the taste for savings are correlated with permanent income, then the usual type of regression we run in economics may attribute to differences in permanent income what is really the effect of differences in tastes.

This is a serious problem because there is some sociological evidence that different income classes do have different tastes for saving. As Pierre Martineau has remarked:

It seems that many economists overlook the possibility of any psychological differences between individuals resulting from different class memberships. It is assumed that a rich man is simply a poor man with more money and that, given the same income, the poor man would behave exactly like the rich man. The *Chicago Tribune* studies crystallized a wealth of evidence from other sources that this is just not so, and that the Lower-Status person is profoundly different in his mode of thinking and his way of handling the world from the Middle-Class individual. . . . Lower-Status people typically explain why one should save—why the act of saving is important. On the other hand, Middle-Class people do not, as if saving is an end-in-itself, the merits of which are obvious and need not be justified. . . . Here are some psychological contrasts between the two different social groups: *Middle Class:* pointed to the future. His viewpoint embraces a longer expanse of time. . . . stresses rationality. . . . Lower status: pointed to the present and past, lives and thinks in short expanses of time. . . . nonrational essentially. . . . very much concerned with security and insecurity.[8]

Since there exists at present no adequate way of measuring tastes, there are only three possible ways of handling this problem. One is to abandon all hope, to conclude that the proportionality hypothesis, at least at present, is not refutable. And since (as will be shown below) there is no valid evidence supporting it either, there is nothing one can say about it. Thus, if one takes this approach, one of the important issues in consumption function theory would have to be shelved until one has a good way of measuring tastes.

The second alternative is to argue that while the taste variable may have *some* effect, its effect is so small that it can be ignored. While this approach is certainly convenient, there is no evidence that it is correct.

But there is still another approach. This is to say that if differences in permanent income are always found in combination with differences in tastes, then let us treat permanent income and tastes as one single variable. This procedure is, of course, most defensible if differences in tastes are themselves caused by changes in permanent income, and if the relationship between permanent incomes and tastes is a stable one.

Fortunately, the fact that one is combining an income and a tastes variable does not reduce the applicability of the new theories to some practical problems; in fact, the opposite is sometimes the case. Thus, consider one of the applications of the permanent income theory discussed by Friedman: evaluating the effect of income redistribution as a way of changing the average propensity to consume.[9] Clearly, what is relevant here is the existence of differences in the average propensity to consume of various permanent income classes, regardless of whether these differences are due to differences in permanent income per se, or to differences in tastes.

The same *may* be true for long-run predictions of the saving-income ratio. If the correlation of savings tastes with permanent income is the same for secular changes in permanent income as it is for cross-section differences in permanent income, then no harm is done, if, in the cross-section data, one has estimated the combined effects of permanent in-

8. "Social Classes and Spending Behavior," reprinted in Martin Grossack (ed.), *Understanding Consumer Behavior* (Boston, Christopher Publishing House, 1964), pp. 134–47. See also Louis Schneider and Sverre Lysgaard, "The Deferred Gratification Pattern," *American Sociological Review*, Vol. 18, April 1953, pp. 142–49, and the literature cited therein.

9. Milton Friedman, *A Theory of the Consumption Function* (Princeton, Princeton University Press, 1957), p. 237.

come and tastes. To be sure, the correlation of permanent incomes and tastes may well be different for secular changes in permanent income than it is in cross-section studies. But there is little reason to think that tastes do not change at all with secular changes in permanent incomes. Hence, even if one could somehow hold tastes constant and estimate the pure relationship between permanent income and the average propensity to consume, this relationship *may* well be a worse guide to the effects of secular income changes than the combined effect of changes in permanent income and in tastes.

I have therefore used cross-section tests, which necessarily combine taste effects with income effects, in my tests of the proportionality hypothesis. This may seem improper since the proportionality hypothesis is formulated in the new theories without explicit reference to tastes. But the adherents of the new theories have implicitly included tastes along with permanent income effects in their own empirical tests and, what is more, they generally do not warn the reader of any potential bias created by the taste effect. Hence, they implicitly combine the direct effect of permanent income, and its indirect effect through taste differences, into one single variable they call the effect of differences in permanent income.[10] Moreover, as already pointed out, when discussing the policy implications of his theory, Friedman did not separate taste effects from income effects either.

So much for the proportionality hypothesis. Another problem of testability arises in connection with Friedman's hypothesis that the marginal propensity to consume transitory income is zero. But since this problem can be discussed best in direct connection with Friedman's theory, I have deferred discussion of it until the next chapter.

Another problem relates to the definition of consumption. The new theories of the consumption function generally define consumption in the "use" sense; that is, they count as consumption not the purchase of consumer goods, but only their actual destruction by use. (In principle this treatment should be extended to all goods; in practice, due to data problems, the adherents of the new theories confine it only to consumer durables.) Therefore, they count as consumption only the purchase of nondurables plus the depreciation on the household's stock of durables. In this book I have *not* done this, but rather have defined consumption in the conventional way as the purchase of consumer goods. To evaluate a theory which defines consumption in one way by tests which define it in another way may seem silly, but there is a good reason for it: the scarcity of data for the "use" concept of consumption. This fact shows up not only here, but also in the work of the adherents of the new

10. This is not true, however, for what I have called below the Pennsylvania School.

theories. They, too, used many tests based on the conventional definition of consumption. In fact, this is the case for the great majority of the tests used by Friedman himself. And, as Friedman has remarked: "I cannot very well accept [a test using the conventional definition of consumption] when it works and reject it when it does not." [11] The adherents of the new theories have essentially used both definitions of consumption, one in the formal exposition of their theories, and the other in much of their testing of these theories. Since I am concerned here with the empirical tests of the theories, my use of the conventional definition of consumption does not really depart very far from practice of the supporters of the new theories.

As mentioned above, my reason for choosing the conventional definition of consumption is mainly that this is the definition for which many more data are available. Household budget surveys, the source of most of my data, do not employ the "use" definition of consumption, and had I decided to work with this definition I could only have employed tests using aggregate time series data.[12] As will be shown in Chapter 9, such tests are hardly conclusive.

11. "Savings and the Balance Sheet," Oxford University Institute of Economics and Statistics, *Bulletin,* Vol. 19, May 1957, p. 126.
12. Some economists have tried to avoid his problem by using nondurable expenditures. But defining consumption as nondurable expenditures does not provide a good proxy for the "use" definition of consumption since it excludes the depreciation of the household's stock of durables. As a rough approximation, one can assume that the household's stock of durables is constant—that is, that depreciation is equal to new purchases. If this is even approximately so, then the conventional definition of consumption provides a better estimate of the "use" definition of consumption than does the definition of consumption as nondurable consumption. For any test of the proportionality hypothesis the conventional definition is, therefore, probably substantially superior to the "nondurables" definition of consumption. However, for testing the hypothesis that consumption out of transitory income is zero, the nondurables definition may be better. This is so because depreciation of a household's stock of durables *may* bear little relation to its transitory income, so that the marginal propensity to consume transitory income through depreciation *may* be close to zero. Hence for the marginal propensity to consume transitory income, the use definition of consumption is perhaps approximated better by the nondurables definition than by the conventional definition. But the superiority of the nondurables definition on this score is not very important, for as will be shown below, the hypothesis that the marginal propensity to consume transitory income is zero is not really testable. Turning to the third hypothesis of the new theories, the lag hypothesis, the nondurables definitions, like the conventional definition, is bad because nondurable consumpion may have a different lag than use consumption. (It is not true, incidentally, that nondurable consumption necessarily has a shorter lag than total use consumption. One of the important items of nondurable consumption, rent, presumably has a long adjustment lag.)

In any case, I believe that little is lost by using the conventional definition of consumption. The permanent income theory claims that when consumption is defined in the "use" sense, then the permanent income elasticity of consumption is unity and the transitory income elasticity of consumption is zero. A definition which makes important parameters equal to unity and zero is convenient, and if the permanent income theory were actually correct, then the "use" definition of consumption might be the better one. But, as will be shown below, even for the "use" definition of consumption, there is no evidence that it is indeed valid.

Quite apart from the new consumption function theories, the "use" definition of consumption is frequently considered to be superior to the conventional definition because it corresponds more precisely to the meaning attached to consumption in economic theory.[13] This idea is certainly true as far as it goes, but it neglects the fact that the "use" definition is still very far from the theoretically correct one. One reason for this is that to apply the "use" definition of consumption correctly, it is not sufficient to subtract from total consumption expenditures on consumer durables as defined in the data. One would have to subtract certain semi-durables and even some nondurable goods and services.[14] The data necessary to do this are generally not available. Second, the "use" definition of consumption ignores the fact that certain consumer expenditures, such as some expenditures on education, should not be included in consumption. Third, intergenerational transfers create a problem, one which is almost unmanageable on an empirical level. Insofar as families expect their children to care for them later in life, some of their expenditures on children should be treated as saving rather than as consumption.[15] And similarly some of the expenditures which children undertake on behalf of their parents should be considered as repayments of debts, that is, as saving.[16] Thus, even if one measures consumption in accordance with the "use" definition, the

13. Moreover, households may *think* of their durable purchases not as consumption but as saving.

14. On services as durables, see Milton Friedman, *The Optimum Quantity of Money* (Chicago, Aldine Publishing Co., 1969), p. 49.

15. Thus Friedman has argued that expenditure on children is part of saving. "Reply to Comments on 'A Theory of the Consumption Function,'" in Lincoln Clark (ed.), *Consumer Behavior* (New York, Harper and Brothers, 1958), Vol. 3, p. 463.

16. Moreover, there is the fact that our household data do not include capital gains and gifts in income. Hence, if consumption is derived by subtracting saving from income, as is frequently the case, for some households consumption is seriously overstated. (And since households receiving capital gains tend to be high-income households, this overstatement may create a serious bias.)

resulting data are far removed from what is called consumption in economic theory. Employment of the "use" definition in place of the conventional definition moves one only part of the way toward the "correct" definition.

To be sure, half a loaf is better than none, and if the "use" definition did not suffer from any disadvantages, it would, despite the above short-comings, be superior to the conventional definition. But the "use" definition does in fact have serious shortcomings. One obvious one, already discussed, is the absence of household data. But even if the data were available, one might still prefer the conventional definition of consumption. The conventional definition relates consumption to actual expenditures, and so it relates directly to the demand for labor. This makes it useful for many practical macroeconomic problems. Thus, when Friedman came to discuss the practical implications of his theory, these turned out to be situations in which the conventional definition of saving is generally more relevant than the "use" definition.[17]

On the other hand, it must be admitted there is something to be said for the "use" definition, too. If one is concerned with measuring consumption from a welfare point of view then the "use" definition is superior to the conventional definition.[18]

Finally, there is another point. This is that the adherents of the new consumption function theories, even when they have employed the "use" definition of consumption in their empirical work, have not been really consistent. If one includes the depreciation of durables in consumption, then one should also include the services which the household obtains from its stock of durables in income. None of them have done this. Hence, when they have regressed "use" consumption on conventionally measured income, they have employed neither the "use" definition nor the conventional definition in a logically consistent manner, but have really worked with a peculiar hybrid which lacks any theoretical significance.

I hope that this has convinced the reader that it is legitimate to follow Friedman's usual procedure and to test the new consumption function theories by data employing the conventional definition. If not, the reader can look upon the tests presented below as tests not of the permanent income theory and life cycle hypothesis per se, but as tests of a series of propositions which differ from these theories in their definition

17. Milton Friedman, *A Theory of the Consumption Function, op. cit.,* pp. 233–39.

18. Another issue is raised by the practical problem of predicting consumption expenditures. It may well be the case that one can predict consumption better by predicting durable and nondurable expenditures separately. But this procedure does not correspond to the use definition of consumption since it leaves out depreciation on durables.

of consumption. Since these propositions are important ones—regardless of whether or not one treats them as parts of the new consumption function theories—they are worth testing in any case. Moreover, insofar as my results are invalid as tests of the new consumption function theories, this applies only to the new tests I present below. In my evaluation of the previous tests, I am using the same consumption concept used originally in these tests. Hence, one of my conclusions—that there is no evidence at all supporting the full permanent income theory and life cycle hypothesis—is unaffected by this definitional problem.

Although there is much to be said against coining new terms, it is worthwhile to develop a few special terms to save verbiage in what follows. I will use the phrase, "measured income theories" to denote the absolute income theory and the relative income theory.[19] I will use the term "wealth theories" not only as a generic term to refer to Friedman's theory but also as a broader term to include the life cycle hypothesis and the rest.[20] The term "strict or full permanent income theory" will designate Friedman's theory in distinction to the standard income theory or the life cycle hypothesis. Finally, unless otherwise specified, when referring to "wealth," I will mean nonhuman wealth only.

19. Above I have referred to these theories as "traditional theories." The term "measured income theories" is better since the term "traditional theories" could also be taken to mean the theory developed by Irving Fisher, a theory which in many ways is the same as the permanent income theory. I have used the designation "measured income theories" because in contrast to the permanent income approach, they assume that consumption is a function of measured income.

20. I am using the term "wealth theories" because the use of wealth either directly, as in the life cycle hypothesis, or indirectly, as in the permanent income theory, is really the hallmark of the new theories.

Two

THE THEORIES

Before taking up the various tests of the permanent income approach, it is necessary to be clear about what is being tested. This chapter gives a brief description of the various theories encompassed by the term "wealth theories." Since I am concerned in this book with empirical tests I will describe these theories only to the extent needed to understand the empirical tests and will not take up the refinements which have appeared in the literature in recent years, often in connection with growth models. But to see these theories in the proper context, one must first look at their background—that is, at the theories prevailing at the time when the permanent income approach was developed.

Previous Theories

As is so frequently the case, a discussion of a modern economic theory should start with the work of Irving Fisher. Fisher described the factors causing households to save in the context of a multi-period model.[1] Two characteristics of Fisher's model relate it to the modern wealth theories. One is Fisher's explicit focus on the rationality of savings decisions. Fisher's households save purposefully. This contrasts with the subsequent treatment of saving by Keynes. The second way in which Fisher's theory resembles the contemporary wealth theories is that Fisher explicitly used a multi-period model and showed no sympathy for the notion that saving can be explained by current income alone.

Although Fisher's work is sometimes looked upon as the fountainhead of the permanent income theory, what Fisher taught was not the strict permanent income theory. He strongly rejected one of its important components, the proportionality hypothesis:

1. Irving Fisher, *The Theory of Interest* (New York, Augustus Kelley, 1961). For a comparison of Fisher's and Marshall's approach to the theory of saving, see Sten Thore, "Marshallian Saving Theory," *Statsøkonomisk Tidsskrift*, Vol. 77, September 1963, pp. 143–64.

In general, it may be said that, other things being equal, the smaller the income, the higher the preference for present over future income. . . . It is true, of course, that a permanently small income implies a keen appreciation of future wants as well as of immediate wants. . . . This influence of poverty is partly rational, because of the importance, by supplying present needs of keeping up the continuity of life and thus maintaining the ability to cope with the future; and partly irrational, because the pressure of present needs blinds a person to the future.[2]

Fisher's discussion of saving was more or less brushed aside by the Keynesian revolution. To be sure, in the *General Theory* Keynes did devote three pages to a discussion of savings motives, but the main thrust of Keynesian theory dealt with consumption rather than with saving. Hence, there is a tendency in the Keynesian literature to treat saving as a residual rather than as something to be explained by a multi-period model. And if one focuses on consumption rather than on saving then one is much less likely to concern oneself with the problem of the relevant time period than if one focuses on saving. This is so because although the motives for saving necessarily involve more than one period, the motives for consumption relate to the current period. By stressing consumption rather than saving, Keynes set the stage for ignoring the question of the time period. Hence, economists tended to follow the line of least resistance by using the unit of time in which the data happen to come—usually a year.

Although Keynes did not stress the savings motives discussed by Fisher, he did follow Fisher in rejecting the proportionality hypothesis:

The fundamental psychological law upon which we are entitled to depend with great confidence both a priori from our knowledge of human nature and from the detailed facts of experience, is that men are disposed, as a rule and on the average, to increase their consumption as their income increases, but not by as much as the increase in their income. . . . This is especially the case when we have short periods in view, as in the case of so-called cyclical fluctuations of employment during which habits, as distinct from more permanent psychological propensities are not given time enough to adapt themselves to changed objective circumstances. For a man's habitual standard of life usually has the first claim on his income, and he is apt to save the difference which discovers itself between his actual income and the expense of his habitual standard.[3]

While Keynes' statement that past consumption habits affect current consumption may, at first glance, suggest something fairly similar to the permanent income theory, it is really a quite different theory, a habit persistence theory. It is previous consumption rather than long

2. *Ibid.*, p. 72.
3. *The General Theory of Employment, Interest and Money* (New York, Harcourt Brace, 1936), pp. 96–97.

run income which Keynes had in mind. He was most explicit on this point.[4]

But while the absolute income theory, as Keynes' formulation came to be called, differs fundamentally both from the preceding theory of Fisher and from the subsequent permanent income theory, Keynes did employ certain elements of the wealth theories. One is that he considered changes in the stock of wealth to have an important effect on consumption.[5] Another is that he thought the propensity to consume to be much less for transitory income ("windfalls") than for permanent income.[6] Although these qualifications blur the sharp edges of the contrast between the absolute income theory and the permanent income approach, there does remain the fact that Keynes brushed aside, without much ado, the logically compelling analysis of Fisher. Excessive regard for the writings of other economists is hardly a characteristic of the *General Theory*.

In the 1940s the credibility of the absolute income theory was severely challenged by two developments; one was the failure of the theory's forecasts of postwar consumption, and the other was Kuznets' demonstration that the average propensity to consume had not risen secularly. These developments set the stage for the emergence of the relative income theory, which reached its full formulation in the work of Franco Modigliani and James Duesenberry.[7]

The relative income theory treats the proportionality hypothesis in a quite different way from Fisher and Keynes. It does *not* assume that a low income, in and of itself, makes households less likely to save. If all households lived in a vacuum, then their average propensities to consume would be independent of their mean incomes. But, house-

4. In discussing "changes in expectations of the relation between the present and the future level of income," Keynes wrote, "we must catalogue this factor for the sake of formal completeness. But whilst it may affect considerably a particular individual's propensity to consume, it is likely to average out for the community as a whole. Moreover, it is a matter about which there is, as a rule, too much uncertainty for it to exert much influence." *Ibid.*, p. 95.

5. See Boris Pesek and Thomas Saving, *Money, Wealth and Economic Theory* (New York, Macmillan Co., 1967), Chapter 1.

6. *Op. cit.*, p. 58.

7. Franco Modigliani, "Fluctuations in the Saving-Income Ratio: A Problem in Economic Forecasting," in Conference on Research in Income and Wealth, *Studies in Income and Wealth*, Vol. 11 (New York, National Bureau of Economic Research, 1949); James Duesenberry, *Income, Saving and the Theory of Consumer Behavior* (Cambridge, Harvard University Press, 1949). My discussion of the relative income theory is based on Duesenberry's work because Modigiliani, being primarily concerned with an empirical test, did not spell out his underlying theory.

holds are influenced by the consumption of other households. Hence, at any one moment of time, low income households—trying to keep up with their neighbors—have a higher average propensity to consume than do high income households. Since the higher propensity to consume of low income households results only from an emulation effect, there is no reason to expect the average propensity to consume to fall as income rises secularly. But households are not simply comparing themselves to other households; they are also comparing their current consumption with their previous consumption level, more specifically with the consumption level they achieved at their last income peak. Hence, the average propensity to consume falls in upswings and rises in recessions.

This theory, too, bears some similarities to the wealth theories. First, it agrees with the permanent income theory in rejecting Fisher's and Keynes' hypothesis that the lower a household's income, the more intensely does it feel current wants relative to future wants. Hence, in their explanation of the secular stability of the saving-income ratio, there is no real difference between the relative income theory and the permanent income theory. Instead, the difference between the two theories shows up primarily in a cross-section context. If one compares at any one moment of time households with different permanent incomes, then the relative income theory asserts—and the permanent income theory denies—that the higher permanent income households have the lower average propensity to consume. One can therefore look upon the relative income theory as a theory which modifies the permanent income theory by introducing an emulation effect, an effect which negates the proportionality hypothesis. Conversely, one can look upon the permanent income theory as a naïve model theory which asserts that there is no systematic relationship between a household's relative income and its propensity to consume. The relative income theory, by contrast, is a theory which attempts to improve on such a naïve model by adding an emulation effect.

Apart from the proportionality hypothesis the relative income theory and the permanent income approach differ in the lag mechanism they use. The relative income theory is a habit persistence theory—that is, a theory in which consumption depends upon the household's memory of previous consumption levels.[8] Expected future income plays no role in this theory. In the permanent income theory, on the other hand,

---

8. The relative income theory is, of course, just one of a number of habit persistence theories. Another well-known one is that of T. M. Brown, "Habit Persistence and Lags in Consumer Behavior," *Econometrica*, Vol. 20, July 1952, pp. 355–71.

households have no difficulty in changing their past consumption habits —in principle (abstracting from uncertainty and capital rationing) a dollar of discounted future income may be just as important as a dollar of past or present income.[9] This difference about the role of future income is a much more important distinction between the two theories than is the fact that the relative income theory uses as the lagged variable only past peak income whereas the permanent income theory uses a distributed lag. In fact, Duesenberry has now accepted a distributed lag formulation.[10] Thus, the two main differences between the relative income theory and the permanent income theory are (1) the validity of proportionality hypothesis in a cross-section context, and (2) the underlying mechanism responsible for the lag, that is, habit persistence vs. rational utility maximization. The particular specification of the lag is a less important issue.

Despite these differences it is often not easy to distinguish between the empirical implication of these two theories. In many cases they have similar implications so that it is hard to find feasible empirical tests which distinguish between them. Indeed, this is one of the biggest difficulties in testing the permanent income theory.

Part, but only a part, of this problem is conceptual. Sometimes the empirical observations explained by the permanent income theory can also, with some effort, be explained by the relative income theory. Yet in some of these cases the explanation of the observed phenomena, while clear and obvious from a permanent income theory standpoint, is not at all clear and obvious if one starts out from the relative income theory. Someone familiar with the permanent income theory can adapt his explanation to fit the relative income theory, but it is probable that

9. To be sure, Margaret Reid has pointed out that a habit persistence effect is not inconsistent with the permanent income theory, but it is not itself a part of this theory. *Housing and Income* (Chicago, University of Chicago Press, 1962), p. 72.

10. Duesenberry has stated that the use of current income and lagged consumption (the Koyck-Nerlove regression) in the place of current and past peak incomes gives "equally satisfactory empirical results." Moreover, this formulation "has certain analytical advantages and it seems reasonable to make consumption depend upon a moving average of past incomes rather than on the income of a single past year." *Business Cycles and Economic Growth* (New York, McGraw-Hill, 1958), pp. 177–78. In any case, Duesenberry's original formulation using past peak incomes is not useful for postwar data, because due to the mildness of cycles in disposable personal income, the past peak of income occurs generally in the immediately previous year. Hence the relative income theory equation cannot be adequately distinguished in this way from an absolute income theory using the incomes of two years.

someone who does not know the permanent income theory would not be able to explain the observation with the help of the relative income theory. Since a theory is a way of organizing thought, as well as a set of specific propositions, I have, rather arbitrarily, treated such cases as confirming the permanent income theory. To be sure, the question whether the relative income theory can explain some empirical observation then becomes a matter of judgment rather than a hard and fast fact, but the use of personal judgment is not unusual in this sort of work.

The Emergence of the Wealth Approach

While the wealth approach finds its fullest expression in the writings of Brumberg and Modigliani and Friedman, the underlying ideas occurred also to a number of other economists.[11] Indeed, the wealth approach was very much in the air in the 1940s and 1950s. While such conjectures in intellectual history are usually dangerous, it seems to me that there were a number of factors responsible for this. One was the greater availability of budget studies and the substantial effort which went into analyzing and using these data. Economists working with these data were confronted by the fact that in each year the lowest income class dissaved substantially. Obviously this could hardly represent a stable situation for these households, and it had to be explained by the fact that from one year to the next many households shifted between income classes.[12] Such "transients" created a bothersome problem for anyone trying to use these budget data to explain household behavior. However, most economists treated the problem created by these transients as merely a nuisance responsible for some biases in their results rather than as the centerpiece for a new theory of the consumption function.[13]

Another factor which may have contributed to the growth of permanent income ideas was the recognition of the great pervasiveness of the "regression toward the mean" phenomenon. In 1945 Friedman and Kuznets had demonstrated that the incomes of independent professionals showed a definite regression toward the mean, thus focusing the pro-

11. My purpose in this section is to give the flavor of some of the research which preceded the publication of the full-fledged versions of the wealth theories rather than to allocate credit among the various developers.

12. To be sure, this fact had been noted earlier. The first instance I have come across was in 1902: Massachusetts, Bureau of Statistics of Labor, *Thirty-second Annual Report* (Boston, 1902), pp. 303–6.

13. For example, in 1951 I started (but never completed) a paper arguing that the usual tax burden studies overstate the regressivity of a sales tax because they fail to make an allowance for transients. However, I was not farsighted enough to go beyond this small point and to grasp the permanent income approach per se.

fession's attention on income fluctuations.[14] In addition, the idea that consumption may depend, in part, on the incomes of years other than the current year was gaining more adherents; it was firmly embedded in the relative income theory and, in addition, was used independently of that theory.[15] Finally, there was the very important fact that Kuznets had shown that the average propensity to consume had not fallen over time. While this fact could, of course, be explained by the relative income theory, it probably made most economists more receptive to a new approach to the consumption function.

Accordingly, we find a number of economists in these years stating permanent income theory ideas. For example, as early as 1943 Kuznets wrote:

The outlay of a family unit . . . during a given year (month, week, etc.) . . . may well be affected by its income over a much longer interval. The composition, absolute and relative, of a family's budget and its other activities are affected by receipts not only in a given year but also in preceding years and perhaps also by those expected in the immediate future. . . . This statement becomes more self-evident when the erratic and temporary variable character of some income flows is considered. . . . Can anyone seriously contend that an income of only $800 in a given year properly measures the effect of income upon the outlay, political views, or welfare of an entrepreneurial family that has been accustomed to an annual average income of some $5,000 for two decades? Or that the effects of this $800 income are similar to those of a family that has been accustomed to an $800 annual income? . . . The entrepreneurial family could not maintain its usual standard of living on $800, while the other could.[16]

In 1947 William Vickrey suggested that, due to the fluctuations of incomes, it would be better in expenditure studies to classify families by total expenditure levels rather than by income. In his view:

The distortions produced by using annual income as a basis for classification are moderately important when the distribution of income is considered, and extremely serious when savings and expenditure patterns are considered and an attempt is made to derive a propensity to con-

14. *Income from Independent Professional Practices* (New York, National Bureau of Economic Research, 1945).

15. See, for example, Ruth Mack, "The Direction of Change in Income and the Consumption Function," *Review of Economics and Statistics,* Vol. XXX, November 1948, pp. 239–58.

16. "The Why and How of Distribution of Income by Size," in Conference on Research in Income and Wealth, *Studies in Income and Wealth,* Vol. 5, *Income Size Distributions in the United States,* Part 1 (New York, National Bureau of Economic Research, 1943), p. 26. As is discussed in Chapter 11, in the same year Richard Sterner explained differences in the Negro-White savings ratio partly by invoking the difference between permanent and transitory income in the same way as was later done by Friedman.

sume function. . . . *The usual figures on the concentration of savings greatly overstate the savings of persons at the upper economic levels, and marginal propensity to consume figures are generally too low.*[17]

In the same year Dorothy Brady and Rose Friedman wrote:

Inasmuch as the farm families are entirely in the entrepreneurial group, it is not unreasonable to assume that the year to year fluctuations in the income of the individual families are greater for farm than for nonfarm families. Expenditures and savings are without doubt dependent upon the expectation of a continuation of a given level of income. . . . In other words, were the data to show average savings in relation to average income for some period, say four or five years, the savings of farm families would not differ so much from the level characteristic of non-farm families.[18]

Around the same time Frank Hanna suggested:

The manner in which an individual's or a family's income changes from year to year may have an important bearing upon its economic behavior. Will a family that has enjoyed an annual income of $20,000–25,000 for several years react to an annual income of $3,500 in the same way as a family that has never before received so much? . . . The expenditure patterns of three families in the $3,500–3,600 income group may differ markedly according to whether they had received more or less, or approximately the same amount the preceding year. And perhaps, they will vary also with what the families expect to receive in the following years.[19]

One of the very important economists contributing to the development of the permanent income theory was Margaret Reid.[20] She distinguished clearly between permanent and measured income as follows:

If expenditure curves were available from classifications by what families regard as the permanent component of their incomes, it might be possible to isolate forth short and long runs effects of income change. . . . Without a suitable measure of the permanent component of income it is impossible to measure the effect of income on differences in expendi-

17. "Resource Distribution Patterns and the Classification of Families," in Conference on Research in Income and Wealth, *Studies in Income and Wealth*, Vol. 10 (New York, National Bureau of Economic Research, 1947), pp. 273–74 (italics added).
18. "Savings and the Income Distribution," in Conference on Research in Income and Wealth, *Studies in Income and Wealth*, Vol. 10, *ibid.*, p. 262.
19. "The Accounting Period and the Distribution of Income," in Conference on Research in Income and Wealth, *Studies in Income and Wealth*, Vol. 9, *Analysis of Wisconsin Income* (New York, National Bureau of Economic Research, 1948), p. 156.
20. As Friedman pointed out in the preface to *A Theory of the Consumption Function*, it was Miss Reid who urged him to write the book. In fact, Friedman referred to the book as being "in essential respects a joint product" of a group consisting of Dorothy Brandy, Rose Friedman, Margaret Reid, and himself (p. ix)

tures among families at a given time or their response to income change when it does occur.[21]

Moreover, Miss Reid is the author of a very important early test of the permanent income theory.[22] Although she did not publish this test herself, it was cited by Modigliani and Brumberg as well as by Friedman in their publications.[23]

Last, but by no means least, there is the remarkable work of Sir Roy Harrod, who perhaps can lay valid claim to being an originator of the life cycle approach rather than merely an anticipator of it. In 1948, in his famous *Towards a Dynamic Economics,* Harrod presented a theory of saving which quite explicitly used a multi-period framework.[24] In this theory households save in part to leave an estate, but more importantly they save to take care of their years of retirement. This "hump" saving, as Harrod called it, is zero in a stationary economy, since the dissaving of old households just cancels the positive saving of younger households. But in any economy in which population or productivity are growing hump saving is positive. This theory, which received little attention for many years—perhaps because it was so much in advance of its time—has since been revived by Franco Modigliani as a version of the life cycle hypothesis.

While a number of economists were stressing the fact that consumption depends on the income of more than one year, other economists were busy introducing wealth into the consumption function. As already pointed out, this started with Keynes and was developed further by Pigou and many other economists such as Gardner Ackley and James Tobin. To some extent their theories could be considered as part of the "wealth theories." However, one must draw a line of demarcation somewhere, and I will not discuss these approaches here because they merely added a wealth variable to the consumption func-

21. "Effect of Income Concept upon Expenditure Curves of Farm Families," in Conference on Research in Income and Wealth, *Studies in Income and Wealth,* Vol. 15 (New York, National Bureau of Economic Research, 1952), pp. 146–47.

22. "The Relation of the Within-Group Transitory Component of Income to the Income Elasticity of Family Expenditures," unpublished manuscript.

23. Franco Modigliani and Richard Brumberg, "Utility Analysis and the Consumption Function: An Interpretation of Cross-Section Data," in Kenneth Kurihara, *Post-Keynesian Economics* (London, George Allen and Unwin, 1955), pp. 419–21. Milton Friedman, *A Theory of the Consumption Function* (Princeton, Princeton University Press, 1957), pp. 191–94.

24. (London, Macmillan and Co., 1948), pp. 35–62. Harrod was not the first to note the effect of age on saving. Phelps has pointed to Cassel as showing the effect of age on saving ("Population Increase," *Canadian Journal of Economics,* Vol. 1, August 1968, p. 499), and the idea was much discussed in the stagnation thesis debate of the late 1930s and the 1940s. However, Harrod brought out the great importance of hump saving.

tion without integrating it into a complete wealth theory of the consumption function.

Hamburger's Theory

Although the wealth theories of the consumption function are generally associated with the names of Friedman, Modigliani, Brumberg, and Ando, the credit for presenting the first complete version of the wealth theories belongs to William Hamburger.[25] Hamburger's theory contains all the hallmarks of the full-scale wealth theories. Thus, he criticized contemporary consumption function studies for ignoring the fact that saving is done for future consumptions. In his model the household is quite explicitly choosing its consumption stream to maximize utility over time. Moreover, he introduced the various concepts which were later used by Friedman and Modigliani and associates—human wealth, nonhuman wealth, and expected income. In addition, he worked with the "use" concept of consumption. Thus, he made "use" consumption a function of the wage rate, total wealth, per capita wealth, the average wage rate, and possibly of per capita consumption.[26]

Hamburger tested his hypothesis by time series regression. For time series regression he used the proportionality hypothesis. However, for a cross-section comparison of households with different levels of income and wealth, he allowed for the *possibility* that, because of Duesenberry's emulation effect, the proportionality hypothesis might not hold. Hamburger's theory, like the permanent income theory but unlike the life cycle hypothesis, allows for an estate motive, and Hamburger treated this estate motive with greater care than did the other proponents of the wealth theory.[27]

The Life Cycle Hypothesis

The life cycle hypothesis,[28] developed and tested by Richard Brumberg, Franco Modigliani, and Albert Ando, is one of the two best known

25. Hamburger developed his theory in his dissertation, "Consumption and Wealth" (University of Chicago, 1951), and published it in two papers, "The Determinants of Aggregate Consumption," *Review of Economic Studies*, Vol. XXII, No. 57, pp. 23–34, and "The Relation of Consumption to Wealth and the Wage Rate," *Econometrica*, Vol. XXIII, January 1955, pp. 1–17.

26. "Consumption and Wealth," *op. cit.* The reason Hamburger included per capita wealth and the average wage rate in the consumption function is that these variables are proxies for the income of potential heirs and hence affect the bequest motive for saving.

27. In the following chapters, I have not dealt directly with Hamburger's test. This is due to data problems rather than to any weakness of his theory.

28. In talking of the permanent income *theory* and the life cycle *hypothesis* I am merely following conventional terminology, and do not wish to suggest that the epistomological standing of these two theories differs in any way.

versions of the "new" theories of the consumption function.[29] It breaks fundamentally with the measured income theories by going back, in a Fisherian manner, to the basic theory of consumer behavior:

A really important lesson can be learned by taking a fresh look at the traditional theory of the household; according to this theory there need not be any close and simple relation between consumption in a given short period and income in the same period. The rate of consumption in any given period is a facet of a plan which extends over the balance of the individual's life, while the income accruing within the same period is but one element which contributes to the shaping of such a plan. This lesson seems to have been largely lost in much of the empirically oriented discussion of recent years, in the course of which an overwhelming stress has been placed on the role of current income or of income during a short interval centering on the corresponding consumption interval, almost to the exclusion of any other variable.[30]

Far from stressing only the current period's consumption, Modigliani, Brumberg, and Ando explicitly included future as well as current consumption in their utility function. They assumed that the individual maximizes his utility function "subject to the resources available to him, his resources being the sum of current and discounted future earnings over his lifetime and his current net worth. As a result of this maximization the current consumption of the individual can be expressed

29. The sources for the life cycle hypothesis are: Richard Brumberg, "Utility Analysis and Aggregate Consumption Functions: An Empirical Test and Its Meaning," unpublished dissertation, Johns Hopkins University, 1953; Brumberg's posthumous "An Approximation to the Aggregate Savings Function," *Economic Journal*, Vol. XLVI, March 1956, pp. 66–72; Franco Modigliani and Richard Brumberg, "Utility Analysis and Aggregate Consumption Functions: An Attempt at Integration," (unpublished manuscript), 1952; Franco Modigliani and Richard Brumberg, "Utility Analysis and the Consumption Function: An Interpretation of Cross-Section Data," in Kenneth Kurihara, *Post Keynesian Economics* (Brunswick, N.J., Rutgers University Press, 1954), pp. 388–436; Franco Modigliani and Albert Ando, "Tests of the Life Cycle Hypothesis of Savings," Oxford University, Institute of Economics and Statistics, *Bulletin*, Vol. 19, May 1957, pp. 99–124; "The 'Permanent Income' and 'Life Cycle' Hypothesis of Saving Behavior: Comparison and Tests," in Irwin Friend and Robert Jones (eds.), *Consumption and Saving*, (Philadelphia, University of Pennsylvania Press, 1960), Vol. 2, pp. 49–174; and their "The 'Life Cycle' Hypothesis of Saving," *American Economic Review*, Vol. LIII, March 1963, pp. 55–84; Franco Modigliani, "The Life Cycle Hypothesis of Saving, The Demand for Wealth and the Supply of Capital," *Social Research*, Vol. 33, Summer 1966, pp. 160–217; and "The Life Cycle Hypothesis of Saving and Intercountry Differences in the Saving Ratio," in W. Eltis, M. Scott and J. Wolfe (eds.), *Induction, Growth and Trade, Essays in Honor of Sir Roy Harrod* (Oxford, Clarendon Press, 1970), pp. 197–225.

30. Franco Modigliani and Richard Brumberg, "Utility Analysis and the Consumption Function: An Interpretation of Cross-Section Data," *op. cit.*, pp. 391–92.

as a function of his resources and the rate of return on capital with parameters depending on age." [31]

So far the theory is quite general. But the life cycle theorists then made it more specific by adding two assumptions. One of these is the absence of an estate motive so that households save only for the sake of consuming later in their lifespan, but not for the sake of passing wealth on to their heirs.[32] The second assumption is the proportionality hypothesis—that is, that contrary to the measured income theories the allocation of consumption over time is independent of the level of income. This assumption is justified by Modigliani and Brumberg as follows:

Suppose that, in the expectation that his total resources would amount to v_t, and with a given interest rate, our individual had decided to distribute his consumption according to the pattern represented by $\bar{c}_r$. Suppose further that, before carrying out his plan, he is led to expect that his resources will amount not to v_t but, say to $v_t + \Delta v_t$. Should we then expect him to allocate the additional income to increase consumption in any specific period of his remaining life (e.g., his early years, or his late years, or his middle years), relative to all other periods, or can we expect him to allocate it so as to increase all consumptions roughly in the same proportion?

We are inclined to feel that the second alternative is fairly reasonable; or, at any rate, we are unable to think of any systematic factor that would tend to favor any particular period relative to any other. And for this reason we are willing to assume that the second answer, even if it is not true for every individual, is true on the average.[33]

The life cycle theorists do not consider these two assumptions as really basic to their approach, and do not hold them very firmly. As far as the proportionality hypothesis is concerned, the passage just quoted is certainly far from being dogmatic. Elsewhere Modigliani and Ando wrote that, while the proportionality hypothesis is "in a very real sense the essence of the Friedman model," for the life cycle hypothesis, it is "less essential," and "could be relaxed by making explicit allowance for an inheritance motive." Relaxing this assumption would have the effect of "reducing, but not destroying altogether the empirical content" of the life cycle hypothesis.[34]

31. Albert Ando and Franco Modigliani, "The 'Life Cycle' Hypothesis of Saving," *op. cit.*, p. 56.

32. As Modigliani and Brumberg pointed out, once uncertainty is introduced into the model there is an additional motive, the precautionary motive for saving. However, they felt that the introduction of uncertainty makes no material difference for their theory.

33. "Utility Analysis and the Consumption Function: An Interpretation of Cross-Section Data," *op. cit.*, p. 395.

34. "The 'Permanent Income' and 'Life Cycle' Hypothesis of Saving Behavior: Comparison and Tests," *op. cit.*, p. 76. I am not at all sure that

The assumption that there is no estate motive for saving is also not critical, but is merely a simplifying assumption:

It has a good deal of a priori plausibility within the range of incomes that are adequately covered by most family budget studies, but we are ready to concede that it is less plausible as a general feature of saving behavior. It is, therefore, important to stress that what gives theoretical as well as empirical content to the M-B-A model is not the absence of an estate motive, but the notion of life planning plus the postulate that. . . . [the propensity to consume total resources] is uncorrelated with lifetime consumption.[35]

In an earlier study, Modigliani and Brumberg had pointed out that one can relax the assumption of no bequests and instead make "either of two more realistic alternative assumptions." [36] One is that planned bequests are proportional to the household's income, and the other that planned bequests rise more than in proportion to the household's income. They conceded that "the proportion of total resources planned for bequests may well tend to be greater for individuals with 'large' resources. If this is so, the individual consumption function will not be a linear function of total resources, at least for sufficiently high values of this variable.[37] However, they went on to argue that even if planned bequests rise more than in proportion to the household's income, the *aggregate* consumption function "may well" still be homogeneous. This is so because "the proportion of total resources earmarked for bequests is likely to be an increasing function of the individual's resources *relative to the average level of resources of his age group,"* and this, together with the assumption that the inequality of income within each age group is constant, yields an aggregate consumption function which obeys the proportionality hypothesis.[38]

In the life cycle model, net saving is composed of three components. First there is one component which is equal to a constant proportion of lifetime income. This component is independent of the level of lifetime income and of age. Second, households save a part of their transitory receipts, a part which depends upon the household's age but not on its income. The reason why households consume a part of their transitory receipts is that they plan to run down their assets to zero at

---

Modigliani and Ando are correct in seeing in the proportionality hypothesis the "essence" of Friedman's theory.

35. *Ibid.*, pp. 106–7. Elsewhere they wrote that there "probably" is an estate motive "at least for the high income and/or self-employed groups." "The 'Life Cycle' Hypothesis of Saving," *op. cit.*, p. 73.

36. "Utility Analysis and Aggregate Consumption Functions: An Attempt at Integration," *op. cit.*, p. 59.

37. *Ibid.*, p. 60.

38. *Ibid.*, p. 60 (italics in original).

the time of death. Hence, a household with, say ten years to live, will consume one tenth of the windfall each year. (By contrast, in the permanent income theory model, households do not consume any part of the windfall because they plan to pass assets on to their heirs.) Third, there is another component of saving, a component which depends upon the difference between the household's actual and desired stock of assets.[39]

On an empirical level, the life cycle hypothesis makes consumption, defined in the "use" sense, a function of expected nonproperty income and initial assets. Expected nonproperty income is, of course, not easily measured. One possibility suggested by Ando and Modigliani is to use simply current nonproperty income, with perhaps a scale factor added. A slightly more sophisticated measure is to add a trend term. Another alternative is to make allowance for the fact that the business cycle introduces a discrepancy between actual income and expected long run income. A way of catching this effect is to introduce into the consumption function an additional, employment-related, term. When Ando and Modigliani fitted their consumption function to aggregate data, they used two functions, one containing just nonproperty income and start-of-period assets, the other adding to these variables another term $\frac{L}{E} Y$ where L is the labor force, E is employment, and Y is, of course, income.[40]

As the reader is undoubtedly aware, the life cycle hypothesis is remarkably similar to the permanent income theory. The difference between them is partly a matter of exposition, such as the life cycle hypothesis' greater emphasis on the underlying utility function, its greater stress on family size as an important variable, and its explicit use of a term for nonhuman capital. In part, it is a matter of the firmness with which certain postulates are held. Beyond this they differ in the way in which they approach the empirical data, the life cycle hypothesis using a stock approach and the permanent income theory using a flow approach. Given the paucity of household wealth data, the life cycle hypothesis tends to rely for empirical testing much more on aggregate time series data than does the permanent income theory.

On a substantive level, there is one significant difference between the two theories. Since in the life cycle hypothesis households consume all their assets over their lifetime, this hypothesis has a testable implication for the relation between age and consumption which it does not share

39. Franco Modigliani and Albert Ando, "Utility Analysis and the Consumption Function: An Interpretation of Cross-Section Data," *op. cit.*, p. 405.

40. Albert Ando and Franco Modigliani, "The 'Life Cycle' Hypothesis of Saving," *op. cit.*, pp. 60–62.

with the permanent income theory. As already mentioned, in the life cycle hypothesis consumption out of a windfall is a function of age whereas in the permanent income theory (where households do not consume their wealth but pass it on to their heirs) it is not.[41] But there is a serious complication here. As Landsberger has pointed out, the proposition that consumption out of windfalls is a function of age is not a necessary implication of a utility function homogeneous in consumption.[42] Rather it follows from a much less basic assumption made by Modigliani and associates, the assumption that households plan to consume their wealth at an even rate over their remaining lifespan. Consequently, if the empirical data were to refute the postulated relationship between the propensity to consume windfalls and age, only a particular specification, rather than a basic point, of the life cycle hypothesis would be damaged. Hence, the proposition that the marginal propensity to consume varies with age does not actually provide a good way of testing the life cycle hypothesis vis-à-vis the permanent income theory. This should not be surprising. The two theories are essentially similar and differ only in details. Hence any test which tries to distinguish between them cannot deal with a basic issue, but must focus on their detailed specification.

The life cycle hypothesis starts with the fairly general idea that, subject to a resources constraint, households distribute their consumption over their lifetime to maximize utility. The model is then made more specific by introducing the assumptions that there is no estate motive and that the proportion of their resources which households consume each year is independent of the level of these resources. But, as also pointed out above, the life cycle theorists have stressed that these assumptions are not really basic. What is fundamental to their approach is that in making consumption decisions, households look beyond the current period and consider their whole expected lifetime.

In a subsequent article, Franco Modigliani has developed this idea

41. Another difference between the two theories mentioned by Modigliani ("The Life Cycle Hypothesis of Saving, the Demand for Wealth and the Supply of Capital," *op. cit.*, p. 170n) is that the life cycle hypothesis implies that the saving ratio tends to rise with income growth, whereas Friedman suggested that a rapid rise in income may lower the saving ratio. This is so because if income is expected to continue its rapid rise, current income is low relative to permanent income. As Modigliani pointed out, the opposite is the case for older households whose stock of saving relative to current income is reduced by income growth. And in the life cycle hypothesis the dissaving of these households relative to average income is therefore lowered by income growth. Hence income growth raises net saving.

42. Michael Landsberger, "The Life Cycle Hypothesis: A Reinterpretation and Empirical Test," *American Economic Review*, Vol. LX, March 1970, pp. 175–83.

further in what may be called a "broad" version of the life cycle hypothesis.[43] Starting with the entirely reasonable assumption that income tends to dry up before death, he showed that in a stationary economy net saving would be zero because the dissaving of old households would just offset the positive saving of other households. But if there is growth in either population or productivity, then saving will be positive. And it turns out that for growth rates similar to those actually experienced by the United States in recent decades, the implied saving ratio is very similar to the actually observed saving rate.[44] The long run savings function implied by this theory is $S_t = aY_t - bA_{t-1}$ where S is saving, Y is labor income and A is assets. Turning to the cyclical behavior of the saving function, the theory implies that the saving ratio will tend to fluctuate countercyclically.

These results do not require the absence of a bequest motive or validity of the proportionality hypothesis. They will hold if planned bequests are an increasing function of an individual's resources relative to the resources of other individuals in his age group, and if further the distribution of resources is stable within each age group. As Modigliani pointed out: "this assumption will be recognized as a variant of the so-called 'relative-income' hypothesis, but applied to aggregate life consumption rather than to short run consumption decisions." [45] In dealing with the short run consumption function, Modigliani again turned to the relative income theory by replacing the trend of income term in the equation for the asset-income ratio by a "rachet" term (last year's income). I shall refer to this new analysis of Modigliani's as the "broad" version of the life cycle hypothesis to distinguish it from the more specific "narrow" version discussed previously.

It is worth noting that Duesenberry in the relative income theory did take account of the fact that much saving is for retirement, writing:

A considerable part of all saving is done with a view to future liquidation. All those people who save in order to have assets to spend in

43. "The Life Cycle Hypothesis of Saving, the Demand for Wealth and the Supply of Capital," *op. cit.* This excellent article is, I believe, not as well known as it should be. It contains a very significant discussion of the extent to which past capital formation can be explained by the supply of saving rather than by the demand for capital. This has important implications for the Keynesian system viewed as a long-run theory. Although this article is the first detailed exposition of this analysis, its basic idea first appeared in Modigliani and Brumberg's 1952 manuscript, cited above.

44. But recently Michael Farrell has shown that if one makes reasonable changes in Modigliani's assumptions one obtains quite different savings rates. ("The Magnitude of 'Rate-of-Growth' Effects on Aggregate Savings," *Economic Journal*, Vol. LXXX, December 1970, pp. 873–94.

45. *Op. cit.*, p. 172.

retirement, or to provide for dependents in the event of death, plan to liquidate their savings in the future. We have little information on the relative importance of these motives for saving, but no one will deny that a very large part of saving is done either for retirement or protection of dependents.[46]

Moreover, in the context of the absolute income theory, the importance of dissaving by the aged had been noted earlier by George Terborgh in his criticism of the stagnation thesis.[47]

Thus the "broad" hypothesis does not differ nearly as much from the measured income theories as does the "narrow" hypothesis. This does not mean that it contains nothing new, for with the exception of Harrod, economists had not realized prior to the publication of the life cycle hypothesis just how important this "hump saving" actually is. For example, while Keynes did refer to saving for retirement, he did so in the context of listing the various motives for saving and did not single out saving for retirement for special attention. Before the development of the wealth theories, most economists were unable to appreciate the significance of hump saving because of their general failure to look upon saving as requiring a multi-period analysis.

Since the "broad" hypothesis lies in between the measured income theories on the one hand, and the "narrow" life cycle hypothesis and the permanent income theory on the other, it is not clear whether or not this "broad" hypothesis should be taken up in a book dealing with the wealth theories. There is much to be said for doing so, but I decided against it. I made this decision not out of any lack of respect for this theory—in fact I have high regard for it—but rather because the amount of material to be covered is already so large that I did not want to add to it by taking up the "broad" hypothesis. Although some of the tests discussed below provide some information on the "broad" hypothesis, to discuss it fully would have involved a great deal of additional work.

Modigliani, Ando, and Brumberg are not the only ones to have espoused a life cycle theory. John Arena presented a model in which he added a bequest motive to the life cycle hypothesis, and in addition brought capital gains into the analysis as an explicit variable.[48] He adapted the theory to a single period model by saying that within each period households have a certain wealth target. This wealth target is a function of expected income, expected capital gains, and age.

46. *Income, Saving and the Theory of Consumer Behavior* (Cambridge, Harvard University Press, 1949), p. 41

47. George Terborgh, *The Bogey of Economic Maturity* (Chicago, Machinery and Allied Products Institute, 1945), pp. 60–63.

48. "The Wealth Effect and Consumption," *Yale Economic Essays*, Vol. 3, Fall 1963, pp. 251–304.

The Permanent Income Theory

Since Friedman's permanent income theory is surely the best known version of the wealth theories, I will discuss it only briefly, stressing those aspects of the theory relevant for the subsequent tests. Friedman followed Fisher in assuming strictly rational behavior. He first abstracted from uncertainty and capital rationing, and he assumed that the household has an infinite life, with its wants remaining constant over time. Given these assumptions the amount which a rational household consumes each year depends only on its discounted (human plus nonhuman) wealth and on the rate of interest. There is no reason at all why the household should allow the time pattern of its receipts to have any effect on the timing of its consumption.[49] Instead of letting the dating of receipts determine its consumption pattern, the rational household allocates its consumption over time so that the marginal rate of substitution between this year's consumption and next year's consumption is equal to the rate of interest. Thus, the time pattern of its consumption depends only on (1) the rate of interest and on (2) the household's tastes, or more precisely on its preference for current over future consumption.

The above does not tell us how the household's allocation of consumption over time is affected by its wealth. Clearly, since the rate of interest is given, any effect which the size of its wealth stock has must operate through the taste variable. And there is nothing in economic theory which tells us how tastes are affected by the stock of wealth.[50] It is therefore tempting to make the simplest possible assumption, which is that tastes are independent of the stock of (human plus nonhuman) wealth. This is the famous proportionality hypothesis, which is the most controversial aspect of the permanent income theory. Friedman justified it as follows:

Doubling, let us say, the level of consumption in year 1 may diminish in some sense the urgency of additional consumption in year 1 relative to consumption in year 2, which, by itself, would tend to lower the additional year 2 consumption required to compensate the consumer unit for giving up one dollar of year 1 consumption; however, if the level of consumption in year 2 is simultaneously doubled, this would have the opposite effect, diminishing the urgency of additional consumption in year 2 relative to consumption in year 1, and so, by itself,

49. Consumption is defined here in the "use" sense rather than in the conventional way.

50. As pointed out above, Fisher and Keynes and Duesenberry did make statements about how the size of wealth (or income) affects the taste for current vs. future consumption, but to do so they had to step outside economic theory and bring in psychological factors.

tending to raise the amount of year 2 consumption required to compensate the consumer unit for giving up one dollar of year 1 consumption. These two effects need not exactly offset each other; but there seems no a priori reason why the first should systematically or generally tend to exceed the second or conversely; the things being compared are the same stuff, differing only in dating; it is hard to see any reason why this difference in dating should have an asymetrical effect. There seems nothing unreasonable, therefore, in supposing the two effects exactly to offset one another, and this is surely the simplest hypothesis. We shall, therefore, tentatively accept it subject as always, of course, to the possibility that empirical evidence will be discovered that turns out to be inconsistent with it.[51]

There are several things which should be emphasized about this passage. First, the proportionality hypothesis is *not* a necessary implication of rational behavior, but is merely a simplifying assumption which is not inconsistent with it. This becomes obvious if one restates the hypothesis as saying that the income elasticity of saving is equal to unity; economic *theory* per se cannot tell us much about the size of the income elasticity of an item.[52] Second, Friedman did not allow into the analysis the kind of psychological and sociological factors which caused Fisher, Keynes, and Duesenberry to reject the proportionality hypothesis. Third, there is the tentative way in which Friedman introduced this proportionality hypothesis. Far from asserting it as a necessary implication of his theory, he suggests it as merely something which, if true, would conveniently simplify it.

The above analysis has made rather rigid assumptions: absolute certainty, no capital rationing, and an infinite life for the households. But when Friedman relaxed these assumptions, he found no reason to change his basic conclusions. The introduction of uncertainty complicates the analysis by eliminating the sharp distinction between tastes and opportunities. There is now the possibility that:

additional factors . . . may produce departures from the shape of the consumption function. . . . However, on the present level of analysis, there seems no way to judge whether these factors would tend to make consumption a larger or a smaller fraction of wealth the higher the absolute level of wealth. Accordingly, this effect of uncertainty establishes no presumption against the shape assigned to the consumption function, and thus casts no shadow on the "simplicity" that recommends it.[53]

51. *A Theory of the Consumption Function* (Princeton, Princeton University Press, 1957) p. 13.

52. The fact that the proportionality hypothesis is equivalent to saying that the income elasticity of consumption is equal to unity is something worth noting since many of Friedman's tests discussed below are formulated in terms of income elasticities.

53. *Ibid.*, p. 15.

A second effect of uncertainty (when combined with the elimination of the no capital rationing assumption) is that a new motive for holding wealth, the contingency reserve motive, enters the picture. Moreover, since nonhuman wealth is much more liquid than human wealth, a dollar of nonhuman wealth provides the household with more security than a dollar of human wealth. Hence, the higher the household's ratio of nonhuman to human wealth, the less it feels impelled by the security motive to undertake more saving. Thus, the saving ratio depends, in part, on the ratio of human to nonhuman wealth.

The assumption of infinite life—or what comes to the same thing, the assumption that a household attaches as much importance to the consumption of its heirs as to its own consumption—can, according to Friedman, be abandoned without any serious change in the theory. However, as is shown in the life cycle hypothesis, if one drops this assumption, then one would expect households to consume part of their transitory receipts each year.

As the name implies, the permanent income theory is formulated primarily in terms of permanent income rather than wealth. The reason for this is the measurement problem. While nonhuman wealth can be measured fairly well, there are no adequate data on human wealth. Friedman formulated the permanent income concept in three ways. One is that permanent income is whatever the household thinks that it is.[54] The other is that permanent income is equal to the household's wealth times the relevant discount rate. The third is that permanent income consists of a trend component plus an exponentially weighted average of past incomes with geometrically declining weights.[55] Friedman may seem open to criticism for having three different definitions of permanent income. But such criticism is not valid. The three definitions can coexist peacefully because they are on different levels of abstraction. The first, "psychological" definition is clearly the best one in the sense that it is closest to what, according to the permanent income theory, does determine consumption. However, since expectations are not sufficiently measurable to make this definition empirically workable, this "expectational" definition must, for empirical work, be approximated by the "objective definition" of human plus nonhuman wealth times the discount rate. While this definition can be used for

54. "The permanent income component is to be interpreted as reflecting the effect of those factors that the unit regards as determining its capital value or wealth. . . . It is analogous to the 'expected' value of a probability distribution." *Ibid.*, p. 21.

55. For an interpretation of permanent income as a geometrically weighted average of past (Hicksian) income see M. A. Arak and Alan Spiro, "The Relationship between Permanent Income and Measured Variables," *Journal of Political Economy*, Vol. 79, May–June 1970, pp. 652–60.

some tests, such as tests which require only a relative ranking of house-holds by permanent income, it too suffers from serious measurement problems. The third definition avoids these measurement problems, but it is really not so much a definition of permanent income as a fairly crude estimation scheme.[56]

In sharp contrast with permanent income there is *measured* income. It is tempting to dismiss the definition of measured income by calling it simply income as measured by the usual statistical data, both cross-section household data and aggregate time series. But this is not quite correct. Measured income corresponds more closely to what might be called "net receipts" than to what is usually called "income" in the data. This is so because Friedman included in measured income such items as capital gains and receipts of inheritances, items which our data do not include in income.[57] This has an important implication for some empirical tests of the permanent income theory. Since the meas-ured income theories do not include in income such windfalls as capital gains, a test which shows that these windfalls are saved rather than consumed fails to distinguish between the permanent income theory and the measured income theories.

The difference between measured income and permanent income is "transitory" income. Such transitory income is uncorrelated with perma-nent income. When dealing with a group of households one has the choice of treating the magnitude of transitory income either as inde-pendent of permanent income or as proportional to permanent income. Although Friedman prefers the latter, he used both treatments, calling the former the arithmetic variant of his hypothesis and the latter the logarithmic variant.[58]

Symbolically, the permanent income theory makes use of the fol-lowing four identities and behavior equations, where Y is income, C is consumption, i the rate of interest, w the ratio of human to nonhuman

56. Thus Friedman defended his use of an exponentially declining weight-ing pattern by saying that this is the approach used by Phillip Cagan in his study of hyper-inflation and that this "may perhaps make the use of this pattern seem somewhat less arbitrary." *Op. cit., p.* 143.

57. See Milton Friedman, "Comments" in Irwin Friend (ed.), *Consump-tion and Saving* (Philadelphia, University of Pennsylvania Press, 1960), p. 194. In his empirical work, Friedman did not include windfalls in income, data being generally not available.

58. Corresponding to transitory income there is transitory consumption. Although Friedman discussed transitory consumption in his theoretical chap-ters, unlike transitory income, it does not play a significant role in the em-pirical tests which make up the bulk of his book. This is as it should be. The data considered by Friedman refer to groups of households, and when one groups households, transitory consumption, unlike transitory income, essentially cancels out.

wealth, u a randomly distributed variable, R the correlation coefficient, and where m, p, and t denote respectively the measured, permanent, and transitory components of income and consumption.[59]

(1) $Y_m \equiv Y_p + Y_t$

(2) $C_m \equiv C_p + C_t$

(3) $C_p = K(i,w,u)\,Y_p$

(4) $R_{y_t y_p} = R_{c_t c_p} = R_{y_t c_t} = 0$ [60]

The relation between permanent and transitory income involves a very complex problem, the "horizon." The interpretation of the horizon has an important implication for any test of one of the major components of the permanent income theory, the hypothesis that transitory income is saved rather than consumed. Hence, this aspect of the theory must be discussed in detail here.

The term "horizon" can be used to signify at least three different concepts. One is an adjustment period in the sense that if a household receives a stream of transitory income for a number of years, it adjusts its expectations of permanent income, and by the end of the horizon period it has incorporated this initially transitory income in its expected

59. Milton Friedman, *A Theory of the Consumption Function, op. cit.,* pp. 26–30. The following is the arithmetic variant of the theory. The logarithmic variant is the same except that in (3) the Y_p term is additive rather than multiplicative and that C, K and Y are logs.

60. The assumption that permanent and transitory income are uncorrelated has been challenged by James Holmes, who pointed out that this independence is not consistent with Friedman's derivation of permanent income from a time trend and past incomes. ("A Condition for Independence of Permanent and Transitory Components of a Series," *Journal of the American Statistical Association,* Vol. 66, March 1971, pp. 13–15 and "The Independence of Permanent and Transitory Components of a Series Where the Permanent Component Is a Weighted Average of Measured Values" unpublished paper read at the Econometric Society meetings, July 1971.) This analysis has been carried further by Donald Ebberler who investigated cases where measured income is generated by a stable first order autoregressive process. He showed that Friedman's assumption of zero correlation between permanent and transitory income can be justified in the case of negative binomial weights with permanent income taken as the two period arithmetic average of measured income. (See Donald Ebberler, "Measuring the Permanent Component of a Series for Serially Correlated Observations," Claremont Economic Papers #18, September 1971; "Measuring the Permanent Components of a Series with a Finite Weighting Scheme," Claremont Economic Papers #17, September 1971; "A Note on the Independence of the Permanent and Transitory Components of a Series," Claremont Economic Papers #14, August 1971; "On the Measurement of the Permanent Component of a Series," Claremont Economic Papers #6, July 1971.) Unfortunately, these papers reached me too late for me to take these conclusions into account in my own work.

permanent income. The second interpretation is that a household looks ahead for a number of years measured by the horizon and takes its permanent income as some sort of average of its measured income during this period. Third, one can look at the horizon as a discount rate. Suppose that a household receives some transitory income, and in accordance with the permanent income theory, it invests it. Since the yield on this investment is permanent income to the household, its permanent income goes up by its receipt of transitory income times the relevant discount rate.

In his book Friedman was not clear about which of these three concepts he was using. Although he was thinking primarily in terms of the discount rate interpretation, this fact was not apparent to many readers, and Friedman himself was misled at one point.[61] Since then, however, he has made it clear that he thinks of the horizon as being the reciprocal of the discount rate, rather than as a planning period.[62]

Since Friedman estimated the horizon as being about three years, his implied discount rate is $33\frac{1}{3}$ percent.[63] While, at first glance, a $33\frac{1}{3}$ percent discount rate may seem quite unreasonable, Friedman defended it as follows:

A yield *r* of $33\frac{1}{3}$ percent per year . . . may seem radically out of line with market yields. . . . However, it should be kept in mind that we are treating the value of nonpecuniary returns from particular assets as an addition to permanent income, consumption and measured income. For this reason, *r* is to be taken as the market yield only on assets yielding no nonpecuniary returns. Rates paid on installment contracts, small loans, etc., are not strikingly out of line with an estimated subjective rate of $33\frac{1}{3}$ percent. . . . If [the $33\frac{1}{3}$ percent rate] seems drastically out of line with widely quoted market rates of interest, it should be kept in mind that these rates apply only to a very limited range of assets; that most future receipts whose discounted value constitutes wealth comes from assets that cannot be readily bought and sold or for which buying and selling prices differ widely.[64]

Thus, if a household receives a dollar of transitory income, it is entirely consistent with the permanent income theory if it increases its

61. See Milton Friedman, "Windfalls, the 'Horizon' and Related Concepts in the Permanent Income Hypothesis," in Carl Christ (ed.), *Measurement in Economics: Studies in Mathematical Economics and Econometrics in Memory of Yehuda Grunfeld* (Stanford, Stanford University Press, 1963), p. 22.

62. *Ibid.*, pp. 3–11. For example, if the discount rate is ten percent, so that the increase in permanent income is equal to one tenth of the transitory income receipt, then the horizon is ten years.

63. Robert Holbrook has argued that Friedman's own empirical tests suggest a horizon of less than three years. This point is discussed in Chapter 3 below.

64. *Ibid.*, p. 13n and p. 25.

consumption by 30 cents.[65] These 30 cents do not represent consumption of transitory income per se; rather they are consumption out of the increment in permanent income which, in turn, consists of the permanent yield of the dollar of transitory income.

While this formulation is unexceptionable as formal economic theory, it creates a very serious problem for empirical testing of the permanent income theory. It may well be that Friedman's hypothesis that all transitory income is saved is at present simply not an empirically testable proposition. The reason for this is that if we observe that a household spends 30 cents when it receives a dollar of transitory income, this observation can be interpreted in two ways. One is to follow Friedman and to say that all of the 30 cents represents the permanent income yielded by the dollar times the marginal propensity to consume. The other way is to say that only a part of the 30 cents represents consumption out of the permanent yield and that the other part is simply expenditure out of the transitory income receipt itself.

The way to distinguish between these two possibilities is to have an independent estimate of the yield on transitory income. But Friedman does not tell us how to obtain such a figure.[66] There is no way of knowing whether a 30 cent increase in consumption in response to a dollar

65. The yield on a dollar of transitory income raises permanent income by 33 cents, and given a marginal propensity to consume permanent income of 0.9, consumption increases by 30 cents.

66. One interesting attempt to measure the horizon has been undertaken by Frank Stafford. He regressed the consumption of graduate students on their future earnings as estimated from variables such as their field of study. Stafford undertook many such regressions using different discount rates. The best fit was obtained for discount rates of about 24 percent. But unfortunately, as Stafford pointed out, other discount rates gave fits which were almost as good. In any case, Stafford did not treat this as a disconfirmation of Friedman's 33.3 percent rate since his estimate is downward biased because his equation did not make any allowance for the secular growth of professional earnings. (Frank Stafford, "Graduate Student Income and Consumption," unpublished Ph.D. dissertation, University of Chicago, 1968, pp. 250–51.) However, in addition to this downward bias, Stafford's estimate also contains an upward bias. This is so because a graduate student surely must feel considerable uncertainty about his expected earnings compared to the earnings of other graduate students. One would expect a discount rate which contains an allowance for that much uncertainty to be substantially higher than the discount rate which represents the average expected yield of transitory income. Hence, Stafford's analysis does not really give us a good estimate of the discount rate which could be compared with Friedman's 33.3 estimate.

Warren Weber estimated the discount rate of households in a study of the interest elasticity of consumption. However, since his estimates of the rate at which households discount future consumption ranged from −31.4 percent to 1.5 percent, they cannot be used here. (Warren Weber, "The

increase in transitory income confirms or disconfirms the permanent income theory. And the same is true if the empirical tests would show that more than 30 cents are consumed when transitory income increases by one dollar. To be sure, if one would observe that, say, 70 cents are consumed, one might argue that this is much too large a figure to represent merely the yield from the transitory income. However, this would leave one open to the charge of casual empiricism. Thus, there seems to be no way at present in which the data can really disconfirm Friedman's hypothesis that all transitory income is saved. But, eventually, someone might discover a reliable way of estimating the discount rate directly, and then Friedman's hypothesis would be testable. Hence, since it is testable in principle, it cannot be dismissed as a metaphysical, rather than a scientific, hypothesis. However, economics is an impatient science; propositions which are testable in principle but not testable in the foreseeable future are of little use. For this reason, in the tests reported below I will devote little attention to the zero marginal propensity to consume transitory income. I will devote some attention, however, to the question of by how much consumption does increase when transitory income goes up, regardless of whether this is consumption out of permanent or transitory income. This question deals with an important parameter for many policies (for example, the effects of a transitory tax change), and from a policy point of view it is immaterial whether the observed change in consumption is explained as consumption out of transitory income directly or as consumption out of the yield on transitory income.

Before leaving the permanent income theory, it might be worth summarizing briefly the hypotheses to be tested. They are that (1) consumption is a function of long-run ("permanent") income, (2) permanent consumption is proportional to permanent income, and (3) the propensity to consume transitory income is zero. However, as just pointed out, the last of these can be tested only by seeing if the data confirm it—it is at present not a disconfirmable proposition.[67]

Effect of Interest Rates on Aggregate Consumption," *American Economic Review,* Vol. LX, September 1970, pp. 591–600.)

Another possibility is to ask households about their discount rate, either directly or indirectly. (Cf. Julian Simon and Carl Barnes, "The Middle-Class U.S. Consumption Function: A Hypothetical-Question Study of Expected Consumption Behavior," Oxford University, Institute of Economics and Statistics, *Bulletin,* Vol. 33, 1971, pp. 73–80.) There is, of course, the problem that the way households actually behave and the way they say they do may differ.

67. This asymmetry comes about in the following way. If the data were to show that a dollar of transitory income raises consumption by, say 4 cents, this would suggest strongly that transitory income is not being con-

In testing these hypotheses, I will follow Friedman in one important respect. Friedman, with his strong stress on simplicity, has argued that the permanent income theory is simpler than its rivals because it allows one to avoid the cumbersome multivariate consumption functions which many economists have fitted. According to Friedman, many of the variables used in these large consumption functions are primarily permanent income proxies. In testing his theory I will go along with Friedman and use simple consumption functions. This is more a matter of necessity than of preference—in many cases I do not have the data needed to fit extensive multivariate functions.

Other Wealth Theories

Having discussed the two best known versions of the wealth theories, I now turn to some of the lesser known ones. Since these have generally been presented only in very brief versions by their authors, they can be summarized quickly.

Alan Spiro has developed a theory in which saving is a function of the discrepancy between actual and desired wealth with desired wealth being, in turn, a function of the income level.[68] Hence, consumption depends on the stock of wealth and current and past income. Since wealth consists of accumulated savings plus capital gains, Spiro was able to eliminate wealth from this consumption function. His consumption function requires that the coefficients of past incomes sum to unity. As Spiro pointed out, this theory is not inconsistent with the permanent income theory or with the relative income theory.

Richard Stone and D. A. Rowe developed a consumption function which combines the permanent income theory and the life cycle hypothesis.[69] Their measure of permanent income embodies an adjustment mechanism whereby permanent income changes by a constant proportion of the difference between last year's permanent income and this year's measured income. They used the same technique to distinguish between measured and permanent wealth. Permanent consumption they took to be a linear homogeneous function of permanent income and permanent wealth. In addition to this permanent component, consump-

---

sumed, since we know that the discount rate is at least 4 percent. On the other hand, if it is 30 cents or 50 cents which is being consumed, we have really no way of saying whether this is greater than the discount rate times the marginal propensity to consume.

68. Alan Spiro, "Wealth and the Consumption Function," *Journal of Political Economy,* Vol. LXX, August 1962, pp. 339–54; and "The Direction of Change in Consumption during Business Cycle Contractions," *Journal of Political Economy,* Vol. LXXI, October 1963, pp. 470–80.

69. "A Postwar Expenditure Function," *Manchester School,* Vol. XXX, May 1962, pp. 187–201.

tion also has a transitory component which is a homogeneous linear function of transitory income and of government policy measures influencing consumption.[70]

The approach used by Harold Lydall is one wherein households save to achieve a certain wealth target.[71] This wealth target he took to be a fixed ratio to the household's consumption. The household does not necessarily attempt to reach this target ratio within any one year, but rather may move each year only part of the way toward it. From these assumptions Lydall derived a savings function using wealth and income in the following way: $S = aY - bW$.

Richard Ball and Pamela Drake have argued that:

> The *new consumption theorists,* however, have produced a theory of the consumption function that unifies the effects of asset holdings and measured income through the concept of normal or permanent income. The cost of this achievement is to impose upon the individual consumer a rigorous course of intertemporal utility maximization, simple to assert, but difficult to execute. Many of the complicating factors, such as the choice of interest rate to use in formulating life-time plans, have to be abandoned at an early stage in order to permit workable empirical formulations, and the question arises as to whether this journey has been really necessary.
>
> There is, however, a more serious difficulty. . . . If an individual adjusts his future consumption to his initial asset holdings and present value of expected income from human wealth, we are essentially deprived of the notion of an excess or undesired holding of assets.[72]

Ball and Drake, therefore, presented a rival theory in which households are shortsighted and accumulate wealth primarily from the precautionary motive. The household's utility function, therefore, has two arguments, consumption and wealth. They assumed that the utility function is homogeneous in degree one, and derived from their utility function the following consumption function: $C_t = (1 - q)Y_t + qC_{t-1}$. This has some similarity with the widely used Koyck-Nerlove function, but it differs from it in two ways—the intercept is zero and the sum of the income and lagged consumption coefficients should be unity. This, as will be shown below, turns out to be an extremely useful property in testing their theory.

Another theory has been advocated by three economists at the University of Pennsylvania, Jean Crockett, Irwin Friend, and Paul Taub-

70. Stone and Rowe introduced the policy variable because they were dealing with British data, and British policy has, at times, tried to affect consumption directly.

71. H. F. Lydall, "Saving and Wealth," *Australian Economic Papers,* Vol. 2, December 1963, pp. 228–50.

72. "The Relationship between Aggregate Consumption and Wealth," *International Economic Review,* Vol. 5, January 1964, pp. 63–64.

man, whom I will refer to collectively as the "Pennsylvania School."[73] They have been concerned primarily with empirical work, and have given only brief justifications of their consumption functions without spelling out their theory in any great detail.[74] They have used a concept of "normal income," which is similar to Friedman's permanent income in that it represents long run income. However, they have employed a much less elaborate technique than Friedman to measure this normal income, frequently using just the trend of income.[75] Moreover, in their model, transitory income—that is, the difference between measured income and the income trend—enters the consumption function, though the propensity to consume is less for transitory than for normal income. In some of their work they have included in the consumption function the difference between actual wealth and desired wealth, with desired wealth taken as a function of normal income. In addition, they have, at times, used a taste variable.

Sten Thore has analyzed the effect of price changes on consumption.[76]

73. I have called this theory the "normal income theory" since it uses the term "normal income," as a counterpart to Friedman's permanent income. This use of the term "normal income" differs from that of Michael Farrell ("The New Theories of the Consumption Function," *Economic Journal*, Vol. 69, December 1959, pp. 678–96); Farrell used the term "normal income" in a much broader sense to include Friedman's permanent income.

74. The literature on this theory is quite scattered. See Irwin Friend, "The Propensity to Save in India," in D. H. Butani and P. Singh (eds.), *Economic Development: Issues and Policies* (Bombay, Vora and Co., 1966), pp. 153–71; Paul Taubman, "Permanent and Transitory Income Effects," *Review of Economics and Statistics*, Vol. XLVII, February 1965, pp. 38–43; Jean Crockett, "Income and Asset Effects on Consumption: Aggregate and Cross-Section," in Conference on Research in Income and Wealth, *Studies in Income and Wealth*, Vol. 28, *Models of Income Determination* (Princeton, Princeton University Press, 1964), pp. 97–132; Irwin Friend and Paul Taubman, "The Aggregate Propensity to Save: Some Concepts and Their Application to International Data," *Review of Economics and Statistics*, Vol. XLVIII, May 1966, pp. 113–23; Paul Taubman, "A Synthesis of Saving Theories with Special Reference to the Components of Personal Saving," unpublished Ph.D. dissertation, University of Pennsylvania, 1964; Irwin Friend, "The Propensity to Save in Argentina" (unpublished manuscript).

75. Irwin Friend has defined "normal income" as follows: "the expected value of the annual household income over whatever time span is most relevant to the consumption decision and asset goals of the household. . . . The span which is most relevant to the average family for most decisions is an open question. In the present state of our knowledge it may be not much longer than a single year or as long as the entire working life of the household head." "The Propensity to Consume and Save in Argentina," unpublished manuscript, pp. 9–10n.

76. *Household Saving and the Price Level* (Stockholm, National Institute of Economic Research, 1961).

To do this he developed a model which is more general than the permanent income theory and the life cycle hypothesis, and bears considerable resemblance to the normal income theory published subsequently by the Pennsylvania School. It does not assume that the income elasticity of consumption is unity for permanent income and zero for transitory income, though it does assert that it is greater for permanent than for transitory income. This model pays much attention to the role of assets and to the composition of assets, particularly to real balances. Since this model is really a special case of the wealth theories, one specifically oriented to a particular question, the effect of price level changes, I will not deal with it specifically. However, the tests discussed below do have a bearing on it.

The late Richard Halfyard developed another wealth theory, a theory which starts from a general equilibrium framework.[77] Since this theory can be discussed better in connection with his empirical work, I will delay discussion of it until Chapter 7.

Clower and Johnson formulated a theory which does not look at the saving motives of households and assumes that households have only limited foresight and short memories.[78] Their utility function has consumption and wealth holdings as its arguments. After manipulating this utility function, they derived the proposition that consumption is a function of wealth only.

The Standard Income Theory

The original idea of the wealth approach, prior to the development of the full scale wealth models, was simply that the income elasticity of consumption is greater for permanent income than for transitory income. However, there was no presumption that it is unity for permanent income and zero for transitory income. On the other hand, some of the wealth theories reviewed above have made these assumptions. One way of evaluating these theories is to see whether or not they represent an improvement over the original, much more moderate, ideas. I will, therefore, use as a counterpoise to the permanent income theory, and to the life cycle hypothesis, a much more moderate theory which I have called the "standard income theory." This theory asserts that the income elasticity of consumption is greater for permanent income than for transitory income, but that it is neither unity for the one nor zero

77. "The Determinants of Aggregate Consumption Expenditures in the United States, 1929–61," unpublished Ph.D. dissertation, University of California at Los Angeles, 1964.

78. "Income, Wealth and the Theory of Consumption," in J. N. Wolfe (ed.), *Value, Capital and Growth, Papers in Honour of Sir John Hicks* (Edinburgh, University Press, 1968), pp. 45–96.

for the other. It also claims that there is *some* lag in the consumption function, but that this lag is substantially shorter than the lag found by Friedman or Modigliani. Finally, this theory is agnostic about the use of a nonhuman wealth term in the consumption function. One way to look at this theory is to say that it represents a synthesis of the wealth theories and the relative income theory. It is in essence a *partial* permanent income theory.

Whenever one is confronted with a dispute between two theories, an easy way out is to say that "the truth lies in between." This sounds like a bromide. To make the standard income theory have any real significance, it is necessary to go beyond such a banality, and to specify more precisely where the truth does lie between the wealth theories and the measured income theories. For example, a theory which asserts that the permanent income elasticity of consumption is less than unity, but that it might well be as high as 0.99, would hardly be much of a contribution. To have significance, the standard income theory must differ sharply from the wealth theories on the one hand and the measured income theories on the other. I have therefore tried to make the standard income theory more specific by making it lie somewhat closer to the relative income theory than to the permanent income theory. More specifically, I claim that although the marginal propensity to consume *is* greater for permanent income than for measured income, the measured income theories do provide somewhat better estimates of the marginal propensity to consume *permanent* income than does the permanent income theory.[79] In other words, the proportionality hypothesis involves a somewhat greater error than does the simple identification of permanent and measured income. Moreover, while there is a lag in the consumption function, it is relatively short. Thus, in some regressions reported below, current income receives roughly 70 percent of the total weight, and the income of the current and past two years accounts for nearly all the weight.

The standard income theory accepts the underlying microeconomics of the wealth theories but modifies these theories in several ways. One is to drop the proportionality hypothesis. This hypothesis was introduced both by Modigliani and associates and by Friedman merely as a convenient simplification. They adopted this simplification because it was not disputed by their tests. But, as will be shown below, it is strongly refuted by subsequent tests. Fortunately, however, the abandonment of the proportionality hypothesis does not really do any serious damage to the underlying approach of the wealth theory.

79. Thus, on a scale where the validity of the proportionality hypothesis is denoted by zero and the validity of the measured income theories by unity, my measure is 0.6 or 0.7.

A more important proposition of the major wealth theories is lifetime averaging—extended by Friedman into the life of future generations. Here one should draw some distinction between the more modest view that lifetime income has some effect on consumption and the more specific view that households spread consumption evenly over their lifetime. (This rigorous view implies the validity of the proportionality hypothesis because if all households do consume their incomes evenly over their lifespans, then given equal lifespans they must all consume the same proportion of lifetime income each year regardless of their income level.) The standard income theory accepts a modest version of lifetime averaging, but not the specific one of full scale averaging.

The rigorous lifetime averaging model is solidly based on sound microeconomic foundations. But this does not suffice to validate it, because the microeconomic theory which underlies it abstracts from a number of factors which could invalidate lifetime averaging as an adequate description and explanation of household behavior. One of these is the assumption of perfect (or at least "adequate") foresight. If households do not know their future income, and find it even difficult to make an informed guess about it, they may simply treat current income as a proxy for permanent income.[80] In this case, while it would still be formally correct to say that consumption depends upon perceived permanent income, there would be little purpose in doing so. The second reason why households may not average their incomes over the lifetimes is the existence of capital rationing. Since households generally start their life with few assets and with incomes below their lifetime average they may simply not be able to act in the way in which the life cycle hypothesis or the permanent income theory predict. Or, insofar as they are *able* to do so, the high cost of borrowing may prevent them from actually doing it. Third, psychological time preference (Pigou's "telescoping faculty") *may* cause households to behave differently than life cycle models predict.

The possibility of lifetime averaging is, of course, one of the bases of the assumption that there is a lag in the consumption function. But it is not the only basis; a lag could also occur because of a delay in people's perception of income changes, or because of past consumption habits. The existence of three reasons for a lag creates a very serious problem which is usually ignored in discussions of the consumption

80. Thus Michael Farrell has suggested that households with fluctuating incomes may consume on the basis of their long-run income expectations, while those with stable incomes may follow a convenient rule such as always consuming, say, 90 percent of their measured incomes. (Michael Farrell, "The New Theories of the Consumption Function," *op. cit.*, pp. 681–92.)

function. I have not been able to solve it, and it is probably the most serious loose end of the standard income theory. One would expect both the delay in perceiving income changes, as well as the stickiness of past habits, to create a fairly short lag, lasting perhaps just two or three years. On the other hand, lifetime averaging creates a much longer lag. Now it is clear that, *to some extent,* there is a long lag in the consumption function. The very obvious phenomenon of saving for retirements shows it. In addition, there may also be a short adaption lag, due to income perception or habits. Thus, we should really look for two quite different lags. This creates a serious statistical problem. Like everyone else I have looked for a single lag and I found a short one. Our statistical techniques make it difficult to look for two different lags at the same time and I have not done so.[81] Hence, the short lag I mentioned above does not really tell the full story. In this respect the standard theory is seriously incomplete.

Finally, there is the propensity to consume transitory income. This I have already discussed implicitly and indirectly above. If households follow a strict lifetime averaging model then they will simply save transitory income. But because of uncertainty and capital rationing, households may consume a substantial part of their transitory income.

Since the standard income theory is really only a very heavily toned down version of the permanent income theory and life cycle hypothesis, I have not presented any formal microtheory for it. The reader can easily see from the above what such a theory would look like—all he has to do is to take the permanent income theory and abandon its restrictive assumptions.

Before leaving the description of the standard income theory, I have to make a confession. I did not follow the proper procedure of formulating the theory precisely at the outset before testing it. Instead, I started with the presumption that the truth lies in between the wealth theories and the measured income theories. I then allowed the tests described below to make the theory more specific.

I claim no originality for the basic idea of the standard income theory. As discussed above, it was essentially formulated by Simon Kuznets, William Vickrey, Frank Hanna, Dorothy Brady, Rose Friedman, and Margaret Reid. Moreover, except for its agnosticism with respect to the wealth term, it is really the same as the normal income theory advo-

---

81. However, it *is* possible, though difficult, to estimate two lags. For example, in a related field, the demand for money, Edgar Feige did succeed in measuring two distinct lags. ("Expectations and Adjustment in the Monetary Sector," American Economic Association, *Papers and Proceedings,* Vol. LXXVII, May 1967, pp. 462–73). But I lack the requisite econometric skills.

cated by the Pennsylvania School. All I have done is to (1) specify the theory somewhat more precisely, (2) test it empirically, and (3) show that it is consistent with all the valid empirical evidence which has been adduced both for and against the wealth theories.

Comparison of Wealth Theories

To conclude this survey of the wealth theories it might be useful to try combining them. As stated above, the basic idea of these theories is that consumption depends upon human and nonhuman wealth rather than upon the flow of income received in any one year. Given certain assumptions, this basic idea can be developed as an implication of utility maximizing. And, in the life cycle hypothesis, Modigliani and associates have spelled out in detail how such a wealth theory of consumption can be derived from the general utility theory. However, it is difficult to test such a theory because of the paucity of data on human wealth, and even on nonhuman wealth. Hence, while the life cycle theorists have offered a number of empirical tests, their comparative advantage has been in the development of the formal theory of household saving.

By contrast, Friedman, in the permanent income theory, has stressed empirical testing. Although he did provide a theoretical framework for the theory—a framework based on Fisher's analysis—Friedman focused most of his attention on the testing of this theory rather than on its formal development. And his tests are generally tests which fit the life cycle hypothesis as well as the permanent income theory.

It is therefore possible to combine the two main wealth theories. One can treat the life cycle hypothesis as setting out the microeconomic framework of the approach, and the permanent income theory as a reformulation of it which is more amenable to testing. To be sure, such an attempt to combine the two theories does overstate their similarities. There is *some* conflict between them. Thus the life cycle hypothesis assumes that households plan to use up their assets over their lifetime, while the permanent income theory assumes that they wish to pass them on to their heirs. But this difference, as well as the other differences discussed earlier, are really rather minor when compared to the important ways in which both of these theories differ from the measured income theories.

The other wealth theories usually contain only briefer discussions of the underlying theoretical framework than either the life cycle hypothesis or the permanent income theory. Since the theory of household equilibrium is quite general these wealth theories have been able to take off from it in various directions. Usually they have suggested that the household's utility function contains wealth as well as consumption, and this simple notion can be developed in several ways. Thus, the Pennsylvania School includes the discrepancy between desired and actual wealth, as well as normal and transitory income, in the consumption function, while Ball and Drake manipulate this utility function in a way which makes consumption a function of current income and lagged consumption.

The general ideas of the wealth theories are therefore much broader than the specific propositions usually associated with the permanent income theory and the life cycle hypothesis. In a general sense, the wealth theories are valid if consumption depends upon human and nonhuman wealth, or translated into flow terms, if consumption is more closely related to long-run income than to current income, and if the coefficients of long-run and current income differ substantially. The more controversial aspects of these theories—such as the proportionality hypothesis, the zero transitory income elasticity, and Friedman's specific lag pattern—are nonessential rather than essential points when one considers the overall approach of the wealth theories. I shall argue below that all three of these specific propositions are not supported by the evidence, and yet that the wealth theories provide an immense step forward in our understanding of consumption and saving behavior.

Some Implications of the Wealth Theories

The wealth theories have a number of implications for both economic analysis and economic policy.[82] One important implication relates to forecasting consumption. Obviously an adherent of, say, the permanent income theory predicts consumption from a different equation than does an adherent of the measured income theory. To be sure, a common technique which has been used in consumption functions, even by those who do not accept the permanent income theory, has been to include the previous period's consumption as an independent variable. Via the Koyck transformation this can be rationalized as making consumption a function of permanent income. In this respect, acceptance of the permanent income theory may not change the consumption function actually fitted, but instead provides a justification for what would otherwise represent the inclusion of a variable on a different basis.

Another implication of the wealth theories relates to income distribution. If the proportionality hypothesis is correct, then the distribution of permanent income does not affect the proportion of income consumed. Hence, one of the variables frequently cited as a determinant of consumption can be excluded, and one potential policy tool, income

82. Many of the implications discussed here were spelled out by Friedman (*A Theory of the Consumption Function, op. cit.,* pp. 233–39).

redistribution, turns out to be useless.[83] An unequal distribution of income cannot validly be criticized as leading to "underconsumption," nor defended as necessary for a high saving rate.

The wealth theories also have a number of implications for more conventional fiscal policy. One of these relates to the effect of a temporary change in tax rates. The standard prescription for countercyclical fiscal policy is that income taxes should be raised in inflationary periods and lowered during recessions. But if the public anticipates frequent income tax changes then the wealth theories suggest they will not be very effective. If consumption depends on permanent rather than on transitory income, then as taxes are temporarily reduced the public will increase its "use" consumption only by the tax saving times the yield it obtains by investing this tax saving multipiled by the marginal propensity to consume. To be sure, in addition to its effect on "use" consumption, a temporary tax cut also changes the household's purchases of durables. But, on the whole, temporary tax changes, particularly if they are announced as merely temporary, are less effective if the wealth theories are correct than if the measured income theories are valid.

The wealth theories also tell us something about the burden of taxation, specifically sales taxes and other taxes which are shifted forward. The traditional treatment of a sales tax has been to assume that the tax is paid by each income class in proportion to its consumption. But this looks at the tax burden as a proportion of measured, and not permanent, income. If the proportionality hypothesis is correct, the burden of a completely general sales tax is proportional to after-tax permanent income.[84]

Another implication for fiscal policy relates to the burden of the

83. Although income distribution has not been given much emphasis in recent professional discussions of the consumption function, at least in part because income distribution is a stable variable, it is discussed in undergraduate textbooks. For instance, see Frederick Brooman and Henry Jacoby, *Macroeconomics* (Chicago, Aldine Publishing Co., 1970), pp. 119–23; John Lindauer, *Macroeconomics* (New York, John Wiley and Sons, 1968), pp. 24–25; David Rowan, *Output, Inflation and Growth* (London, Macmillan, 1968), p. 159; Edward Shapiro, *Macroeconomic Analysis* (New York, Harcourt Brace & World, 1966), pp. 222–27.

84. See D. G. Davies, "Progressiveness of a Sales Tax in Relation to Various Income Bases," *American Economic Review*, Vol. L, December 1960, pp. 987–96. Another example of the use of the wealth theories in discussing a specific tax is the use of a life cycle model in analyzing the impact of wealth taxes. See A. B. Atkinson, "Capital Taxes, the Redistribution of Wealth and Individual Saving," *Review of Economic Studies*, Vol. XXXVIII, April 1970, pp. 209–29.

public debt. The life cycle hypothesis, and by implication some of the other wealth theories, suggest that debt financing does make future generations worse off. This is so because debt financing, in contrast to tax financing of government expenditures, raises the public's stock of wealth because the public holds more government securities. If, as seems likely, taxpayers do not take the increased service cost of this debt into account in computing their net wealth, debt financing raises household wealth and hence reduces the saving rate so that less wealth is passed on to future generations.[85]

In addition to these implications for fiscal policy the wealth theories also have important implications for the stability of the economic system. One of these is that the short-run multiplier is relatively small because a temporary increase in income is largely saved. Another implication is the light they throw on the Pigou effect, supporting the classical proposition that a price flexible system tends toward full employment.[86] Labor economics is still another field in which the wealth theories are useful since they can help to explain the amount of labor supplied by the household.

The wealth theories also have implications for economic development. They suggest that the saving ratio is not likely to be any lower in less developed countries. However, it is worth noting that this conclusion is not peculiar to the wealth theories. Unless there is an international emulation effect—and there very well may not be one—the relative income theory too does not imply that a low level of income for a country is associated with a low saving ratio.

Still another implication of the wealth theories deals with the relation of saving and age. If the life cycle hypothesis is correct, households dissave all their assets in old age so that the rate of population growth is an important determinant of the saving ratio. Although it has long been known that population growth has an important effect on the overall saving ratio, the measured income theories have not developed this relationship to the same extent as the life cycle hypothesis. Given the present emphasis on curbing population growth this aspect of the wealth theories is an important one.

In recent years numerous growth models have been developed. In constructing these growth models one must make some assumptions

85. See Franco Modigliani, "Long-Run Implications of Alternative Fiscal Policies and the Burden of the National Debt," *Economic Journal,* Vol. LXXI, December 1961, pp. 730–55.

86. For an application of the permanent income theory to the measurement of the real balance effect, though with a much lower discount rate than Friedman's, see my "The Empirical Significance of the Real Balance Effect," *Quarterly Journal of Economics,* Vol. LXIII, May 1959, pp. 275–91.

about the effect of income growth on the saving rate. Here the wealth theories and the relative income theory have a common implication—a stable saving ratio—while the absolute income theory implies a saving ratio which rises with the level of income. In addition, growth models frequently rely on the effect of wealth on the saving ratio. Here, too, the wealth theories are obviously relevant.

Then, there is the implication of the wealth theories for the macro-economic distribution theory. This theory takes the marginal propensity to consume to be zero for capitalists and unity for workers. This is obviously an idealization, but for the theory to be useful there must be a great gap between the marginal propensity to consume of the two classes. While the wealth theories do not talk about the propensities to consume of different *classes,* the proportionality hypothesis is very inhospitable to such a large difference. This does not mean that the proportionality hypothesis necessarily denies the existence of differences in the propensities to consume of capitalists and workers. A difference in the saving ratio need not, after all, be the result of a difference in income, but could result, for example, from a tendency of particularly thrifty people to become entrepreneurs.[87] But, at the very least, the proportionality hypothesis raises the question whether there actually is a significant difference between the saving ratios of capitalists and workers. Someone who takes the proportionality hypothesis seriously would be inclined to ask adherents of the macroeconomic distribution theories to provide empirical evidence for something which these theories treat as almost self-evident.[88]

The implications discussed so far are those of the full permanent income theory and life cycle hypothesis. They are not those of the standard income theory; the implications of this theory essentially lie in between those of the full permanent income theory and life cycle hypothesis on the one hand, and the relative income theory on the other.

87. Corporate saving creates another possible reason why the marginal propensity to consume might be less for capitalists than for workers, but, certainly in the life cycle hypothesis, corporate saving is treated as imputed personal saving by households, which offset such saving by reducing their personal saving.

88. The existence of a difference in the propensities to consume of capitalists and workers is also relevant for the double-switching debate, so that the wealth theories have an important message for this seemingly far-removed branch of economics. See G. C. Harcourt, "Some Cambridge Controversies in the Theory of Capital," *Journal of Economic Literature,* Vol. VII, June 1969, pp. 396–98.

Part Two
PREVIOUS TESTS

INTRODUCTION

As discussed in Chapter 1, to reach agreement on the wealth theories one must examine existing tests critically. Such an examination must be sharply distinguished from mere description. It must not only try to determine whether a particular test contains errors, but must also go on to see whether the test, if valid, supports only say, the permanent income theory, or whether its results can also be explained by other theories such as the relative income theory or the standard income theory. And in those cases where the test supports the standard income theory, one must ask further whether it gives estimates of the parameters for such a theory.

As I have argued in Chapter 1, such a critique of existing tests should cover *all* the tests which have been undertaken. In fact, one has to look beyond formal tests, and also examine empirical findings which have relevance even if their authors did not present them as tests of the wealth theories. (In what follows I will use the term "tests" to include such pieces of evidence.) However, I am not covering all the tests in Part II; certain tests of the permanent income approach which consist of fitting consumption functions to aggregate data can be discussed best in Part III, and I shall postpone their discussion until then.

The first chapter of this Part, Chapter 3, deals with the various tests presented by Milton Friedman. Friedman has provided many more tests than anyone else has done since. As one sees different tests in the current issues of journals, it is easy to forget that Friedman offered no less than sixteen tests in his original presentation of the theory. In view of the many tests he presented and of their importance, I have devoted a special chapter to his tests. Chapters 4 through 6 then deal with the evidence presented by other investigators, both friends and foes of the theory. (I have included the tests undertaken by Franco Modigliani and associates in these chapters rather than giving them a separate chapter because they offered fewer tests than did Friedman.) Although this is not really part of the permanent income theory as originally presented, some economists have applied the permanent income theory to corporate saving, and, in addition, corporate saving may have some bearing on the propensity to consume of households. I have dealt with this topic only briefly and have relegated it to Appendix III.

In evaluating the various tests I did not discuss the results of each test vis-à-vis all the many variants of the wealth theories taken up in Chapter 2. To do so would have been very tedious. Instead I have discussed their results in the context of the full permanent income theory and the standard income theory. Since the other variants of the wealth theories share many of the characteristics of these theories, such a procedure is adequate in most cases. In those cases where a test throws light on a characteristic specific to one of the other wealth theories, I have, of course, taken this up.

In discussing each test I have tried to point out any serious weaknesses it seems to have. If I have not given any explicit criticism of a test, it is because I could see nothing wrong with it. Since my purpose here is to *evaluate* the tests rather than merely describe them, I have prepared tables classifying each test as valid or invalid. These tables may be found at the ends of Chapters 3, 5, and 6; the results of Chapter 4 are shown in the table at the end of Chapter 5.

Three

FRIEDMAN'S TESTS

In this chapter I take up each and every test of the permanent income theory presented by Milton Friedman in his pathbreaking *A Theory of the Competition Function*.[1] My purpose is to classify all his tests into four groups: (1) those which are invalid, (2) those which are valid, but support also the measured income theories, (3) those which do not support the measured income theories but are consistent with the standard income theory, and (4) those tests which support the full permanent income theory against all the other theories. As I will try to show, this last category is an empty box.

Friedman presented a wide variety of tests, the results of which are *consistent* with his theory. But most of the tests are no more than this; they do not require a full permanent income theory to explain the observations.[2] They are tests of the direction only, rather than rigorous tests of the full theory. By "tests of direction" I mean tests which show

1. (Princeton, Princeton University Press, 1957.) Apart from the tests contained in this book, the only other empirical evidence for the permanent income theory given by Friedman consists of his discussions of tests undertaken by other economists. These discussions are taken up in the following two chapters. Throughout this chapter, references to "Friedman, *op. cit.*" relate to his book. There is a difficulty in taking up the various tests given by Friedman: it is not clear what should be treated as a test of the theory and what should be treated merely as an obiter dictum. I believe that I am covering everything which can be considered a separate test.

2. I am by no means the first to have noticed this point. Thus Robert Ferber in his survey of consumption function literature has pointed out that it has been found that many of Friedman's tests are consistent with other theories, too. ("Research on Household Behavior," *American Economic Review,* Vol. LII, March 1962, p. 31.) A similar point was made earlier by Hendrick Houthakker. ("The Permanent Income Hypothesis," *American Economic Review,* Vol. XLVIII, June 1958, p. 399). Michael Farrell has argued that while Friedman's cross-section evidence is consistent with his theory, this "does not go very far towards confirming the hypotheses." ("The New Theories of the Consumption Function," *Economic Journal,* Vol. LXIX, December 1959, p. 689.)

that two coefficients differ in the *direction* predicted by the permanent income theory, but not necessarily by the *amount* predicted by the theory. The reason for this is that usually there is not enough information available to allow the permanent income theory to predict the magnitude of the difference. To show that any particular test confirms the standard income theory as well as the full permanent income theory, all that is therefore necessary is to show that the standard income theory makes the same prediction about the direction of the difference between the two coefficients.

Such an almost page-for-page criticism as I am undertaking here may seem unduly contentious and carping. I would therefore like to state at the outset, not as a matter of politeness, but as a matter of sincere belief, that I consider Friedman's book to be one of the outstanding performances in modern economics. The tests he presents are truly ingenious; to show their limitations is by comparison a pedestrian task. All that my criticisms really amount to is the claim that Friedman has gone too far, that his evidence is consistent with less dramatic conclusions than the ones he drew.

I will now take up Friedman's tests in the order in which they are given in his book, and to faciliate cross references, I will use his section headings. But before taking up each test individually, it may be useful to explain a technique which Friedman used in several tests. This is the comparison of the proportion of the income variance due to permanent elements with the income elasticity of consumption. According to the full permanent income theory the income elasticity of consumption is unity for permanent income (proportionality hypothesis), and zero for transitory income (assumption that all transitory income is saved). The income elasticity of consumption for measured income is, of course, a weighted mean of the unitary elasticity for permanent income and the zero elasticity for transitory income. Hence, the actually observed income elasticity for measured income tells us the relative weights of permanent and transitory elements in the income variance. For example, if this elasticity is 0.80, then 80 percent of the observed income variance must be due to differences in permanent income and 20 percent to differences in transitory income. This method of inferring from the measured income elasticity of consumption the proportion of the income variance due to permanent elements is the basis of several of Friedman's tests.

Temporal Changes in Inequality of Income

The first piece of evidence which Friedman presented is not a test based on the details of statistical observation, but relies on the well-known stylized fact that the distribution of income has not become more unequal over time. Both the absolute and relative income theories assert that the "rich" are saving a larger percent of their income than the "poor." If so, as time goes by, the rich should receive an increasing share of property income, and hence of total income. Here is one implication of these theories which seems to be sharply and dramatically contradicted by the evidence.

But Friedman's analysis assumes that differential savings rates are the only factor to be considered and that there are not offsetting effects on the distribution of income. With the help of a growth model it is possible to analyze the stability of the income distribution along a balanced growth path, taking account of several factors such as population growth, and taxation. Such an analysis has been undertaken by Joseph Stiglitz.[3] He showed that with a linear, *but not necessarily homogeneous,* savings function (as well as with a nonlinear one), as the economy moves along the balanced growth path the distribution of income and wealth will become asymptotically equal. This provides a counter-example to Friedman's argument that the fairly constant distribution of income and wealth implies the validity of the proportionality hypothesis.

Consumption-Income Regressions for Different Dates and Groups

Temporal Differences. Under this rubric Friedman considered several different empirical observations. First, there is the fact that various budget studies since 1888–1890 show roughly similar average propensities to consume, and hence illustrate that the saving-income ratio has not been rising with the increase in income. Moreover, differences between the income elasticities shown by various budget studies can be explained plausibly by differences in the importance of transitory income components in these budget studies.

The first of these facts is merely another way of showing what is shown so dramatically by the time series data; the time series results and the budget study results are not separate facts, but are merely the same fact, a stable saving-income ratio, observed in two different ways. (Friedman did not claim that it *is* separate evidence—in fact, the title of the chapter begins "The Consistency of the Permanent Income Hypothesis with Existing Evidence.") What *is* additional evidence is the relationship between the income elasticities of consumption and the importance of transitory income components in different budget studies. According to the permanent income theory, the greater the proportion of the difference in measured income, which represents merely a difference in transitory income, the lower should be the income elasticity of consumption. And Friedman showed that transitory elements are

3. J. E. Stiglitz, "Distribution of Income and Wealth among Individuals," *Econometrica,* Vol. 37, July 1969, pp. 382–97.

relatively important in budget studies with a low income elasticity. This agreement between the prediction from the hypothesis and the observation is meaningful evidence for the permanent income theory. But note that this evidence, while perfectly consistent with a full permanent income theory, is just as consistent with the standard income theory.[4]

Differences Between Countries. In addition to looking at budget studies for different times, Friedman also compared budget studies for the United States and Great Britain. He found that the income elasticity of consumption is greater in Britain than in the United States and he explained this by a greater importance in income variance of transitory components in the United States than in Britain.[5]

Friedman based his comparison on two sets of data which come from closely comparable studies, the Survey of Consumer Finances for the United States and the Oxford Institute of Economics and Statistics survey for Britain. The former shows an income elasticity of consump-

4. But it is not consistent with the measured income theories. Since these theories make no use of the distinction between transitory and permanent income, they *imply* that the income elasticities of consumption should be the same in budget studies where transitory income is important and those where it is unimportant.

5. Friedman also discussed differences in the average propensities to consume in the two countries. However, the reasons he gave for these differences are all some distance removed from the permanent income theory. (The reasons are the lower transitory income variance in Britain, and hence the lower demand for nonhuman wealth; the greater provision of security through the government in Britain; and the absence of a capital gains tax in Britain in the period of the budget studies.) All these reasons suggest is that income fluctuations, social security programs, and the tax system may affect the average propensity to consume. But all of this is entirely consistent with the measured income theories, and hence does not allow us to choose between them and the permanent income theory. Moreover, the argument that greater income instability leads to a greater saving ratio in any one year is not really valid for the reason which Friedman himself stated (*A Theory of the Consumption Function, op. cit.,* p. 57) but then ignored. This reason is that, to be sure, a household with much fluctuation of income will have a higher equilibrium ratio of nonhuman wealth to income; but once it has achieved this equilibrium ratio, it has no incentive to save a larger proportion of its income than do other households. The argument that high income variability leads to a high saving ratio assumes, as Friedman pointed out, that the household is not initially in equilibrium, and "that the discrepancy between the existing position and the full equilibrium position is larger the higher the equilibrium level of nonhuman wealth, so that the higher the latter, the greater the pressure to devote current resources to increasing the level of non-human wealth." (*Ibid.,* p. 57.) In addition to comparing the budget studies in the United States and Britain, Friedman also discussed Swedish budget studies. However, he concluded that differences among the studies interfere with such a comparison.

tion for the United States of 0.82, whereas the latter shows an income elasticity of consumption for Britain of 0.87.

But this test suffers from two weaknesses. First, Friedman used the permanent income theory to deduce from the income elasticities that income is less variable in Britain than in the United States. But he then did not go on to determine in any rigorous way whether this deduction is correct.[6] To be sure, he mentioned some reasons why income is *likely* to be less variable in Britain, but these amount to little more than casual empiricism.

The second weakness of this test concerns the data. Friedman, writing before computers became widely used, did his regressions by the graphic method. When I reran his regressions on a computer, it turned out that his results were very accurate. However, they were based on unweighted data; that is, every income class (except the terminal classes which he omitted) obtained the same weight regardless of the number of households in it. Since there is no reason why the basic unit of observation should be an income class rather than a household, I reran the regression weighting each class by the number of households in it.[7] The results are shown in Table 1. I added in this table one British survey which had not been available to Friedman at the time. The weighted data for the three studies show no consistent difference in the income elasticities in the two countries, thus rejecting Friedman's results.[8]

6. See John Johnston, "Review of Friedman, *A Theory of The Consumption Function,*" *Review of Economics and Statistics,* Vol. LX, November 1958, p. 433. However, there is some evidence supporting Friedman. (See Robert Parry, "Separation of Normal and Transitory Components of Income from Cross Section Data," unpublished Ph.D. dissertation, University of Pennsylvania, 1967, p. 175.) But this evidence is based on a comparison of only two budget studies (the 1950 Bureau of Labor Statistics Survey and the 1954 Oxford Institute Survey) and it is not certain that other surveys would show the same result.

7. Surely an income class with say, 20 percent of the population should receive a bigger weight than another class containing only, say 5 percent. One can argue of course, that the data should be weighted by the square root of the number of cases. From the point of view of statistical inference, this would clearly be a better method of weighting. However, weighting by the number of cases has an advantage, too; it gives each income class the same importance as it has in the total.

8. It might be tempting to argue that this test, therefore, rejects the full permanent income theory. But this would be going too far. The difference between the income elasticities shown by the two British studies are very large. It is, therefore, quite possible that the income elasticity is, in fact, lower in Britain than in the United States. Klein and Liviatan attributed the difference found by Friedman in the income elasticities of the two countries to institutional factors. They did, however, support Friedman in some ways

Table 1

Income Elasticities of Consumption,
United States and Great Britain

Country	Unweighted		Weighted by Number of Cases	
	Income Elasticity of Consumption	*Standard Error*	*Income Elasticity of Consumption*	*Standard Error*
United States, 1950	.82	N.A.	.84	.01
Britain, 1951–52	.87	N.A.	.81	.01
Britain, 1952–53	N.A.ª	N.A.	.90	.01

SOURCES: Unweighted data from M. Friedman, *A Theory of the Consumption Function*, p. 41; weighted data based on H. F. Lydall, "National Survey of Personal Incomes and Savings, Part IV." Oxford University Institute of Economics and Statistics, *Bulletin* (October–November 1953), p. 388. L. R. Klein, "Patterns of Savings, the Surveys of 1953–54," in *ibid.*, May 1955, p. 179, and T. P. Hill, "Incomes, Savings and Net Worth," in *ibid.*, May 1955, p. 135; "1951 Survey of Consumer Finances, Part III," *Federal Reserve Bulletin*, August 1951, p. 421.

ª N.A. means not available.

Consumption of Farm and Nonfarm Families. The next comparison which Friedman presented is one of farm and nonfarm households within the United States.[9] The facts to be explained are two: first, the lower average propensity to consume of farmers at any absolute income level, as well as the lower consumption-income ratio for all farmers combined, and second, the farmers' lower income elasticity of consumption. The first of these is due to the fact that since mean income is less for farm than for nonfarm households, *at any given income level* farmers are more likely to have positive transitory income (or less likely to have negative transitory income) than nonfarm households. (The same reasoning applies with regard to the size of the transitory component.) For example, take an income level corresponding to the mean income of

since they believe that both the cross-section studies and time series show a higher income elasticity for the United States, and moreover they agreed with him (though they did not cite any supporting data) that income is more variable in the United States. Lawrence Klein and Nissan Liviatan, "The Significance of Income Variability on Savings Behaviour," Oxford University Institute of Economics and Statistics, *Bulletin,* Vol. 19, May 1957, p. 154.

9. In their original publication of the life cycle hypothesis, Modigliani and Brumberg also used a very brief comparison of farm and nonfarm households, similar to Friedman's discussion of the differences in the income elasticities. John Johnston (*op. cit.*, p. 433) criticized Friedman for not verifying his inference that farm income is more variable. However, there are strong grounds for thinking that farm income is in fact more variable.

nonfarm households. For nonfarm households transitory income is zero on the average. But since this income is above the mean of farmers' incomes, farm households at this income level have, on the average, positive transitory income. Hence, if transitory income is saved, the consumption-income ratio will be less for farmers than for nonfarm households.

But this does not provide a good test of the permanent income theory. To be sure, the lower propensity to consume of farmers at any given income level can be explained by the full permanent income theory, but it can also be explained by the relative income theory. Moreover, since Friedman does not quantify the size of the effect, the standard income theory can explain the observed facts just as easily as the full permanent income theory.

The lower overall propensity to consume of farmers when all income levels are combined was explained by Friedman as a result of farmers experiencing greater income variability than urban households, and possibly by farmers earning perhaps a higher rate of return on their saving. But both of these are extraneous factors from the point of view of the permanent income theory. They can be grafted onto the relative income theory or the absolute theory, and so the lower average propensity to consume of farmers does not differentiate between these theories.[10]

This leaves the difference in the income elasticities—a difference which persists if one weights the data and controls for family size. The fact that the income elasticity of consumption is greater for farm than for nonfarm households is consistent with the permanent income theory, but it does not support the full permanent income theory against the standard income theory. To choose between these two one would have to compare the income elasticities with independently derived data on

10. As James Tobin and Harold Watts have pointed out, "the plausible notion that households with volatile incomes will endeavor to provide themselves with contingency reserves can be accepted even if one is skeptical of the more distinctive propositions of the Friedman and Modigliani-Brumberg theories." "An Evaluation of the Tests," Oxford University Institute of Economics and Statistics, *Bulletin*, Vol. 19, May 1957, p. 161. Moreover, as pointed out above the permanent income theory does not really establish that there is a connection between income uncertainty and a high saving ratio unless one makes two special assumptions. Irwin Friend has argued that the Goldsmith data show a *higher* average propensity to consume for farm than for nonfarm households prior to the mid-1930s. ("Further Comments on 'A Theory of the Consumption Function'") in Lincoln Clark (ed.), *Consumer Behavior* (New York, Harper and Brothers, 1958, Vol. 3, p. 457.) However, Friedman pointed out that this is not so if capital gains are included in income. ("Reply to Comments on 'A Theory of the Consumption Function,'" in the same volume, p. 464.)

income variance. Unfortunately, such data are not available, and hence
this test also is merely a test of direction rather than a test of a specific
implication of the full permanent income theory.[11]

Occupational Characteristics of Families. In the next section of this
book, Friedman considered the saving ratio of nonfarm entrepreneurs
and explained it by essentially similar reasons. Entrepreneurs have a
high saving ratio because income instability gives them a strong incentive
to raise their ratio of non-human wealth to income. Their great income
variability also explains their low income elasticity of consumption.
Other factors which cause entrepreneurs to save more, according to
Friedman, are the higher rates of return on capital for entrepreneurs
than for other households, perhaps also the characteristics of the type
of persons who take up entrepreneurial pursuits and demographic differences (the exclusion of retired households and households who have
not yet become entrepreneurs). These factors explaining the high saving
rate of the self-employed are, of course, entirely consistent with the
measured income theories. The distinctive characteristic of the permanent income theory is its explanation of the difference in the income
elasticity of consumption between self-employed and employees.

Friedman treated it as a self-evident fact that the self-employed have
a much more unstable income than do employees. At first glance this
seems to be obviously correct, surely distribution theory teaches us that
profits are more variable than wages and salaries. But this argument
from income distribution theory is not really applicable. It is not valid
to identify the income of the self-employed with economic profit. The
typical entrepreneur in budget studies is a small businessman who receives mainly what, in the functional income distribution, is classified as
wages. For the small entrepreneur the wage component is probably large
relative to the pure profits component. And this wage component of

11. Friedman did, however, present data for the income variance of
another sample of farm households, as well as for urban households (*op. cit.,*
p. 187). These data show a greater difference between the income variance
of farm and nonfarm households than is implied by the income elasticities
discussed in this section. Hence, these data could be used to support the
standard income theory against the full permanent income theory. However, it would probably be unwise to attach much importance to this since
the income variability data come from a different sample than do the income
elasticity figures.

Robert Clower and Bruce Johnson have argued that Friedman's data for
farm and nonfarm households suggest that the income elasticity of consumption for permanent income is below unity; see "Income and Wealth
and the Theory of Consumption," in J. N. Wolfe (ed.), *Value and Growth,
Papers in Honour of Sir John Hicks* (Edinburgh, University Press, 1968), p.
72. However, since Friedman's data show measured rather than permanent
income, I do not know how to interpret their cryptic remark.

the entrepreneur's income is likely to be more stable than the income of employees because the entrepreneur's employment is stable—surely he is the last man to be fired when business turns down. Hence, it is not really possible to say a priori whether the income of the self-employed is more or less stable than an employee's income.

Unfortunately, little empirical information on relative income variability is available. What the available data do show is that income *may* be somewhat more variable for the self-employed, but *on the whole* they suggest that the difference, if any, is rather minor.[12] And since the difference in income variability is rather small it may not be sufficient for Friedman's test. However, as will be shown in the next chapter, income change data obtained by asking households about their previous incomes are not reliable.

But quite apart from the question whether or not income is, in fact, more variable for the self-employed, there is another consideration. Friedman's test does not deal *directly* with income variability per se. It attributes the smaller income elasticity of the self-employed to the claimed fact that for the self-employed the transitory component accounts for a great *proportion* (and the permanent component for a smaller proportion) of the *total measured income dispersion* than for employees. But the fact that income is more variable for the self-employed than for employees may be offset by the dispersion of *permanent* income being greater for the self-employed, too.

This is agreed to by Friedman:

It is plausible that permanent components differ more widely for business spending units, than for nonbusiness, nonfarm spending units. The crucial question for elasticities, however, is whether differences in the

12. For data from the Survey of Consumer Finances, see Lawrence Klein and Julius Margolis, "Statistical Studies of Unincorporated Business," *Review of Economics and Statistics,* Vol. XXXVI, February 1954, p. 38. Ralph Bristol ("Factors Associated with Income Variability," American Economic Association, *Papers and Proceedings,* Vol. XLVIII, May 1958, p. 288) provides evidence from panel data and the annual *Survey of Consumer Finances* by George Katona, et al, also provides relevant data. Other data from the 1950 Bureau of Labor Statistics Survey and from the Oxford Reinterview Survey are cited in Lawrence Klein and Nissan Liviatan, *op. cit.,* pp. 152–53. See also George Katona and Eva Mueller, *Consumer Response to Income Increases* (Washington, D.C., Brookings Institution, 1968), p. 68, and Lawrence Klein, "Entrepreneurial Saving," in I. Friend and R. Jones (eds.), *Consumption and Saving* (Philadelphia, University of Pennsylvania Press, 1960), pp. 314 and 326–30. Further evidence on relative income variability is given in James Morgan ("Saving and Spending as Explained by All the Variables," in Richard Kosobud and James Morgan (eds.), *Consumer Behavior of Individual Families over Two and Three Years* (University of Michigan, Survey Research Center, Ann Arbor, Mich., 1964), p. 115.

dispersion of permanent components are greater or less than the corresponding differences in the dispersion of transitory components, and
about this there is not much a priori basis for formulating any precise
expectations. What the elasticities tell us is that . . . if the dispersion
of permanent components for business units exceeds that for nonfarm,
nonbusiness units, the dispersion of transitory components does so by
an even larger percentage.[13]

But this argument is dubious. What Friedman did here was not to
use the data to tell us whether the theory is correct, but to assume at
the outset that the theory is right, and to use it to tell us something about
the data, something which cannot be verified directly. To be more specific, since the dispersion of the permanent income components is not
known, the permanent income theory cannot be used to predict, purely
from a knowledge of the dispersion of the transitory components,
whether or not the income elasticity of consumption should be greater
for self-employed or for employee households. So as far as Friedman's
test goes, the lower income elasticity for the self-employed neither confirms nor disconfirms the permanent income theory.[14] But, as will be
shown in Chapter 5, Liviatan's work avoids this difficulty and does confirm either a full permanent income theory or a standard income theory.[15]

Negro and White Families. In discussing farmers, Friedman dealt with
a group whose income is low and variable; in his analysis of the self-
employed, Friedman dealt with a group whose income is high but
variable. He supplemented these tests by taking up a group with a low
income, black households. He pointed to four differences in the saving

13. *Op. cit.,* p. 72.
14. Friedman offered two additional considerations which can be interpreted as a test of the fine structure of the theory. One is that in those
data in which entrepreneurial income is defined as the entrepreneur's withdrawals from the business, the income elasticity is higher than in those
data which measure his income more accurately. But this observed fact
can be explained in another way, too. Entrepreneurs may withdraw more
or less of their firm's earnings depending upon how much they want to spend
on consumption. The second fact is that the dispersion of the permanent
income component (which Friedman estimated on the basis of the permanent income theory) is greater in New York than in other cities considered (Columbus and Atlanta) for salaried business and salaried professional households. Friedman's explanation is that a broader range of activities is open to these households in New York than in other cities, so that
the dispersion of the permanent component is greater in New York. But the
greater range of opportunities presumably also raises the dispersion of the
transitory component, so that one cannot use the permanent income theory
to predict either a greater or a smaller income elasticity for New York.
15. Clower and Johnson, working with a wealth theory have suggested
(*op. cit.,* p. 72) that the entrepreneur's lower income elasticity of consumption may be due to his high ratio of wealth to consumption.

behavior of black and white households. First, at the same measured income the average propensity to consume is greater for white households than for black households. Second, if one considers households at all income levels together, the picture is reversed: the average propensity to consume is greater for black households than for white households. Third, the income elasticities of consumption are approximately the same in each group.[16]

The first of these observations, the greater propensity to consume for white households at any given level of income, is explained by Friedman in the same way as in the case of farmers. At any given level of measured income, households coming from the low income population have more positive (or less negative) transitory income than do households from the higher income group. The fact that black households at all levels of income combined consume a larger percent of their income than do white households is explained by Friedman as a consequence of entrepreneurship being less frequent among blacks, as well as by the exclusion of relief families from the data. The third fact, the similarity of income elasticities, is explained by Friedman as showing that the relative importance of permanent and transitory elements in accounting for income differences is similar in the two groups.

To what extent do these observations provide firm evidence for the permanent income theory? The fact that at any given income level the average propensity to consume is greater for white than black households is consistent not only with the permanent income theory but also with the relative income theory; indeed, it is one of the pieces of evidence which Duesenberry used to confirm this theory. It can even be made consistent with the absolute income theory by arguing, as Tobin among others has done, that the lower average propensity to consume of blacks is due to the fact that dissaving is more difficult for them.[17] Moreover, it is entirely consistent with the standard income theory. And as will be shown in Chapter 11, the standard income theory provides a better explanation of the difference in the propensity to consume at any given income level than does the full permanent income theory.

16. In addition, Friedman showed that the difference between the North and the South in the relative saving behavior of Negroes and whites supports the permanent income theory. However, Friedman qualified this by pointing out that this result "must be regarded with some suspicion as possible being simply a disguised reflection of the restriction of these data to nonrelief families" (*op. cit.*, p. 84). In addition, as pointed out in Chapter 11, there is a very confusing peculiarity of the data on consumption of Southern Negroes. I have therefore not treated this as a test.

17. "Relative Income, Absolute Income and Saving," in *Money, Trade and Economic Growth, Essays in Honor of John H. Williams* (New York, Macmillan, 1956), pp. 143–49.

The similarity of the income elasticities of black and white households is not evidence for the permanent income theory either, since it is also consistent with the measured income theories.

Savings and Age

The next characteristic of saving behavior which Friedman considered is the relation of saving and age. It is basic to the permanent income theory that households attempt to maximize utility by using savings as a buffer against income fluctuations. Since young and old households have incomes which are below their lifetime mean incomes, we would expect young and old households to have a low (or, even negative) saving ratio, and middle aged households to have a high saving ratio. And, generally speaking, this is what the data show. But the correlation between the relative incomes of different age groups and the relative saving ratios is very loose. Friedman explained this by the fact that cross-section data give a bad estimate of the relation of income to age. The mean income presently received by, say, households with a 40-year-old head is not a good estimate of the mean income which will be received in twenty years by a household with a head now aged 20 years, since incomes have a secular trend. Hence, Friedman adjusted the relative incomes received by households in different age groups to take account of this trend. This adjustment improves the correlation, and since this adjustment is one suggested by the permanent income theory, the improvement in the correlation provides some favorable evidence for the permanent income theory. However, the improved correlation is far from perfect. Friedman explained this by the fact that even the adjusted income data do not measure permanent income properly:

the permanent income component is not to be regarded as expected lifetime earnings; it can itself be regarded as varying with age. It is to be interpreted as the mean income at any age regarded as permanent by the consumer unit in question, which in turn depends on its horizon and foresightedness. Accordingly [the adjusted relative income figures] are to be regarded solely as indexes of the ratios of measured income to permanent income.[18]

But this means that what we have here is merely a test of direction rather than of precise magnitude. In other words, the saving ratios of different age groups can be explained not only by the full permanent income theory but also by the standard income theory.[19]

18. *Op. cit.*, p. 93.
19. Friedman went on (pp. 93–94) to compare the relation between his adjusted relative income figures and the saving ratios to the relationship found by Dorothy Brady and Rose Friedman when they plotted the saving ratio against the ratio of measured income to mean income of urban families. These two procedures yield very similar figures, but it is hard to see how this can be interpreted meaningfully as a test.

Effect of Change in Income

The next test which Friedman used is to look at data which classify households by income change. If we group households by income change, we are classifying them to a large extent by their receipt of transitory income. Hence, if the permanent income theory or the standard income theory is right, the consumption functions for these income change groups should differ. The "income decline" group—the group with predominately negative transitory income—should have the greatest average propensity to consume, while the group with the greatest income increase—and hence the most positive transitory income—should have the lowest average propensity to consume. And this is what the data show. However, the relative income theory has the same implication. Hence, this test does not really distinguish between the measured income theories and the permanent income theory.

The income change data can also be used in another test. If we group households by income change—that is, largely by transitory income—then within each income change group differences in transitory income should account for a smaller proportion of the measured income variance than if we consider all households jointly regardless of the income change they experienced. According to the permanent income theory, this implies that the income elasticity of consumption should be greater for the income change groups considered separately than for all households taken together. Again, the data confirm the theory. But this, too, does not support the permanent income theory against the relative income theory, since the relative income theory implies the same thing. According to the relative income theory, the fact that households whose income has fallen are below their peak income raises their consumption relative to income, while households whose incomes have risen may be at their peak income so that a past income peak effect does not raise their consumption. Since households whose income has fallen tend to be in the lower part of the income distribution, the past peak income effect tends to lower the income elasticity of consumption. Hence, the income elasticity is less for all households considered jointly than for any single income change group.

Finally, Friedman was able to derive from the permanent income theory the slope and intercept (or rather a transformation thereof) of the consumption function which should be shown by the data. And the data confirm this implication of the permanent income theory, too. This test is extremely important. It quantifies the prediction of the permanent income theory most precisely, so that it represents a test of the full permanent income theory vis-à-vis the standard income theory, as well as vis-à-vis the measured income theories. This is one of the very few tests which Friedman treated as establishing the permanent income theory precisely rather than as just showing a general consistency between the theory and the data.[20]

But actually this test does not give the permanent income theory the strong support which Friedman believes it does. There is a question whether the theory really gives such a good fit to the data. Friedman used two sets of data, one for farm families in 1940–1942 and one from a Survey of Consumer Finances sample for 1947–1948. In each case he used the permanent income theory to predict for each income change class the regression coefficient of consumption on measured income, and also—in place of the intercept—the income level at which the regression line for the income change class intersects the regression line for the whole sample. Let us look at each of these in turn.

Table 2 shows the predicted and observed regression coefficients for each income change class for Friedman's data, and, at first glance, the similarity of the predicted and actual values is impressive. But what is the proper criterion for judging whether the predicted and observed values are really close enough to confirm the theory? Does the theory really predict well? The way to answer this question is to see to what extent the permanent income theory gives a better prediction of the regression coefficient than does a naïve model.[21] Suppose that one were told only the regression coefficient for the whole sample, and asked to guess at the regression coefficient for each income change class. In the absence of the permanent income theory one would have to give in reply the regression coefficient of the whole sample. Hence, the proper way of seeing whether the permanent income theory predicts well is to compare the prediction error of the permanent income theory with the prediction error which results if one uses the regression coefficient of the whole sample as one's estimate of the regression coefficient for each income change class. In deriving the regression coefficient for each income change class Friedman used as one of the parameters the regression coefficient of the whole sample; hence it is a fair test to determine the extent to which the manipulation of this coefficient suggested by the permanent income theory improves the prediction over what one gets by using this coefficient in its raw form.[22] This is shown

20. "The correspondence, particularly in numerical characteristics, is in some ways the most striking bit of evidence for our hypothesis that has so far been adduced. It is so partly because the comparisons between observation and prediction are for fairly precise implications of the hypothesis that could readily have been contradicted, partly because these implications have not heretofore been drawn from other hypotheses and some have not even been established as empirical generalizations." Friedman (*op. cit.,* p. 109).

21. I am indebted at this point to my former research assistant, Geoffrey Carliner.

22. I used Friedman's own unweighted data since the weights needed to weight each class by its frequency are not available.

Table 2

Prediction of Regression Coefficients
for Income Change Classes

Income Change Class	(1) Predicted by Permanent Income Theory	(2) Observed	(3) Error of Prediction as Percent of Naïve Model Error
Spending Units, 1947–48			
Down more than 25%	.89	.77	240
Down 25% to down 5%	.89	.87	40
Down 5% to up 5%	.89	.88	12
Up 5% to up 25%	.89	.89	0
Up 25% or more	.89	.87	40
All Classes		.82	61[a]
Farm Households, 1940–41			
No change	.23	.29	43
Up 1 class	.23	.27	33
Up 2 classes	.23	.25	20
Up 3 classes	.23	.23	0
Up 4 classes	.23	.24	11
All Classes		.15	25[a]

SOURCE: Columns (1) and (2), Milton Friedman, *A Theory of the Consumption Function*, pp. 102, 106.

[a] Represents sum of errors of the prediction divided by the sum of errors of the naïve model.

in column 3 of Table 2. This column shows that the theory does not predict so well after all. The mean absolute error of the prediction is about 60 percent of the naïve model error for the Survey of Consumer Finances sample, and 25 percent for the farm sample.[23]

It is worth noting that the naïve model which I used as a foil for

23. Friedman argued that except for the class with the greatest income decrease "the observed elasticities are very close to the predicted" (*ibid.*, p. 107). I have therefore undertaken another test excluding this income change class. Since the exclusion of one income change class would change the elasticity of the whole sample, I have used as the naïve model value the unweighted mean of the observed elasticities of each income change class. The mean absolute error of this naïve model turned out to be substantially less than that of the prediction.

Friedman stated that the deviations of the predicted from the observed values are in the direction implied by this theory, but this fact does not furnish a precise test of the theory. Moreover, Friedman suggested another weakness of his results. His use of class means in place of the (unavailable) actual income changes for each family implies that his predicted values of the regression coefficient should be greater than the observed ones—but actually they are lower. As Friedman pointed out, this can be explained in part—but only in part—by a probable negative transitory element in consumption (*ibid.*, pp. 102–3).

the theory is an extremely naïve one. Unlike some of the naïve models which have been used to evaluate time series regressions, it does not imply any specialized knowledge of the behavior of the variable to be predicted, such as its past growth rate. It assumes that we know nothing at all about the way in which the regression coefficients for each income change class differ from the coefficient for the whole sample. It therefore differs sharply from the standard income theory, because this theory implies that the regression coefficient for each of the income change classes should be higher than the coefficient for the whole sample.

The other parameter which Friedman estimated (in place of the intercept) is the income at the intersection of the regression line for the income change class with the regression line for the whole sample. Here I had to change the naïve model somewhat since I don't have a value for the whole sample to use as a naïve model estimate in each income change class. Instead, I used the unweighted mean for all income change classes as my naïve model estimate for each income change class. For the farm data the mean absolute error of the permanent income theory prediction is only 24 percent of the corresponding error of the naïve model, but for Survey of Consumer Finances data the theory's mean absolute error is equal to 94 percent of the naïve model error.[24] Again, it should be emphasized, the naïve model is indeed a very naïve one.

Thus for both parameters the permanent income theory gives a better fit than one gets from "no theory at all," which is what the naïve model amounts to. But for the Survey of Consumer Finances data, the fit leaves very substantial room for improvement, and for the farm data it is by no means perfect either.[25] Hence this test does not really support the full permanent income theory.

24. In addition to the two parameters just discussed, Friedman also calculated average consumption in each income change class. The prediction of the permanent income theory here is that this is similar for all income change classes, while the measured income theories predict that it is positively related to the magnitude of the income change. For the farm sample, such a positive relationship is apparent. Friedman attributed it to the bias which results when the data are classified, not by percentage income change but by the absolute amount of the income change, as is the case for the farm sample. But this bias does not exist in the Survey of Consumer Finances sample, where income change is measured on a percentage basis. Friedman argued that these data show average consumption as being "much the same for the various income-change classes" and as having "no systematic relation to income change" except in the greatest income decrease class, where it may reflect an age effect (*ibid.*, p. 107). But actually, even for the remaining four income change classes the coefficient of ranked correlation between average consumption and income change is 0.35. While this is not significant, it is a correlation in the direction predicted by the measured income theories.

25. Unfortunately, it is not possible to see whether the standard income theory gives a better fit than the full permanent income theory. To predict

Recent Long-Period Estimates of Aggregate Savings for the United States

In this section Friedman provided a general discussion of the secular constancy of the saving ratio. Here he pointed out that there is no tendency for the fraction of income consumed to fall secularly—a fact quite consistent with the permanent income theory. He went beyond this general statement by looking at the observations which deviate from the long-run consumption function. In inflationary war years actual consumption is below predicted levels, as are the observations for two years of relatively great peacetime prosperity, 1902 and 1905. In all of these years one would expect transitory income to be positive and, hence, the permanent income theory predicts what the data show: a high ratio of saving to income. Conversely, all the observations which show consumption above the predicted level are years of deep depression "and there is no year that clearly deserved to be so designated that is excluded from the list." [26] Clearly, this is what the permanent income theory would predict. But this evidence is consistent not only with the permanent income theory but also with the relative income theory and the standard income theory. Hence it is not really evidence for the permanent income theory. And Friedman agreed that it was not "very strong evidence for the hypothesis." [27]

Friedman then took up the reasons for the secular stability of the saving ratio. He pointed out that this stability, while consistent with the permanent income hypothesis, is in no way required by it. "So the observed rough constancy . . . is about as much of a puzzle as substantial variations in it would be." [28] (It is worth noting that the same is true for the relative income theory.) Friedman then explained this constancy as the result of mutually offsetting factors such as changed family size and the importance of farm income.

Regression of Consumption on Current Income

Next, Friedman presented an ingenious test based on the change in the income elasticity that occurs if one lengthens the period covered. The rationale of this test is the following: Compare two consumption functions fitted to aggregate data, one covering a fifty-year period and

---

the regression coefficient for the income change classes on the basis of the standard income theory, one would need to know such parameters as the correlation coefficient of transitory income and consumption. This information is not available. I am indebted for this point to my former research assistant Adil Kanaan.

26. *Ibid.*, p. 119.
27. *Ibid.*, p. 119.
28. *Ibid.*, p. 120.

the other a five-year span. Over the fifty years covered by the first consumption function, most of the change in income which has taken place represents economic growth—that is, a change in permanent income. In the five-year consumption function a much smaller proportion of the income change is due to economic growth, and a much larger proportion of the income variation represents transitory factors. Hence, if the permanent income theory is correct, and the income elasticity of consumption does measure the proportion of the income change which is accounted for by the permanent component of income, one would expect the fifty-year consumption function to show a greater income elasticity of consumption than does the five-year function. Moreover, Friedman developed a much more specific test from this approach, and on the assumption that the trend is the only factor accounting for the change in permanent income, he computed the rise in the income elasticity which should result from lengthening the period.

And the data *do* show that the income elasticity of consumption increases as one lengthens the period over which it is fitted. However, the increase in the income elasticity is not as great as could be predicted on the assumption that all the change in permanent income is due to a stable secular trend. Friedman concluded: "This is as it should be. For factors other than secular trend produce differences in permanent income so that the computed figures are estimates of the maximum effect to be expected, on our hypothesis, from lengthening the period. It would be most disturbing if the observed effects exceeded these maxima; the fact that they do not lends some minor additional support to our hypothesis." [29] The fact that the income elasticity increases as one lengthens the period covered is strong evidence either for the full permanent income theory or for the standard income theory, but it does not distinguish between them.

The second part of Friedman's test does quantify his predictions and furnishes a *potential* test of the full permanent income theory versus the standard income theory. However, the results of the test fail to distinguish between the two. Friedman found that the observed income elasticities are less than the predicted ones, and then explained this by the fact that one of the assumptions he made to obtain the predicted elasticities is not fully met. Now the fact that the assumption is not met would certainly lead to *some* discrepancy between the actual and predicted elasticities, but there is no way of telling whether it accounts for all of the discrepancy. Part of the difference between the actual and the predicted results may be the fault of the special assumption, and part may well be the fault of the hypothesis being tested. Thus, all in

29. *Ibid.*, p. 128.

all, this test, too, does not distinguish between a full permanent income theory and the standard income theory.[30]

Friedman then applied a similar technique to derive another ingenious test, one based on the form of the data. He compared the income elasticity one obtains from aggregate data with the income elasticity which one gets from per capita data. Using aggregate data means using per capita income and consumption multiplied by population. Since population is growing at a fairly steady rate, the steady growth component—the permanent component—accounts for a greater percentage of the change in aggregate income than in per capita income. The permanent income theory predicts from this that the income elasticity should be greater when derived from aggregate data than when derived from the same observations expressed on a per capita basis. And this is what we find.

Roughly similar reasoning applies to the comparison of income elasticities computed from deflated and undeflated data. Hence, one would expect the income elasticity to be greater for undeflated magnitudes. Again, the data support the theory. But note that both of these tests are tests of direction only, and are just as consistent with the standard income theory as with the full permanent income theory.

Regressions of Consumption on Current and Past Incomes

This test of the permanent income theory is an extremely important one. What Friedman presented here is, in a way, the most obvious test—he compared the fit of a permanent income theory regression with the fit obtained from two alternative theories. One is the relative income theory—a theory which makes consumption a function of current income and past peak income. The other is an equation used by Mrs. Mack, which makes consumption depend on current income and income of the previous year. This I interpret to be a *modified* absolute income theory.[31]

There are several things worth noting about this test. First, this is the only place where we meet the famous seventeen-year consumption function. In other tests Friedman showed that consumption depends on income of more than the current year. In this test, the length of time is specified very precisely. Second, it is my impression that a number of economists find the permanent income theory implausible because they find it hard to believe that consumption is affected by income of the past sixteen years. This criticism is invalid. What Friedman did is to

30. But see below for a test by Simon and Aigner which avoids this difficulty.
31. In addition, Friedman discussed briefly the results for a simple absolute income theory (*ibid.*, p. 149).

fit an equation using past income of many years with exponentially declining weights. Since he worked it out very precisely, he included all
years which have a weight of *one tenth of one percent* or more. This is
why the function includes what at first seems to be an implausibly long
span of time. The current year plus the past two years together account for almost 70 percent of the weight. Current income plus the income of the past three years account for close to 80 percent of the
weight. The incomes of the last three years included in the seventeen-
year function, on the other hand, each account for only one tenth of one
percent of the weight. As Friedman explained, "the retention of as
many as 17 terms is doubtless an excess of precision. It is dubious that
the results would be appreciably affected by retaining, say, only 9 terms
and adjusting the weight for them to unity." [32]

What is more significant than Friedman's use of seventeen years is
that his results do *not* give strong support to the permanent income
theory. The relative income theory equation fits the data somewhat
better than the permanent income theory. While the permanent income
equation explains 60 percent of the variance not accounted for by
common trend, the relative income equation explains 80 percent.[33]
Friedman accounted for this apparent superiority of the relative income
theory by pointing to a statistical bias: the consumption figures were
obtained by subtracting Goldsmith's saving estimates from the income
figures. This means that the income and consumption data have a common error component. This raises the correlation coefficient, and does
so to a greater extent for a regression equation which attaches a large
weight to current income, as the relative income theory does, than for
a regression equation like the permanent income equation, which puts
relatively little weight on current income. This is perfectly correct, but
it is by no means clear that this bias is great enough to account for *all*
the difference. Friedman showed that it may be that large, "though it is
by no means clear that it is." [34]

But quite apart from the question of which consumption function

32. *Ibid.*, p. 146n.
33. *Ibid.*, p. 148. However, for 1917 and 1918—years not used in fitting
the consumption functions—the permanent income theory does better than
the relative income theory (*ibid.*, p. 151).
34. *Ibid.*, p. 150. He continued: "On statistical grounds alone, therefore,
there is little basis for choosing between the highest previous income equation [relative income theory] and the expected income equation [permanent
income theory]. Despite what seem to me the theoretical defects of the highest
previous income equation, it fits the data better than the aesthetically more
appealing expected income equation, though both fit the data extremely well,
and the difference in fit is of an order of magnitude that can be explained on
purely statistical grounds of spurious correlation."

performs better, Friedman's permanent income regression has been challenged by Colin Wright who reran the Friedman regression, or rather a very close algebraic transformation of it.[35] He used slightly different data than Friedman did and treated the war years differently.[36] In addition, he included a constant in his regression. (Friedman had not included a constant in the regression he reported in detail, but he did include a constant—which turned out to be insignificant—in another regression which yielded fairly similar parameters.)[37] Wright's results differ radically from Friedman's. Instead of attributing 0.33 of the weight to the current year's income, Wright's equations attribute to it a weight ranging from 0.65 to 0.80 depending upon how the war years are treated. As Wright pointed out, if his results are correct "then not only are the original calculations made by Friedman suspect, but the use to which they have been put by Friedman and others needs modification." [38]

To see whether Friedman's or Wright's computations were correct, it was necessary to rerun the regressions. I asked my research assistant, Hal Varian, to do so. The equation he used was exactly the same as Friedman's, and the details of his procedures are described in Appendix II.

Part A of Table 3 shows Varian's results, and they support Friedman rather than Wright. (The small differences, namely that R^2 reaches a peak for a beta of 0.5 instead of 0.4, and that, as shown in Appendix II, k and the constants differ could perhaps be due to rounding, or to some difference in the precise treatment of the war years.) The fact that Wright obtained different results than did Friedman could conceivably be due to his using somewhat different data; but it is likely to be the result of his treatment of the war years. Wright presented several alternative treatments of the war years and they show that these calculations are very sensitive to the way the war years are treated.[39]

The problem created by the war years is the following. Even though these years are not themselves included in the regression one has to

35. Colin Wright, "Estimating Permanent Income: A Note," *Journal of Political Economy,* Vol. 77, September–October 1969, pp. 845–50.

36. Friedman had used Goldsmith's unpublished preliminary estimates while Wright used the published data. Moreover, Wright terminated his regression in 1949 while Friedman did so in 1951, and in addition he did not extrapolate his income series backward for the years before 1897 as Friedman did.

37. Friedman, *op. cit.,* p. 146.

38. Colin Wright, *op. cit.,* p. 846.

39. I am indebted to Phillip Cagan (private communication) for pointing out the great importance of treating the war years precisely as Friedman did and for explaining Friedman's method.

Table 3

R^2 for Various Beta Values

Beta	A. Friedman's Treatment of War Years		B. No Special Adjustment for War Years	
	Without Constant	With Constant	Without Constant	With Constant
		$R^{2\,a}$		
.10	.8961	.9164	.9155	.9203
.15	—b	—	.9289	.9321
.20	.9313	.9436	.9365	.9382
.25	—	—	.9406	.9413
.30	.9464	.9510	.9427	.9429
.35	—	—	.9438	.9438
.40	.9513	.9523	.9446	.9447
.45	—	—	.9450	.9452
.50	.9521	.9522	.9452	.9457
.55	—	—	.9454	.9462
.60	.9514	.9517	.9452	.9464
.65	—	—	.9451	.9467
.70	.9500	.9510	.9449	.9469
.75	—	—	.9445	.9470
.80	.9483	.9503	.9441	.9470
.85	—	—	.9435	.9468
.90	.9465	.9495	.9430	.9468
1.00	.9446	.9486	—	—
1.10	.9427	.9477	—	—
1.20	.9408	.9468	—	—
1.30	.9390	.9459	—	—
1.40	.9373	.9450	—	—
1.50	.9356	.9441	—	—

a Not corrected for degrees of freedom.
b Dash denotes not computed.

use them to calculate permanent income in the postwar years. Friedman's procedure was to use in place of the abnormal income of these war years income in the last prewar year plus a 2 percent growth trend. While this is certainly a defensible procedure it is not the only one; one could simply use the actual incomes of the war years on the argument that income in these years was no more abnormal than it was during the Great Depression. Moreover, while the public may have treated their war time incomes as a poor guide to their permanent income it is by no means clear that they formed their income expectations in the way described by Friedman. To be sure, Friedman's treatment of the war years yields a higher R^2, but the difference between the highest R^2's in the two parts of Table 3 is only 0.0053, hardly a meaningful difference. In any case, I am not arguing that Friedman's treatment of the war years is inappropriate, but merely that the results of this regression are very sensitive to essentially arbitrary decisions. If one uses the actual income of the war years one obtains the quite different results shown in Part B of Table 3. These results show a much shorter lag than Friedman's procedure, and in addition, the constant term is statistically significant though too small to have an economic significance. Friedman's beta implies a mean weighting period of 2.5 years while the regressions in Part B of Table 3 imply a mean weighting period of 1.3 years if there is a constant in the equation and 1.8 years if there is no constant.[40] The fact that one obtains quite different results depending upon the treatment of the war years should not really be surprising. The R^2's for various years are very similar so that a very small difference in procedures can easily determine which year has the highest R^2.

The fact that these regression results are so sensitive to what is essentially an arbitrary and quite trivial adjustment strongly suggests that this method of estimating the lag does not furnish reliable results. The differences in the R^2's for various beta values are too trivial to give this test the robustness it needs to be convincing.

Thus Friedman's permanent income regression is subject to two criticisms. First, it performs worse than a relative income theory regression, and this inferior performance may, or may not, be just the result of a bias. Second, the regression does not establish a clear superiority for any particular beta value. I believe that these two weaknesses invalidate it as support for Friedman's lag structure.[41]

Comparison of Actual and Estimated Income Elasticities of Consumption

The next set of tests which Friedman presented consists of comparing the income elasticity of consumption with the proportion of the measured income variance which is due to the variance of the permanent component as estimated from income data. According to the permanent income theory, the income elasticity of consumption is an indirect measure of the proportion of the variance in measured income which is due to differences in permanent income among the households.[42] Hence,

40. While Friedman's regression attributes 0.33 of the weight to the current year the new regressions give it a weight of 0.53 or 0.55 if there is a constant in the regression and 0.42 if there is not.

41. Moreover, Friedman's regression could be challenged on conceptual grounds since he excluded corporate saving from income and also failed to include the imputed income from durables in income, though he included it in consumption.

42. See p. 60 above.

by comparing the income elasticity of consumption with *independently* derived estimates of the proportion of the measured income variability accounted for by the permanent component, Friedman obtained a set of tests of the permanent income theory. This series of tests has two parts: First, there is a test using general data and then there is a test using specific budget studies for which very detailed information is available.

Friedman first showed that the proportion of the income variability accounted for by the permanent component over any period of years is measured by the coefficient of correlation between the measured incomes of those years. He then presented this correlation coefficient for an impressive array of data, half of it coming from his famous study with Simon Kuznets, *Incomes from Independent Professional Practices*. The correlation coefficients show that

the contribution of the permanent component to the variance of income cannot be set higher than about .85 on the broadest definition of the permanent component, nor lower than about .70 on a rather narrow definition. For a three-year permanent component span—that is, for one year intervening between the years correlated—the relevant value . . . is about .80. The correlation coefficients for farm families are distinctly smaller than for urban families, as general knowledge would lead one to suspect. For the small and unrepresentative samples . . . unfortunately the only ones for which we have data—the coefficient is between .4 and .5 for consecutive years and between .3 and .5 for non-consecutive years with one year intervening.[43]

These figures are similar to the income elasticities computed from budget studies which vary "from .70 to .87 for various groups of non-farm consumer units in the United States, with something like .83 as a reasonably typical value, and . . . .65 and .69 for two samples of farm units.[44]

This close coincidence of the sets of data is impressive and shows that the great importance of transitory income which Friedman assumed throughout his analysis is indeed justified. Moreover, since the two estimates come from quite different sets of data, and are calculated by different methods, such close agreement is unlikely to be merely a coincidence.

But this test, too, supports the permanent income theory only in general terms and fails to distinguish between the full permanent income theory and a standard income theory. The reason for this is that if one assumes, as the standard income theory does, that the income elasticity of consumption is greater for permanent income than for transitory income, but is *not* unity for one and zero for the other, the

43. *Op. cit.*, p. 189
44. *Ibid.*, p. 190.

estimates of the income elasticity of consumption for measured income one obtains are just as consistent with the actually observed data as are Friedman's estimates. This similarity in the implications of the full permanent income and the standard income theories is unsurprising. The standard income theory differs from the full permanent income theory in two ways which are relevant here. One of them is its assumption that the income elasticity of consumption is less than unity for permanent income. This tends to lower its estimate of the income elasticity of consumption out of *measured* income, because it means that the permanent component of measured income is multiplied by a smaller income elasticity than it is in the full permanent income theory. The other way it differs is in its assumption that the income elasticity of consumption out of transitory income is greater than zero, and this works in the opposite direction. The effects of these two assumptions cancel in part, so that the standard income theory and a full permanent income theory can generate similar estimates of the income elasticity of consumption out of measured income. This is so even for some variants of the standard income theory which differ sharply from the full permanent income theory. Since the standard income theory as well as the full permanent income theory are consistent with the observed income elasticity out of measured income (around .83), this test is unable to distinguish between the two.

Table 4 shows the income elasticity of measured income which results from different assumptions about (1) the proportion of the measured income variance accounted for by the permanent income component, (2) the income elasticity of consumption out of permanent income, and (3) the income elasticity of consumption out of transitory income.

For the first of these parameters I chose a set of alternative values which correspond to the range suggested by Friedman for nonfarm households. For the income elasticity of consumption out of permanent income I picked values of 0.9, 0.85, and 0.80. I then took values ranging from 0.4 to 0.7 for the income elasticity of consumption out of transitory income. As the last column shows, the *full* permanent income theory is only one of several possibilities which fit the data.[45]

What is needed to confirm or disconfirm the full permanent income theory are more detailed data, data which measure both the income elasticity of consumption and the correlation of incomes in different years from the same set of budgets, and therefore allow a more precise comparison. If in three different samples, for instance, the income

45. Moreover, Clower and Johnson have suggested that Friedman's explanation does not fit the data well because it implies that the horizon is longer than he claimed it is in other parts of his book (*op. cit.*, p. 83).

Table 4

Income Elasticity of Consumption Calculated
on the Basis of Various Assumptions

Proportion of Variance of Measured Income Accounted for by Variance of Permanent Income	Assumed Income Elasticity of Consumption for		Income Elasticity of Consumption for Measured Income
	Permanent Income	Transitory Income	
.70	.90	.40	.75
.70	.85	.50	.75
.70	.85	.60	.78
.70	.80	.70	.77
.75	.90	.40	.78
.75	.85	.50	.76
.75	.85	.60	.79
.75	.80	.70	.78
.80	.90	.40	.80
.80	.90	.50	.82
.80	.90	.60	.84
.80	.85	.40	.76
.80	.90	.60	.80
.80	.85	.70	.82
.80	.80	.70	.78
.83	.90	.40	.82
.83	.90	.50	.83
.83	.90	.70	.87
.83	.85	.70	.83
.83	.80	.60	.76
.83	.80	.40	.73
.85	.90	.50	.84
.85	.90	.60	.85
.85	.90	.70	.85
.85	.85	.40	.78
.85	.85	.70	.82

elasticity of consumption would be exactly equal to the correlation of incomes, then it would take a peculiar coincidence for the standard income theory to be able to explain this similarity. It could then be rejected in favor of the full permanent income theory.

Friedman provided two such sets of data. First, he used some un-published data of Miss Reid's. These data do not really give a good fit for the full permanent income theory, but suggest a permanent income elasticity of less than unity. Friedman explained this by weaknesses of the data, saying that "the appearance . . . is produced entirely by points for the more dubious set of farm samples" and he therefore excluded them from further consideration.[46] In view of the weakness of the data, Friedman *may* be right in saying that these data should not be treated as contradicting the full permanent income theory. But can they be treated as confirming it? I think not. To get a confirmation for the full permanent income theory, Friedman would have to settle on some objective method of discriminating between the dubious and the acceptable data. If elimination of the dubious data would result in the sample agreeing closely with the prediction of the permanent income theory then, and only then, could the data be treated as confirming the theory. But Friedman did not do this; he merely stated that the data which account for the bad fit are unreliable. But some of the data which give a *good* fit may be dubious too, and so they should also be eliminated. There is no reason to think that if *all* doubtful data were eliminated, the remaining data would necessarily support the full permanent income theory.[47] This is so particularly when one takes into account the fact that the permanent income theory and the standard income theory have fairly similar implications on this type of test so that the inclusion or exclusion of just a few observations could change the results. Hence, this test does not provide valid evidence for the theory.[48] Moreover, as will be shown in Chapter 13, when I applied this test to a sample of Swiss households, I obtained results sharply at variance with those cited by Friedman.

The next set of data which Friedman presented came from the Survey of Consumer Finances, and they show a similarity between the correlation coefficients of incomes in consecutive years and the income elasticity of consumption for three occupations. But this apparent agreement between the prediction of the permanent income theory and the data does not furnish sufficient evidence for the full permanent income theory as against the standard income theory. I compared Friedman's predictions of the measured income elasticity of consumption against

46. *Op. cit.*, p. 192. Friedman stated: "Much of Reid's data are for the farm families analyzed also by Tobin . . . and used . . . in considering the effect of change of income. . . . As noted earlier, there is considerable doubt about the representativeness and accuracy of these data." (*Ibid.*, p. 191.) Yet when discussing his income change test which is based on these data (as well as on Survey of Consumer Finances data), Friedman called the results "in some ways the most striking bit of evidence for our hypothesis that has so far been adduced." (*Ibid.*, p. 109.)

47. Unfortunately, I cannot test for this possibility since the Reid data are unpublished and no longer available.

48. Michael Farrell has raised another point, namely that households willing to maintain account books for a three-year period may be more prone to behave in accordance with the permanent income theory than other households (*op. cit.*, p. 691).

the predictions of three standard income theory models. The permanent income elasticities used in these three models are the same as in Table 4—0.80, 0.85, 0.90—and I assumed that the transitory income elasticity is equal to half the permanent income elasticity.[49] Friedman presented three estimates of the proportion of the income variance due to the permanent component, and I used all three. The results of this comparison of the two theories provides little support for the permanent income theory. Looking at the mean error, the permanent income theory does better than one of the standard income theory models, and worse than the other two. For the median error this result is reversed, and the permanent income theory does better than two of the standard income theory models and worse than the third one.

Moreover, there are problems relating to the estimate of the income elasticity of consumption. First, as Friedman pointed out, his estimate is subject to two serious weaknesses. One is the fact that the saving data from which it is derived cover only changes in liquid asset holdings and in short term debts, so that other forms of saving are thrown into consumption, and second, personal taxes are included in both income and consumption.[50] An additional problem is created by the fact that when consumption is estimated by subtracting saving from income, as it is in these data, there is a common error term in income and consumption, and this imparts an upward bias to the income elasticity of consumption.

The next test used by Friedman is a correlation between saving in two different years. Friedman showed that the permanent income theory predicts that this correlation should be .25, and then stated that the actual correlation is .26, though "such close agreement is to be regarded as an accident." [51] However, there is a problem with this test.

49. I did not select these models after a "fishing expedition"—they are the only ones I tried.

50. *Op. cit., pp.* 194–95. Friedman argued that both of these factors impart an upward bias to the income elasticity. While I agree that the inclusion of taxes in income and consumption does this, I suspect that the limitations of the saving definition gives a downward bias to the income elasticity. Both the change in liquid assets and in short term debts are probably more closely related to transitory income than are other types of saving. Since the elasticity of transitory income with respect to measured income is greater than unity, the two types of saving covered by the data are likely to show a greater measured income elasticity than do other forms of saving. Hence when consumption is derived by subtracting only these two types of saving from income, the overall elasticity of saving is overestimated so that the income elasticity of consumption is probably understated.

51. *Ibid.,* p. 197n. As Friedman pointed out, his estimtae of the correlation from the permanent income theory as .25 is only "a very rough approximation." (*Ibid.,* p. 199).

The correlation is based on a correlation table (a two-way frequency distribution) published by George Katona.[52] This two-way frequency distribution used saving classes without stating the mean of each class. This is relatively harmless for the closed classes where one can use the midpoint of the class, but the two extreme saving classes are open-ended, and here the selection of a midpoint is more arbitrary. To see how sensitive the correlation is to the selection of an arbitrary midpoint for open-ended classes, I reran the correlation (weighted by the number of households) twice, using different assumed midpoints.[53] One run yielded a correlation coefficient of 0.21, the other about 0.19.[54] Undoubtedly had I selected other assumed midpoints I would have obtained Friedman's figure of .26. But the essence of the matter is that making different arbitrary assumptions leads to different correlation coefficients. Hence, one cannot use any particular correlation coefficient one gets from these data in an acceptable test of the permanent income theory. Thus all three comparisons of the income elasticity of consumption and the income correlations derived from the same data fail to provide adequate support for the full permanent income theory.

A Miscellany

In this chapter Friedman considered material which represents "primarily tentative speculations about possible further work rather than records of completed work." [55] Two actual tests, as distinct from suggestions for further work, can be found in this section. One is Friedman's estimate of the consumption elasticity of income, which according to the permanent income theory should be greater than unity. The data generally show that it is, but the measured income theories have the same implication. They imply that the percent of income saved is greater for households with high consumption (and hence higher incomes) than for low consumption households. Since consumption plus saving equals

52. "Variability of Consumer Behavior and the Survey Method," in Lawrence Klein (ed.), *Contribution of Survey Methods to Economics* (New York, Columbia University Press, 1954) p. 71.

53. The two open-ended saving classes are "—25 percent and over" at the lower end and "50 percent and over" at the upper end. In one regression I took the mean of the former class as —30 and the mean of the latter as 60. In the other regression I used assumed means of —50 and 70. I make no claim that these assumed means and hence my correlation coefficients are "right" while Friedman's are "wrong." All I am trying to show is that any correlation coefficients obtained from these data are of questionable accuracy.

54. I ran this regression on two computers using different programs. One gave the correlation coefficient as 0.189, the other as 0.184. (The difference is presumably due to rounding.)

55. *Op. cit.*, p. 200.

measured income, this implies that measured income increases more than proportionately with consumption, so that the consumption elasticity of income is greater than unity.

The second test given by Friedman in this chapter discussed what happens to the income elasticity of consumption if one uses a period shorter than a year. The permanent income theory implies that the income elasticity is less when calculated for a period shorter than a year than when calculated over a full year. Again, the data support the theory. But this, too, is consistent with the measured income theories. Adherents of these theories have generally used a full year period to fit their consumption functions; presumably they would agree that if one takes a very short period, say a month, measured income would not be adequate to explain consumption. On this issue there seems to be no real disagreement between the adherents of the measured income theories and the adherents of the permanent income theory.

Digression on the Horizon

As discussed in Chapter 2, one of the most difficult issues in the permanent income theory is the length, and indeed the meaning of, the "horizon." In several of his tests Friedman claimed to have obtained estimates of this horizon as roughly three years. One of these is the regression of consumption on permanent income discussed above which yielded a two-and-a-half year horizon. However, as pointed out by Holbrook, the actual estimate generated by Friedman's regression is as close to a two-year horizon as to a three-year horizon.[56] In any case, as discussed earlier, Friedman's estimate is questionable.

A second estimate comes from Friedman's comparison of the income elasticity of consumption with a correlation of income over a two-year period and a three-year period.[57] Friedman argued that the correlation covering a three-year span is the closer one to the income elasticity so that the horizon is three years. But Holbrook pointed out that if one excludes one wartime observation this no longer holds true, and a two-year horizon is then as consistent with the data as is a three-year horizon.[58] But note that this supports a two-year horizon only if one accepts the full permanent income theory; it does not tell us what the horizon is in the standard income theory. A third piece of evidence

56. Robert Holbrook, "The Three-Year Horizon: An Analysis of the Evidence," *Journal of Political Economy*, Vol. 75, October 1967, p. 751. As Holbrook further pointed out, Friedman's horizon is not consistent with the income growth rate he used.

57. The three-year correlation is a correlation of incomes in years 1 and 3 with year 2 omitted.

58. *Ibid.*, p. 753.

for the three-year horizon comes from Friedman's comparison of the correlation of the income elasticity of consumption with the correlation of incomes using Miss Reid's farm data. Friedman stated that the correspondence between the data and the hypothesis is closer for the three-year data than for the two-year data. But if one accepts the standard income theory in place of the full permanent income theory, this provides no evidence for a three-year horizon. Since none of Friedman's evidence is able to show that the full permanent income theory is superior to the standard income theory, one can hardly take the three-year horizon as established. Friedman's final piece of evidence in support of the three-year horizon is his correlation of saving in two years—the last of the tests discussed above. But as pointed out, this test should be rejected because of a data problem.[59]

Conclusion

In this chapter I have examined every test presented by Friedman in his *A Theory of the Consumption Function*. The results summarized in Table 5 are mixed. On the one hand, only three tests turned out to be completely invalid, though one other is invalid in part. On the other hand, *none of the tests support the full permanent income theory in the sense of showing that the income elasticity of consumption is zero for transitory income and unity for permanent income.* In fact, the majority of the tests are not even concerned with these two hypotheses; all they deal with is the existence of a lag in the consumption function, and whether or not the income elasticity of consumption is greater for permanent than for transitory income. In other words, a substantial majority of the tests represent attempts to confirm *either* the full permanent income theory *or* the standard income theory as against the measured income theories without even attempting to distinguish between the two.

A large number of tests show that certain observed characteristics of the consumption function can be explained by either the full permanent income theory or the standard income theory. However, many of these same characteristics can be explained also by the relative income theory, and some even by the absolute income theory. This does not mean that these tests are therefore useless. To establish the validity of the permanent income theory or the standard income theory it is necessary to show that these theories can explain those observed phenomena which the measured income theories can explain, and that they can also explain other observations which the measured income theories cannot explain.

59. However, a test of Landsberger's discussed below suggests a horizon of about three years.

Table 5

Summary of Results of Tests—Friedman's Evidence

Test	Hypothesis Tested[a]	Invalid	Results Explicable by Permanent Income Theory and also by		
			Absolute Income Theory	Relative Income Theory	Standard Income Theory
1. Stability of income distribution	P		x	x	x
2. APC.'s of various budget studies	D				x
3. Difference in income elasticities, U.S. and U.K.	D	x			
4. Difference in APC and income elasticities, farm and nonfarm households	D				x
5. Differences in APC and income elasticities, self-employed and employees	D	x[b]			
6. Black-white saving differences	D		x	x	x
7. Relation of age and saving	L, D				x
8. Effect of income changes	P, Z, D	c		x	x
9. Secular stability of saving ratio	P		e	x	x
10. Differences in saving ratios of various years	D			x	x
11. Effect of lengthening period	D				x
12. Effect of form of data	D				x
13. Regressions of consumption on current and past income	P, Z, L	x[d]			x
14. Similarity of income elasticities and correlation of incomes	P, Z, D				x
15. Consumption elasticity of income	D		x	x	x
16. Income elasticity of consumption, period shorter than a year	D		x	x	x

[a] The following code is used: D, difference in permanent and transitory income elasticities of consumption. L, lag hypothesis made explicit. P, proportionality hypothesis. Z, zero income elasticity for transitory income. Actually, the lag hypothesis is covered in every one of these tests since it is implicit in the separation of permanent and transitory income.

[b] Test is invalid as given by Friedman, but is valid in the form used by Liviatan and discussed in Chapter 5. It, too, is consistent with the standard income theory.

[c] Invalid for hypotheses P and Z, but not for D.

[d] Slight change in treatment of war years yields higher value for beta.

[e] Consistent with absolute income theory if wealth is introduced into the consumption function.

As Table 5 shows, there are a number of confirmed predictions made by the permanent income theory and the standard income theories which are not also predictions of the measured income theories. They are (1) the differences in average propensities to consume of various budget studies, (2) the higher income elasticity of farm households, (3) the relation of age and saving,[60] (4) the effect of lengthening the period covered, (5) the effect of the form of the data, and (6) the similarity of the income elasticities of consumption and the correlation of incomes. Six such successes are enough to validate a theory—in fact, in establishing the widely popular relative income theory, Duesenberry used fewer tests than this.

However, the theory which is established by these tests is not necessarily the full permanent income theory. The standard income theory can do the job as well. Actually, only five of the tests deal with the proportionality hypothesis, and they fail to establish it. Similarly, only three tests deal with the proposition that the transitory income elasticity is zero, and they, too, fail to support this proposition. What the tests *do* show is that there is *some* lag in the consumption function and that the income elasticity of consumption is greater for permanent than for transitory income. Both of these hypotheses are ones which the full permanent income theory shares with the standard income theory. Hence, all of the valid evidence presented by Friedman is consistent with both of these theories. Later on in this book I will discuss several tests which do distinguish between them.

60. This test is the only one which shows consumption as affected by income expectations as well as by past income, thus supporting the permanent income theory and the standard income theory against a habit persistence theory.

Four

OTHER PREVIOUS TESTS, I

Introduction

In the previous chapter I discussed Friedman's tests; in this and the following chapter I shall take up the tests performed by other economists. However, I will not be covering all the tests in these two chapters; I will postpone tests dealing with international data until Chapter 6 and certain time series regression tests until Chapters 7 and 8.[1] The great majority of the tests covered in this and the following chapter are cross-section tests, that is, tests using household budgets.

There are many such tests extant, and to impose some order on this material I have classified them into broad groupings. These groups are, of course, somewhat arbitrary, and what is just as bad, they do not really allow one to impose very *much* order on this material. This is not surprising since the tests were performed by numerous economists, working independently of each other, and they form a patchwork of largely independent points rather than a unified whole.

The groupings I have used are: (1) effect of windfalls, (2) narrowing cells, (3) group means, (4) stable versus fluctuating income, (5) direction of income change, (6) time series tests, (7) disaggregation (8) self-employed versus employees, (9) propensity to consume from monthly data, (10) income profiles, (11) temporarily low incomes, (12) instrumental variables, (13) errors in variables tests, (14) other tests with two or three year data, (15) occupation versus measured income, (16) effect of assets, (17) distribution of net worth, (18) classification by relative income, (19) age and consumption, (20) hypothetical questions, and (21) (invalid) miscellaneous tests. The results of all of these tests are summarized at the end of Chapter 5.

1. I am excluding a test by Robert Brown and Franklin Fisher since it is more convenient to discuss it in Chapter 11, and a test by Vakil, which I discuss in Chapter 10.

The Effect of Windfalls

The NSLI Dividend. An obvious way of testing the permanent income theory is to identify a particular item of transitory income and then to measure the marginal propensity to consume out of this transitory income item; that is, to measure the effect of a windfall.[2] One such test was proposed by Friedman himself, who suggested using the dividend received in 1950 by veterans holding a National Service Life Insurance policy (NSLI).[3] This dividend was unexpected, and hence qualifies as a windfall, or transitory income. Since a big budget study for 1950 is available, this affords a possibility of testing the permanent income theory.

Ronald Bodkin undertook this test and noted some rather surprising results; the marginal propensity to consume was (insignificantly) *greater* for the NSLI windfall than for regular income.[4] This was so regardless of

2. In addition to tests by what is usually thought of as windfalls, there are also a number of tests which use transitory income in time series regressions. These tests are discussed in the last section of this chapter.

3. *A Theory of the Consumption Function* (Princeton, Princeton University Press, 1957), p. 215.

4. "Windfall Income and Consumption," *American Economic Review*, Vol. XLIX, September 1959, pp. 602–14. Bodkin's results were supported by Robert Jones, who found that the marginal propensity to consume food, housing, and clothing was as great, or greater, for the dividend than for regular income. (American Economic Association, *Papers and Proceedings*, Vol. L, May 1960, pp. 584–92.) Actually, Bodkin was not the first to take Friedman up on this issue. Earlier Irwin Friend stated, though without detailed documentation, that among the dividend recipients "over one half reported using the dividend exclusively to purchase goods and services" ("Further Comments on 'A Theory of the Consumption Function,'" in Lincoln Clark, ed., *Consumer Behavior,* New York, Harper and Brothers, 1958, Vol. 3, pp. 457–58). But as Friend pointed out, this evidence is weak for three reasons; first, durables are included in consumption; second, what people say they do may not correspond to what they actually do; and third, the study does not have a control group which did not receive the dividend. Moreover, the actual use of the dividend may be quite misleading. A household may use the dividend to purchase an item which it otherwise would have purchased in any case. It would then report that it "used" the dividend for consumption, whereas in reality the dividend may have had no effect on consumption. It is not at all unlikely that households used the liquidity they obtained from the dividend receipt to purchase items they would have bought in the absence of the dividend as soon as they had built up their liquidity sufficiently. A related test cited by Friend, who calls it a "weak test," was to ask households what they did when they cashed their terminal leave bonds when they became redeemable in 1947. Thirty-two percent reported buying nondurables, 26 percent said they bought durables, and the remainder reported "saving and other purposes" (*ibid.,* p. 458). But Friend pointed out that households may not have considered the receipt from these

whether consumption was defined conventionally, or whether durables were excluded.

Friedman responded to this sharp challenge. He pointed out that Bodkin's results appear to be highly implausible, and that the NSLI dividend may be a proxy for permanent income, so that its coefficient does not measure the effect of windfall income on consumption.[5] The size of the dividend depended upon the length of time over which the policy had been in force (and hence the veteran's age) as well as the size of the policy, two variables presumably correlated with permanent income. Friedman then used the permanent income theory to derive the correlation of the dividend and *permanent* income. After allowing for this correlation the regression coefficient of the dividend falls to 0.493.[6] By contrast, the predicted value according to the permanent income theory is 0.3 while Bodkin's original estimate for nondurable consumption is 0.723. Friedman then proceeded in his reconciliation by arguing that the dividend payment actually received in 1950 was not considered by the recipients a single once-for-all receipt. Inquiry among some people who had received this dividend (a process Friedman admitted was "casual empiricism") showed that "when the first large payment was made, recipients were apparently told, or could infer, that additional annual payments would be forthcoming." [7] Subsequent payments were about one fifth of the size of the initial payments. Given the 33⅓ percent discount rate used in the permanent income theory, the present value of the subsequent payments is three-fifths of the initial payment, so that a dollar of initial payment really corresponds to a windfall of $1.60. Dividing the coefficient of the dividend, 0.493 by 1.6 yields a true coefficient of .31, a value uncannily close to the .30 predicted by the permanent income theory.

In his reply, Bodkin challenged Friedman's statement that the policyholders had any reason to expect the 1950 dividend to be followed by other ones. A check with the Veterans Administration showed that:

It was made quite clear to the recipients that this was a special dividend, and that no mention was made about any future dividends. . . . The

bond sales as transitory income. Quite apart from this, this evidence does not contradict the permanent income theory for two reasons: the "remainder" includes almost half the sample, and it ignores those households who did not cash in their bonds, and hence saved them.

5. "Comments" in Irwin Friend and Robert Jones (eds.), *Consumption and Saving* (Philadelphia, University of Pennsylvania Press, 1960), Vol. II, pp. 197–98. This point was developed further by Malcolm Fisher, who showed that it can account for Bodkin's results (Malcolm Fisher, "Empirical Tests of the Permanent Income Hypothesis," unpublished paper, 1960, pp. 10–15).

6. *Ibid.*, p. 203.

7. *Ibid.*, p. 198.

statement form which accompanied the dividend check . . . characterized by government austerity, carried no suggestion that any future dividend payments would be made. Consequently, one could argue that, in 1950 at least, the greater part of the dividend recipients were unaware of the future dividend receipts that they were about to receive.[8]

This suggests that Friedman's adjustment to the coefficient to bring it down from .493 to .31 is unwarranted.

In a subsequent paper Roger Bird and Ronald Bodkin took account of Friedman's criticism that the dividend is correlated with permanent income.[9] They analyzed the same data as before, plus some additional data, but introduced into the regressions a set of variables which either act as proxies for permanent income or are themselves determinants of consumption. Their results were now quite different from those originally obtained by Bodkin. For nondurables the marginal propensity to consume is now .498 for measured income, and .383 for the NSLI dividend.[10] For neither, consumption including durables or for nondurable consumption, do the data reject—at the 5 percent significance level—the proposition that the marginal propensity to consume is the same for measured income and for the NSLI windfall. Hence, the absolute income theory survives this test. On the other hand, the permanent income theory can be rejected only if consumption is defined conventionally, but not if consumption is defined as nondurable consumption. Bird and Bodkin, therefore, concluded: "the outcome is inconclusive. Our results are clearly consistent with an absolute-income hypothesis, while they do not decisively refute a strict [permanent income hypothesis, they] suggest a loose [permanent income theory] with a mild propensity to spend transitory income." [11] Bird and Bodkin did not allow for the possibility that *some* recipients

8. Ronald Bodkin, "Rejoinder" in Friend and Jones, *op. cit.*, Vol. II, p. 209. However, as Bodkin points out, in actuality a second dividend *was* paid in 1951, and regular dividends started in 1952. Bodkin also argued that even if dividend recipients expected further dividends they would not know the size and timing of these future payments and hence Friedman's calculations are not applicable.

9. "The National Service Life Insurance Dividend of 1950 and Consumption: A Further Test of the 'Strict' Permanent Income Hypothesis," *Journal of Political Economy*, Vol. LXXIII, October 1965, pp. 499–515.

10. *Ibid.*, p. 507. For the conventional definition of consumption the marginal propensity is .695 for measured income and .646 for the windfall (*ibid.*, p. 506). Bird and Bodkin also fitted regressions not to the individual observations but to their means in each location. The resulting marginal propensities to consume the dividend generally exceeded unity, a result which Bird and Bodkin rejected as "highly implausible" (*ibid.*, p. 510). They suggested that it might be due to interference by a regional effect on consumption, or to dividends being a strong proxy for permanent income.

11. *Ibid.*, pp. 508, 511.

may have expected to receive further dividends, and to this extent their test is not really fair to the strict permanent income hypothesis.[12]

Windfalls in the Oxford Survey. The NSLI dividend is not the only windfall which has been used to test the permanent income theory. Using data from the Oxford survey, Lawrence Klein and N. Liviatan fitted a regression equation explaining the noncontractual saving-income ratio.[13] They found that windfalls, expressed as a percent of income, had a *negative* coefficient. This suggests not only that windfalls are all consumed, but that the receipt of a windfall reduces other noncontractual saving.[14] However, this evidence is far from convincing. As both Malcolm Fisher and Ronald Bodkin pointed out, there is some question whether the items which Klein and Liviatan call windfalls are really windfalls in the sense of the permanent income theory.[15] These items are life insurance benefits, gambling gains, cash gifts, cash legacies, postwar credits, and other lump sum receipts. Life insurance benefits are not transitory income. Somewhat more questionably, Bodkin argues that gambling winnings are not transitory income either, because to the professional gambler, winnings represent permanent income. It is, of course, impossible to tell what proportion of gambling winnings are received by professionals, or by amateurs so gifted that these winnings are a regular source of income. But, on the other hand, quite apart from the issues involved in the permanent income theory, one would expect gambling winnings to be negatively related to the saving-income ratio. It is highly plausible that heavy gamblers are people whose personality is such that they tend to have a low saving-income ratio. Bodkin also objected to the inclusion of cash legacies in windfalls, since the heirs may have

12. There is still another budget study test of the effect of the insurance dividend. Albert Ando and E. Cary Brown looked at the residuals from their time series regression equation to see if these residuals suggest that the dividend was consumed. The results for the regression using yearly data were inconclusive, while the results of the quarterly regression appear to suggest "that the dividend payment, an unexpected windfall income, was spent with some delay, if at all." (Albert Ando, E. C. Brown, R. M. Solow, and J. Kareken, "Lags in Fiscal and Monetary Policy," in Commission on Money and Credit, *Stabilization Policies,* Englewood Cliffs, N.J., 1963, p. 134.) Since the point at issue, in this chapter, is not the lag in the consumption function but whether transitory income is consumed at all, this study does not provide strong evidence for either view.

13. "The Significance of Income Variability on Savings Behavior," Oxford University, Institute of Economics and Statistics, *Bulletin,* Vol. 19, May 1957, pp. 156–60.

14. Klein and Liviatan interpreted their result as showing windfalls going into consumption since it is highly unlikely that windfalls go into contractual saving.

15. Malcolm Fisher, "A Reply to the Critics," Oxford University, Institute of Economics and Statistics, *Bulletin,* Vol. 19, May 1957, pp. 189–90, and Ronald Bodkin, "Windfall Income and Consumption," *op. cit.,* p. 604.

anticipated such legacies so that they are not transitory income. The treatment of gifts as transitory income creates another problem. A household may receive a gift *just* because its transitory income is negative or because it has special consumption needs in that year. Both of these factors would tend to reduce the saving-income ratio. If so, there is likely to be a spurious negative correlation between the receipt of gifts and the saving-income ratio. Too many of the windfall items used by Klein and Liviatan are therefore suspect, and their test should be rejected.[16]

The Israeli Reparations Payments. Bodkin's original test stimulated Mordechai Kreinin to undertake a test using another type of windfall.[17] This windfall was the German reparations payment received by Israelis in 1957–1958. These payments were not anticipated well in advance and were non-recurrent. They were substantial, their mean value being close to one year's income. Kreinin ran a regression similar to Bodkin's and found a very low marginal propensity to consume this windfall. For the conventional definition of consumption, the marginal propensity to consume was .167 (standard error 0.156) for the windfall and 0.857 (standard error 0.105) for regular income. Excluding durable goods purchases from consumption changed the windfall coefficient only slightly, to 0.156.[18]

Subsequently Michael Landsberger undertook a similar but more detailed analysis using four Israeli surveys.[19] His results, too, showed a substantially smaller marginal propensity to consume for windfalls than for measured income, ranging from 0.15 to 0.25.[20] He got roughly similar results when he calculated the marginal propensity to consume not by comparing households at different income levels but by using the change in income and consumption shown by his two-year reinterview data.[21]

Kreinin's favorable results for the permanent income theory were chal-

---

16. The inadequate definition of transitory income also creates trouble for Klein and Liviatan's argument that "having read through numerous questionnaires, especially those of a sample of recent heirs, we conclude that many people spend sudden unexpected gains on travel, entertainment, and other luxuries in addition to durable goods." *Op. cit.*, p. 156. The increase in these expenditures may result not from a receipt of transitory income but from an increase in the household's liquidity as an illiquid asset (expectation of an inheritance) is transformed into a more liquid form of an actual receipt.

17. "Windfall Income and Consumption—Additional Evidence," *American Economic Review*, Vol. LI, June 1961, pp. 388–90.

18. *Ibid.*, p. 389.

19. *Restitution Receipts, Household Savings and Consumption Behavior in Israel* (Jerusalem, Research Department, Bank of Israel, 1970).

20. *Ibid.*, p. 30. For nondurable consumption his coefficients ranged from 0.10 to 0.22.

21. *Ibid.*, p. 35.

lenged by Bodkin, who raised several issues. First, he argued that foreign exchange regulations "provided a powerful incentive for the recipient *not* to spend these receipts" [22] as did expectations of devaluation. Second, these restitution payments "might be considered analogous to insurance receipts as they were intended to be partial compensation . . . for losses sustained by the individual in the past." [23] Third, the effect of previous hardships experienced by the recipients is likely to give them a low marginal propensity to consume. Finally, Bodkin doubted that these receipts were really unanticipated.[24]

But Bodkin's analysis in turn was very effectively challenged by Michael Landsberger.[25] Landsberger tested Bodkin's hypothesis that personality characteristics of restitution payment recipients are responsible for their tendency to save these payments. He did this by running separate regressions for households receiving reparations and those receiving only other types of windfalls. The results showed no significant difference in the regression coefficients of windfalls in the two groups.[26] Second, Landsberger showed that for the year *prior* to the windfall receipt, the

22. "Windfall Income and Consumption; Comment," *American Economic Review*, Vol. LIII, June 1963, p. 445.

23. *Ibid.*, p. 447.

24. *Ibid.*, p. 447.

25. "Windfall Income and Consumption; Comment," *American Economic Review*, Vol. LVI, June 1966, pp. 534–39. Kreinin too questioned Bodkin's argument, saying that it is essentially based on suppositions rather than on hard evidence. "Windfall Income and Consumption: Further Comment," *American Economic Review*, Vol. LIII, June 1963, p. 448.

26. Bodkin in his reply ("Windfall Income and Consumption: Reply," *American Economic Review*, Vol. LVI, June 1966, pp. 540–45) objected to this test because, since most Israelis are refugees, "one might well expect the same sense of thriftiness, caution, and orientation towards security to characterize most of the citizens of this country, not only restitution-payment recipients" (*ibid.*, p. 544). But this hypothesis is readily tested. If it were correct, one would expect the Israeli saving ratio to be unusually high, and this is not the case. See Richard Albin, "Household Saving in Israel," Oxford University Institute of Economics and Statistics, *Bulletin*, Vol. 28, May 1966, pp. 130–43. Bodkin also pointed to institutional differences between the United States and Israel which could account for the divergent results and make Kreinin's findings inapplicable to the United States. One factor is the much greater degree of inflation in Israel, and another is the difference in the availability of consumer goods. If the first of these points is considered correct, this would imply that the permanent income theory may be valid if prices rise at the rate of 6 percent per year, but not if they are stable—a rather disruptive hypothesis, which, in the absence of any supporting evidence, I will disregard. The continual shortage of consumer durables is a more plausible explanation. Conceivably households did not spend their windfalls upon receipt, but only did so later on when the durables were available. However, Bodkin provided no evidence that this is what actually occured.

marginal propensity to consume this windfall was not significantly different from zero, thus denying Bodkin's contention that the windfall payments were anticipated, and hence raised consumption in prior years. Landsberger also pointed out that the foreign exchange regulations referred to by Bodkin could account for only a 20 percent saving from these windfalls since at the time Israelis were permitted to spend abroad only 20 percent of their total receipts. Finally, Landsberger answered Bodkin regarding the fear of devaluation in two ways. He pointed out that households expecting devaluation were able to hold their liquid assets in a form linked to the exchange rate. Moreover, he ran regressions for reparations received subsequent to the 1962 devaluation, when presumably there was no longer any expectation of further devaluation, and again the marginal propensity to consume windfalls is very low.[27]

Having disposed, quite conclusively I think, of Bodkin's points, Landsberger went on to fit regressions for households with different ratios of windfalls to ordinary income. The data show a strong tendency for the marginal propensity to consume to fall as the ratio of windfalls to ordinary income rises.[28]

The windfalls discussed by Kreinin were a much larger proportion of income than those analyzed by Bodkin. This, Landsberger suggested, accounts for the difference in the results obtained by Bodkin and Kreinin. In his reply to Landsberger, Bodkin tested this hypothesis for his insurance dividend data, and found *no* significant differences in the propensity to consume large and small windfalls.[29] However, this test is open to question. As was discussed above, when Bird and Bodkin held other variables constant, they obtained a quite different result than Bodkin had in his original regressions. It may well be the case that if Bodkin had held these other variables constant he would have found a difference between large and small windfalls. A technique which gives a misleading result in one analysis is suspect when applied subsequently to a similar problem. But it is worth noting that a study by R. C. Doenges, confined to a single locality, also found a significant association between the size of the windfall and the propensity to save it, thus supporting Landsberger's conclusion.[30]

27. Landsberger, "Windfall Income and Consumption: Comment," *op. cit.*, pp. 536–38
28. *Ibid.*, pp. 538–39. A greater propensity to consume for small than for large windfalls fits the wealth theory of consumption suggested by Clower and Johnson in their "Income, Wealth and the Theory of Consumption," in J. N. Wolfe (ed.), *Value, Capital and Growth, Papers in Honour of Sir John Hicks* (Edinburgh, The University Press, 1968), p. 65.
29. "Windfall Income and Consumption: Reply," *op. cit.*, pp. 540–45.
30. R. Conrad Doenges, "Transitory Income Size and Savings," *Southern Economic Journal*, Vol. XXXIII, October 1966, pp. 258–63. Doenges also

In a subsequent study dealing mainly with the life cycle hypothesis (which I shall soon discuss) Landsberger fitted regressions using both restitution payments and "other windfall income" to Israeli data for 1957–1958 and 1963–1964.[31] The coefficients for both types of windfalls were small, no higher than would be expected on the basis of the permanent income theory.

But there is considerable doubt whether the findings of Kreinin and Landsberger really support the permanent income theory as against the measured income theories. The point at issue is the proper interpretation of the measured income theories. Do these theories assert that windfall items, such as reparation payments, are consumed, or do they agree with the permanent income theory that they are saved? As Landsberger quite rightly pointed out, the measured income theories have been vague as to what should be included in income.[32] He argued:

In view of the obscurity of the Traditional Approach on this point, we have chosen to present here its extreme, or perhaps naive, interpretation. This is done so as to underline the confrontation between this approach and the Wealth Theories. However . . . the interpretation of the empirical results is not at all affected by such a presentation.[33]

Granted the fact that the measured income theories do not give a clear-cut definition of income, it is not really necessary to settle the issue by making an arbitrary assumption. The evidence of the *General Theory* suggests that Keynes did *not* include windfalls in income. Thus, Keynes specifically excluded entrepreneurial windfalls (defined as unexpected changes in the value of equipment) from the net income concept since a dollar of windfalls has less effect on consumption than a dollar of net income. In addition, he described changes in the money value of wealth as a factor changing the propensity to consume.[34] Moreover, he defined income as follows:

Our definition of *net income* comes very close to Marshall's definition of *income,* when he decided to take refuge in the practices of the Income Tax Commissioners and—broadly speaking—to regard as income what-

---

ran a regression of saving on windfalls and found a marginal propensity to save of .996, a finding which appears to support the permanent income theory. However, these results are suspect because Doenges did not include ordinary income in his regression. Since ordinary income and windfalls are correlated (R. C. Doenges, private communication) a regression of saving on windfalls is likely to reflect, at least in part, the saving of ordinary income, so that there is an upward bias in the regression coefficient.

31. "The Life Cycle Hypothesis—A Reinterpretation and Empirical Test," *American Economic Review,* Vol. LX, March 1970, pp. 175–83.

32. *Restitution Receipts, op. cit.,* pp. 24–25

33. *Ibid.,* p. 25.

34. *The General Theory of Employment, Interest and Money* (New York, Harcourt Brace, 1936), pp. 57–58, 92–93.

ever they, with their experience, choose to treat as such. . . . It also corresponds to the money value of Professor Pigou's most recent definition of the National Dividend.[35]

Since reparations payments are not considered income by the British income tax and are not included in Pigou's definition of national income,[36] it follows that the Kreinin-Landsberger results are entirely consistent with the measured income theories.[37] The real question is not how households react to what the measured income theorists call windfalls, but rather whether the measured income theorist's distinction between income and windfalls is valid. In other words, can one predict consumption successfully from measured income, or does one have to draw the line instead between permanent income on the one hand and transitory income including windfalls on the other?

None of this denies in any way the substantive import of Kreinin's and Landsberger's estimates of the effect of reparations payments. A complete theory of the consumption function would contain not only estimates of the marginal propensities to consume income but also estimates of the marginal propensity to consume windfalls, a figure which may well differ for various types of windfalls. Kreinin's and Landsberger's estimation of the marginal propensity to consume one type of windfall is a useful contribution to our substantive knowledge of the consumption function. Whether or not it contradicts the measured income theories is merely a doctrinal dispute devoid of practical relevance.

Other Windfalls. Another paper provoked by Bodkin's original paper is a study by Miss Reid. She tried to extend the Bodkin analysis by relating the item called "other money receipts" in the BLS household expenditure survey to saving, expenditures for autos, expenditures for furnishings and equipment, and other expenditures.[38] She did this in the belief that the NSLI dividend showed up in "other money receipts," a

35. *Ibid.,* p. 59.

36. Pigou defined net income as "the whole of the annual output minus what is needed to maintain the stock of capital intact," "Net Income and Capital Depletion," *Economic Journal,* Vol. XLV, June 1935, p. 235.

37. As Bodkin has pointed out, windfalls are not the same thing as transitory income. ("Windfall Income and Consumption: Reply," *op. cit.,* p. 544n). I know of no place where the relative income theorists have discussed the definition of income. Since they did not discuss it in their critique of the absolute income theory, I assume that they accepted the Keynesian definition of income.

38. Margaret Reid, "Consumption, Saving, and Windfall Gains," *American Economic Review,* Vol. LII, September 1962, pp. 728–37. Another (unpublished) contribution to the debate by Miss Reid has been to suggest that the receipt of the dividend may have stimulated house purchases, and that these house purchases increased consumption in the short run and saving in the long run. See Robert Ferber, "Research on Household Behavior," *American Economic Review,* Vol. LII, March 1962, p. 31n.

belief which, as Roger Bird pointed out, is mistaken.[39] Miss Reid then reworked her analysis using instead of "other money receipts," mean "military payments" received in 58 cities.[40] The dependent variables were durables (furnishings and equipment plus autos) in one equation, and all other consumption expenditures in the other equation. The results showed that the marginal propensity to purchase durables was much greater for military payments than for regular income, being .622. On the other hand, the marginal propensity to consume nondurables (items other than furnishings and equipment and autos) was lower for these military payments than for other income (.580 vs. .831).[41] A marginal propensity to consume windfalls of .580 is consistent with the *standard* income theory. If consumer durables are excluded from consumption, the permanent income theory predicts consumption of roughly twenty-four cents resulting from a dollar of windfall income.[42] The measured income theories, on the other hand, predict the same propensity to consume as for other income, in this case .831. The observed marginal propensity to consume is quite close to the midpoint (.54) of these two estimates. Since the standard errors are not given, however, it is not possible to say whether the data reject either the conventional theories or the permanent income theory.

In any case, there is a serious weakness in Miss Reid's study. This results from her using "military payments" as an example of transitory income. The items which compose "military payments" are mustering-out pay, dependency allotments, retirement pay, survivor and service-connected disability pay, unemployment insurance, other allowances, bonuses, and war insurance refunds.[43] Mustering-out pay was a fully anticipated receipt which would, therefore, not qualify as transitory in-

39. Roger Bird, "Consumption, Savings and Windfall Gains: Comments," *American Economic Review*, Vol. LIII, June 1963, pp. 443–44. "Other money receipts" are "inheritances and occasional large gifts of money from persons outside the family . . . and net receipts from the settlement of fire and accident policies" (p. 443). Nothing is known about the breakdown of "other money receipts" among these items. If inheritances are the dominant part, the high marginal propensity to save reported by Miss Reid is not surprising.

40. "Consumption, Savings and Windfall Gains: Reply," *American Economic Review*, Vol. LII, June 1963, pp. 444–45.

41. *Ibid.*, p. 444.

42. As Bird and Bodkin (*op. cit.*, p. 505n) pointed out, the permanent income theory's prediction of the increase in the consumption of nondurables per dollar of transitory income is obtained by multiplying 0.3 by the ratio of nondurables and services to total consumption. Since this ratio is not given by Miss Reid for her data, I used the ratio given by Bird and Bodkin for their data.

43. Reid, *op. cit.*, p. 444n.

come at the time of receipt. The next three items are permanent income. Unemployment insurance indicates that the household has negative transitory income. Only the last item is clearly positive transitory income. Thus, the marginal propensity to consume military payments is a mixture of the marginal propensity to consume permanent and transitory income. If the marginal propensity to consume is, in fact, higher for permanent than for transitory income, then Miss Reid's estimate of the marginal propensity to consume military payments is an overstatement of the marginal propensity to consume transitory income.

The marginal propensity to purchase durables shown by Miss Reid's equation is surprisingly high, and this tends to support the permanent income theory. However, it is subject to a bias which may be quite serious. Since military payments included mustering-out pay, the recipients presumably include a disproportionate number of newly discharged veterans.[44] Since they are reestablishing their civilian life, it is not surprising that their purchases of furnishings and equipment and autos are high. This consideration is reinforced by the fact that the marginal propensities to spend military payments on both types of consumption together is greater than unity (1.2), a fact which fits the view that veterans were re-equipping themselves with civilian goods. All in all, this test of Miss Reid's is quite consistent with a standard income theory, but does not really provide disconfirming evidence for either the full permanent income theory or for the measured income theories.

Some other evidence on the use of windfalls is a finding of George Katona. He reported the result of asking households the following question: "Suppose you had some extra money—say an amount equal to one week's wages or salary . . . what would you do with this money?" [45] Forty-two percent of the sample said that they would save it.[46] This, of course, is consistent with the standard income theory. However, it does not provide good evidence against a full permanent income theory, because people's statements of what they would do under hypothetical cir-

44. Miss Reid's observations were not individual households, but city averages. The greater the proportion of newly discharged veterans in a city, the greater presumably was the average military payment received.

45. George Katona, *Private Pensions and Individual Savings* (Ann Arbor, Survey Research Center, University of Michigan, 1965), p. 47.

46. The sample was limited to complete families "with the head in the labor force and aged 35 to 64 with a family income of $3000 or more." *Ibid.*, p. 8.

Other polls like this have shown a savings response of one-half to 86 percent. See Hadley Cantril and Mildred Strunk, *Public Opinion 1935–46* (Princeton, Princeton University Press, 1951), p. 68; National Association of Bank Women, *Money and the Young Wage Earner* (National Association of Bank Women, 1967), p. 28. See also the Simon-Barnes study cited below (p. 179)

cumstances is not necessarily a reliable indication of what they actually do. Moreover, the question was worded rather generally.

Many economists have felt disappointed with the effect of the 1968 surtax. It seemed as though this surtax did not have much effect on consumption. One possible explanation, given by Robert Eisner, is that this tax was a temporary one. According to the permanent income theory or life cycle hypothesis, a temporary tax would have only a relatively small effect on nondurable consumption. Hence, this seems to be a case where the permanent income theory and the life cycle hypothesis can explain the observed events so that these theories are confirmed.[47]

But this view has been challenged by Arthur Okun.[48] What Okun did was to take four econometric models not using a permanent income theory approach (the Data Resources Inc. model, the Michigan model, the O.B.E. model, and the Wharton model) and to see how well they can explain the behavior of consumption in the surtax period. Specifically, Okun formulated the problem as follows: suppose that the permanent income and life cycle theories are correct. If so, one should forecast consumption from an income total which ignores the surtax.[49] This is what Okun called the "zero effects view." On the other hand, assume that the surtax was fully effective. In this case one should predict consumption from an income total which is adjusted for the surtax. This he called the "full effects view." Okun then used his four econometric models to generate predictions of consumption on both the zero effect and the full effect views to see which is closer to actually observed consumption, and to what extent the surtax was effective; that is, the extent to which the surtax had the same effect as other income changes. For nondurable consumption and services one of the models (the Data Resources Inc. model) showed the surtax as 69 percent effective, and the other three models showed it as 100 percent or more effective. Similarly, for durables other than autos, the surtax was close to 100 percent effective. However, for autos both the full effect and the zero effect views underpredicted actual consumption. Apparently some factor, either excluded or not given sufficient weight in these models, raised automobile purchases. Okun then combined the three consumption components to es-

47. "Fiscal and Monetary Policies Reconsidered," *American Economic Review,* Vol. LIX, December 1969, pp. 897–905; and "What Went Wrong," *Journal of Political Economy,* Vol. 79, May–June 1971, p. 632. Eisner was concerned with the effect of a temporary tax in general terms, and hence did not try to estimate the marginal propensity to consume windfalls.

48. "The Personal Tax Surcharge and Consumer Demand," *Brookings Papers on Economic Activity,* 1971, No. 1, pp. 167–204.

49. Note, however, that on Friedman's assumption, a one-dollar transitory income change, via its effect on permanent income, changes consumption by thirty cents.

timate the effect of the surtax on overall consumption. To do so he assumed that the effect of the surtax must lie in between zero and 100 percent as measured by the zero effects and the full effects view and he therefore reduced any estimates outside the zero and 100 percent range to zero or 100 percent. On this assumption the effect on total consumption ranged from 63 percent to 80 percent in the four models (with an unweighted mean of 75 percent). But if one does not restrict the values to the 0–100 percent range then the effects range from 34 percent in one model to 133 in another (with a mean of 67 percent). These values are entirely consistent with the standard income theory.

However, I believe that this experience with the surtax does not furnish acceptable evidence on the wealth theories. It seems that some special factor influenced automobile purchases and if it had not been for this factor, the data might well have rejected the permanent income theory and life cycle hypothesis completely. But for reasons given by Okun, any evidence they would provide against these theories is highly suspect. One is that the public may have been skeptical that the tax would really be only temporary. Past experience with "temporary" taxes makes such skepticism plausible. Second, the tax increase represented only a very small percent of income, and a previously discussed study of Landsberger's suggests that small windfalls may be more readily consumed than large ones.[50] Hence, I conclude that this evidence from the surtax does not provide an adequate test of the wealth theories.

Windfalls and the Horizon. Finally, there is a study by Michael Landsberger in which he took as his *point of departure* the proposition that windfalls are saved, and used data on consumption, income, and windfalls to estimate the horizon.[51] Specifically, Landsberger's model is one in which households consume only out of their human and nonhuman wealth. In such a model, when a household receives a windfall gain and increases its consumption, this increase in consumption represents consumption out of the yield on this windfall. The magnitude of this yield, as Landsberger showed, is equal to the relative size of the marginal propensity to consume out of income and the marginal propensity to consume from windfall receipts minus unity. By doing such calculations with Israeli reparation receipts in five surveys, Landsberger

50. In his discussion of Okun's paper ("Comment and Discussion" in *ibid.,* p. 209) Eisner argued that the four econometric models really include permanent income theory effects because they include lagged income or consumption terms. However, as Okun pointed out, these terms do not differentiate between a permanent and transitory income change (*ibid.,* p. 210). They fit in better into a habit persistence theory than into a permanent income theory.

51. "Consumer's Discount Rate and the Horizon: New Evidence," *Journal of Political Economy,* Vol. 79, November–December 1971, pp. 1346–59.

obtained estimates of the discount rate which are consistent with Friedman's. His estimates of the horizon varied from two to six years.[52]

This is a very neat test of Friedman's horizon, given Friedman's (and Landsberger's) assumption that the windfall is treated entirely as capital so that households consume only its yield rather than the windfall itself. But the change in consumption which is associated with the observed windfall can also be interpreted as consumption out of the windfall itself —the data permit both interpretations. Hence, Landsberger's test of Friedman's horizon is a test of a particular specification of theory, but not a test of the theory itself.

Summary. To summarize, this set of tests has not been very successful on the whole. The Bird and Bodkin study invalidates the results of the original Bodkin study without providing any clear-cut results itself. The study by Klein and Liviatan founders on their bad definition of transitory income. The Kreinin and Landsberger results, while interesting for their own sake, are not really relevant to the choice between the permanent income theory and the measured income theories.[53] Miss Reid's findings also suffer from a bad definition of transitory income, and Katona's data on what households think they would do with additional receipts are only weak evidence. Eisner's study too, does not furnish reliable evidence supporting the permanent income theory. And Landsberger's test is a test of the specification rather than of the theory itself.

The Narrowing Cells Test

Friedman proposed the following tests: suppose we take a sample of households and divide them into subgroups based on some characteristic correlated with permanent income. Within each of these subgroups, differences in permanent income among households have, in part, been eliminated, and hence (if the variance of transitory income is the same), the *proportion* of the measured income variance accounted for by transitory elements is greater within each of these subgroups than it is for the whole sample. A similar thing applies if one divides these subgroups into still smaller groups. And since the income elasticity of consumption is zero for transitory income, the income elasticity of consumption out of

52. In addition to dealing with total consumption, Landsberger also estimated horizons from the expenditures on individual commodities.

53. The reason for this, as discussed above, is that a lower marginal propensity to consume windfalls than ordinary income is entirely consistent with the measured income theories. The propensity to consume windfalls, therefore, provides only a one-way test. A showing that the marginal propensities are the same for windfalls and for ordinary income refutes the permanent income theory, but a showing that they are substantially different does not confirm this theory.

measured income should fall towards zero as one breaks the total sample into finer and finer subgroups.[54]

This test was performed by Hendrick Houthakker in his review article of Friedman's book, and his results rejected the permanent income theory.[55] However, in a comment on this article Robert Eisner pointed out that Houthakker had committed an error by not weighting his data correctly.[56] Eisner then presented the coefficients resulting from a correct weighting procedure and they showed that, as the permanent income theory predicts, the income elasticity declines as one narrows the cells. Houthakker agreed that his method had been faulty, but argued that Eisner's revised results do not really confirm the permanent income theory.[57] "While the results . . . do go *in the direction* predicted by Friedman, this is not by itself a confirmation of the hypothesis." [58]

But as William Fellner has pointed out, the results of Eisner's test are consistent with the relative income theory, too.[59] According to the relative income theory the demonstration effect raises the consumption of households with an income below the mean, and lowers the consumption of households with an income above the mean.[60] This lowers the income

54. *A Theory of the Consumption Function, op. cit.,* p. 216.

55. Hendrick Houthakker, "The Permanent Income Hypothesis," *American Economic Review,* Vol. XLVIII, June 1958, pp. 396–404.

56. "The Permanent Income Hypothesis: Comment," *American Economic Review,* Vol. LVIII, December 1958, pp. 978–79. In a following comment Friedman expressed his agreement with Eisner ("The Permanent Income Hypothesis: Comment"), in *ibid.,* pp. 990–91. See also Dennis Aigner and Julian Simon, "A Specification Bias Interpretation of Cross-Section vs. Time Series Parameter Estimates," *Western Economic Journal,* Vol. VIII, June 1970, pp. 144–62. Eisner's criticism is also applicable to earlier attempts to test the permanent income theory in this way. In their comment on Malcolm Fisher's study ("Exploration in Savings Behaviour," Oxford University Institute of Economics and Statistics, *Bulletin,* Vol. 18, August 1956, pp. 201–78), James Tobin and Harold Watts argue that in Fisher's data there is no "striking tendency" for a narrowing of the class cells to have the effect predicted by the permanent income theory. ("An Evaluation of the Tests," Oxford University Institute of Economics and Statistics, *Bulletin,* Vol. 19, May 1957, p. 163.) Another test by narrowing the cell means, again not weighting the results (and hence subject to Eisner's criticism), can be found in Harold Watts, "Long-Run Income Expectations and Consumer Saving," in Thomas Dernburg, Richard Rosett, and Harold Watts, *Studies in Household Economic Behavior* (Yale University Press, 1958), pp. 137–38.

57. "The Permanent Income Theory: Reply," in *ibid.,* pp. 991–93.

58. *Ibid.,* p. 922.

59. "Relative Permanent Income: Elaboration and Synthesis," *Journal of Political Economy,* Vol. LXVII, October 1959, pp. 508–11.

60. Fellner's argument is somewhat different from the above. In his version of the relative income theory, households not only try to keep up with

elasticity of consumption. And since the demonstration effect is stronger within a group than between groups it lowers the within-group elasticity more than the between-group elasticity. Eisner's findings are, therefore, quite consistent with the relative income theory, and hence cannot be used to support the permanent or the standard income theory against the relative income theory.

Test by Group Means

Early Tests. In his refutation of Houthakker's test Eisner undertook an additional test.[61] This is to classify households by some variable correlated with permanent income, such as occupation or type of city, and to compute mean income and consumption for households within each occupation or city type. By looking not at incomes of individual families but at these means, one eliminates much of the transitory income differences among households. Within each group some households have positive, and some negative, transitory income so that transitory income differences, in good part, cancel out. The difference in mean income between the groups then represent, mainly, differences in permanent income. If *all* the differences between the mean incomes of various groups would represent differences in permanent income, then the income elasticity of consumption measured from these group means should, according to the permanent income theory, be unity. However, according to Eisner, not all transitory elements are eliminated completely by using the mean income of groups as the unit of observation. It is not implausible that certain groups have positive and other groups negative transitory income in a particular year. Such transitory elements in the group means are particularly likely in a year which witnessed a change from recession to inflation, such as 1950, the year to which Eisner's data relate. Hence, if the income elasticity of consumption calculated from the group means is less than unity, this does not necessarily contradict the permanent income theory.

In Eisner's view this test strongly confirms the permanent income theory. Using nine different city classes the income elasticity measured between cities is .995—"about as close to unity as anyone could wish." By comparison, the weighted within-city income elasticity is .715. Using occupation instead of city-size class as the permanent income variable by which to classify households, the income elasticity measured between occupations is 0.798 compared with an elasticity of 0.727 for households

---

their neighbor's consumption, they also try not to get too far above it. This "brake effect," as Fellner calls it, is really not needed to support the argument made above. As long as the consumption of low income households is raised by a demonstration effect, the income elasticity is lowered.

61. *Op. cit.,* pp. 981–85.

classified by measured income.[62] Although Eisner concluded that these results support the permanent income theory, he conceded that "our results are consistent as well with the hypothesis that consumption is positively related to temporary components of income, but not as positively related as it is to the permanent component." [63]

In his reply Houthakker emphasized the fact that most of the elasticities calculated from the group means are less than unity, and did not accept Eisner's explanation that this divergence is due only to transitory income elements influencing the group means.[64] This criticism seems applicable to the occupational grouping where the elasticity calculated from the group means is only .798, but is hardly applicable to the city-class coefficient, which is .995.[65] Thus, in this test the permanent income theory appears to predict very well indeed for geographic differences, but badly for occupational differences. This, moreover, is not a peculiarity of Eisner's data, but shows up also in other tests using class means. Chapters 10 and 12 below deal with geographic and occupational tests in greater detail. They show that the results of both types of tests are consistent with the standard income theory.

Another test based on cell means, one which actually preceded the Eisner test, was undertaken by Irwin Friend and Irving Kravis, who compared the average propensities to consume of high income and low income occupational groups.[66] They found a substantial negative correlation—the coefficient of ranked correlation being 0.81, so that the proportionality hypothesis fails to pass this occupational test.

The Modigliani-Ando Tests. A whole battery of tests using group means were performed by Franco Modigliani and Albert Ando.[67] They used numerous ways of classifying households. First, they grouped them by city type, then by education, third by occupation, and fourth by age. They then grouped households by housing expenditure, and followed this up grouping households this way within education and occupation groups. They also grouped households by expenditures on personal insurance

62. *Ibid.,* pp. 983–84. Eisner also classified households by age and by two-way classifications.

63. *Ibid.,* p. 984.

64. Houthakker, "The Permanent Income Hypothesis: Reply," *op. cit.,* p. 993.

65. The third grouping into age classes seems inadmissible—see p. 110n below—so that the size of the coefficient is irrelevant.

66. "Consumption Patterns and Permanent Income," American Economic Association, *Papers and Proceedings,* Vol. XLVII, May 1957, pp. 544–46.

67. "The 'Permanent Income' and 'Life Cycle' Hypothesis of Saving Behavior: Comparison and Tests," in Irwin Friend and Robert Jones, *Consumption and Saving* (Philadelphia, University of Pennsylvania, 1960), Vol. II, pp. 123–66.

and by city type within occupational groups. Each of these will be discussed in turn.

Unlike Eisner they assumed that the differences in the group means for city classes result entirely from differences in permanent income, so that the income elasticity of consumption computed from these group means should be unity, or randomly distributed around this value.

Not surprisingly, they obtained the same result from the city type test as did Eisner; again the income elasticity calculated from group means was very close to unity, thus supporting the proportionality hypothesis. Their next test dealt with households classified by educational level. Here the income elasticity calculated from the class means is only 0.858, which is very close to the income elasticity of 0.847 for all households together calculated from measured income classes, so that the permanent income theory fails this test.[68]

The third classification principle, occupation, leads to a similar result. The income elasticity calculated from the group means is only slightly higher (0.870 or .880)[69] and is again close to the value calculated from the measured income classes (0.847). Modigliani and Ando admitted that "the gulf between this new estimate and unity is so wide that it seems impossible to reconcile this result" with the proportionality hypothesis.[70]

They then took up an age classification and this gave an income elasticity measured between group means of 0.880, but when they eliminated those households without a full-time earner, it jumped to 0.963. However, age is not a proper classification principle, a fact which Modigliani and Ando conceded.[71]

68. Modigliani and Ando stated that the life cycle hypothesis, unlike the strict permanent income theory, does not require an income elasticity of unity because of the correlation of education and age. But they also pointed out that these data contradict the life cycle hypothesis as well.

69. There appears to be a misprint. In the text Modigliani and Ando give the elasticity as .870, while their table (p. 129) shows it as .880.

70. *Ibid.*, p. 135.

71. "This criterion, in contrast to the three previous ones, cannot be regarded as satisfactory even prima facie. It is open to suspicion in terms of the Friedman model since age is one of the variables explicitly mentioned by Friedman as likely to affect systematically the value of k. It is even more objectionable in terms of the [Modigliani, Brumberg-Ando] model." (*Ibid.*, p. 135.) Despite this statement, Modigliani and Ando in summarizing the upshot of these tests do include the result of the age grouping test, though they added that "the relevance of this test is somewhat open to question." (*Ibid.*, p. 136.) This is an understatement. Modigliani and Ando used still another grouping, tenure, but stated that "this criterion is obviously not a satisfactory one. . . . For this reason the value of [the income elasticity] is not even worth computing, and the data are reported primarily for reference." *Ibid.*, pp. 135–36.

Modigliani and Ando then stated that the failure of the proportionality hypothesis on the education and occupation tests may be due to the correlation of educational status and occupation with some other variable which is, in turn, correlated with the saving ratio. "This explanation," they argued, "is consistent with the favorable results obtained with city class. . . . Yet we can hardly accept [the proportionality hypothesis] merely on the ground that we can't quite reject it. The tests of this section do establish at least a prima facie case against its validity." [72]

Modigliani and Ando, therefore, looked for another classification variable, one which would not only provide independent evidence but might also throw some light on the failure of the proportionality hypothesis to pass the occupation and the education tests. If it could be shown that *within* each of the occupation and education groups, the income elasticity of consumption calculated from some group means is unity, then this would suggest that the less than unitary elasticity found between occupation or education groups is due to some variable correlated with occupation or education.

Modigliani and Ando, therefore, classified households by housing expenditure (rent for renters and value of house for homeowners). They pointed out that housing expenditure involves a long-run consumption decision and is, therefore, closely related to permanent income.[73] And when they classified families by housing expenditure, the elasticity of consumption with respect to housing expenditure was practically unity.

Next, Modigliani and Ando used housing expenditure as a proxy for permanent income to see if it explains their previous results for education and occupation groups. Therefore, they classified households *within* education and occupation classes by housing expenditure, and measured the elasticity of consumption with respect to housing expenditures within each of the education and occupation classes. The results they obtained from this grouping by expenditures were not clear-cut. While many of them supported the proportionality hypothesis, in two cases (self-employed homeowners and the homeowning salaried professionals) the hypothesis is rejected.

But all of the tests using housing expenditures as a permanent income proxy are invalid. Modigliani and Ando have confused a *functional* rela-

---

72. *Ibid.*, pp. 137–38.
73. While this assumption is certainly plausible, it is not beyond challenge. In his review of Margaret Reid's *Housing and Income*, Robert Ferber argued that families may lack the financial resources to purchase a house in keeping with their permanent incomes, and that they may not be able to estimate their permanent incomes correctly. *American Economic Review*, Vol. LIV, March 1964, pp. 214–15. See also Sherman Maisel and Louis Winnick, "Family Housing Expenditures: Elusive Laws and Intrusive Variances," in Irwin Friend and Robert Jones, *op. cit.*, Vol. 1, pp. 392–94.

tion with a *proportional* relation. They argued that since housing expenditures *depend* upon permanent rather than transitory income, they are an adequate proxy for permanent income. But to be an adequate proxy for permanent income, a functional relationship is not enough. What their tests require is something more than this, namely that housing expenditures be *proportional* to permanent income. If housing expenditures are not proportional to permanent income, then the elasticity of consumption with respect to housing expenditures does *not* measure the permanent income elasticity of consumption. Suppose, for example, that the permanent income elasticity of housing expenditures is 0.9, and suppose further that the permanent income elasticity of total consumption is 0.9, too. If so, the elasticity of consumption with respect to housing expenditures is 1.0, and the Modigliani-Ando method of using housing expenditures as a proxy for permanent income shows the proportionality hypothesis as valid when in fact it is invalid. If, and only if, the permanent income elasticity of housing expenditures is itself unity would it be correct to use it as a permanent income proxy in the way Modigliani and Ando do. And there is no reason to think that the permanent income elasticity of housing is, in fact, unity or very close to it.[74] Hence, Modigliani and Ando's numerous tests based on housing expenditures are invalid.[75] Modigliani and Ando supplemented their analysis by classifying

74. See Frank de Leeuw, "The Demand for Housing: A Review of Cross-Section Evidence," *Review of Economics and Statistics,* Vol. LIII, February 1971, pp. 1–11; Margaret Reid, *Housing and Income* (Chicago, University of Chicago Press, 1962), p. 6; T. H. Lee, "Housing and Permanent Income: Tests Based on a Three-Year Reinterview Survey," *Review of Economics and Statistics,* Vol. L, November 1968, pp. 480–90; T. H. Lee, "More on the Stock Demand Elasticities of Non-Farm Housing," *Review of Economics and Statistics,* Vol. XLIX, November 1967, pp. 640–42; and "The Stock Demand Elasticities of Nonfarm Housing," *Review of Economics and Statistics,* Vol. XLVI, February 1964, pp. 82–89; Richard Muth, "The Demand for Nonfarm Housing," in Arnold Harberger (ed.), *The Demand for Durable Goods* (Chicago, University of Chicago Press, 1960), p. 72; and "The Stock Demand Elasticities of Non-Farm Housing," *Review of Economics and Statistics,* Vol. XLVII, November 1965, pp. 447–49; Sherman Maisel and Louis Winnick, *op. cit.,* pp. 392–94; David Laidler, "Income Tax Incentives for Owner-Occupied Housing," in Arnold Harberger and Martin Bailey (eds.), *The Taxation of Income from Capital* (Washington, D.C., Brookings Institution, 1969), p. 71. Sherman Maisel, James Burnham and John Austin, "The Demand for Housing: A Comment," *Review of Economics and Statistics,* Vol. LIII, November 1971, pp. 410–13.

75. Moreover, as Modigliani and Ando pointed out, using an expenditure item as a permanent income proxy means that the dependent variable (total consumption) and the independent variable have a common error term, thus biasing the results. However, they showed that the bias was not large in this case.

households by another permanent income proxy, personal insurance expenditures. But once again the confusion of a functional relationship with a proportional one invalidates the analysis.[76]

In addition to these tests by housing and insurance, Modigliani and Ando used still another method of subclassifying households, city type. In each of two occupational groups, the self-employed and the salaried professionals, they classified households by city type, and calculated the income elasticity within each of the two occupations using as their permanent income proxy the mean income of the particular occupation in each city type. They found income elasticities of substantially less than unity for both occupations, so that this test rejects the proportionality hypothesis.[77]

Modigliani and Ando concluded from all of this that their results support the life cycle hypothesis to the extent that the income elasticity of consumption is greater when households are classified by a permanent income proxy than it is when they are classified by measured income. However, they agreed that the proportionality hypothesis "is not fully supported by the results of our tests" arguing that it is supported by some of the tests, but not by others.[78] But if one leaves aside the clearly invalid use of housing expenditures as a permanent income proxy, the proportionality hypothesis is supported only by the city type classification. On the other hand, it is rejected by the tests which classified households by education, by occupation, and by city type within two occupations. Thus, all in all, the Modigliani-Ando tests really reject, rather than support, the proportionality hypothesis.

Other Tests. A study by Asimakopulos using Canadian data found a similar result for location.[79] He looked at households grouped by location (regions and cities), family type, and age of head. The income elasticities

76. Since insurance is a savings item, the bias discussed in the preceding footnote operates in the direction of raising the elasticity. Since insurance expenditures are a substantial proportion of saving, it can be large.

77. *Op. cit.,* pp. 158–60. Modigliani and Ando suggested a possible explanation for this low elasticity (*ibid.,* p. 158n). This is that the suburbs which tend to have relatively high incomes also tend to have a high frequency of home ownership. Home ownership, they argued, causes an understatement of consumption since depreciation of the house is not counted. However, if one leaves the suburbs aside and looks at the remaining city types, there is still a negative correlation between the mean income and the consumption-income ratio. The ranked correlation coefficient is significant at the 5 percent level despite an (insignificant) negative ranked correlation between income and the home ownership proportion.

78. *Ibid.,* p. 167.

79. "Analysis of Canadian Consumer Expenditure Surveys," *Canadian Journal of Economics and Political Science,* Vol. XXX, May 1965, pp. 222–41.

calculated from the grouping by location varied from 0.816 to 1.216 with an unweighted mean of 0.997. The income elasticities calculated from family type groups were also close to unity, while the elasticities computed from age groups were somewhat lower. But family type and age of head are not good classification criteria. One would expect these variables to have an independent effect on consumption so that these elasticities confound income effects and "taste" effects. For example, only some of the higher consumption of large families can be attributed to the higher income of larger families; surely some is due to differences in tastes ("needs").[80] Hence, among these tests only the ones using location are really reliable. Thus these Canadian data support a conclusion found for U.S. data; when computed from geographic groups, the income elasticity is approximately unity.[81]

In another study, Harold Guthrie compared the permanent income theory with the absolute income theory and the relative income theory.[82] To test the permanent income theory he divided his sample into sixty-five relatively homogeneous subgroups, and called the difference between a household's income and the average income of its subgroup transitory income. For permanent income he used the average of the household's subgroup. He obtained good results in his regression equations with the permanent income theory, but the correlation coefficients were, on the whole, no higher than they were for the absolute and relative income theories. This was also true when Guthrie used these theories to explain not the saving ratio but the percent of income spent on durables. However, this can hardly be treated as a disconfirmation of the permanent income theory. Some of the difference between a spending unit's income and the average income of its group surely represents differences in permanent income rather than in transitory income. The fact that Guthrie did not get a better fit for the permanent income theory than for the other theories (for which his specifications were much better) *could,* therefore, be the result of a bad specification of transitory income.[83]

In a study to be discussed later on, Harold Watts divided a sample of households into groups based on variables, such as occupation, which are correlated with long-run income. He plotted mean income of these groups and their propensity to save, and his scatter diagram suggests a

80. Thus Asimakopulos wrote that "for the Family Type and Age of Head classifications . . . it is more difficult to assume that consumption behavior is unaffected by the classification criteria." *Ibid.,* p. 241.

81. Asimakopulos himself considers this test to be "rather inconclusive." *Ibid.,* p. 241.

82. Harold Guthrie, "An Empirical Evaluation of Theories of Saving," *Review of Economics and Statistics,* Vol. XLV, November 1963, pp. 430–33.

83. Guthrie concedes that the appropriateness of this test is "open to question." *Ibid.,* p. 432.

rather weak positive correlation between group income and the saving ratio.[84]

Arnold Zellner compared the average propensities to consume of households classified by education.[85] He found that the households with higher education, and hence a higher income, had a lower average propensity to consume.[86] However, he pointed out that this does not necessarily refute the proportionality hypothesis since it could be due to differences in family size, to greater availability of saving opportunities for the better educated, to inclusion of durables expenditure in consumption, or to the effect of education on the taste for savings.

Ramachandra Ramanathan dealt with households in a single Indian city, Delhi, classifying households by education and age.[87] He found that the marginal propensity to save is substantially lower for permanent income than for transitory income (defined as the difference between the household's actual income and the mean income of its group). However, the marginal propensity to save transitory income was less than unity, so that Ramanathan claimed to have rejected Friedman's hypothesis that all transitory income is saved. Since Ramanathan included consumer durable purchases in saving in one of his definitions of saving, this failure of the full permanent income theory cannot be dismissed as due to transitory income being spent on durables. However, there is another difficulty. While some of the difference between a household's measured income and the mean income of its group is transitory income, some of it surely does represent permanent income. Moreover, according to Friedman receipt of transitory income raises consumption indirectly because it raises per-

84. Harold Watts, "Long-Run Income Expectations and Consumer Saving," in Thomas Dernburg, Richard Rosett, and Harold Watts, *Studies in Household Economic Behavior* (New Haven, Yale University Press, 1958), p. 140.

85. "Tests of Some Basic Propositions in the Theory of Consumption," American Economic Association, *Papers and Proceedings*, Vol. L, May 1960, p. 568.

86. Zellner divided his sample by age and home ownership status. Actually, for renters the positive correlation between education and the average propensity to consume is rather questionable. Zellner's data are supported, on the whole, by Morgan's tabulation of the saving ratios of households classified by occupation. Only one group (education of less than eight years) is out of line. Morgan also presented saving ratios adjusted by holding a number of variables constant. Here the picture is less clear, a fact which is not surprising since some of the variables Morgan held constant are themselves permanent income proxies. (See James Morgan, "An Analysis of Expenditure and Saving," in Richard Kosobud and James Morgan, *Consumer Behavior of Individual Families over Two and Three Years*, University of Michigan, Survey Research Center, Ann Arbor, 1964, p. 130.)

87. "Estimating the Permanent Income of a Household: An Application to Indian Data," *Review of Economics and Statistics*, Vol. L, August 1968, pp. 383–88.

manent income. When one combines these two factors, they *may* suffice
to explain the low propensity to save transitory income without abandon-
ing the strict permanent income theory. Nonetheless, it is interesting to
see what Ramanathan's findings imply for the relative marginal propensities to consume permanent and transitory income. For the conventional
definition of consumption, the marginal propensity to consume transitory
income is 87 percent of the marginal propensity to consume permanent
income.

Another important result reached by Ramanathan is his support for
the Pennsylvania School's normal income theory. In his regressions the
coefficient for the difference between desired and actual wealth was
nearly always significant.

In a previous study I dealt with the average propensities to consume of
households in various manual occupations in the nineteenth century.[88]
These occupations, taken two at a time, can be ranked by permanent income. In ten of the fourteen cases the occupation with the higher permanent income had the lower average propensity to consume, thus rejecting the proportionality hypothesis at the 10 percent significance
level.[89] Since all the households covered were those of manual workers,
differences in cultural values which may interfere when other groups are
compared, are here a minimum.

The tests discussed so far used as a proxy for a household's permanent
income the mean income of a group, such as an occupational group, to
which the household belongs. Irwin Friend used a generalized version of
this method. He estimated the normal income of Indian urban households
by using simultaneously the mean income for the household's occupation,
education, mother tongue, and size of town.[90] He then used this normal
income estimate, together with transitory income, to explain saving.
Both of these variables turned out to be significant, and the marginal
propensity to save was twice as great for transitory income as for measured income.[91]

Subsequently Robert Parry employed the same method to investigate
the propensities to save in the United States (1950), Britain (1954), and

88. Thomas Mayer, "The Permanent Income Theory and Occupational
Groups," *Review of Economics and Statistics,* Vol. XLV, February 1963,
pp. 16–22.
89. If one includes one rather doubtful case the score becomes eleven out
of fifteen. All this relates to renters. If one includes homeowners—a procedure which creates some data problems—the score is eighteen out of
twenty.
90. "The Propensity to Save in India," in D. H. Butani and P. Singh (eds.),
Economic Development: Issues and Policies (Bombay, Vora and Co., 1966),
pp. 153–70.
91. *Ibid.,* pp. 165–66.

Israel (1957–1958).[92] He used the following characteristics: occupation, education, age, location, number of earners, family size, sex, income change, a housing expenditure variable, race (for the U.S.), net worth, and housing tenure.[93] The last two variables measure not only normal income but also saving tastes, and Parry ran two sets of regressions, one including and one excluding them. The results were dramatic. The marginal propensity to *save* was roughly two to four times as great for transitory income as for permanent income.[94] The implied marginal propensities to consume are shown in Table 6.

But note that the method used by Friend and Parry understates the extent of the difference between the propensities to consume normal and transitory income. The technique of separating normal from transitory income is by no means perfect; on the contrary, there is some evidence that it is not very effective. Robert Holbrook, who as far as I know was the first to use this method of estimating permanent income, found that it gave results inferior to those obtained by using the household's past and present incomes as an estimator of permanent income.[95] Hence, some of what is called transitory income by Friend and Parry is really permanent income. This mixing of permanent and transitory elements must lead to an understatement of the difference between the two propensities to consume. The fact that much transitory income is shown as consumed in Parry's study cannot, therefore, be used to disconfirm the permanent income theory. Rather this study reinforces the result that any theory which does not distinguish between permanent and transitory income is inadequate.

Summary. To summarize, there have been numerous tests using the

92. "The Separation of Normal and Transitory Components of Income from Cross-Section Data," unpublished Ph.D. dissertation, University of Pennsylvania, 1967.

93. For Britain, Parry could not use education and number of earners. For Israel he added two other variables, continent of birth and length of residence in Israel.

94. Parry also ran regressions for durable purchases and these regressions show that by no means all the consumption of transitory income takes the form of durables.

95. Robert Holbrook, "Alternative Models of Consumer Behavior: The Permanent Income Hypothesis and the Life Cycle Hypothesis," unpublished Ph.D. dissertation, University of California, Berkeley, 1965, p. 58.

The reason why this method of using the mean income of many groups is more precarious than using the income of a single group is that it is more ambitious. It tries to isolate the permanent income of each individual household separately. (This permanent income estimate for each household is then used in a regression equation to explain the household's saving.) When using the mean income of a single group, as a measure of the *mean* permanent income of its members, no attempt is made to isolate the permanent income of each household. All that is assumed is that within each group positive and negative transitory income cancels.

Table 6

Marginal Propensity to Consume Normal and Transitory Income

| | (1) | (2) | (3) | (4) | (5) | (6 |
| | | Using all Normal Income Proxies | | | Excluding Housing Variable and Wealth | |
Country	Normal Income	Transi- tory Income	(2) as Percent of (1)	Normal Income	Transi- tory Income	(5) as Percent of (4)
United States	.91	.60	66	.90	.65	72
Great Britain	.85	.74	87	.88	.73	83
Israel	.86	.73	85	.88	.72	82

SOURCE: Based on Robert Parry, "Separation of Normal and Transitory Components of Income from Cross-Section Data," unpublished Ph.D. dissertation, University of Pennsylvania, 1967, pp. 139–40.

mean income of groups as a proxy for the permanent or normal income of its members. These tests show that the income elasticity of consumption is greater for permanent than for transitory income. While this finding agrees with the permanent income theory or the standard income theory, and supports them as against the absolute income theory, it does not really support them against the relative income theory since the relative income theory has the same implication. If consumption depends upon past peak income as well as on current income, the income elasticity of consumption is also higher if one classifies households by current income than if one classifies them by the mean income of their group. The fact that some low income households are below their income peak, and some high income households are above their income peak, lowers the income elasticity of consumption. But when households are classified by the mean income of their group presumably much of this effect cancels out; the mean income of a low income group may be at its peak level even though many households with that income are below their individual income peaks. Hence, the relative income theory, too, predicts that the income elasticity of consumption is less when calculated from the mean incomes of groups than when calculated from the current incomes of each household.

Turning to the proportionality hypothesis, these studies show that if the mean income of a locality is used as a proxy for the permanent incomes of households in that locality, the income elasticity of consumption is approximately unity, as the permanent income theory predicts. But for other groupings of households, there is no evidence supporting the proportionality hypothesis; instead the evidence overwhelmingly rejects it. Thus except for the case of the geographic grouping of households, discussed in Chapter 12, these tests reject the proportionality hypothesis, and support the standard income theory rather than the permanent income theory. But they also support the relative income theory.

Comparison of Families with Fluctuating and Stable Incomes

The Friend-Kravis Test. Another test, due to Irwin Friend and Irving Kravis, is the comparison of households with stable and with fluctuating incomes.[96] The expenditure survey they used asked families whether their income was relatively constant between 1949 and 1950 and whether they expected about the same income in 1951. Households with stable incomes for these three years presumably are closer than other households to their permanent income. Therefore, income differences among them reflect differences in permanent income to a much greater extent than is true for other households. Hence, if the permanent income theory is correct, the income elasticity of consumption should be greater for these stable income households than for others. Note, however, that there is only a loose relation between income stability and permanent income. For some households, a rising income may be the normal thing, and for others (particularly retired households) a declining income may be normal. For such households the receipt of the same income in three years would not denote the absence of transitory income.[97] To be sure, in deriving permanent income, Friedman used the income of previous years, but this formulation is meant to apply only to whole groups of households and not to individual households.

Leaving this point aside, Friend and Kravis found that:

Only for the lowest income groups, where the consumption-income ratios of the constant income families are substantially lower than those of the nonconstant income families, are the findings reasonably consistent with these theories. . . . The data even show some tendency for the consumption income ratios of the "constant" income families in the upper income groups to be lower than the corresponding ratios of the "nonconstant" income families in these groups—the reverse of the results which would be expected from the assumption that the transitory component of income will not be consumed.[98]

Let us look at the data—shown in Table 7—in some detail. As Friend and Kravis assert, the consumption-income ratio of the constant income families does decline markedly with rising income. This indicates either

96. Irwin Friend and Irving Kravis, *op. cit.,* pp. 536–55.
97. See Jean Crockett, "Income and Assets Effects on Consumption: Aggregate and Cross Section," in Conference on Research in Income and Wealth, *Studies in Income and Wealth,* Vol. 28, *Models of Income Determination* (Princeton, Princeton University Press, 1964), p. 106.
98. *Ibid.,* p. 544. I have reversed the order of the two parts of this quotation.

that the proportionality hypothesis is invalid or that the "constant income families" do not really receive their permanent income. The latter alternative could be defended in two ways, either by arguing that the relevant period for measuring permanent income is more than three years, or that households who say that their income is *relatively* constant really experience quite a bit of income fluctuation, too.[99]

To evaluate the second of these arguments, let us suppose that households did use quite a broad range in saying that their incomes were constant. Assume for example, that among these families with allegedly constant income, recorded 1950 income was, on the average, 10 percent below permanent income in the $1,000–2,000 income class, and 10 percent above permanent income in the $7,500–10,000 class. This could then account, on permanent income theory assumptions, for much of the difference in the consumption-income ratio of these two income classes.[100] Admittedly, the assumption that on the average the constant income families in the $1,000–2,000 income bracket had more than 10 percent

99. See the "Comment" on the Friend-Kravis paper by Alfred Oxenfeldt (American Economic Association, *Papers and Proceedings,* Vol. XLVII, May 1957, p. 572).

100. Let S be saving, k the proportion of permanent income which is consumed (by permanent income theory assumptions it is equal for all income classes), Y_p permanent income, and Y_m measured income. Let the subscripts 1 and 2 indicate the lower and upper income classes respectively. On the permanent income theory assumption that all transitory income is saved, and on the further assumption of 10 percent transitory income in each class, the saving of the lower and upper income classes, respectively, can be written as:

$$S_1 = (1 - k)Y_{p_1} - .1Y_{m_1}; \; S_2 = (1 - k)Y_{p_2} + .1Y_{m_2}.$$

One can eliminate Y_p from these equations, since by assumption Y_p is 110 percent of Y_m in the lower income class, and .90 percent in the upper class. Eliminating Y_p and dividing by Y_m to get the saving-income ratio yields:

$$\frac{S_1}{Y_{m_1}} = 1.1(1 - k) - .1 \text{ and } \frac{S_2}{Y_{m_2}} = .9(1 - k) + .1.$$

Subtracting $\frac{S_1}{Y_{m_1}}$ from $\frac{S_2}{Y_{m_2}}$ to get the difference in the saving income ratio between these two income groups, gives $.2 - .2(1 - k)$. Now in these data, where saving is probably understated, $1 - k$ is .05 when durables are excluded from saving. Hence, on the above assumptions, there would be a 19 percentage point difference in the saving-income ratios of the two income classes. As can be seen from Table 7, the actual difference between the second lowest and second highest classes is 25.4 points, so that in this case, three quarters of the difference in the consumption-income ratios can be accounted for. To be sure, this involves some overstatement of the adjustment since I am not allowing for the fact that part of transitory income is spent for durables.

Table 7

Average Propensity to Consume for Stable
Income and Fluctuating Income Families

| | Percent of Income Consumed [a] | |
Income	Constant Income Families	Nonconstant Income Families
Under $1000	153.1	251.3
1000–1999	106.5	121.2
2000–2999	102.7	108.9
3000–3999	99.4	103.5
4000–4999	96.1	100.5
5000–5999	94.1	96.9
6000–7499	88.3	92.4
7500–9999	81.1	85.7
10,000 up	63.7	68.7

SOURCE: Based on I. Friend and I. Kravis, "Consumption Patterns and Permanent Income," American Economic Association, *Papers and Proceedings*, Vol. XLVII, May 1957, p. 545.

[a] Including durable purchases.

negative transitory income, while households in the $7,500–10,000 income class had more than 10 percent positive transitory income is not only a special case, but one that may lack plausibility. Why should such households state that their income is stable? However, there is some empirical evidence that households claiming no income change actually *do* experience some income change. As James Morgan has pointed out:

Validity studies have shown a tendency for people to remember the past as much more like the present than it really was. Memory questions about short-run changes will elicit "no change" responses from one-fourth to one-third of the respondents, whereas computations based on two interviews with the same people show only one-sixth or one-seventh with income changes of less than 5 percent. In addition, for a substantial number of respondents (more than a tenth) a comparison of the two interviews reveals disagreement even about the direction of the change.[101]

A similar finding was subsequently reported by Robert Holbrook:

The respondents were twice asked about their 1960 income. . . . In the second instance, respondents were given the option of reporting "same as 1961 income" or giving an actual dollar figure. There was a strong tendency to report no change rather than to provide such a figure, and

101. "The Anatomy of Income Change," in Richard Kosobud and James Morgan, *Consumer Behavior of Individual Families over Two or Three Years* (Ann Arbor, Survey Research Center, University of Michigan, 1964), p. 19.

even when an amount was named it was frequently quite wide of the mark.[102]

Thus, there is a strong possibility that the failure of families to specify income changes may lead to a serious bias. Hence, this test of Friend and Kravis cannot really be treated as evidence against the permanent income theory.

Moreover, there is an aspect of the data which Friend and Kravis ignored. Assume that mean transitory income is negative in the lower end of the income distribution and positive at the upper end, but that this difference is less for the "constant income" families than for other families. The permanent income theory then predicts that the consumption-income ratio falls faster as one goes up the measured income scale for the families whose income is not constant, than for the constant income families; in other words, that the income elasticity is greater for the families with the stabler income. This is, in good part, what the data show. The consumption-income ratio generally does decline less for the constant income families than for others until one reaches the $6,000 level, a range encompassing close to 90 percent of all families in this sample. In fact, even if one takes the whole distribution the same principle holds overall. For constant income families, the consumption-income ratio falls from 153.1 percent for the lowest income class to 63.7 percent for the highest income class, a drop of 89.4 percentage points. For the other families the corresponding difference drops by 182.6 percentage points.[103]

But note that this is consistent with the relative income theory as well as with the permanent income theory, as can easily be seen by changing the language of the above argument. If instead of talking about positive and negative transitory income, one talks instead of current income being above or below peak income, one has a relative income theory explanation in place of a permanent income theory explanation.

In any case, there is another puzzling characteristic of these data, which serves to weaken the Friend and Kravis argument. In every income class the "stable income families" have a lower consumption-income ratio than do the other families. It is not at all clear why the "stable income families" should save more. It suggests that these two sets of families may

102. "Alternative Models of Consumer Behavior: The Permanent Income Hypothesis and the Life Cycle Hypothesis," *op. cit.*, p. 35.

103. If one excludes the very lowest income class from the comparison, the difference is 42.8 percentage points for the stable income families and 52.5 percent for the other families. To be sure, in the top income classes this tendency does not hold, and the consumption-income ratio falls faster for the constant income households than for other households. I can think of no reason for this reversal; conceivably it merely represents sampling fluctuations, though this is not very plausible.

differ in other relevant ways, quite apart from income instability. If so, this test is questionable on yet another ground.

All in all, these data do little damage to the permanent income theory. If one allows for the possibility that there is substantial income variability even for the so-called "stable income" families, they do not disconfirm the permanent income theory or the standard income theory.

Other Tests. In another study Crockett and Friend used data from the same source.[104] Holding constant a number of variables which affect saving, they compared the marginal propensities to consume of stable income and fluctuating income families. This comparison was unfavorable for the permanent income theory. But among the variables which Crockett and Friend held constant was education, a good proxy for permanent income. In fact, education may be a better measure of permanent income than is the measured income of constant income families. If the educational variable picks up much of the permanent income difference among households, then one should not treat, as Friend and Crockett do, the coefficient of the measured income for stable income families as a measure of the propensity to consume permanent income.

Miss Reid, using mainly data for farm families, found results which differed sharply from those of Friend and Kravis.[105] She found that households with relatively stable incomes had income-expenditure curves with a steeper slope than did families with fluctuating incomes. In fact she went much further than this—she found that when she took families with sharply fluctuating incomes and classified them by income in any *one* year, households in various income classes in that year "on the average spent about the same amount," thus sharply contradicting the measured income theories.[106] But this is not as surprising as it may seem at first. It is a well-known fact that the income elasticity for farm households is very low so that consumption differences among farm households with different incomes are very small. This fact was used by Friedman in one of his tests discussed in the previous chapter. Presumably Miss Reid's data are the ones also used by Friedman, and, as was discussed in Chapter 3, unless certain observations are eliminated from the sample, they do *not* support the proportionality hypothesis.[107]

---

104. "Rejoinder," in Friend and Jones, *Consumption and Saving,* Vol. I, *op. cit.,* pp. 171–73.

105. "Savings by Family Units in Consecutive Periods," in Walter Heller, Francis Boddy, and Carl Nelson (eds.), *Savings in the Modern Economy* (Minneapolis, University of Minnesota Press, 1953), pp. 219–20.

106. *Ibid.,* p. 219.

107. Since Miss Reid's paper is only a brief summary of her results, it does not contain the data or their sources.

In a subsequent publication Miss Reid reported the following results:

Using data from annual surveys of spending units reporting income and savings for both 1947 and 1948, I selected spending units with at least two persons in 1948 and reporting income of 1948 within ten percent of income of 1947. . . . It included 146 units ranging in income for 1948 from under $1,000 to over $35,000. For this set the elasticity of expenditures with respect to income, with variables in log form, was .98 whereas that of the entire set with at least two persons was .85 and for the unstable set .80.[108]

Miss Reid considered this test superior to the Friend-Kravis test since data on actual income reported in surveys covering consecutive years give a more accurate picture of income changes than do responses to a question about income stability.

The income elasticity of 0.98 which Miss Reid obtained for the sample of households with relatively constant income appears to support the proportionality hypothesis. But, as Miss Reid pointed out, there is a bias in her income elasticities.[109] Hence, this evidence does not provide firm support for the proportionality hypothesis. However, since the bias is likely to be less for the stable income families than for the others, her finding that the income elasticity is greater for households with relatively stable income than for others cannot be dismissed in this way, and it does provide evidence for the permanent income theory, the standard income theory, or, as pointed out above, for the relative income theory.

Miss Reid's favorable conclusions for the permanent income theory, or the standard income theory, are supported by the implications of some work by James Morgan. Morgan worked with a subsample of "normal income" households—that is, a sample which eliminated households with relatively high transitory income. As Klein and Liviatan pointed out, his data favor the permanent income theory since the marginal propensity to consume is higher for the "normal income" subsample than for the

108. "Comments" in Friend and Jones, *Consumption and Saving, op. cit.*, Vol. I, pp. 151–52.

109. *Ibid.*, p. 152n. The bias results from the fact that the original data did not give consumption, but only income and saving. If one derives consumption by subtracting saving from income, income and consumption have a common error term. Miss Reid stated that this problem is likely to be relatively minor for the sample of households with stable income since large errors in income are likely to cause a difference of more than 10 percent in the reported incomes for the two years and hence serve to exclude the household from the sample. But it is certainly possible that some households made the same error in both years. Another problem is that Miss Reid's study is based on a two-year horizon, whereas Friedman believes that a three-year horizon is the relevant one for his theory. However, as discussed above, it is by no means clear that Friedman is correct in this.

whole sample.[110] But this evidence, too, is consistent with the relative income theory.

To summarize these results, Friend and Kravis's unfavorable evidence for the permanent income theory is open to serious question. The Crockett-Friend test suffers from the weakness that Crockett and Friend held a permanent income proxy constant, while one of Miss Reid's tests furnishes support for a full permanent income theory, the standard income theory, or the relative income theory, as do the Friend-Kravis data. Morgan's data, as used by Klein and Liviatan, also support one of these theories. All in all, this set of tests does not distinguish properly between the permanent income theory and the relative income theory.[111]

Direction of Income Change

Numerous studies of consumption and saving classified households by the *direction* of past or expected income changes to see if these variables help to explain the saving ratio. At first glance these studies, often undertaken without direct reference to the permanent income theory, appear to furnish a good test of this theory. Upon a closer look, however, this is not so. There are two reasons for this. One is that such data are highly unreliable. As has been pointed out above, households make large errors in estimating past income changes. Similarly, a household's prediction of future income changes is often wide of the mark. One reinterview study found that only 44 percent of the sample predicted the *direction* of their income change correctly, and even for these 44 percent there were large errors in the magnitude of the change.[112] To be sure, what is relevant for the permanent income theory is not the actual change but the expected change in income. But given such large errors in prediction, many households presumably are quite uncertain about their income ex-

110. Lawrence Klein and Nissan Liviatan, "The Significance of Income Variability on Savings Behavior," Oxford University Institute of Economics and Statistics, *Bulletin,* Vol. 19, May 1957, p. 157.

111. The results of this test are consistent with the habit persistence theory as well. In a stable income group a high income household is likely to have had a high consumption level in the previous year, and hence, according to the habit persistence theory, its consumption should be high in the current year, too. And similar reasoning applies to a low income household in the constant income group. Hence, the income elasticity of consumption is likely to be high in the stable income group, higher than among families with greater income fluctuations.

112. These results are based on a small sample. See Donald Gratehouse, "A Reinterview Study Showing Correlation between Income and Expenditures Based on the Ability to Anticipate Income One Year in Advance," American Statistical Association, Business and Economics Section, *Proceedings,* 1966, pp. 377–85

pectations, and a question about these expectations may therefore serve in large part to separate households into optimists and pessimists. Optimists and pessimists are likely to have different saving ratios because of personality differences, differences which may well confound any attempt to test the permanent income theory in this way.[113] Specifically, they are likely to bias the results in favor of the permanent income theory.[114]

Moreover, quite apart from errors in the data, there are serious limitations on the use of income change data for testing the permanent income theory. Consider first data on income changes from the previous year to the survey year. If it should turn out that households whose income has increased over the previous year have a high saving ratio, this would be simple for the permanent income theory to explain. Their income has risen, and this can be taken as an *indication* that their current measured income exceeds their permanent income. But if the data show the opposite —that is, a low saving ratio for households experiencing an income increase, this would not necessarily disconfirm the permanent income theory. Households whose income has risen over the past year *may* have a current income which is less than their permanent income. This is so because not all transitory income elements are due to short-term factors which are eliminated within one year. Factors such as unemployment may influence income over a two year period. The mere fact that income is rising does not prevent it from being below the household's permanent income level. Hence the household's income expectations for the next year do not provide adequate information to test the permanent income theory.

Fortunately, James Morgan has provided data—shown in Table 8— on income expectations over a ten-year period.[115] Here the problem of interpretation is less severe. As the permanent income theory predicts, households expecting an income increase have a lower saving ratio than households expecting stable income. However, households expecting an income decline have the lowest saving ratio. If one takes a short horizon

113. See Jean Crockett, "Income and Asset Effects on Consumption: Aggregate and Cross Section," in Conference on Research in Income and Wealth, *Studies in Income and Wealth*, Vol. 28, *Models of Income Determination* (New York, Columbia University Press, 1964), p. 106.

114. Pessimists are more likely than optimists to expect income decreases; at the same time they are likely to feel a greater need to save, with the result that there probably is a spurious correlation between high saving and expectations of income decrease in the sample.

115. In addition to the data shown in this table, Morgan also gave saving ratios when many of the variables affecting saving are held constant. But since many of these variables are proxies for permanent income, these adjusted saving ratios are not useful for testing the permanent income theory.

Table 8

Two-Year Saving Rates
by Income Anticipations Over the Next Ten Years

Income Anticipations over Next Ten Years[a]	*Two-Year Total Saving Rate, Class Mean Percent*	*Number of Cases*
Income will go up	11.6	496
Income will stay about the same	12.9	104
Income will fall (including will retire)	9.4	55
Income will fluctuate	16.2	52
Answer N.A. or inappropriate: head is retired or housewife		246
Grand mean	11.4	

SOURCE: James Morgan, "An Analysis of Expenditure and Saving," in Richard Kosobud and James Morgan, *Consumer Behavior of Individual Families over Two and Three Years* (University of Michigan, Survey Research Center, Ann Arbor, 1964), p. 133.

[a] The question asked early in 1961 was: "During the next ten years, do you think your earnings will rise gradually, go up and down from year to year, or fall, or what?"

this fact is hard to explain. But, if one assumes a long horizon, as Modigliani and associates do, or as Friedman does in his discussion of age and saving, then it is quite possible that these households expecting an income decline over the next ten years are currently, on the average, receiving less than their permanent income. In those occupations where income starts to fall prior to retirement, this would not be a surprising pattern.[116]

The inability to serve as a test of the wealth theories also applies to another set of income change data, data which classify households, at one and the same time, by past income changes and by expected income changes. Such data seem to allow one to isolate transitory changes in income. On the one hand, households with an income increase over the previous year who expect a *decrease* in the next year have positive transitory income. On the other hand, households with an income decrease in the current year followed by an expected income increase have negative transitory income. But it would do little good to compare households with transitory income changes thus defined to households with

116. The high saving ratio for households with fluctuating income seems to support Friedman's contention that such households are high savers. But Morgan did not define fluctuating income in the way Friedman did, but included households expecting a stable increase in income followed by a stable decrease. Moreover, the adjusted saving ratios (that is, adjusted for the effects of other variables) which are relevant when one is testing for the effect of income fluctuations rather than for permanent income, show a lower saving ratio for fluctuating income households.

"permanent" income changes—that is, households who expect the income movement to continue, or at least not be reversed, over a two-year
period. As already discussed, two years is too short a period in which to
measure permanent income adequately; many of the households who
expect the previous income change to continue from the previous year
into the next year receive transitory income. To be sure, one would expect that on the average the transitory component is less important for
households who expect the previous year's income change to continue
than for those who expect it to be reversed, but this separation of households into those with permanent and transitory income changes is not
clear-cut. When one combines this with the fact that income change data
are in general quite inaccurate, there is little purpose in undertaking such
a comparison.

Another possibility would be to compare households with transitory
income increases and decreases with all other households. But such a
comparison would prove little. The prediction that households with
temporary income increases save more than the average of households,
many of whom did not get an income increase, is a prediction which is
not specific to the permanent income theory. The absolute income theory,
at least in its *General Theory* version, the relative income theory, and the
habit persistence theory all share this prediction.[117]

117. This leaves the possibility of comparing the permanent income
theory and the habit persistence theory by seeing whether households react
symmetrically to income increases and income decreases. But while the
data give some support to the asymmetrical habit persistence theory, this
support is far from clear-cut. One study by Katona ("Effect of Income
Changes on the Rate of Saving," *Review of Economics and Statistics*, Vol.
XXXI, May 1949, p. 101) seems to support the asymmetrical habit persistence theory since the effect on saving is clearer for negative transitory income than for positive transitory income, but this is hardly very strong
evidence. Lawrence Klein's data ("Statistical Estimation of Economic Relations from Survey Data," in L. Klein and J. Morgan, eds., *Contributions of
Survey Methods to Economics, op. cit.*, pp. 215, 225) appear to support the
asymmetrical habit persistence theory, but since Klein dealt with residuals
from regressions—regressions which included many permanent income proxies—this is perhaps not a fair test. Thore's data (*Household Saving and the
Price Level, op. cit.*, pp. 182–84) do not show the predicted pattern for either
income increases or decreases, a fact *perhaps* explained by the small number
of households in each cell. Finally, there is a table of Morgan's ("An
Analysis of Expenditure and Saving," in Richard Kosobud and James
Morgan, *op. cit.*, p. 116). His data show that households with negative
transitory income deviate more from the mean saving ratio of the whole
sample than do households with positive transitory income, thus suggesting
an asymmetry. But since the number of households in the relevant cells is
fairly small and since Morgan does not give standard errors, one cannot tell
if this asymmetry is significant.

The problem of using income change data is less for data which cover three years rather than two years, as most income data do. Margaret Reid and Marilyn Dunsing have analyzed the Cochrane-Griggs three-year income change data used by Friedman in one of his tests.[118] Unlike Friedman, they did not test a very precise and specific implication of the permanent income theory, but they did show that transitory income and the saving ratio were correlated. Moreover, they pointed out that Ruth Mack's interpretation of these data in terms of a habit persistence theory could not account for the fact that households whose income went up had a low saving ratio in the initial year before income rose. Thus this test supports the permanent and standard income theories against the relative income theory.

There is, however, one piece of evidence on income expectations which does contradict the permanent income theory. When a sample of households was asked what changes they expected in their income, 108 said that they expected their income to be much higher, and 80 of those (74 percent) said that they expected this to make a big difference in their consumption, while 28 said it would make no difference in their consumption.[119] The fact that 74 percent stated that they plan to raise their consumption substantially contradicts the permanent income theory and life cycle hypothesis.[120] To be sure, this is not very strong evidence because people's statements about what they will do are an imperfect guide to what they actually do, but nonetheless this survey provides at least weak evidence against the permanent income theory and life cycle hypothesis. However, it does employ the conventional definition of consumption.

Time Series Tests

A number of economists have tested the life cycle hypothesis and related wealth approaches by regressing consumption on wealth and other variables. These tests are discussed in Chapter 8. In addition, some economists have run regressions using Friedman's permanent income concept. I will deal with these regressions in Chapter 7. Here I am dealing only with some of these time series regressions.

118. "Effect of Variability of Incomes on Level of Income—Expenditure Curves of Farm Families," *Review of Economics and Statistics,* Vol. XXXVIII, February 1956, pp. 90–96. In addition to the three-year income change data, they discussed also two-year income changes.

119. Ronald Freedman and Lolagene Combs, "Economic Consideration in Family Growth Decisions," *Population Studies,* Vol. XX, November 1966, p. 209.

120. The behavior of the other 26 percent does not contradict the relative income theory since these may be households whose income is below its previous peak.

In his review of Friedman's book Marc Nerlove was concerned primarily with the applicability of the permanent income theory to the demand functions for individual commodities.[121] But in addition he tested Friedman's proportionality hypothesis by using a Koyck-Nerlove transformation of a logarithmic consumption function. If the proportionality hypothesis is valid then, in a logarithmic consumption function, the sum of the income coefficient and the lagged consumption coefficient should equal unity. Nerlove's regression rejected this hypothesis of unity at the 1 percent significance level. He qualified this result, however, by pointing out that he used the conventional definition of consumption, and that the possibility of serial correlation does "warrant caution." [122] In addition, Nerlove found that the income elasticity of consumption rose when he lengthened the period over which he fitted the regression, a fact which is consistent with the permanent income theory "and suggsts that some transitory components of income may be affecting the regression." [123] Hence, Nerlove's test of the proportionality hypothesis, while unfavorable to this hypothesis, probably does not provide *strong* evidence against it.

Since permanent income, while hard to observe, is correlated with employment, one way of formulating and testing the permanent income theory is to use employment as a permanent income proxy. In fact, the use of employment or unemployment to explain saving or consumption antedates the permanent income theory by many years.[124] It was used by Franco Modigliani in his classic paper on the relative income theory as well as by Raymond Goldsmith in 1953.[125] Arguing that the saving ratio, or consumption, depends on the employment ratio is of course consistent not only with the permanent income theory, but also with the relative income theory.

A more recent test of a permanent income theory using employment

121. "The Implications of Friedman's Permanent Income Hypothesis for Demand Analysis," *Agricultural Economics Review,* Vol. X, January 1958, pp. 1–4.

122. *Ibid.,* p. 10.

123. *Ibid.,* p. 10.

124. The first use of unemployment to analyze saving probably was a study published in 1937 in Czech by K. Maiwald. It is described in his "The Effects of Maintained Consumption in the Unemployed Sector," *Economic Journal,* Vol. LXV, March 1955, pp. 89–106.

125. Franco Modigliani, "Fluctuations in the Saving-Income Ratio: A Problem in Economic Forecasting," Conference on Research in Income and Wealth, *Studies in Income and Wealth,* Vol. 11 (New York, National Bureau of Economic Research, 1949), pp. 384–92; Raymond Goldsmith, "Trend and Structural Changes in Savings in the Twentieth Century," in Walter Heller, Francis Boddy, and Carl Nelson (eds.), *Savings in the American Economy,* *op. cit.,* pp. 145–46.

data was undertaken by Jacob Mincer.[126] Using the consumption-income ratio as the dependent variable, Mincer fitted an equation using an employment measure.[127] In addition, he fitted to the same data an algebraic transformation of Friedman's permanent income measure and a relative income equation. Another equation he fitted took account not only of employment fluctuations but also of changes in productivity by using in place of employment the trend value of income as a measure of normal income. Such a trend of income equation can be interpreted not only as a permanent income approach but also as a relative income approach. As Mincer pointed out, it is similar to the Modigliani-Duesenberry relative income equation, but it uses the deviations of income from its trend in place of the relative income theory's deviations from the past income peak. He obtained the coefficients of determinations shown in Table 9. This table shows that if purchases of durables are excluded from consumption, the employment equation and the trend of income equation do about equally well and are superior to all the equations tested. On the other hand, if consumer durables purchases are included in consumption, the Modigliani-Duesenberry relative income equation does best.[128] Since I am primarily interested in the latter concept, I conclude from this that the relative income theory performs best.

Mincer's regression coefficients measure the marginal propensities to consume out of transitory income as well as the difference between the marginal propensities to consume for measured and permanent income. As Table 9 shows, the marginal propensity to consume transitory income is quite substantial.[129] Mincer pointed out that this marginal propensity to consume transitory income can be reconciled with the permanent income theory by interpreting it as reflecting not the direct effect of transitory income but the indirect effect of transitory income working through expectations of changes in permanent income, though "substantively, such rephrasing is nothing more than semantics." [130] In any case, the

126. "Employment and Consumption," *Review of Economics and Statistics,* Vol. XLII, February 1960, pp. 20–26.

127. Such a function was also fitted by Albert Ando and E. C. Brown in a subsequent publication. See Albert Ando, E. C. Brown, R. M. Solow, and John Kareken, "Lags in Fiscal and Monetary Policy" in Commission on Money and Credit, *Stabilization Policies* (Englewood Cliffs, N.J., Prentice Hall, 1963), pp. 117ff.

128. As discussed in Chapter 3 (p. 78) this does not necessarily disconfirm the permanent income theory.

129. Moreover, Mincer suggested that his employment equation which is shown in Table 9 understates the marginal propensity to consume for transitory income since it makes no allowance for changes in the workweek. Mincer, *op. cit.,* p. 25n.

130. *Ibid.,* p. 26.

Table 9

Marginal Propensity to Consume

	Including Durable Purchases			*Excluding Durable Purchases*		
Equation	R^2	*MPC out of Trans. Income*	*Trans. MPC as Percent of Perm. Income MPC*	R^2	*MPC out of Trans. Income*	*Trans. MPC as Percent of Perm. Income MPC*
1909–1949[a]						
Employment equation[b]	.84	.43	70	.92	.25	51
Trend of income equation	.82	.48	51	.91	.35	39
Friedman permanent income equation	.79	.46	46	.89	.34	37
Modigliani-Duesenberry equation[c]	.89	.44	44	.87	.30	33
1929–1956[d]						
Employment equation	.82	.41	67	.92	.38	58
Trend of income equation	.83	.60	63	.92	.36	40

SOURCE: Based on Jacob Mincer, "Employment and Consumption," *Review of Economics and Statistics*, Vol. XLII, February 1960, p. 25.

[a] Based on Goldsmith Data, excludes war years.

[b] Mincer presented two employment equations, one based on a man-hour series and one based on a population series. I have used the latter, which is the one he prefers.

[c] Equation is a modified variant of the original Modigliani-Duesenberry equation; it uses peak consumption in place of peak income.

[d] Based on Department of Commerce data, excludes war years.

marginal propensities to consume transitory income, particularly when consumption is defined in the conventional way, are high enough to agree with the standard income theory.

The unemployment rate has also been used by M. A. Arak and Alan Spiro in a paper dealing with Friedman's analysis of the adjustment in income expectations.[131] Friedman's model treats the difference between actual receipts and expected receipts as causing wealth revaluations which are proportional to the discrepancy between actual and expected receipts. Arak and Spiro, on the other hand, have households revalue their human plus nonhuman wealth in accordance with the utilization rate of this

131. "The Relationship between Permanent Income and Measured Variables," *Journal of Political Economy*, Vol. 79, May–June 1971, pp. 652–60.

wealth, for which the unemployment rate serves as a proxy. Their model, fitted to "use" consumption, performs better than the Friedman model.[132]

A set of saving functions has been fitted by Paul Taubman.[133] Taubman was concerned primarily with seeing what happens if one uses different sets of data to measure personal saving. One of these is the generally used Department of Commerce saving figure; the other, also from the Department of Commerce National Income Accounts, derives saving from the investment and net exports figure, which implies that the statistical discrepancy is allocated either to income or to consumption but not to saving. The third concept uses the SEC financial liquid saving total, and adds Department of Commerce estimates for other savings items to it. Taubman fitted a regression using normal income, transitory income, and net worth to these three estimates of saving for the years 1951–1965.[134] Table 10 shows his results for these three savings measures as well as for two hybrids: Clearly, there is a shocking difference in the marginal propensities to save depending upon the data used. This would not be such a serious problem if it were possible to decide in some way which set of data is the most accurate. However, this is not the case. Hence, Taubman concludes that:

There is no statistical test to determine which series is better except in one sense. . . . In principle, if one data source—but not another—gave answers unacceptable in terms of the a priori considerations dictated by economics, we could eliminate the series. . . . But none of the responses violate all saving theories. . . . The conclusion, thus, is quite pessimistic. For the saving function, one of the most basic elements in macro-economics, the dynamic and cyclical characterization depends upon our choice of measurement of a given concept and we do not know which measurement is correct.[135]

In view of this one must conclude that all savings functions and consumption functions fitted to national income data should be treated as doubtful. If the discrepancies among the series are so bad for recent years (1951–1965) one's faith in functions fitted to data reaching back to, say 1905, is put to a severe test. Fortunately, the marginal propensities to

132. In addition, they argued that one of the coefficients in the Friedman model is not confirmed by the data. This disconfirmation is due only to the constant term not being significant. But the fact that a term is not significant does not really mean that the data throw it out; given a larger sample it might well be significant.

133. Paul Taubman, "Personal Saving: A Time Series Analysis of Three Measures of the Same Conceptual Saving," *Review of Economics and Statistics,* Vol. XLX, February 1968, pp. 125–29.

134. Taubman measured normal income by using Fisher's method of lagged regression, using four years weighted in a 0.4, 0.3, 0.2, 0.1 pattern.

135. *Ibid.,* pp. 128–29.

Table 10

Marginal Propensities to Save and Consume
Obtained from Three Savings Measures

Savings Measure	Marginal Propensity to Save from			Marginal Propensity to Consume Trans. Income as Percent of Marginal Propensity to Consume Normal Income
	Trans. Income	Normal Income	First Year Income	
1. Using SEC savings data	.60	.20	.43	50
2. Dept. of Commerce direct estimate	.36	.07	.23	69
3. Using SEC savings data and income adjusted by subtracting the difference of Commerce and SEC saving	.66	.16	.45	40
4. Derived from investment data	.32	.11	.23	76
5. Derived from investment data adding statistical discrepancy to income	.41	.11	.28	66

SOURCE: Based on Paul Taubman, "Personal Saving: A Time Series Analysis of Three Measures of the Same Conceptual Series," *Review of Economics and Statistics*, Vol. XLX, February 1968, p. 128.

consume show smaller (percentage) variations than do the marginal propensities to *save,* and for all four regressions the marginal propensities to consume transitory income lie between 40 percent and 76 percent of the marginal propensities to consume normal income.

Prem Laumas fitted permanent income theory consumption functions to Canadian data.[136] One function made permanent consumption (derived as a moving average of past consumption) a function of permanent income (obtained by fitting Friedman's permanent income equation to the data). The other equation made transitory consumption a function of transitory income. The mean lag he found for permanent income was fairly similar to Friedman's. However, his coefficient for consumption out of transitory income was significant, and his marginal propensity to consume transitory income was 59 percent of the marginal propensity to consume permanent income if durables are included, and 42 percent if durables are excluded.

136. "A Test of the Permanent Income Hypothesis," *Journal of Political Economy*, Vol. 77, September–October 1969, pp. 857–61.

But this paper has been severely criticized by James Holmes.[137] Holmes pointed out that Laumas' derivation of transitory consumption from a moving average of measured consumption is not consistent with the permanent income theory. Holmes, therefore, fitted different regression equations to the Canadian data—equations in which both permanent and transitory income jointly determine permanent consumption. He did this twice; once for consumption defined to include durables expenditures, and once defined to exclude them. In the latter case, his data did not allow him to reject the permanent income theory since the propensity to consume transitory income was, in all four regressions, at or below Friedman's estimate of 0.3. (This differed from the results discussed below that he obtained from U.S. data.)

However, when durables are included in consumption there is trouble. The marginal propensity to consume permanent income is now significantly greater than unity. This is, of course, contrary to the permanent income theory as well as to the measured income theories. As Holmes has pointed out[138] what has gone wrong is that Laumas had left the

137. "On Testing the Permanent Income Hypothesis," Discussion Paper 170, Department of Economics, State University of New York at Buffalo, 1971 (mimeographed). In a paper ("A Test of the Permanent Income Hypothesis—Comment") which unfortunately reached me too late to cover adequately, Balvir Singh criticized Laumas' study on several grounds. One is that, given the imperfect separation of permanent and transitory elements, the inclusion of permanent income and consumption elements along with the transitory ones creates correlation between Laumas' transitory income and consumption. Second, in estimating permanent (and hence transitory) consumption Laumas used an R^2 criterion. This is not appropriate because the dependent variables differ in various regressions. Third, ordinary least square methods assume that transitory consumption is uncorrelated with transitory income, which is, of course, contrary to Laumas' findings. Fourth, the common trend component of transitory income and consumption creates spurious correlation.

138. James Holmes, private communication. Before leaving these two tests with Canadian data, it might be worth discussing the consumption functions of the Canadian econometric model RDX 1. These consumption functions, at first glance, seem to support the permanent income theory. They include permanent income and transitory income, and permanent income is more important than transitory income. But the permanent income series used in this model includes only seven calendar quarters. (See John Helliwell, L. Officer, H. Shapiro, and I. Stewart, *The Structure of RDX 1, Bank of Canada, Research Study No. 3,* Ottawa, Bank of Canada, 1969, pp. 36–38, 60.) Hence, it is far removed from Friedman's concept and is, in this way, more in accord with the standard income theory than with the permanent income theory. However, since the Canadian model does not deal with consumption as a whole, but fits separate consumption functions for durables, nondurables and services, it cannot be used to derive coefficients for the

secular growth coefficient out of his formulation of permanent income, and Holmes had used his weights merely normalizing them. Since the growth rate in Canada was very high during the period covered this lead to an overstatement of the marginal propensity to consume permanent income. This, of course, invalidates Holmes' results.

James Holmes also undertook a similar study for the U.S. using almost exactly the same data as Friedman did in his time series regression.[139] He regressed consumption on both permanent and transitory income twice, once assuming that the error term is normally distributed and once assuming that there is a first order Markov process operating on the error term. In both regressions the transitory income term was significant at the 1 percent level. The marginal propensity to consume transitory income was 30 percent of the marginal propensity to consume permanent income in one regression and 44 percent in the other. Hence the full permanent income theory is once again disconfirmed.[140] And since Holmes employed the "use" definition of consumption, and in fact used almost exactly the same data as Friedman, this result cannot be attributed to a "wrong" definition of consumption.

A number of consumption and saving functions using permanent income have been fitted to Indian data. Mrs. Chounhury fitted various consumption functions using current and lagged income, consumption, permanent income (defined as a two-year average of income), transitory income, and wealth.[141] Unfortunately, she had data for only thirteen years so that her standard errors are very high. Not surprisingly, her lagged income and consumption terms were therefore not significant (except in one case where the lagged income term had the wrong sign). Her estimate of the marginal propensity to consume transitory income was very high, exceeding the marginal propensity to consume permanent income in about half the cases. This may well be the result of the way she defined permanent and transitory income. When permanent income is defined as the average of two year's income, current income and the previous

---

standard income theory. A function fitted to separate consumption components may yield quite different results than a function fitted to total consumption.

139. "Direct Test of Friedman's Permanent Income Theory," *Journal of the American Statistical Association*, Vol. 65, September 1970, pp. 1159–62.

140. Holmes also correlated permanent and transitory income, and contrary to Friedman's assumption, the correlation coefficient was positive and significant at the one percent level.

141. "Income, Consumption, and Saving in Urban and Rural India," *Review of Income and Wealth*, Series 14, March 1968, pp. 37–56. Since using a two-year moving average amounts to using income of the current year and the past year, this function is not really different from Mrs. Mack's version of the absolute income theory.

year's income get the same weight, whereas in Friedman's formulation current income has a larger weight than the previous year's income. Hence, some of what Friedman would call permanent income is included in her transitory income. Her wealth coefficients were significant in some regressions and not in others. K. L. Gupta, in his critical note on this study, fitted his own regressions.[142] Again the lagged income and consumption terms were insignificant. Gupta used three-year moving averages as well as the trend of income as measures of permanent income, and again the marginal propensity to consume is greater for transitory income than for permanent income. I presume that this too is the result of the way permanent and transitory income are defined.[143]

In another study Gupta defined permanent income as either a two-year, or three-year, moving average, and ran regressions explaining saving on both aggregate and per capita levels.[144] Unfortunately, the two ways of estimating permanent income give widely divergent results. The three-year moving average results in a negative marginal propensity to save transitory income, while in the case of the two year moving average the marginal propensity to save transitory income is positive.

In view of their rather special ways of defining permanent income, none of these studies provides an adequate test of the permanent income theory. And given the short run of data used in two of the studies, and the divergence of their results, they do not really give reliable estimates of the marginal propensities to consume permanent and transitory income, quite apart from the problem of defining permanent income.

Another possibility is to compare normal income with certain types of income which we know a priori to be transitory. This was done by R. M. McInnis working with Canadian time series.[145] In Canada, changes in

142. "Income, Consumption and Saving in Urban and Rural India: A Note," *Review of Income and Wealth,* Series 16, December 1970, pp. 379–88. My discussion of this paper deals only with Gupta's result for urban and rural households combined, since Mrs. Chounhury has pointed out that Gupta's separation of income into rural and urban is faulty ("A Rejoinder to the Note by Prof. K. L. Gupta on 'Income, Consumption and Saving in Urban and Rural India,' " *Review of Income and Wealth,* Series 16, December 1970, pp. 389–90)

143. However, even so, it is surprising that Gupta's marginal propensity to consume transitory income is equal to unity when permanent income is obtained from the three-year moving averages. In the calculations using the trend of income it is a more reasonable figure, a figure which is less than once its standard error above the marginal propensity to consume permanent income.

144. "Personal Saving in Developing Nations: Further Evidence," *Economic Record,* Vol. 46, June 1970, pp. 243–49.

145. The Friedman Hypothesis and the Relationship between Consumption and Income in Canada (unpublished paper).

the value of farm inventories are an important component of income. Since they depend largely on harvest conditions, they represent primarily transitory income. The exclusion of changes in the value of farm inventories from the Canadian national income figures should thus raise the income elasticity of consumption. But the data show exactly the opposite. McInnis explained this by a capital rationing effect. Since the credit system is very imperfect, an increase in the value of his inventories does not give the farmer more cash, but a decrease in farm inventories as he sells them does so. To be sure, this is a special case and McInnis concluded that "This evidence cannot be considered of very great importance. It arises from a peculiar situation . . . highly imperfect capital markets in that sector give rise to an adverse result." [146] But all the same, this study, even if it deals with a special case, serves as a warning that credit rationing *may* play a more important role than is assumed in the permanent income theory.

Ralph Husby has fitted what is essentially a relative income, or standard income theory, consumption function in an attempt to explain the apparent contradiction between time series and cross-section data.[147] He fitted a regression using a lagged consumption term to time series data in order to obtain a coefficient for the lagged consumption term. He then used this coefficient from the time series regression as prior information in a regression fitted to the 1960–61 BLS cross-section data. In this regression he included, along with income, an income squared term which turned out to be significant. His results suggest that consumption is a nonlinear function of income but that the function shifts upwards over time due to the effect of past income (for which past consumption is a proxy). It is tempting, but unwise, to interpret the significance of the negative income squared term as a rejection of the proportionality hypothesis. Keeping in mind that the lagged consumption term picks up much of the effect of permanent income, the income term and the income squared term pick up, to a large extent, the effect of transitory income. Since transitory income is presumably an increasing function of measured income as one goes up the income scale, the significance of the income squared term does not contradict the proportionality hypothesis for permanent income.[148]

146. *Ibid.,* p. 23.
147. "A Nonlinear Consumption Function Estimated from Time-Series and Cross-Section Data," *Review of Economics and Statistics,* Vol. LIII, February 1971, pp. 76–79.
148. The negative coefficient of the squared income term merely indicates once again that positive transitory income is relatively more important in the upper income groups.

James Bonin used seasonal variations in OASDHI (social security) payments as his measure of transitory income.[149] Since there is a ceiling to the amount of earnings which are liable to OASDHI contributions, for many employees these deductions cease at a certain date during the year. Insofar as employees anticipate this pattern it does not represent transitory income. However, as Bonin pointed out, because of legislative changes in the ceiling on taxable wages, as well as wage changes, it is likely that the date at which these payroll deductions cease is not accurately anticipated by many employees. More questionably, Bonin operated on the assumption that *all* of these OASDHI changes represent unanticipated, and hence transitory, income. Bonin then regressed consumption of durables, nondurables, and services on these OASDHI contributions as well as a number of other variables. He did not regress the actual dollar amounts, but instead used the seasonal adjustment values of these variables (that is, the difference between the seasonally unadjusted values and the adjusted values), deflated for population as well as for GNP growth and price changes. Given the large degree of error attached to seasonal adjustment techniques, the use of seasonal adjustment coefficients as the variables to be regressed does of course raise a question.

Bonin's results were dramatic, and he claimed that they support a loose version of the permanent income theory. The marginal propensity to consume changes in OASDHI contributions (transitory income) was 2.36 for durables, 0.59 for nondurables, and -0.35 for services. While the first of these coefficients is statistically significant, the other two are not. The very high marginal propensity to consume durables is surprising. It implies that when a household receives a dollar of transitory income, it not only put none of it into financial savings (that is, into assets other than consumer durables), but it actually reduces its financial savings. Using the conventional definition of consumption, Bonin's results show a marginal propensity to consume transitory income well in excess of unity.[150]

Such a high marginal propensity to consume is, of course, contrary to the measured income theories, as well as the standard income theory. One could argue that it does not directly contradict the permanent in-

149. "Consumption, Durable Goods Spending and Changing OASDHI Seasonality," *American Economic Review*, Vol. 58, June 1968, pp. 468–76. Bonin also used other seasonal income change items in his regression, but pointed out that they may be anticipated and hence may not represent transitory income. (*Ibid.*, p. 472.)

150. For the conventional definition of consumption one can also use Bonin's (unpublished) results for total consumption. They also show that the coefficient is significantly above unity. Given the "use" definition of consumption, this problem does not exist.

come theory or the life cycle hypothesis because these theories employ the "use" definition of consumption.[151] But this argument is not convincing. Although the permanent income theory is formulated in terms of "use" consumption, most of the data it employs in various tests define consumption in the conventional way. Hence, while Bonin's findings do not contradict the permanent income *theory* per se, they do contradict most of the empirical evidence used for this theory. Thus, we face the choice of either rejecting much of the work that has been done on consumption functions, or rejecting Bonin's results. The latter appears preferable. Bonin regressed not actual consumption and income figures but rather their seasonal adjustment coefficients. Since it is well known that seasonal adjustment coefficients are subject to substantial error, any results based on regressing seasonal adjustment coefficients may well contain large errors.[152]

To summarize this set of tests, Nerlove's results reject the proportionality hypothesis, but because of serial correlation, its evidence is not very strong. Mincer's results, however, are not favorable for the permanent income theory since they show that the relative income theory does better, at least for the conventional definition of consumption. Arak and Spiro's results suggest that the full permanent income theory is misspecified. Taubman's study neither confirms nor disconfirms the permanent income theory, but instead shows that time series tests are inherently very weak. Holmes' work with U.S. data again disconfirms the strict permanent income theory. McInnis's findings are contrary to both the permanent income theory and the standard income theory. But since they can be explained as being due to a special factor—capital rationing having an unusually strong effect in his data—they really do not disconfirm either theory. The results of Bonin's study, on the other hand, are inconsistent with all the consumption functions, but are themselves open to question. Similarly the tests of Chounhury and Gupta are not usable for the purpose at hand. The upshot of all of this is that the permanent income theory is disconfirmed by these tests while the standard income theory is supported.[153]

151. Some rough calculations I have made suggest that if one adjusts Bonin's figures to a "use" definition of consumption they are not necessarily inconsistent with the hypothesis that only the permanent income which results from investing the transitory receipt is consumed.

152. See Marc Nerlove, "Spectral Analysis of Seasonal Adjustment Procedures," *Econometrica*, Vol. 32, July 1964, pp. 241–87.

153. In a series of papers Richard Stone has fitted permanent income and wealth consumption functions to British data. While some yielded a lower propensity to consume transitory than permanent income, in one of them he obtained the opposite result. And When K. Hilton and D. H. Crossfield repeated one of Stone's regressions with later data they too obtained a higher

Rather than summarize the results of all the tests discussed in this chapter at this point, I have delayed this summary until the end of Chapter 5.

---

propensity to consume transitory than permanent income ("Short-Run Consumption Functions for the U.K., 1955–66," in Kenneth Hilton and David Heathfield, *The Econometric Study of the United Kingdom*, New York: Augustus Kelley, 1970, pp. 89–93). This result may be due to the use of both wealth and permanent income in the same regression with the wealth coefficient picking up some of the effect of permanent income. As Hilton and Crossfield pointed out (*ibid.*, p. 89n), the inclusion of both wealth and permanent income in a regression equation is questionable because permanent income is itself a proxy for wealth.

Five

OTHER PREVIOUS TESTS, II

Disaggregating the Consumption Function

One of the early tests of the permanent income theory consisted of looking at the income elasticity of various types of commodities. Friend and Kravis used this test to estimate the *permanent* income elasticities of consumption.[1] According to the permanent income theory, the measured income elasticity of consumption for any commodity gives a biased estimate of its *permanent* income elasticity because the income elasticity is zero for transitory income. This bias in the permanent income elasticity of particular commodities is shown by the extent to which the measured income elasticity of total consumption falls short of unity. Hence, to turn an income elasticity calculated from measured income into a permanent income elasticity one merely has to multiply it by unity and divide by the measured income elasticity of total consumption.

Friend and Kravis did this for several commodities and then compared their elasticities to those they obtained using the stable income families discussed above. For these families, they argued, given a three-year horizon, measured income is close to permanent income, so that the measured income elasticity is a good estimate of the permanent income elasticity. If the horizon is more than three years, the income elasticities derived from families with three-year constant incomes should fall in between the one-year elasticities and the permanent income elasticities derived in the way described. The permanent income theory passes this test, but does so barely. "If the permanent income theory squeezes past our test, it does not escape without serious question. The elasticities for the three-year-constant-income group, are without exception, much closer to the single year than to the permanent income elasticities." [2] But as pointed out above, the use of the measured income

1. "Consumption Patterns and Permanent Income," *American Economic Review*, Vol. XLVII, May 1957, pp. 546–50.
2. *Ibid.*, p. 549. The commodities considered by Friend and Kravis (food,

of stable income families as a measure of their permanent income may result in substantial error. Hence the fact that the permanent income theory barely passes this test is consistent both with the theory being right and with its being wrong.

Another test using expenditures on individual commodities as well as on total consumption was undertaken by Asimakopulos, who used family size as an instrumental variable.[3] However, his results were not very definite, and in any case family size is a poor proxy for permanent income since it probably has independent effects on consumption.

Landsberger investigated the question whether the same discount rate is applicable to various commodities and found that it is.[4] What he did was to calculate for a particular commodity the ratio of the marginal propensity to consume for measured income and for windfalls. Since the marginal propensity to consume windfalls is equal to the discount rate (needed to transform it into permanent income) times the marginal propensity to consume permanent income, it is possible to derive the discount rate for various commodities by regressing consumption on windfalls and on income, and then taking the ratio of the two regression coefficients. One of the main rivals to the permanent income theory, the habit adjustment theory, predicts that these ratios should differ since habits adjust at varying rates. The permanent income theory, however, does not have this implication.[5] Landsberger found that the difference in the discount rates for various commodities is not significant at the 5 percent level, so that the permanent income theory passes this test. Note, however, that this does not necessarily reject the habit persistence theory. Since this theory does not tell us how much variation there should be in the ratio of the two regression coefficients for various

clothing, housing and auto expenses) accounted for over 60 percent of total consumption. Friend and Kravis also presented another test in this paper, a test which compares the consumption patterns of high and low savers. However, as the authors pointed out, the results are not clear-cut (*ibid.*, p. 552).

3. "Analysis of Canadian Consumer Expenditure Surveys," *Canadian Journal of Economics and Political Science,* Vol. XXXI, May 1965, pp. 231–35.

4. "Consumer's Discount Rate and the Horizon: New Evidence," *Journal of Political Economy,* November–December, Vol. 79, 1971, pp. 1346–59.

5. However, one could easily add to the permanent income theory the assumption that, though total consumption is governed by permanent income independently of past consumption habits, the composition of total consumption is affected by habits and by differences in adjustment lags. Failure on this test would, therefore, not damage the permanent income theory. Perhaps I should add that this juxtaposition of the permanent income theory and the habit persistence theory is my own interpretation of Landsberger's findings. He did not use this framework.

commodities, one cannot say whether the data reject it or not. However, it does suggest that habit persistence is not very important.[6]

One fact which provides some general support for the permanent income theory is that a number of studies have found that permanent income can be used to explain the demand for individual commodities and even for children.[7] While this is, of course, consistent with the permanent income theory, it does not really provide an adequate test of the theory, since it *could* be the case that consumption of certain durables depends upon permanent income while total consumption depends more on measured income. Thus none of these tests based on expenditures for particular consumption items appears to be conclusive, in the sense of rejecting either the permanent income theory or its rivals.[8]

Self-Employed versus Employee Households

One of Friedman's tests, discussed in Chapter 3, is to compare the marginal propensities to consume of self-employed and other households. This test was repeated by Malcolm Fisher using British data.[9] His re-

6. Landsberger presented one other test using individual commodities. It shows that, as for total consumption, the marginal propensity to consume individual commodities is several times greater for income than for windfalls.

7. See Frank de Leeuw, "The Demand for Housing: A Review of Cross-Section Evidence," *Review of Economics and Statistics,* Vol. LIII, February 1971, pp. 1–10; Arnold Harberger (ed.), *The Demand for Durable Goods* (Chicago, University of Chicago Press, 1960), chaps. 2–4; Frank Stafford, "Student Family Size in Relation to Current and Expected Income," *Journal of Political Economy,* Vol. 77, July–August 1969, pp. 471–77. See also Ronald Freedman and L. Coombs, "Economic Considerations in Family Growth Decisions," *Population Studies,* Vol. XX, November 1966, pp. 197–222. For a survey of the literature relating the demand for money to permanent income see David Laidler, *The Demand for Money* (Scranton, Pa., International Textbook Co., 1969), chap. 8. However, earlier Marc Nerlove had found that the permanent income theory is not useful for determining demand for some individual commodities and had concluded that a Marshallian demand model with both income and prices lagged does better. (Marc Nerlove, "The Implication of Friedman's Permanent Income Hypothesis for Demand Analysis: A Review," *Agricultural Economics Research,* Vol. XX, January 1968, pp. 1–14.)

8. Earlier J. D. Sargan had argued that the proportionality hypothesis implies the income elasticities of all the individual commodities are unity too. But this is incorrect. (See W. M. Gorman, "Professor Friedman's Consumption Function and the Theory of Choice," *Econometrica,* Vol. 32, January–April 1964, pp. 189–97.) Expenditures on individual items were also used by Landsberger in a study of the horizon discussed above, and by Barton, Theil, and Leenders in a study discussed below.

9. Malcolm Fisher, "Explorations in Savings Behavior," Oxford University Institute of Economics and Statistics, *Bulletin,* Vol. 18, August 1956, p. 233. Fisher went beyond the confines of Friedman's test by bringing the age

sults were similar to Friedman's. To recapitulate briefly the criticisms raised above in connection with Friedman's test: it is by no means certain that entrepreneurs really face greater income uncertainty than do employees, and even if they do, this might be offset by a greater dispersion of the permanent component.[10]

In an ingenious paper Nissan Liviatan undertook a more elaborate analysis of the difference in the income elasticity of the self-employed and of employees.[11] There are two ways to explain this difference: One is to argue, as Friedman did, that the transitory income element accounts for a larger share of income variability among the self-employed than among employees. The second explanation is that the self-employed have a greater incentive to save. Although it may seem virtually impossible to find a test which distinguishes between these two explanations, Liviatan has found such a test. This is to compare not the income elasticity of consumption, but the consumption elasticity of income. If one classifies households not by income class but by consumption class, then there is no transitory income bias and hence no reason why households with fluctuating incomes should have a greater consumption elasticity of income than do households with stable incomes. However, if the self-employed have a different saving behavior because they have a greater incentive to save, this should show up as a

---

variable into the comparison. He found that the saving-income ratio of the self-employed was especially high for very young households and for those households close to retirement. He explained this by the fact that the self-employed face their greatest income uncertainty in their early years when they are just "setting up in business," and later "when through increasing age they endeavor to counter declining resilience."

10. There are two related pieces of evidence worth discussing. One is a finding of Fisher's (*ibid.*, pp. 249–50) that the ratio of consumption to liquid assets is abnormally high both at the top and bottom of the income distribution. Fisher explained this by the fact that income is abnormally unstable for these groups. (This income instability is a reflection of the regression towards the mean which is so basic to the permanent income theory.) The second point, raised by Michael Farrell ("The New Theories of the Consumption Function," *Economic Journal*, Vol. LXIX, December 1959, p. 690) is that Fisher's data show a high income elasticity of consumption for British manual workers, a fact which Farrell found hard to reconcile with their limited income instability as shown by American data. But the fact that the proportion of American manual workers who had an increase in income over the previous year is relatively low is hardly conclusive evidence that British manual workers do not have a high degree of income instability. For example, fluctuations in the amount of overtime work might well differ.

11. "Tests of the Permanent-Income Hypothesis Based on a Reinterview Saving Survey," in Carl Christ (ed.), *Measurement in Economics: Studies in Mathematical Economics and Econometrics in Memory of Yehuda Grunfeld* (Stanford, Stanford University Press, 1963), pp. 32–35.

difference in the consumption elasticity of income. Hence if the consumption elasticity of income is similar for the self-employed and for employees it follows that the difference in their income elasticities of consumption is explained by a difference in income variability. Liviatan calculated the consumption elasticities of income for an Israeli 1957/58 —1959/60 reinterview sample, as well as for the British savings data used by Malcolm Fisher. In both cases the difference between the self-employed and employees is very substantially less for the consumption elasticity of income than it is for the income elasticity of consumption. This supports the permanent income theory explanation of the difference in the income elasticity of consumption, and hence provides supporting evidence for this theory.[12] In another test, discussed below, Liviatan used the previous year's income as a proxy for permanent income and found that the marginal propensities to consume permanent income were remarkably similar for employees and the self-employed. However, this remarkable similarity may, in part, result from a bias.[13]

The fact that the permanent income theory is able to explain at least a substantial part of the difference in the consumption behavior of employees and the self-employed must be treated as supporting evidence

12. Liviatan's analysis also disposed of a criticism of the permanent income theory raised by Fisher, who had argued that the low marginal propensity to consume of managerial households has to be reconciled with their presumed income stability. ("Exploration in Savings Behavior," *op. cit.*, p. 233.) Their consumption elasticity of income is not out of line with that of other occupations shown by Liviatan's data (*op. cit.*, p. 35). Bernard Saffran has made the interesting point that Liviatan's results indicate that the quasi-permanent component is much greater for the self-employed than for employees and that the length of the horizon for these two groups is different. (See Bernard Saffran, "Estimation of Some Structural Parameters in Friedman-Type Consumption Functions," unpublished Ph.D. dissertation, University of Minnesota, 1963, p. 49.) Not surprisingly, Liviatan's analysis does not fully explain the difference in the saving behavior of the self-employed and employees. Leland has suggested that this is so because it does not take account of the fact that greater uncertainty of income gives the self-employed a greater incentive to save. Leland also argued, more generally, that the fact that the proportionality hypothesis holds in time series data, but not in cross-section data, can be explained the same way. If in cross-section studies income uncertainty rises with income, then the higher saving ratio of the high income groups may be due to their greater uncertainty rather than to their higher incomes. But this argument ignores the fact that cross-section data confined to employees (where income and uncertainty are negatively correlated) also reject the proportionality hypothesis. See Hayne E. Leland, "Saving and Uncertainty: The Precautionary Demand for Saving," *Quarterly Journal of Economics*, Vol. LXXXII, August 1968, p. 471.

13. This bias, which is discussed below, is the common error term in income and consumption. The error term is presumably larger for the self-employed than for employees.

for it.[14] However, this evidence does not distinguish between the full permanent income theory and the standard income theory.

Estimates of the Propensity to Consume Transitory Income Based on Monthly Data

In a test with data on Norwegian salary earners, Harold Watts used income over two years to represent permanent income, and monthly deviations from this two-year mean to measure transitory income.[15] He found that "those with temporary deviations of income from more long-term levels show substantial deviations of consumption expenditure from 'normal' levels. The effect of a given short-term deviation was generally smaller than that of a similar differential in long-term level, and was different depending on the sign of the deviation." [16] He pointed out, however, that there are two qualifications. One is the fact that the transitory income he measured consisted of routine changes in income. Households may react quite differently, for instance, to a temporary tax change when they might know how long it would last. Second, it is possible that there is spurious correlation between transitory income and consumption. Insofar as transitory income receipts are due to seasonal factors, or other predictable factors (in which case they should not really be considered transitory income), households may shift expenditures they would make in any case to coincide with the receipt of extra income. However, Watts considered it unlikely that this spurious correlation is "important enough to explain the whole apparent effect of transitory income." [17]

These results give some support to the standard income theory vis-à-vis the full permanent income theory.[18] But in view of the qualifi-

14. In a previous chapter I pointed out that the direct evidence on the relative income instability of self-employed and employees does not, on the whole, indicate much greater income instability for the self-employed. But there is *some* evidence of greater income instability in a number of the studies cited in Chapter 3, and that may suffice to reconcile these studies with Liviatan's findings.

15. "An Analysis of the Effects of Transitory Income on Expenditure of Norwegian Households," *Statsøkonomisk Tidsskrift*, Vol. 81, December 1967, pp. 136–61. It is also available as Cowles Foundation Discussion Paper No. 149.

16. *Ibid.*, p. 160. The sign of the deviation of income is relevant because households reacted more readily to positive transitory income than to negative transitory income.

17. *Ibid.*, p. 161.

18. In Watts' simplest and most restrictive model, the coefficient of transitory income is about one-third of the coefficient of "permanent income." Note, however, that this "permanent income" is defined as two-year income, and hence on the more usual definition of a permanent income it contains

cations just mentioned, their disagreement with the full permanent income theory does not provide convincing evidence against it. As regards the measured income theories, Watt's findings, though interesting for their own sake, cannot be used to disconfirm them. Measured income theorists have *not* claimed that a month is a long enough span to measure the normal relation of income and consumption. Hence, a relatively low marginal propensity to consume for monthly income deviations does not disconfirm the measured income theories.[19]

Japanese employees receive a very substantial bonus in two months of the year. This bonus is variable, depending as it does on the firm's profitability. Hence, the permanent income theory and the standard income theory predict that its income elasticity of consumption should be low in cross-section data. T. Mizoguchi has found that the data do support this prediction.[20] Time series data, on the other hand, show that the Japanese income elasticity of consumption is not unusually low.[21] This does not contradict the permanent income theory because one would expect the time series income elasticity to be unusually low only if the year-to-year fluctuations in aggregate bonus income were unusually large. Hence, once again, the wealth theories are able to explain a puzzling contradiction between cross-section and time series data.

While on the subject of the Japanese bonus, it is worth noting that the permanent income theory has also been used by Shinohara and Mizoguchi to explain the secular rise in the saving-income ratio of Japanese workers.[22] They explained this rise by the concomitant rise in

---

some transitory income. Hence, for the more usual definition of permanent income the difference between the permanent and transitory income coefficients would presumably be greater. However, there is an offsetting factor. Insofar as some of the transitory income receipts were anticipated, Watts' measure of transitory income contains a permanent income component and this tends to understate the difference in the two coefficients.

19. Watts is not the only one who used monthly data. Jean-Claude Eicher (*Consommation et Epargne*, Paris, Robert Goez-Girley, 1961, p. 136) compared consumption functions fitted to monthly and yearly data. The monthly data showed a bigger gap between the average and marginal propensities to consume than did the yearly data. Similarly, T. Yasunaga found that the consumption function has a higher intercept when fitted to monthly than to yearly data. (This study is reported in Toshiyuki Mizoguchi, "The Permanent Income Hypothesis and the Workers' Consumption Function in Japan," Tokyo, Committee for Translation of Japanese Economic Studies, mimeographed, pp. 4–5.) For the reason given above none of this disconfirms the measured income theories.

20. Toshiyuki Mizoguchi, *Personal Savings and Consumption in Postwar Japan* (Tokyo, Kinokuniya Bookstore Co., 1970), p. 72.

21. *Ibid.*, p. 72.

22. M. Shinohara, *Growth and Cycles in the Japanese Economy* (Tokyo Kinokuniya Bookstore, 1962, pp. 235–36), and T. Mizoguchi, "Time Series

the ratio of bonuses (transitory income) to total income. But this assumes that the secular rise in bonuses was not predicted as well as the secular increase in ordinary income. It is not clear why this should be the case.

Test by Group Income Profiles

Let us now examine testing by group income profiles.[23] Harold Watts has presented another ingenious test of the permanent income theory.[24] Working with Survey of Consumer Finances data (which unfortunately exclude mortgage repayments from saving) he divided his sample into a large number of groups based on the household's employment status, education, occupation, location, age, and race. He fitted separate savings functions for each of the 187 groups he obtained in this way, and then asked two questions: first, do the savings functions for the various groups have different parameters, and second, can any such differences be explained by the long-run income expectations of households within each group? For example, compare young households in manual and professional occupations. We know that the households headed by professionals can expect greater income increases as they get older than can households headed by manual workers. Hence, if consumption does depend upon expected income, one would predict the saving-income ratio of young professional households to be lower than that of young manual worker households at the same income level.

Watts' data do show differences in the saving functions of various groups, a fact which cannot be explained by a naïve absolute income theory or a relative income theory. The next step is to see if these differences can be explained by the relation between expected income and current income. The results are moderately favorable to the hypothesis:

The demographic variables of age, occupation, race, education and location which . . . "determine" the relation between current and ex-

Analysis of the Consumption Function in Japan by Occupational Groups," *Hitotsubashi Journal of Economics,* Vol. 9, February 1969, pp. 13–35. In another study Shinohara had tried to use the rise in transitory income relative to permanent income to explain the rise in the saving ratio of farmers. However, Mizoguchi disconfirmed this hypothesis (*ibid.,* p. 29).

23. In addition to the studies discussed in this section the group income profiles method was also used by R. Ramanathan (*loc. cit.*). However, he obtained similar results using the cell mean method and preferred that method.

24. "Long-Run Income Expectations and Consumer Saving," in Thomas Dernburg, Richard Rosett, and Harold Watts, *Studies in Household Economic Behavior* (New Haven, Yale University Press, 1958), pp. 103–44. Actually Watts was not testing primarily the permanent income theory here; most of his effort was devoted to seeing if expected income influences consumption, rather than to testing a more restrictive permanent income theory.

pected income, are empirically correlated with saving behavior. More precisely, they interact with the "economic" variables, income and liquid assets holdings. Furthermore, much of the interaction that is found can be interpreted more reasonably by the expected-income hypothesis than by the simpler theories that assume a much shorter income horizon. The hypothesis has not been effective in explaining some of the observed and presumably significant interactions. Such failure might be damning if a superior alternative hypothesis were at hand—until one is proposed, however, the positive evidence must be emphasized. . . . The results do suggest that adoption of the simplifying assumptions that are used in similar contexts by Friedman and Modigliani-Brumberg would have been unfortunate. There may be no equally convenient assumptions that will adequately represent the behavior of individual decision makers. If not, more complicated theories, perhaps combining parts of the "absolute," "relative," and "expected" income hypothesis must be formulated.[25]

On the whole, these results support—in moderation—the permanent income theory, in a rather general version, and the standard income theory. The fact that the support is not stronger could perhaps be attributed, at least in part, to the fact that the saving data exclude an important form of saving, mortgage repayments. This test has a great advantage over many other tests because by using expected income rather than past income it provides a sharp differentiation between the permanent income theory and the standard income theory on the one hand, and the habit persistence theory and the relative income theory on the other. By showing that expected income plays a role in consumption decisions, this test disconfirms the theories which omit future income.

In the previous chapter I discussed a study in which R. Ramanathan classified households by permanent income groups. He carried this analysis further by estimating the permanent income of each group on the basis of time series data on the income trends of each group.[26] He also introduced a wealth effect by taking the difference between actual wealth and estimated desired wealth, as well as an interaction effect between this wealth term and income. Applying this model to Indian data he found (for different groupings, and for different assumed discount rates applicable to future income) marginal propensities to *save* transitory income which ranged from 0.08 to 0.27. Such low marginal propensities to save hardly support the permanent income theory. However,

25. *Ibid.*, pp. 142–43.
26. R. Ramanathan, "Measuring the Permanent Income of a Household: An Experiment in Methodology," *Journal of Political Economy*, Vol. 79, January–February 1971, pp. 177–85. See also his "Estimating the Permanent Income of a Household: An Application to Indian Data," *Review of Economics and Statistics*, Vol. L, August 1968, pp. 383–88. In my discussion below I relied on the former paper since it is later.

his marginal propensities to save permanent income were lower than those for transitory income, ranging from −0.05 to 0.10. These results are, of course, not inconsistent with the standard income theory.[27] And since Ramanathan used a different method than did Friedman to segregate permanent from transitory income, his results do not, strictly speaking, really disconfirm the full permanent income theory.

Temporarily Low Incomes

One group of households whose current incomes are clearly below their permanent incomes are graduate students, and Frank Stafford has used a sample of graduate students in two tests of the permanent income theory.[28] His first test consisted of looking at the components of the income of graduate students. Certain types of income, such as income from current employment, are highly correlated with the future income of graduate students, while certain other income types, such as the spouse's earnings, are not. If the permanent income theory or the standard income theory are valid, one would expect the marginal propensity to consume to be positively correlated with the relative importance of the income components closely related to future income. And this is what the data show. Moreover, if one groups households by field of study then, since this reduces the error variance, one would expect the marginal propensity to consume to be higher, particularly for those income types which are a good proxy for permanent income. And again, this is confirmed by Stafford's data.

In a second test Stafford regressed consumption on a number of variables including variables measuring the household's expected future earnings. And this test shows that future earnings do affect current consumption. Moreover, the intercepts of Stafford's regressions were usually not significantly different from zero at the 5 percent level, a fact which, as he pointed out, is consistent with the proportionality hypothesis. However, while most of the intercepts in his various regressions are not *significantly* different from zero, they are positive in the substantial majority of cases and a few are significantly positive. Hence Stafford's results are entirely consistent with the proportionality hypothesis being wrong.[29] Hence, I conclude that Stafford's work sup-

27. Since the range of the estimates of the propensities to consume is so large, the fact that Ramanathan's estimates do not disconfirm the standard income theory does not, of course, provide much support for it.

28. Frank Stafford, "Graduate Student Income and Consumption," unpublished Ph.D. dissertation, University of Chicago, 1968.

29. Stafford also found that graduate students are, on the average, net savers. This is hard to reconcile with the permanent income theory or life cycle hypothesis. Stafford's explanation is the existence of high borrowing

ports both the full permanent income theory and the standard income theory against the measured income theories, but does not distinguish between them.

Graduate students are people whose income is temporarily low. Another group of households whose incomes were temporarily low were farm households during the Great Depression. A. P. Barten, H. Theil, and C. T. Leenders tested the permanent income theory by looking at a sample of Dutch farmers' budgets during 1935–1936.[30] They used the rental value of the farmer's land as a proxy for permanent income, and calculated the "rental value" elasticity of consumption as well as the measured income elasticity. In a semi-log regression the two elasticities were similar, but in a log regression the rental value elasticity was higher. Since one has no good way of choosing between the types of regressions, this test neither confirms nor disconfirms the permanent and standard income theories. All in all, this set of tests supports the standard income theories, but does not disconfirm the full permanent income theory.

Income or Consumption as Instrumental Variables

Another set of tests is based on data from households interviewed in consecutive years. These tests use the previous year's income or consumption as an instrumental variable. One such test was undertaken by Nissan Liviatan, who used data from an Israeli survey which interviewed the same households in two consecutive years.[31] The rationale behind this test is the following: Assume that there is no correlation between the transitory elements of income in the two years. The permanent elements, however, are correlated, so that *measured* income in year *one* serves as a proxy for *permanent* income in year *two*. And similarly the measured income of year two can serve as a proxy for the permanent income in year one. The results which Liviatan obtained by this technique were disappointing for the permanent income theory. To be sure, in three of the four cases covered, the marginal propensity to consume turned out to be higher for permanent income than for measured income, but the difference, though significant at the 1 percent level in

---

costs. But such capital rationing does not fit in well with the permanent income theory, though to be sure, one can hardly treat graduate students as representative of the typical household in the extent of capital rationing.

30. "Farmers' Budgets in a Depression Period," *Econometrica*, Vol. 30, July 1962, pp. 548–64.

31. "Tests of the Permanent-Income Hypothesis Based on a Reinterview Savings Survey," *op. cit.*, pp. 46–48.

two cases, was substantial in only one of the four cases. Hence the result of this test is unfavorable for the full permanent income theory. But it does support the standard income theory against the measured income theories.

In his reply to Liviatan, Friedman pointed out a statistical bias.[32] Liviatan's original data were not income and consumption data, but income and saving data. To get his consumption estimates Liviatan had to subtract saving from income. Now suppose that there is an error in the income figure, so that it is too large. When consumption is obtained by subtracting saving from this overstated income, consumption is overstated, too. As a result consumption and current income have a common error term. This raises the regression coefficient for current income relative to that of the other year's income which does not have this upward bias. And Friedman pointed out that reasonable errors in incomes would suffice to account for Liviatan's results.

In addition, Friedman challenged Liviatan's assumption that the horizon is essentially only two years. This assumption is needed for Liviatan's test, because if it does not hold, transitory income in the two years is correlated, so that one year's measured income is not a good instrumental variable.[33] Friedman concluded that in view of the weaknesses in Leviatan's test, his conclusion that the permanent income elasticity of consumption is less than unity, is "suggestive, but hardly very strong evidence." [34]

In his reply Liviatan agreed with Friedman in principle, but stated that Friedman really has no evidence that the error in income is large enough for the common error term to bias the results seriously.[35] But given the large errors which do seem to occur in budget studies, this is not a convincing argument.

There is another weakness in Liviatan's study, as well as in many other studies, which results from his deriving consumption by subtracting saving from income. The notion that consumption is equal to income minus saving is simply *not* correct for budget study data. The reason for this is the anomalous treatment of certain capital gains, inheritances, and gifts. They are treated as saving since saving is estimated by comparing the value of assets at the beginning and the end of the year, but they are not included in income. Hence, if one sub-

32. "Note on Nissan Liviatan's Paper," in *ibid.,* pp. 59–63.
33. In a previous test, discussed below, Liviatan had concluded that the horizon was only two years, but Friedman had pointed out an error in this test.
34. *Ibid.,* p. 62.
35. "A Reply," in *ibid.,* pp. 63–66.

tracts saving from income to obtain consumption, consumption will be understated. It may well be the case that these "non-income" receipts are more closely correlated with permanent income than with measured income and they are probably received largely by high income groups. If so, the marginal propensity to consume is understated more for permanent income than for measured income. It is hard to know how important this understatement is. It is a common procedure, one which was probably followed in this survey, to exclude households with abnormal saving ratios from the sample. Moreover, many, probably most, households do not have major "non-income receipts." But for some households, they may be very substantial. Since in fitting a regression one minimizes the *square* of the deviation, the regression coefficient can be strongly influenced by a few relatively very large errors. Hence, it is possible that the understatement of consumption has a significant effect on the income elasticity, and this might conceivably invalidate Liviatan's results, as well as results reached by others who used saving data to obtain consumption estimates.

In another test Liviatan used *consumption* of the "other year" as the instrumental variable.[36] Liviatan pointed out that this test is unbiased if the transitory elements in *consumption* are uncorrelated, but is biased in favor of the permanent income theory if the correlation between transitory consumption in the two years is positive. He considered such a positive correlation to be likely. "After all the dividing line between two consecutive years is arbitrary, and therefore the same factors which cause a discrepancy between actual Y or C and their permanent components in the first year are likely to continue to operate (though to a smaller extent) in the second year." [37] The results of this test, while they do not support the proportionality hypothesis, are closer to the prediction of the permanent income theory than to the prediction of the measured income theory. But since, as just pointed out, a positive correlation of transitory consumption in the two years could bias the results in favor of the permanent income theory, this evidence should not be treated as a disconfirmation of the measured income theories.

In his reply Friedman took this test of Liviatan very seriously. He pointed out that the bias resulting from the correlation of transitory consumption in the two years need not *necessarily* favor the permanent income theory. If the correlation is negative instead of positive—not an impossible situation—then the bias would be *against* the permanent income theory. However, he concluded that this was not a plausible explanation of Liviatan's results and that "if these results should be confirmed for other bodies of data, they would constitute relevant and

36. *Op. cit.*, pp. 50–53.
37. *Ibid.*, p. 51.

significant evidence that the elasticity of the permanent components [of income and consumption] is less than unity." [38]

Errors in Variables

From a statistical point of view the permanent income theory is essentially an errors-in-variables approach; that is, it is a theory which asserts that a regression of consumption on measured income produces biased results because income is measured with an error, the error being transitory income. Hence, one way of testing the permanent income theory—a way suggested by Friedman—is to use an errors-in-variables approach. [39]

This has been done by Bernard Saffran, who used two models. One of them is a one-way components of variance model developed by Tukey. In the second model Saffran relaxed the unrealistic assumption made in the first model that the transitory components of income for all years are independent. To do this he extended Tukey's analysis into a two way bivariate components of variance analysis. He used 270 urban nonentrepreneurial households for whom he had data for two consecutive years. [40] He worked with both the conventional definition of consumption and the "use" definition. [41] He made separate estimates for homeowners and others since he had to measure consumption in different ways for these two groups.

The results, shown in Table 11, are unfavorable for the proportionality hypothesis. All of the point estimates show an income elasticity of less than unity, and for homeowners as well as for the whole sample one can reject the proportionality hypothesis at the 1 percent probability level. However the fact that the basic data he used were derived from a cluster sample means that the confidence intervals are not quite broad enough. But as Saffran pointed out, there is some rough evidence available on the magnitude of this bias and it suggests that it is too small to affect his results. Hence, this test, too, can be treated as disconfirming the proportionality hypothesis.

In an ingenious paper Julian Simon and Dennis Aigner developed another errors-in-variables model, one which does not require data for

38. "Note on Nissan Liviatan's Paper," *op. cit.*, p. 63.

39. See Milton Friedman, *A Theory of the Consumption Function, op. cit.*, pp. 217–18.

40. "Estimation of Some Structural Parameters in Friedman-Type Consumption Functions," unpublished Ph.D. dissertation, University of Minnesota, 1963.

41. However, he did not include the imputed income from durables (other than houses) in income due to data problems. Saffran included gifts and inheritances in income so that the problem of "non-income receipts" discussed in the previous section does not arise.

Table 11

Estimates of Permanent Income Elasticities of Consumption,
by Conventional and Use Definitions

Consumption	First Estimate			Second Estimate			Number of House-holds
	Elasticity	Confidence Interval		Elasticity	Confidence Interval		
		95%	99%		95%	99%	
Conventional Definition							
Homeowners	.90	.85–.95	.83–.97	.89	.83–.94	.81–.96	176
Others	.93	.86–1.01	.84–1.03	.97	.90–1.05	.88–1.08	82
Total Sample[a]	.90	.86–.94	.85–.95	.90	.86–.95	.85–.96	270[a]
Use Definition							
Homeowners	.87	.82–.92	.81–.93	.89	.84–.94	.83–.96	176
Others	.94	.88–1.00	.86–1.02	.96	.90–1.03	.88–1.05	82
Total Sample[a]	.91	.88–.94	.86–.96	.93	.90–.97	.88–.98	270[a]

SOURCE: Bernard Saffran, "Estimation of Some Structural Parameters in Friedman Type Consumption Functions," unpublished Ph.D. dissertation, University of Minnesota, 1963, p. 95.

[a] Includes some households which could not be classified by homeownership.

two or more years but instead uses the correlation of incomes as well as information on the weights which each year has in permanent income.[42] They employed this model to test the proportionality hypothesis by seeing how much of the difference between the marginal propensity to consume measured income and the average propensity to consume could be explained as due to errors in variables. They used several tests. One dealt with the slopes of the consumption function in cross-section budget studies. They showed that the observed slopes, when combined with Friedman's weight pattern and information on the correlation of incomes, imply that about two-thirds of the gap between the marginal propensity to consume measured income and the average propensity to consume is due to the use of measured income in place of permanent income.[43] In a second test, working with what they admit are very bad data, they made separate estimates for farm families and urban families.

42. "Cross-Section and Time Series Tests of the Permanent-Income Hypothesis," *American Economic Review*, Vol. LX, June 1970, pp. 341–52. In another more basic paper, Aigner and Simons developed a general relationship between time series and cross-section data in which the permanent income approach is just a special case. "A Specification Bias Interpretation of Cross-Section vs. Time Series Parameter Estimates," *Western Economic Journal*, Vol. VIII, June 1970, pp. 144–61.

43. The measure used by Simon and Aigner is what, in Part IV, I am calling the "prediction coefficient." Their results do not really reject the proportionality hypothesis.

Here only half the gap is eliminated, but as they pointed out, this could be due to the weakness of the data.

Simon and Aigner then took up one of Friedman's time series tests, the one which consisted of comparing the income elasticities obtained from long and short time series. Although Friedman was not able to quantify the effect to be expected, and dealt only with the direction of the effect,[44] Simon and Aigner were able to quantify it. For the two time series they compared, the actual values bracketed the expected values, thus supporting the proportionality hypothesis. Simon and Aigner explained the difference between this result and their earlier results from cross-section data by suggesting that a Duesenberry effect may be operative in cross-section situations, or that there has been a secular upward shift in the propensity to consume.

Simon and Aigner then reversed the analysis and tried to see what lag pattern would be required to support the proportionality hypothesis. Whether or not the resulting lag pattern is plausible is something they left for the reader to decide.[45] However, their own conclusion was that the proportionality hypothesis is not valid, and that there is a relative income effect operating.[46]

All in all, this study supports the standard income theory. In the cross-section data the proportionality hypothesis did not hold even if one uses Friedman's weights. And, as was discussed in Chapter 3, Friedman's weights are questionable; alternative, just as defensible, weights decline more rapidly than Friedman's weights.[47] Since the introduction of shorter lags into the Simon-Aigner model works against the proportionality hypothesis, the gap between the marginal propensity to consume permanent income and the average propensity to consume *may* therefore be actually greater than is claimed by Simon and Aigner.

Other Tests Using Two- or Three-Year Data

Other tests, too, have used two- or three-year data.[48] Liviatan fitted lagged consumption functions containing current income and the previ-

44. See p. 75 above. Friedman had quantified it, but pointed out that this quantification would be valid only if the secular trend were the only factor determining permanent income.

45. For a cross-section marginal propensity to consume permanent income of 0.75, the weights of the various years are the same as Friedman's.

46. They also undertook a test using Klein's comparison of the saving-income ratio derived from one-year data and two-year data. However, as will be shown below, this comparison of Klein's is defective.

47. As is shown in Chapter 9 various other methods of lagged regressions also yield shorter lags than those implied by Friedman's weights.

48. In addition to the tests considered in this section there are a number of other tests using two-year data, but since these tests are not valid, I have left them to a later section of this chapter.

ous year's consumption to three sets of budget study data (one Israeli and two U.S.) giving income and saving for two years.[49] His results were highly unfavorable for the permanent income theory. The lagged consumption term is unimportant compared to current income. In addition, his results reject the proportionality hypothesis and show only a short lag. However, Liviatan concluded his paper on a note of caution, pointing out that he derived consumption by subtracting saving from income, which, for the reason given above, biased the results. Moreover, there is the "non-income receipts" bias discussed earlier.

In an attempt to integrate the permanent income theory and the absolute income theory, Paul Taubman fitted regressions using permanent income, measured income, and transitory income.[50] Taubman used three measures of permanent income. One is a simple average of income for the two years covered by his data; the second is Fisher's method of lagged regression; and the third is Koyck's method. His data give income and financial savings (plus gross savings through the purchase of durables) of a sample of households for two years. Unfortunately, they exclude mortgage repayments from saving, but this is balanced, at least to some extent, by the fact that depreciation on the house is not counted as dissaving. This study is very important for the question whether the marginal propensity to save transitory income is unity. This is so because it included the purchase of durables in saving, and in addition—unlike other studies giving estimates of the propensity to save transitory income—it used one definition of permanent income, the Koyck transformation which is closely related to Friedman's definition of permanent income. Taubman's results, shown in Table 12, are broadly in line with the prediction of the standard income theory, though because of the large standard errors they cannot be treated as rejecting the full permanent income theory.[51]

In an earlier study Taubman had worked with a stock adjustment model of saving explicitly focusing on the normal income theory, and using, in addition to normal income and transitory income, past peak income, initial stocks, and a habit variable.[52] His data, based on a small

49. "Estimates of Distributed Lag Consumption Functions from Cross-Section Data," *Review of Economics and Statistics,* Vol. XLVII, February 1965, pp. 44–53.

50. "Permanent Income and Transitory Income Effects," *Review of Economics and Statistics,* Vol. XLVII, February 1965, pp. 38–43.

51. In addition to the data shown in Table 12 Taubman provided a breakdown by age. For the Koyck regressions the marginal propensities to save transitory income were 0.38 for the 18–34 age group, 0.81 for the 35–54 age group and 0.71 for the 55 and over age group (*ibid.,* p. 42).

52. "A Synthesis of Saving Theory with Special Reference to the Components of Personal Saving," unpublished Ph.D. dissertation, University of Pennsylvania, 1964.

Table 12

Estimates of the Marginal Propensity to Save Permanent and Transitory Income*

Lagged Regression Method Used	MPS, Permanent Income		MPS, Transitory Income			*Difference Divided by Standard Error*	*MPS Trans. Income as Percent of MPS Perm. Income*	*MPC Trans. Income as Percent of MPC Perm. Income*
	Coefficient	*95 Percent Confidence Interval*	*Coefficient*	*95 Percent Confidence Interval*				
Simple Average of Two Years' Income	.37	.34 to .40	.50	.36 to .64		1.5	135	.79
Fisher's Method	.37	.34 to .40	.56	.33 to .79		1.5	151	.70
Koyck's Method	.40	N.A.	.63	N.A.		N.A.	158	.62

SOURCE: Based on Paul Taubman, "Permanent and Transitory Income Effects," *Review of Economics and Statistics*, Vol. XLVII, February 1965, p. 42 (last two columns added).
* Purchases of durable goods included in saving, but mortgage payments are excluded.

sample, cover only certain types of saving, excluding saving through life insurance, pension funds, mortgage transactions, and home purchases.[53] Taubman used two variants of saving, one including and one excluding the purchase of durables. His results indicate that past peak income is important, so that income increases and decreases have sharply asymmetrical effects. If one excludes durables from saving, holds past peak income constant, and looks primarily at cases of income decreases, then the marginal propensity to *save* is about unity for normal income—and less than half of that for transitory income. The unitary marginal propensity to save is, of course, highly implausible and casts doubt on this regression equation. However, if past peak income is allowed to vary by the same amount as normal income, then the difference between the marginal propensities to save transitory and normal income is fairly small (0.23 vs. .17 respectively in one estimate). If one includes durables in saving the marginal propensity to save becomes 0.31 for normal income and 0.42 for transitory income.[54] This is a fairly small difference, and if the items excluded from saving were added, it might well be even smaller. This evidence can hardly be said to support the permanent income hypothesis. However, strictly speaking, this study cannot be used as firm evidence against the full permanent income theory since it uses "normal income" rather than permanent income as defined by Friedman. It is certainly *possible* that Friedman's permanent income equation, if fitted to these data, would explain them better than do Taubman's regressions, and would have the predicted coefficients. This is, of course, not testable because income data are not available for enough years.

In another study Crockett and Friend explained saving over a two-year period by using, in addition to that period's income, mean income over a five-year period, net worth, age, a taste variable, and "historical income"—that is, the mean income of two years much further in the past.[55] Their focus was not on the permanent income theory but on the normal income theory. Among their findings are: (1) "historical income" does badly; (2) on the whole, normal income does not do as well in the regressions as does current (two years) income; (3) the elasticity of saving with respect to short run normal income exceeds

53. By excluding items like life insurance saving and mortgage repayments, Taubman's data probably overstate the difference between the propensities to save normal and transitory income. In addition, "non-income receipts" create a problem.

54. *Ibid.*, pp. 178, 181.

55. Jean Crockett and Irwin Friend, "Consumer Investment Behavior," in Universities-National Bureau Conference on Economic Research, *Determinants of Investment Behavior*, R. Ferber (ed.) (New York, National Bureau of Economic Research, 1967), pp. 15–127.

unity; (4) for these two-year saving data, the marginal propensity to save is "somewhat greater" for transitory income than for normal income; and (5) the evidence for the asset adjustment model is mixed.

The fact that "historical income" performs badly does not contradict the strict permanent income theory, since this is not the way in which Friedman measures permanent income. And the same thing applies to the fact that normal income—that is, the unweighted mean of five-year income—does not do as well as two-year income. However, the finding that the normal income elasticity of saving exceeds unity creates more difficulty for the full permanent income theory. Crockett and Friend measured normal income by using an unweighted five-year average of income, which means that they gave less weight to current year income than does Friedman. Hence, one can hardly argue that their income elasticity for saving is above unity because they included transitory elements excluded by Friedman in his income measure. There is, however, still a possible "out." What is of interest for the permanent income theory is not saving, but consumption. As pointed out above, due to inclusion in the saving data of receipts other than income, one cannot, strictly speaking, derive the marginal propensity to consume from a knowledge of the marginal propensity to save. But this argument, which could also be used against some of Friedman's tests, is not very convincing.[56]

In a dissertation concerned primarily with determining the proportion of permanent income or total (human plus nonhuman) wealth being saved, Robert Holbrook evaluated the strict permanent income theory, the life cycle hypothesis, and the absolute income theory.[57] Since, as pointed out in Chapter 2, the permanent income and life cycle theories are so similar, one might ask what it means to choose between them. What Holbrook did was to deal with the issue of the detailed specification of the two theories. In other words he tried, to the extent permitted by his data, to set up regressions which represent the particular regression equations used by Friedman on the one hand and by Modigliani and associates on the other, and then to see which predicts better. Thus, his life cycle equation followed Modigliani in assuming that current labor income can be used as a measure of expected labor income, and that nonhuman wealth should be included along with current labor income in the regression equation.

56. Since the Crockett-Friend measure of normal income is rather arbitrary, their finding that normal income does worse than two-year income does not really disconfirm the normal income theory.

57. "Alternative Models of Consumer Behavior: The Permanent Income Hypothesis and the Life Cycle Hypothesis," unpublished Ph.D. dissertation, University of California, Berkeley, 1965.

Holbrook's data provided household income for three years and also saving for two years combined. Holbrook first estimated permanent income from the mean incomes of various groups to which the household belonged and from its wealth. This method turned out to be less satisfactory than his alternative estimate of permanent income from current and past incomes of the household.[58] He used Friedman's method of lagged regression, but did not include Friedman's 2 percent steady growth rate. In one regression he allowed the data to determine the length of the lag. The resulting lag is much shorter than Friedman's, being just over one year.[59]

To test the life-cycle hypothesis Holbrook had to estimate human wealth. He did this by a technique similar to that used by Watts. He estimated the median income of various groups by age class, and then assumed that each household will, in the future, earn the same proportion of the median income of its groups as it did in the years covered by the data. To find the present value of these future earnings Holbrook needed a discount rate. He used the rate which equalized the marginal propensities to consume human and nonhuman wealth. For nonhuman wealth he used two variants, one including and one excluding the present value of Social Security benefits. As a challenger to the permanent income theory and life cycle hypothesis Holbrook used an absolute income theory embodying the same "other" variables (such as family size and wealth) as he had used for the other two theories.

The results are shown in Table 13. They suggest that the permanent income theory specification is somewhat better than the absolute income theory specification, though the difference is not very great. But this victory of the permanent income theory is qualified by the fact that in Holbrook's version of this theory the consumption lag is much shorter than in Friedman's version, thus draining the theory of much of its contribution. It is, in fact, tempting to argue that the combination of the very limited superiority over the absolute income theory, combined with the short lag, means that this test is unfavorable to the permanent income theory. But the short lag cannot really be used to disconfirm the permanent income theory because Holbrook derived his consumption figures by subtracting saving from income. As was discussed above, this biases the results in favor of current income. The same problem results in a downward bias of the errors shown for the absolute income

58. In an article discussed in Chapter 3, Holbrook had shown that the horizon is shorter than Friedman believes so that three year's income data are sufficient.

59. His weights for the first eight quarters are: 0.22, 0.17, 0.13, 0.10, 0.08, 0.06, 0.05, and 0.04. *Ibid.,* p. 53.

Table 13

Comparison of Residuals from Equations

Equation	Root-Mean-Square Residual	Mean Residual
Absolute Inc. Theory		
(1)	2610	−41[a]
(2)	2579[a]	290
(3)	2613	46
(4)	2698	439
Permanent Inc. Theory		
(1)	2564	−16[a]
(2)	2558[a]	305
(3)	2575	304
(4)	2566	57
Life Cycle Hypothesis		
(1)	3167	−152
(2)	3166	−431
(3)	3081[a]	−58
(4)	3353	−25[a]

SOURCE: Robert Holbrook, "Alternative Models of Consumer Behavior: The Permanent Income Hypothesis and the Life Cycle Hypothesis," unpublished Ph.D. dissertation, University of California, Berkeley, 1965, p. 110.
[a] The minimum value of each criterion for each model.

theory, so that the superiority of the permanent income theory over that theory is understated.

The life cycle hypothesis does badly in this test and is distinctly inferior to the absolute income theory on the root-mean-square criterion, though it is superior on the mean absolute error criterion. As Holbrook pointed out, its mixed performance could be due to his particular specification of the theory, "but it is hard to imagine a method of measuring human resources essentially different from the one we have used." [60] Compared to the full permanent income theory specification, the life cycle specification is inferior on the root-mean-square residual criterion, but for the mean residual criterion the matter is more complex. The permanent income theory is superior in the sense that its best equation has a lower mean residual than does the best equation for the life cycle

60. *Ibid.*, p. 110. For the comparison of the life cycle hypothesis with the absolute income theory the downward bias in the errors of the absolute income theory is not important. This is because in estimating human wealth, Holbrook used as one factor the ratio of the household's income to the median incomes of its groups. This means that the error in the current income term is also present in the human wealth term used in the life cycle hypothesis regression.

hypothesis, but considering all four equations for each theory, the median of the mean residuals is less for the life cycle hypothesis than for the permanent income theory. However, it is not implausible to argue that each specification should be judged on the basis of the equation which gives it the best performance, and if one takes this line, then Holbrook's test shows the strict permanent income theory specification to be superior to the life cycle specification. Finally, it is worth noting that the equation which gives the best fit for the life cycle hypothesis is one which does not set the intercept equal to zero, thus rejecting the proportionality hypothesis.[61]

In a subsequent study Robert Holbrook and Frank Stafford carried forward the analysis of these three-year data by using a generalized errors-in-variables model.[62] This model does not require a knowledge of a household's permanent income, but can work with only an estimate of the variance of transitory income. They allowed for the secular growth of permanent income by using the technique developed by Watts and described above.

The results were startling; they appear to provide strong support for the full permanent income theory. They support the proportionality hypothesis and the zero propensity to consume transitory income. (In addition, Holbrook and Stafford found that the propensity to consume differs for incomes from various sources.)

But these results, important for their own sake as they are, do not relate to the permanent income theory. This is so because of the way in which Holbrook and Stafford defined saving. They included the purchase of durables in saving, but, except for automobiles, they did not subtract depreciation (or any other measure of services of the household's stock of durables) from saving. What they therefore measured is something quite different from saving on either the conventional or the "use" definition of saving. This can be seen most easily by looking at the average propensity to consume. The Holbrook-Stafford definition of this parameter amounts to $\dfrac{C + D}{Y - D - D_a}$ where C is the "use" definition of consumption, D is the imputed services from durables other than autos (i.e., depreciation), D_a the imputed services from autos, and Y is income including an allowance for the use of durables. Using this concept of consumption, an income elasticity of unity may emerge even if the income elasticity of consumption, defined as "use" consumption, is less than unity. Similarly, from the viewpoint of the conventional defi-

61. *Ibid.*, p. 98.

62. "The Propensity to Consume Separate Types of Income: A Generalized Permanent Income Hypothesis," *Econometrica*, Vol. 39, January 1971, pp. 1–22.

nition of consumption, the Holbrook-Stafford results can be explained by their inclusion of consumer durable purchases in saving. The resulting marginal propensity to consume, therefore, bears little relation to the marginal propensity to consume when consumption and income are defined in either of the two acceptable ways, and is, in face, a hybrid that differs from the consumption concept used in any of the consumption function theories.

I now turn to two tests which used farm households exclusively. One of these, a test by Miss Reid, actually preceded the publication of the full scale wealth theories.[63] She used the fact that for farm families, temporary variations in farm expenses are an important factor influencing transitory *net* income. She therefore expressed farm operating expenses in each net income class as a ratio to farm operating expenses in the net income class just below it. This ratio is a proxy measure for the proportion of the income difference between these two income classes which is due to transitory elements, since if expenses are high it is probable that a temporary factor has raised them, and hence has depressed net income. If the income elasticity of consumption is greater for permanent than for transitory income, then there should be a positive correlation between the income elasticities calculated between the two adjacent income classes and the farm expense ratio. And this is what the data show.

In a subsequent test Miss Reid and Miss Dunsing used three-year farm budgets classified by income change.[64] They calculated the income elasticity of consumption in one year for subsamples of households grouped by incomes in another year. These elasticities were lower than the income elasticity obtained for the whole sample. The permanent income theory (or standard income theory) explanation of this is that when households are classified by a permanent income proxy, such as the previous year's income, the remaining differences among households within each of these classes are primarily differences in transitory income, and hence the income elasticity is relatively small. A similar conclusion emerged when they calculated the income elasticity of consumption twice, once using the income of the current year and once using the mean income of all three years.

Thus there have been many tests using household data for two or

63. "Effect of Income Concept upon Expenditure Curves of Farm Families," in Conference on Research in Income and Wealth, *Studies in Income and Wealth*, Vol. 15 (New York, National Bureau of Economic Research, 1952), pp. 164–68.

64. "Effect of Varying Degrees of Transitory Income on Income Elasticity of Expenditures," *Journal of the American Statistical Association*, Vol. 53, June 1958, pp. 348–59. The data used in this study are the same ones used by Friedman in his income change test.

three years. Liviatan's test tends to reject the full permanent income theory, although because of data problems it is not good evidence, as Liviatan himself recognized. A study by Taubman supports the standard income theory against the permanent income theory, but because of the large standard errors it too does not provide good evidence. An earlier study of his supports the normal income theory. However, it too cannot really be used to disconfirm the permanent income theory because of the difference between normal income and permanent income. Crockett and Friend's tests of the normal income theory are also unfavorable for the permanent income theory, though again this result is not strong. But Holbrook does provide important evidence contrary to the life cycle hypothesis. The Holbrook-Stafford study, on the other hand, does not furnish valid evidence, for or against, the permanent income theory. Finally, two tests using farm data support either the full permanent income theory or the standard income theory.

Thus none of these tests, taken individually, provides really convincing evidence against the full permanent income theory. However, since so many of these tests provide circumstantial evidence against the permanent income theory, I think that the upshot of these tests is to provide weak disconfirmation for the full permanent income theory, and to confirm the standard income theory.

Occupation versus Measured Income

One puzzling observation which the permanent income theory and the standard income theory are able to explain is the difference in the saving ratios of households receiving the same measured income but belonging to different occupations. At the same *measured* income households in the better paid occupations have a smaller saving ratio than do households in lower-paid occupations. In a noteworthy early anticipation of the permanent income theory, Mrs. Mack explained that this could be the result of income change and transitory income.[65] At a lower income level households affiliated with a high income occupation are likely to have negative transitory income. The opposite is true for

65. Ruth Mack, "Direction of Change in Income and the Consumption Function," *Review of Economics and Statistics*, Vol. XXX, November 1948, pp. 246–47. James Morgan elsewhere gave the savings residuals for different occupations, and they do *not* show a meaningful and consistent difference. ("Factors Related to Consumer Saving When It Is Defined as a Net Worth Concept," in Lawrence Klein, ed., *Contribution of Survey Methods to Economics, op. cit.*, p. 131, and "Analysis of Residuals from 'Normal' Regressions," in *ibid.*, p. 170.) But this can be explained by the fact that Morgan held so many proxy variables for permanent income constant that there were not enough permanent income differences left to allow an occupational grouping to segregate households by permanent income.

households belonging to a low income occupation but having a high measured income in the survey year. However, a comparison of the saving ratios of salaried professionals and skilled wage workers in the 1950 BLS Survey shows the opposite result.[66] But in view of the weaknesses of the 1950 data, Mrs. Mack's results are probably the more reliable.[67]

In any case, Mrs. Mack's results do not support the permanent income theory against the relative income theory, since this theory, too, can explain the observed behavior—with, or without—using Fellner's "brake effect." Insofar as households treat others in the same occupation as their "peer group," the higher paid manual worker, for example, is under less pressure to consume than, say a professional man with the same income, and hence he saves more.[68] Thus, this piece of evidence supports the permanent income theory or the standard income theory against the absolute income theory, but not against the relative income theory.

The Effect of Assets

General Aspects. A great deal of empirical work has been undertaken relating wealth to consumption. But not all of it is relevant to what I have called the wealth theories of consumption. This is so because, as pointed out in Chapter 2, the absolute income theory, at least in some versions, introduces a wealth term in the consumption function. Hence a test which shows that wealth affects consumption does not really confirm the wealth theories vis-à-vis their rivals.[69] But if a test were to show that wealth (i.e., nonhuman wealth) has no effect on consumption, this would be important evidence against some of the wealth theories. In addition, there is a question about the nature of this effect. Different versions of the wealth theories introduce wealth into the consumption function in various ways. Hence, it is possible to test some

66. The data are given in W. Eizenga, *Demographic Factors and Savings* (Amsterdam, North Holland Publishing Co., 1961, pp. 70–71). He stated that the saving behavior of other occupational groups (for which he did not give the data) can be explained by the permanent income theory. But since he did not quantify the test the standard income theory too could presumably explain the data. *Ibid.*, pp. 82–83.

67. See Franco Modigliani and Albert Ando, "The 'Permanent Income' and the 'Life Cycle' Hypothesis of Saving Behavior: Comparison and Tests," in Irwin Friend and Robert Jones (eds.), *Consumption and Saving* (Philadelphia, University of Pennsylvania Press, 1960), Vol. II, pp. 51–73.

68. Cf. Werner Paschke, *Bestimmungsgründe des Persönlichen Sparens* (Berlin, Ducker and Humbolt, 1961), p. 172.

69. To be sure, the relative income theory does not employ a wealth term, but it could readily be modified by adding one.

of these variants by looking in some detail at the role which wealth plays in the consumption function. I will, therefore take up now the various budget study tests using wealth. The time series tests I will defer until Chapter 8.

Since few budget studies provide information on wealth holdings, it is tempting to use liquid assets—which are reported in more budget studies—as a proxy for wealth. But liquid assets are not an adequate proxy for wealth. Holbrook used both wealth *and* liquid assets in his consumption functions and found that their coefficients had different signs! Liquid assets holdings were positively related to consumption, while total wealth had a negative coefficient.[70]

Other studies which have included a wealth term obtained mixed results. Thus Richard Kosobud found a positive effect of wealth on consumption for low income households, but not for high income households.[71] Melander and Maynes argued that wealth has a positive effect on consumption, but Crockett and Friend in numerous regressions got wealth coefficients which were generally insignificant.[72] Harold Lydall included wealth in a series of consumption functions and his wealth coefficients were in many cases insignificant, and when they were significant they frequently had the wrong sign.[73] In Sten Thore's study of Swedish data, a similar thing occurred: wealth was not generally significant and sometimes had the wrong sign.[74]

In her more detailed analysis, Mrs. Projector allowed for an age effect. Her regressions for all households together gave similar results to Thore's, but when she fitted separate regressions for various age groups, she found a positive effect of wealth on consumption, "although the pattern is somewhat erratic." [75] But it would not be correct to argue from this that the failure of a positive wealth effect to show up in other

70. "Alternative Models of Consumer Behavior," *op. cit.,* pp. 66, 96–97.

71. "Effect of Alternative Measurement of Wealth and Income Variables upon Consumer Saving Relationships: Some Evidence from a Panel," American Statistical Association, Business and Economics Section, *Proceedings,* 1964, pp. 36–38.

72. E. R. Melander, "Longer-Term Saving: Some Models and Their Empirical Evaluation," unpublished Ph.D. dissertation, University of Minnesota 1966; E. R. Melander and E. S. Maynes, "A Cohort Analysis of the Longer Term Saving Function," paper read at the December 1967 Econometric Society Meetings; J. Crockett and I. Friend, "Consumer Investment Behavior," *op. cit.,* pp. 15–127.

73. "Saving and Wealth," *Australian Economic Papers,* Vol. 2, December 1963, pp. 241–43.

74. *Household Saving and the Price Level* (Stockholm, National Institute of Economic Research, 1961), pp. 70–74.

75. *Survey of Changes in Family Finances* (Washington, D.C., Board of Governors, Federal Reserve System, 1968), p. 26.

studies is due to their ignoring age differences among households. This would not be correct because Holbrook used an age variable in his regressions, and despite this he found a negative effect of wealth on consumption. Crockett and Friend also included an age variable in many of their regressions, and these results too did not support the wealth effect. When they broke their data down by age, the wealth coefficients usually had the right sign, but all the coefficients with the right sign were insignificant. One must therefore conclude that the empirical evidence on the wealth effect is conflicting.

The reason for this is not hard to find. It is a taste variable. Households with a thrifty disposition have a high saving ratio, and in addition, as a result of past saving, they also have a high stock of wealth. Hence the data show a spurious correlation between the stock of wealth and a low propensity to consume.[76] Thus, if the wealth coefficient is not positive, as is required by the permanent income theory, this can be explained away as merely the result of a spurious correlation. This interpretation is supported by the fact that a study by Simon and Barnes, to be discussed later on, which asked respondents to *imagine* differences in their wealth holdings, and is therefore not subject to the taste bias, does show a positive effect of wealth on consumption.

But unfortunately, the taste variable cannot be dismissed quite this easily. It *could* be the case that tastes are not exogenous—that an increase in wealth creates a greater taste for wealth and hence raises saving. If so, the wealth theories are invalid or at least incomplete. George Katona has argued that as households accumulate more wealth their taste for wealth increases because of an "aspiration effect." [77] There is some evidence for this. In the United States, though not in Canada, households covered by private pension plans save, quite apart from the pension plan, at least as much, and perhaps somewhat more, than households not covered by pension plans.[78] It is hard to know how

76. See Sten Thore, *op. cit.,* pp. 70–76, and James Morgan, "Analysis of Residuals from 'Normal' Regressions," in Lawrence Klein (ed.), *Contributions of Survey Methods to Economics* (New York, Columbia University Press, 1954), p. 185; Lawrence Klein, "Statistical Estimation of Economic Relations from Survey Data," in *ibid.,* p. 201. Two of these authors also invoked the "aspiration effect."

77. See George Katona, *The Powerful Consumer* (New York, McGraw-Hill, 1960), pp. 130–37.

78. George Katona, *Private Pensions and Individual Saving* (Ann Arbor, Survey Research Center, University of Michigan, 1965); Phillip Cagan, *The Effect of Pension Plans on Aggregate Saving, Occasional Paper No. 95* (New York, National Bureau of Economic Research, 1965), pp. 4–5; and William Waters, "The Effect of Pension Plan Membership on the Level of Household Non-Pension Plan Wealth," paper read at the Econometric Society Meetings, December 1966, pp. 7–8, 11. The last of these relates to Canada.

much importance to attach to this fact. It *could*—in part—be due to an aggregation problem.[79] Or it could very well be the case that pension plans generate a much more powerful aspiration effect than do other forms of wealth, so that for most forms of wealth, the aspiration effect is swamped by the more traditional substitution effect of economic theory. Another factor is that pension plan equity is an extremely il-liquid form of wealth, and hence may lead to less consumption than do other forms of wealth.[80]

And so I conclude, though somewhat uneasily, that this budget study evidence has not invalidated the general presumption of the wealth theories about the effect of wealth on consumption. However, it does perhaps raise a question about the specific nature of this effect, and about the stress which is placed upon it in the life cycle hypothesis, the normal income theory, and the rest. Now let us look at some specific tests of the wealth theories.

Specific Aspects. The stock of wealth is given a prominent place in the Pennsylvania School's normal income theory, using as it does a stock adjustment version of the wealth effect. But in a cross-section study by two members of this school, Jean Crockett and Irwin Friend, this model did not perform well despite the fact that Crockett and Friend tried to adjust for differences in saving tastes.[81] The wealth adjustment model is invalidated if the adjustment process is so slow that asset disequilibrium has little effect on the saving rate within any one year. And their findings do not reject such a slow adjustment:

A puzzling result of our analysis is the conflicting evidence relating to the planning span for total asset accumulation. While we are disposed to believe that the relevant period is relatively short, i.e., a period ef-fectively much shorter than the earning span, there is as much evidence to contradict as to support this supposition. On the other hand, the significance of the initial asset coefficient in the parabolic saving form and the fact that this coefficient is significantly different from one in the

79. See Robert Schoeplein, "Effect of Pension Plans on Other Retirement Saving," *Journal of Finance,* Vol. XXV, June 1970, pp. 633–37. Schoeplein, working with Canadian data, obtained results similar to Cagan's in a re-gression for all households combined. But when he separated households by income class he found some substitution between pension saving and other saving. When he used Katona's technique on his data, he found substitution, both for all households combined, and for households separated by income class. However, in this case too, the substitution effect was less in the regres-sion combining all households.

80. To be sure, households can usually offset the illiquidity of their pen-sion wealth by holding other parts of their wealth in more liquid form; however, for some households lack of liquidity probably does reduce con-sumption.

81. "Consumer Investment Behavior," *op. cit.,* pp. 84–85.

logarithmic asset form tend to support our lagged adjustment model as opposed to a model which considers initial assets irrelevant.[82]

Mrs. Projector, too, experimented with a wealth adjustment model.[83] And again the results did not give strong support to this approach. The parabolic income term which results from making the desired asset stock a function of income was

highly significant in the youngest age group only. In the age group 35–44 the coefficient of Y is negative, leading to negative marginal propensities to save with respect to income above about \$20,000 or above about \$4,000 when net worth is introduced into the equation. The net worth coefficients are small with the exception of the age group 35–44 in which the coefficient is about 0.10 with a positive sign.[84]

The speed of adjustment in this model is slower than that found by Crockett and Friend. In the Crockett-Friend model about two-thirds of the gap between desired and actual assets is eliminated in about six years,[85] while in the Projector model one-third to one-half of the gap is eliminated in this period.[86] However, there is the possibility that the speed of adjustment is understated in both studies due to a bias in the net worth term.[87]

On the other hand, when Ramanathan tested a stock adjustment model for wealth against Indian data, he found that it yielded a higher coefficient of determination than he obtained when he used just a simple wealth term.[88] But since, as pointed out above, a taste variable is likely to distort a regression using a simple wealth term, and is less likely to do so in a stock adjustment model, this evidence is not conclusive. All in all, the normal income theory, although not refuted by these tests, can hardly claim to derive strong support from them.

Michael Landsberger used a wealth variable in a life cycle hypothesis framework.[89] He made consumption in Israel a function of human plus

---

82. *Ibid.*, p. 127.

83. *Op. cit.*, pp. 28–31.

84. *Ibid.*, p. 29.

85. For the self-employed the proportion of the gap eliminated is somewhat larger.

86. *Ibid.*, p. 30. While Crockett and Friend used five-year income in their regressions, Mrs. Projector used only current income, though she found that introducing the previous year's income made little difference.

87. *Ibid.*, p. 29n.

88. R. Ramanathan, "Estimating the Permanent Income of a Household: An Application to Indian Data," *Review of Economics and Statistics,* Vol. L, August 1968, pp. 383–88.

89. "The Effect of Windfall Income on Consumption and Composition of Saving, and Its Implications on the Income Concept of the Consumption Function," unpublished Ph.D. dissertation, Hebrew University, Jerusalem, 1968, chap. VI.

nonhuman wealth.[90] After running a linear regression he looked at the residuals to see if they gave any indication of nonlinearity. He did this to test the proportionality hypothesis for which linearity is, of course, a necessary but not a sufficient condition. For the five sets of data he used, the linearity hypothesis was rejected at the 5 percent level in two cases.[91] In addition, the pattern of the deviations from unity is not very close to what one would expect if consumption is less than proportional to total human and nonhuman wealth. Looking at separate groups of households did not change the results, and in addition a similar result emerged for the relation of consumption and the size of restitution payments. However, this does not really support the proportionality hypothesis as distinct from a linearity hypothesis because Landsberger included an intercept in his regression.

The Distribution of Net Worth

There is another way in which asset holdings can be used to test the proportionality hypothesis. If this hypothesis is correct, then, holding age constant, net worth should be the same proportion of permanent income in each permanent income class. This implication has been tested by Jean Crockett and Irwin Friend,[92] and another test of it is presented in Chapter 15. Crockett and Friend used both the Federal Reserve wealth survey for 1962 as well as a special Survey of Consumer Finances reinterview sample. The first of these sources gives only the measured income of households, and Crockett and Friend therefore had to assume that 1962 measured income was close to normal income. The second source, however, gives a five-year income history of each household and Crockett and Friend used this five-year income as a measure of the household's normal income.

They used both sets of data in regressions to calculate the income elasticity of net worth. For the Survey of Consumer Finances data they classified households into separate groups on the basis of employment status and age. In some of their regressions they included as independent variables age, historical household income (the average of 1947 and 1955 income), five-year household income, mean group income for five years, current income, previous net worth, and an estimate of

90. He first ran a regression of consumption on measured income, nonhuman wealth, and restitution payments. He then used the coefficients obtained from this regression to estimate the discount rate needed to combine measured income and nonhuman wealth and restitution payments into a measure of human plus nonhuman wealth.

91. For nondurable consumption linearity was rejected in three of the five cases.

92. "Consumer Investment Behavior," *op. cit.*, pp. 45–76.

capital gains. They found that the income elasticities of net worth exceeds unity, thus rejecting the proportionality hypothesis.[93]

In another study Mrs. Projector and Mrs. Weiss fitted a regression equation to the Federal Reserve's wealth data. They found an income elasticity of well over unity (1.74) thus corroborating the Crockett-Friend results.[94] In a subsequent work Mrs. Projector used an asset adjustment model, and here the results were less clear-cut. In the model assuming instantaneous adjustment, the income elasticities for three out of five age groups were below unity (though the mean of these elasticities is above unity), but in the model allowing for delayed adjustment all but one of the income elasticities were above unity.[95]

Using Canadian data, Waters estimated long-run expected income from instrumental variables (mean income of the household's occupation, age, pension plan membership, outstanding life insurance, number of household members employed, and property income). When Waters related wealth holdings (other than pension plan equity) to this measure of permanent income, the income elasticity of wealth was again above unity (1.294). However, Waters suggested that this might be explained by the "appreciation in the value of owner-occupied housing

93. James Tobin in his comments in the same volume "Comments on Crockett-Friend and Jorgenson," *ibid.,* pp. 156–160, challenged this criticism of the proportionality hypothesis. He stated that Crockett and Friend did not control age sufficiently and that the high income elasticity of wealth found by Crockett and Friend reflects wealth accumulated not by saving, but through inheritance and capital gains. However, Friend and Crockett ("Reply to Tobin and Griliches," *ibid.,* p. 171) pointed out, quite correctly, that in some of their regressions they did include an age variable, and in addition, ran some separate regressions for various age groups (age groups which Tobin considered too crude). They suggested that if households receive inheritances they would simply reduce their own saving thus adjusting their stock of wealth to their income. This reply is perhaps more relevant in the context of the normal income theory, with its explicit emphasis on wealth, than in Friedman's version of the permanent income theory, which makes the optimal wealth-income ratio less explicit. More significantly, it does not answer the argument that households may have received an inheritance in the recent past, and hence may not yet have adjusted their stock of wealth. But, in any case, my own test in Chapter 15, which excludes households with inherited assets (though not households with capital gains) shows similar results to the Friend-Crockett study. As far as capital gains are concerned, Crockett and Friend pointed out that the inclusion of a crude proxy for capital gains reduces the elasticity only slightly.

94. Dorothy Projector and Gertrude Weiss, *Survey of Financial Characteristics of Consumers* (Washington, D.C., Board of Governors, Federal Reserve System, 1966), p. 7.

95. They are: 1.73, 2.39, 1.45, 0.63, 1.11. Projector, *op. cit.,* p. 31.

which in turn may have been relatively more important for the higher income groups.[96] All in all, these tests, like so many others, show that the proportionality hypothesis is invalid.[97]

Classification by Relative Income

One of the prominent pieces of evidence in support of the *relative income* theory was the finding of Dorothy Brady and Rose Friedman that the saving ratios of households at various times and in various locations are much more alike if households are classified by their relative income position, such as deciles, than if they are classified by their absolute income. As Modigliani and Brumberg pointed out, this fact fits well into the general framework of a wealth theory. This is so because transitory income as a proportion of measured income is much more apt to be similar in the same income decile than in the same dollar income class. For example, to take an extreme case, a household with a real income of $2,000 had an above-average income in a 1901 budget study but a below-average income in a 1960 budget study. Hence, in this income class mean transitory income was positive in 1901 and negative in 1960. But this is not the case for income deciles. Modigliani and Brumberg recognized, of course, that the relative income theory can explain the same fact, but they claimed that their explanation is superior because it "is much simpler and integrates these findings with many others without recourse to additional postulates." [98] But if I am right, the "additional postulates" of the relative income theory are needed to explain consumption behavior in any case because the proportionality hypothesis is invalid, so that the wealth theory explanation is not really superior.

Age and Consumption

Both the life cycle hypothesis and the full permanent income theory imply particular effects of age on the propensity to consume. However, these effects are more specific and more important in the life cycle hypothesis than in the permanent income theory. Indeed, as pointed out in Chapter 2, the different predictions of the two theories of the effect of age provide the way of choosing between them. Since age is a more

96. Waters, *op. cit.*, p. 8.

97. The only contrary result, the result from the Projector instantaneous adjustment model, seems less reliable than her result from the delayed adjustment model since there is no evidence that households do adjust their asset holdings rapidly.

98. "Utility Analysis and the Consumption Function: An Interpretation of Cross-Section Data," in Kenneth Kurihara, *Post-Keynesian Economics* (London, George Allen and Unwin, 1955), p. 424. However, they did not deny that the relative income theory explanation may have "some validity."

prominent and explicit variable in the life cycle hypothesis than in the strict permanent income theory, it is not surprising that the cross-section tests using age are focused on the life cycle hypothesis.

One of the implications of the life cycle hypothesis is that the income elasticity of consumption falls (and the intercept rises) with age. This is so because an increase in income raises the (expected) amount of future income which can still be earned prior to retirement. The older the household the fewer the number of years of increased earnings relative to years of retirement. Modigliani and Brumberg cited data published by Mrs. Fisher which support this prediction of the life cycle hypothesis.[99]

In one of the early discussions of the permanent income theory and life cycle hypothesis, Malcolm Fisher derived the implication of the life cycle hypothesis for the effect of changes in family size on the saving rate, and he tested this implication, as well as the relation of age and saving, implied by this theory. On the whole, the theory did not perform well on these tests, but the result was not clearcut; Fisher claimed that the theory's "outer fortifications are impaired but not necessarily the citadel itself." [100] In any case, in their rejoinder Modigliani and Ando argued that Fisher had misinterpreted their theory and pointed out other weaknesses in his tests.[101] In his reply Fisher conceded that his introduction of a family size variable into the life cycle model had been faulty because he did not allow for the interaction of family size and age. He conceded Modigliani and Ando's claim that, when interpreted correctly, the age-saving relationship shown by the data "provides an encouraging degree of support" for the life cycle hypothesis.[102]

Michael Farrell investigated whether the life cycle hypothesis is correct in assuming that households consume their assets over their lifetime.[103] By assuming a linear decline in population after the age of 65 and a linear running down of assets he showed that, given stable prices and incomes, a household over 65 years old would hold, on the average, two-thirds of the assets held by a 65-year-old household. This

99. *Ibid.*, pp. 424–25.
100. Malcolm Fisher, "Exploration in Savings Behavior," Oxford University Institute of Economics and Statistics, *Bulletin*, Vol. 18, August 1956, p. 261.
101. "Tests of the Life-Cycle Hypothesis of Saving," Oxford University Institute of Economics and Statistics, *Bulletin*, Vol. 19, May 1957, pp. 99–123. The fact that Fisher misinterpreted the life cycle hypothesis is not surprising, because at the time this theory had not yet been fully spelled out.
102. "A Reply to Critics," in *ibid.*, p. 188.
103. M. J. Farrell, "The New Theories of the Consumption Function," *Economic Journal*, Vol. LXIX, December 1959, pp. 686–87.

is in rough agreement with Goldsmith's data, and thus supports the
life cycle hypothesis. However, as Farrell pointed out, if one looks at
estate tax figures (which, of course, cover only wealthy households)
in place of Goldsmith's figures for all households, then the data do *not*
support the life cycle hypothesis. Thus the life cycle hypothesis holds
overall only because the thriftiness of the wealthy is offset by the im-
providence of the poor. But this does not in any way invalidate the
life cycle hypothesis. A life cycle theorist would expect some households to be thriftier and some to be less thrifty than the theory calls for.
And one would expect that the thrifty households are disproportionately
represented among large wealth holders even if there is no correlation
between income and thriftiness.

Clower and Johnson, working with their own wealth model rather
than a permanent income model, regressed consumption on wealth.[104]
They found that the proportionality hypothesis does not hold for wealth.
Rather, if one classifies households by wealth, consumption is a de-
creasing proportion of wealth as one goes up the wealth scale. They
buttressed this result by pointing out that Goldsmith's data (obtained
from estate tax records) show that households with estates of over
$200,000, unlike those with estates of $60,000 or less, save until death.
But both of these findings could be explained by the fact that a thrifty
disposition leads to a high stock of wealth.

In an analysis of Indonesian data, Allen Kelley and Jeffrey Williamson
found that the saving rates of different age groups could not be explained by the life cycle hypothesis, but they suggested that this might be
due to a special factor, a dramatic postwar increase in education. Moreover, their data do support the life cycle hypothesis in another way.
They show that, as this theory predicts, the marginal propensity to
consume increases with age.[105]

More detailed evidence on the age-saving relationship is available in
a study by Dorothy Projector, who fitted the regression equation of the
life cycle hypothesis to net worth data and found that these data give
only very qualified support to this hypothesis:

The net worth coefficients show the expected rise across the three oldest
age groups. . . . The sign in the 25–34 age group is not in accord
with the life cycle hypothesis and, while the coefficient in the 35–44
group has the expected sign, the coefficient is larger than it should be

104. Robert Clower and Bruce Johnson, "Income Wealth and the Theory
of Consumption," in J. N. Wolfe (ed.), *Value, Capital and Growth, Papers in
Honour of Sir John Hicks* (Edinburgh, The University Press, 1968), pp.
63–65.

105. Allen Kelley and Jeffrey Williamson, "Household Saving Behavior in
the Developing Economies: The Indonesian Case," *Economic Development
and Cultural Change,* Vol. 16, April 1968, pp. 385–403.

relative to the older groups. The income coefficients show the expected decline across the age range 35–64 and the expected increase in the 65 and over group. The pattern for the constant term seems to depart markedly from the expected shape. Perhaps these data can be said to be in accord with a modified life-cycle theory in that the notion of redistributing resources to obtain a desirable pattern of consumption becomes more feasible as the individual ages . . . The failure of the constant term to show a pattern similar to the expected pattern may be related to the assumption about bequests.[106]

The performance of the life cycle hypothesis on this test can be evaluated with the help of a naïve model. For each of the five age groups Mrs. Projector gave an index of the actual and estimated values of the income coefficients, the net worth coefficients, and the constant terms.[107] My naïve model is one which assumes that these parameters have the same value in each age group (a value equal to the unweighted mean for all age groups)—that is, that their value is independent of the theory's prediction of the relation of age and consumption. The life cycle hypothesis did *not* perform better than this naïve model. For the wealth coefficient the hypothesis had a mean error of 24.2 percent as compared to the naïve model's error of 28.7 percent. But for the income term the naïve model had the smaller error (12.8 percent versus 17.8 percent), while for the constant term the two mean absolute errors were almost identical, 69.9 for the hypothesis and 70.3 percent for the naïve model.

Sten Thore has used an age-consumption test for his model which has some similarity with the life cycle hypothesis.[108] In his model age is a measure of the difference between the household's current income and its long-run income. However, as Mrs. Projector has pointed out, his data do not give much support to this model, and the same is true for Mrs. Projector's own data.[109]

Michael Landsberger tested the life cycle hypothesis in another way.[110] Working with Israeli data he took restitution payments as well as "other windfall receipts" and considered whether the marginal propensity to consume these windfalls is, as the life cycle hypothesis asserts, positively related to age. He did it separately for the two younger age groups (18–34, 35–44), where the family size variable does not bias the results against the hypothesis, and for the older age groups (45–54, 55 and over), where it does. He calculated the regressions twice, once for total

106. *Op. cit.*, pp. 22–23.
107. *Ibid.*, p. 21.
108. Sten Thore, *op. cit.*, p. 28.
109. Projector, *op. cit.*, p. 28.
110. "The Life-Cycle Hypothesis—A Reinterpretation and Empirical Test," *American Economic Review*, Vol. LX, March 1970, pp. 175–83.

consumption and once for nondurable consumption. Looking at the younger age groups, the life cycle hypothesis predicts total consumption correctly in two out of the four cases, and nondurable consumption in three out of four cases. For the older households the hypothesis predicts correctly in three out of four cases for either definition of consumption. These results do not seem to confirm the hypothesis. However, Landsberger argued that they actually support it because in all the six cases where the difference is statistically significant the hypothesis is confirmed.

This argument raises a methodological issue. What Landsberger did was to say that we should disregard the insignificant coefficients and look only at the significant ones. But is this legitimate? If the theory had predicted correctly in all cases, then it is correct to focus on the significant coefficients. But since the theory predicted incorrectly in some cases, this procedure is questionable.[111]

Moreover, there is another problem with Landsberger's results. He obtained consumption by subtracting saving from income. His consumption figure is therefore overstated to the extent that households saved indirectly by making gifts to their children. Such gifts are more likely to occur in older households where the children are older, too. Hence there is likely to be a spurious correlation between age and the estimated propensity to consume. This may seem to be a trivial point, but it may be important because some of the differences in the propensities to consume shown by Landsberger are also very small. Even a minor bias, therefore, may affect the results. On the other hand, there is also a bias against the life cycle hypothesis. If these windfalls were anticipated to any extent at all, households may have raised consumption prior to the year of receipt. Due to liquidity considerations, this is more likely to have happened for the older than for the younger age groups. All in all, Landsberger's evidence is suggestive, but it does not provide strong confirmation for the life cycle hypothesis.

Lester Thurow has analyzed optimal consumption expenditures at each age level.[112] He argued that in the younger age groups actual consumption might well be less than that called for by lifetime utility maximization because of capital rationing. He, therefore, decided to look at households which are neither saving nor dissaving, and to treat their level of consumption as reflecting the equilibrium adjustment of life-

111. By analogy consider tossing ten true dice a large number of times. If we just focus on the cases where the results are significantly different from what is expected by pure chance, then our results would tell us that the dice, which we know a priori to be true, are not. (This analogy is, of course, overdrawn because Landsberger's data, unlike the hypothetical dice, support his hypothesis in the majority of the cases.)

112. "The Optimum Lifetime Distribution of Consumption Expenditures," *American Economic Review*, Vol. LIX, June 1969, pp. 324–30.

time consumption to lifetime income. By finding the income level at which different age groups reach this equilibrium point, he derived a curve relating equilibrium consumption to age. His data showed that capital rationing is important—young households consume substantially less than the equilibrium amount. This is an important result for it directly contradicts the life cycle model. However, Thurow's analysis requires that a household's distribution of consumption expenditures does not depend on its income level. This assumption is consistent with the proportionality hypothesis. But if I am correct, and the proportionality hypothesis is in fact invalid, then there is little reason for accepting Thurow's assumption.[113] All in all, then, some of these age tests support the life cycle hypothesis in a general way, but as the results of Mrs. Projector's test show, they do not support the specific predictions of this theory.

Hypothetical Questions

Julian Simon and Carl Barnes have undertaken an interesting and original test of the life cycle hypothesis.[114] Instead of relying on the limited stock of available objective data, they decided to ask a series of hypothetical questions. These questions gave the respondents certain hypothetical information relevant to the life cycle hypothesis, such as income, stock of saving, age, and so on. They asked the respondents how much they would consume under these conditions, and then posed other conditions such as receipt of a windfall. Since the life cycle hypothesis makes specific predictions for such circumstances, they were able to compare the responses they obtained with what the theory predicts.

Several interesting results emerged. First, the consumption level given by the respondents exceeds somewhat the consumption level predicted by the life cycle hypothesis. Second, changes in the hypothetical level of assets do affect consumption. Third, when respondents were told to vary their assumed ages, a strong life cycle effect did show up, but the life cycle effect was less than what the hypothesis predicts. Fourth, when presented with a hypothetical windfall on the one hand and with an equal increase in their stock of saving, respondents were much more ready to spend out of the windfall than out of saving. This failure to

113. See also Brian Motley and Samuel Morley, "The Optimum Lifetime Distribution of Consumption Expenditures: Comment," *American Economic Review*, Vol. LX, September 1970, pp. 738–43; and Lester Thurow's reply, *ibid.*, pp. 744–45.

114. "The Middle-Class U.S. Consumption Function: A Suppositious-Question Study of Expected Consumption Behavior," Oxford University Institute of Economics and Statistics, *Bulletin*, Vol. 33, 1971, pp. 73–80.

treat windfalls and savings alike is of course contrary to the life cycle hypothesis. However, it can perhaps be explained by saying that households think of their assets as being equal to, or less than, the equilibrium amount so that they are reluctant to spend out of these assets. But when they receive a windfall, assets are raised above their equilibrium level, and hence they spend some part of this windfall. While such behavior does not fit the life cycle hypothesis, it does fit other wealth theories which look to the direct utility of wealth, such as the normal income theory and the theories of Lydall and Clower-Johnson.

Another set of questions asked about the reaction to windfalls and other income increments to be received in the future. Such future receipts had little if any effect on current consumption. There are several ways of explaining this. One is that the discount rate is very high. Another is that respondents face severe capital rationing, and hence have to await the actual receipt of a windfall before spending it. Since many of the respondents were middle-class people this is rather unlikely. Another explanation is that people treat future receipts as doubtful even if the question is phrased in terms of a *certain* receipt. Thus while this study supports the general notion of lifetime averaging, it tends to disconfirm some of the specific predictions of the life cycle hypothesis. In this respect its results are similar to those of other tests discussed earlier.

All the same, it does not provide strong evidence, either for or against, the life cycle hypothesis. There are two reasons for this. One is that the sample being small, the standard errors are very large relative to the difference between the actual and the predicted value. Second, as Simon and Barnes conceded, the response to hypothetical questions may not be a good indicator of how people actually react.[115] However, responses to hypothetical questions may give a good indication of how the respondents *think* people react. Since people may well have a fairly good intuitive idea of how people behave, their response to such hypothetical questions may be fairly accurate.[116] Hence, while I do not consider this test as providing a conclusive test of the life cycle hypothesis, I think it provides suggestive circumstantial evidence.

Miscellaneous Evidence

In addition to the tests discussed above, there are a number of other tests and isolated pieces of evidence which can be discussed fairly

115. Friedman specifically rejected Tobin's suggestion of simply asking people how they react to permanent and transitory income changes, "Reply to Comments on *A Theory of the Consumption Function*," in *Consumer Behavior*, Lincoln Clark (ed.) (New York, Harper and Brothers, 1958), Vol. 3, p. 468.

116. This raises serious methodological issues. Followers of Friedman's and of Weber's methodology are likely to see this issue quite differently.

briefly since none of them provide firm evidence for or against the permanent income theory.

The permanent income theory relies upon the regression of incomes toward their mean—in other words, households with a high income in any one year should be more apt to have an income decline than an income increase in the future, while the opposite is true for low income households. This seems a priori plausible and there is a great deal of empirical evidence supporting it.[117] However, it has been challenged by Michael Farrell in his excellent survey article on the permanent income theory.[118] Farrell argued that regression toward the mean may exist for some occupational groups but not for others.

Farrell cited two sets of data. First there are Dutch data which give the current income of a group of manual and clerical workers as well as their average incomes over the previous four years. If regression toward the mean is present, then as one goes up the income scale the ratio of current incomes to previous incomes should rise. Farrell stated that this is what the data show for manual workers, but not for clerical workers. This statement about clerical workers is highly questionable. Actually, for clerical workers, too, the ratio of current income to past average income increases with increasing income except in the top two income classes.[119] These two income classes account for only thirty-three households, 19 percent of the whole sample, so that for the great majority of cases these data *do* show regression toward the mean. The peculiar behavior of the two top income classes may be due to the small number of cases included, or it could perhaps be explained by the fact that the country was under German occupation during the survey year, 1941. It is not unlikely that some of the highly paid clerical workers were previously self-employed businessmen or professionals who had been forced into lower-paid activities as a result of the enemy occupation.[120]

In addition, Farrell cited U.S. data giving the household's estimate

117. See Milton Friedman and Simon Kuznets, *Income from Independent Professional Practice* (New York, Columbia University Press, 1945), chap. 7, as well as the data cited by Mrs. Mack in her "Direction of Change in Income and the Consumption Function," *Review of Economics and Statistics,* Vol. XXX, November 1948, pp. 239–58. See also George Katona, et al., *1962 Survey of Consumer Finances* (Ann Arbor, Survey Research Center, University of Michigan, 1963), pp. 27–29.

118. "The New Theories of the Consumption Function," *op. cit.,* pp. 687–89.

119. The ratios for the seven income classes are: 102, 104, 106, 109, 110, 101, 0.85.

120. Moreover, Farrell pointed out some other weaknesses of these data. As discussed above, income change data based on recall are quite bad.

of its income change over the previous year. These data, unlike other sets of data just like it, do not exhibit regression toward the mean. This could, perhaps, be due to the fact that Farrell's data include the early postwar years (1946–1947, 1947–1948) when conditions were unusual. In any case, these data are entirely consistent with the permanent income theory, since this theory does not require regression toward the mean *within the next year* but uses a longer horizon than that. Thus, Farrell's data do not invalidate the permanent income theory.

Modigliani and Brumberg supported the life cycle hypothesis by referring to a finding by Josephine Staab that the elasticity of consumption with respect to socioeconomic scale variables is greater than the measured income elasticity of consumption.[121] Since one can treat the socioeconomic scale variables as a proxy for permanent income, this shows that the permanent income elasticity of consumption is greater than the measured income elasticity. However, Miss Staab used certain expenditure items, such as newspapers, cars, and radios in establishing her socioeconomic scale.[122] The high elasticity of consumption with respect to the socioeconomic scale *may* therefore reflect nothing more than a taste variable—thriftiness reducing both a family's rating on the socioeconomic scale and its total expenditures.

Arnold Zellner has tested two related implications of the permanent income theory. One is that because of the existence of transitory elements in *consumption,* the consumption elasticity of income should be less than unity. The second implication is that the intercept in a regression of measured income on measured consumption, as well as the intercept in a regression of measured consumption on measured income, should both be positive. His results, while in general agreement with the permanent income theory, do not give it strong support. The results, "which under a generous interpretation meet the requirements of Friedman's theory, cannot be interpreted as seriously supporting the [proportionality hypothesis] against economically important alternatives." [123]

121. "Utility Analysis and the Consumption Function: An Interpretation of Cross-Section Data," *op. cit.,* p. 422n. They also referred to an unpublished study by Miss Reid also cited by Friedman in this connection. (The Staab data come from her "Income-Expenditure Relations of Farm Families Using Three Bases of Classification," unpublished Ph.D. dissertation, University of Chicago, 1952).

122. Staab, *op. cit.,* p. 45.

123. Arnold Zellner, "Tests of Some Basic Propositions in the Theory of Consumption," *American Economic Review,* Vol. L, May 1960, p. 572. One alternative mentioned by Zellner is a theory which, like the standard income theory, asserts that the marginal propensity to consume transitory income is greater than zero, but less than the marginal propensity to consume permanent income (pp. 570–72).

Another test can be devised by comparing the income elasticities of consumption in a single city and in the whole country. Eicher suggested that since economic conditions show greater differences within the whole country than within any single city, one would expect the importance of the permanent component of income variability to be greater for the country as a whole than for a single city. Hence the permanent income theory and the standard income theory predict that the income elasticity of consumption will be greater for the country as a whole than for a particular city. Eicher found that this is so,[124] but this test is of questionable validity. Even if the variance of the permanent component of income is greater for the country as a whole, the same is likely to be true of the transitory component. If both the variance due to permanent income differences and the variance due to transitory income differences are greater in the whole country than in a single city, one cannot say, a priori, which one should have the larger income elasticity of consumption.

Another item of supporting evidence, developed by Jacob Mincer, is the relation between the earnings of the family *head* and saving, keeping *family* income constant.[125] Families with working wives are more likely to have negative transitory income than other families since this may well be the reason why the wife is working. Hence, households where the head's earnings account for a below-average proportion of family income should, according to the permanent income theory, have a low saving-income ratio. This is what the data generally show. But the same fact can be explained without invoking the permanent income theory, because families with working wives may have special consumption "needs" or wishes.

Still another way of testing the permanent income theory is to calcu-

124. Jean-Claude Eicher, *Consommation et Epargne* (Paris, Robert Goetz-Girley, 1961), p. 136. In this book Eicher presented a number of other tests. Thus he fitted a simple consumption function to some German data and found that the intercept is very small and slightly negative, so that the average and marginal propensities to consume are very close. However, since he used measured income and measured consumption, it is hard to see why this fact should confirm the permanent income theory. (Eicher's impression that the data cover the same group of households throughout is erroneous. This is the case only for some of the households in the survey.) There is some variation in the findings of different budget studies. In some the intercept of the consumption function is large, in some it is small. When constructing a theory of the consumption function, one has to use the typical value of the intercept. The fact that it is trivial in one particular budget study does not tell us much unless it can be shown that this particular budget study is more reliable than the others.

125. Jacob Mincer, "Labor Supply, Family Income and Consumption," *American Economic Review*, Vol. L, May 1960. pp. 574–83.

late the correlation of the saving-income ratio and the income level twice, once from data covering a one-year span, and once from data covering a two-year period. According to the permanent income theory, the longer the accounting period over which income is averaged the lower the proportion of income variance accounted for by transitory elements, and hence the lower should be the correlation of the saving ratio and income.[126] In a study using U.S. Survey of Consumer Finance data, Lawrence Klein found support for this prediction.[127] However, when Klein and Liviatan subsequently did a similar comparison using British data they obtained the opposite results, thus leaving the upshot of this test quite uncertain.[128] But Malcolm Fisher pointed out a weakness in these tests.[129] In both tests what is being compared is a correlation over a two-year span with a correlation for only the first of the years covered by the two-year correlation. This is insufficient because it ignores the correlation for the second year. It may well be that for the second year of the two-year period the correlation coefficient is different enough to make the average of the two one-year correlation coefficients either higher or lower than the correlation coefficient obtained from two-year data. Hence this test neither confirms nor disconfirms the permanent income theory. In Chapter 13 I will present the results of a similar test which does not suffer from this weakness.

Nissan Liviatan calculated the marginal propensity to consume in two ways, once from the usual static cross-section data, and once dynamically, by dividing the change in a household's consumption by the change in the household's income over the two years covered by his data.[130] The absolute income theory predicts that these two ways of estimating the marginal propensity to consume yield the same answer. But since some of the income change is only transitory, the permanent

126. To see this, assume that all the income differences are differences in permanent income. The full permanent income theory would then predict a zero correlation of income and the saving rate.

127. "Statistical Estimation of Economic Relations from Survey Data," in Lawrence Klein (ed.), *Contributions of Survey Methods to Economics, op. cit.,* pp. 220–21. Klein's analysis is developed further by Simon and Aigner, *op. cit.,* pp. 347–48.

128. "The Significance of Income Variability on Savings Behaviour," Oxford University, Institute of Economics and Statistics, *Bulletin,* Vol. 19, May 1957, p. 156.

129. Fisher appears not ready to reject the test because of this weakness and believes that the Klein-Liviatan test "makes a point against the Friedman hypothesis" ("A Reply to the Critics," in *ibid.,* p. 194). However, to me his criticism is important enough to invalidate the test.

130. "Tests of the Permanent-Income Hypothesis Based on a Reinterview Savings Survey," *op. cit.,* pp. 38–44.

income theory predicts that the marginal propensity to consume is much smaller when derived by comparing changes in income and consumption between two years than when derived from the cross-section comparison of households with different incomes.[131]

Liviatan's data showed a tendency in the direction predicted by the permanent income theory, but the magnitude was not right. It could, however, be reconciled with the permanent income theory by adding the assumption that the household's expectation of future income varies as it experiences income changes, or that the horizon is substantially longer than two years. These assumptions are, of course, made explicitly in the life cycle hypothesis, so that this test, while unfavorable for the permanent income theory, does not really reject the Modigliani-Ando-Brumberg version.

In another test, Liviatan compared the income elasticity of consumption with the correlation of the household's income in the two years covered by his data.[132] This test, which had also been used by Friedman, strongly confirmed the permanent income theory. But in his comments on Liviatan's paper Friedman rejected both of these tests for reasons explained before, namely the bias which occurs if one obtains consumption by subtracting saving from income.[133] In view of this difficulty neither of these tests can be used as evidence either for or against the permanent income theory.

William Vickrey, one of the precursors of the permanent income theory, had classified households by consumption, and looked at mean income and consumption in each consumption class. Modigliani and Brumberg used these data in one of their tests.[134] If consumption is a linear, homogenous function of permanent income, and is independent of transitory income, then classifying households by consumption class amounts to classifying them by permanent income. The life cycle hypothesis assumes that there is some small consumption out of transitory income, and this implies that classifying by consumption is not quite the same thing, but is very close to, classifying households by permanent income. Hence, its prediction is that the income elasticity of consumption when calculated from households classified by consumption should be close to unity. When Modigliani and Brumberg estimated this elas-

131. Liviatan took the horizon to be two years.
132. *Ibid.*, pp. 35–38.
133. "Note on Nissan Liviatan's Paper," *op. cit.*, pp. 59–61. In his discussion of the second of these tests, Friedman also stated that the two-year horizon used by Liviatan (whose data covered only two years) is too short. This point was discussed in Chapter 3.
134. "Utility Analysis and the Consumption Function: An Interpretation of Cross-Section Data," *op. cit.*, p. 422n.

ticity, they found it to be 0.97 compared to an elasticity of 0.85 obtained from the same households classified by measured income rather than by consumption.[135]

But while the Modigliani-Brumberg technique avoids the bias due to transitory income, it introduces another bias, a bias due to the existence of transitory consumption. Suppose that a household has positive transitory consumption. This tends to shift it to a higher consumption class. Thus in the higher consumption classes there is a factor raising consumption relative to income. And similarly, negative transitory consumption lowers consumption relative to income in the lower consumption classes. Hence, the income elasticity of consumption, when interpreted as a relationship between permanent income and permanent consumption, is biased upwards, and this could explain the high income elasticity found by Modigliani and Brumberg. As Miss Reid pointed out in her discussion of Vickrey's original paper, one should classify households by consumption over several years, not by consumption in any single year.[136]

M. Perrot calculated the ratio of changes in consumption to changes in income with no lag and with a one year lag. In addition, she took the two-year change in consumption divided by the two-year change in income.[137] She classified these ratios as "normal" if they fell into the range of 0.50 to 1.25, and as "abnormal" if they were negative or greater than 2.00. In two of the three periods she analyzed, the ratio based on current income had the fewest abnormal cases. This is entirely consistent with the full permanent income theory and with the standard income theory. In both of these theories the first year's income has more significance than the previous year's income. Hence changes in consumption are more likely to be a reasonably behaving function of current income than of the previous year's income. And the fact that the two-year ratio shows more abnormal cases than the one-year ratio is not inconsistent with these theories either, because while they predict that the marginal propensity to consume will be lower for a two-year period than a one-year period, they do not really predict that it is more likely to lie in the "normal" rather than in the "abnormal"

135. Weighting the data by the number of adult-equivalents in each class does not change the result much. The coefficient is 0.98 with an intercept, and 0.99 if the intercept is omitted.

136. "Comment," in Conference on Research in Income and Wealth, *Studies in Income and Wealth*, Vol. 10 (New York, National Bureau of Economic Research, 1947), p. 315.

137. Marguerite Perrot, *Le Mode de Vie des Familles Bourgeoises*, 1873–1953 (Paris, Librairies Armand Colin, 1961). M. Perrot was not using the material described here to test the permanent income theory, but rather to describe the consumption function.

range. Another finding of M. Perrot supports both the full permanent and standard income theories. This is that the ratio tends to be "normal" more frequently among households with stable incomes than among those with unstable incomes. This reflects, of course, the fact that among stable income households an increase in measured income is more likely to represent an increase in permanent income. However, it is also consistent with an absolute income theory, which like Mrs. Mack's theory uses the incomes of two years. If consumption depends on the income of two years, then the marginal propensity to consume with respect to the current year's income will be more erratic if income fluctuates a great deal than if it is stable.

Conclusion

In this and the previous chapter I have evaluated a large number of tests of the wealth theories. Tables 14 and 15 show the results of all this work. Table 14 is a summary table which treats each type of test as a unit, while Table 15 shows the details for each test.[138]

In column 8 of Table 14, I have given my judgment of the strength of the evidence. I do so with trepidation. These judgments inevitably involve considerable subjective and arbitrary elements—as is, in fact, also the case with regard to some of the decisions (shown in column 1) about the rejection of a test. My justification for presenting these subjective judgments in column 8 is that some readers may find them useful and those who do not can simply ignore them. In any case, it should be clear that my evaluations of these tests in columns 2 or 8 should certainly not be treated as an evaluation of the quality of the analysis they contain. Some truly ingenious tests ran into inevitable difficulties. Moreover, some of the items I have referred to as "tests" were not really conceived as such by their authors, who were dealing with some other problems and not trying to test the wealth theories. Hence, to evaluate their quality on the basis of whether or not they give us valid information about the permanent income theory, or other variants of the wealth theories, would be, to put it mildly, somewhat egocentric.

What is more firmly grounded than these evaluations is the overall message of Tables 14 and 15. They show, first and foremost, that *none* of the tests support the full permanent income theory. All the evidence which is consistent with the full permanent income theory is also consistent with the standard income theory. On the other hand, one of the tests (the future versus past income test) disconfirms the relative income theory, and what is more, none of the evidence disconfirms the basic ideas of the wealth theories—the existence of *some* lag in the

138. I have not included some of the minor tests, such as tests I discussed only in footnotes.

Table 14

Summary of Results of Tests

Test	(1) Hypothesis Tested[a]	(2) No Usable Evidence	(3) Results Disconfirm Full Permanent Income Theory	Results Consistent with Predictions of Full Permanent Income Theory and			(7) Other Wealth Theories	(8) Strength of Evidence
				(4) Relative Income Theory	(5) Standard Income Theory	(6) Not with Relative or Standard Income Theory		
1. Windfalls	D, Z	x						strong
2. Narrowing cells	D			x	x			strong
3. Group means	D, P		x	o	o			strong
4. Stable vs. fluct. income	D, P			x	x			moderate
5. Direction of income change	D, P				d			strong
6. Time series	D, P, Z		x					moderate[h]
7. Disaggregation	P, M						x	strong
8. Self-employed vs. employees	D, P, Z				x			moderate
9. Monthly data	D				x			strong[h]
10. Income profiles	D, E, L				x			strong[h]
11. Temporarily low income	D, E, L				x			moderate
12. Instrumental variables	D, P		x					strong
13. Errors in variables	D, P		x					
14. Other 2- or 3-year data	C, D, L, P, Z, M, N		x				e	strong

No.	Item	Code used[a]					Strength
15.	Occupation vs. measured inc.	D			x		weak
16.	Effect of assets	N		x			moderate[f]
17.	Distribution of net worth	P		x	x		weak
18.	Classification by relative inc.	D		x	x		weak
19.	Age and cons.	C, M					strong[g]
20.	Hypothetical questions	M	x[b]				
21.	Miscellaneous	M	x				

NOTES: Classification of tests as confirming or disconfirming various theories is based on my own conclusion, which may not correspond to that of their author. I have not evaluated tests which confirm the relative income theory as well as another theory. Although tests showing wealth variables to be significant are consistent with the standard income theory, I have not entered them as confirming this theory unless they confirm the standard income theory in some other way as well.

[a] CODE USED: C, life cycle hypothesis. D, difference between permanent and transitory income elasticities. E, relevance of income expectations. L, lag in consumption function tested explicitly. M, miscellaneous. N, normal income theory. P, proportionality hypothesis. Z, zero transitory income elasticity of consumption.

[b] Although this test is interesting and suggestive, I have not treated it as disconfirming any hypothesis for reasons explained in the text.

[c] Geographic groupings seem to contradict standard income theory as well as relative income theory. This is discussed in Chapter 12. Difference in income elasticities of permanent and transitory income is consistent with relative income theory.

[d] For income decreases consistent with standard income theory only if the horizon is long, otherwise disconfirms it.

[e] Disconfirms life cycle hypothesis, but not normal income theory.

[f] Results not favorable for normal income theory.

[g] Results not favorable for life cycle hypothesis.

[h] Rejects habit persistence theory.

189

Table 15

More Detailed Summary of Results

Test	(1) No Usable Evidence	(2) Results Disconfirm Full Permanent Income Theory	Results Consistent with Predictions of Full Permanent Income Theory and			(6) Strength of Evidence
			(3) Relative Income Theory	(4) Standard Income Theory	(5) Other Wealth Theories	
1. Windfalls						
Bodkin	x					
Bodkin-Bird	x					
Klein-Liviatan	x					
Kreinin	x					
Landsberger	x					
Reid	x					
Katona	x					
Eisner	x					
2. Narrowing Cells						
Houthhakker	x					
Eisner			x	x		strong
3. Group Means						
Eisner			x	x[a]		weak
Friend-Kravis		x				strong
Modigliani-Ando		x[a]				strong
Asimakopulos			x[a]	x[a]		weak
Guthrie	x					
Watts		x				weak
Zellner		x				weak
Ramanathan			x	x		weak

190

Study					
Mayer		x			moderate
Friend		x	x		moderate
Parry		x	x		moderate
4. Stable vs. Fluctuating Income					
Friend-Kravis		x	x		weak
Crockett-Friend	x	x			
Reid (1)	x		x		strong
Reid (2)	x	x	x		moderate
Morgan			x		
5. Direction of Income Change					
Morgan			x[d]		weak
Reid-Dunsing			x		moderate
Freeman-Coombs	x		x		weak
6. Time Series					
Nerlove	x	x	x		weak
Mincer			x		moderate
Arak & Spiro	b				
Taubman	x		x		strong
Laumas	x				
Holmes (Canada)	x				
Holmes (U.S.)	x	x	x		strong
Chounhurry	x				
Gupta	x				
McInnis	x				
Husby	x				
Bonin	x				
7. Disaggregation					
Friend-Kravis	x				
Asimakopulos	x				
Landsberger			x		moderate
Miscellaneous Authors (individual commodities)	x				

Table 15 (*Continued*)

Test	(1) No Usable Evidence	(2) Results Disconfirm Full Permanent Income Theory	(3) Results Consistent with Predictions of Full Permanent Income Theory and — Relative Income Theory	(4) Standard Income Theory	(5) Other Wealth Theories	(6) Strength of Evidence
8. Self-employed vs. Employees						
Fisher	x					
Liviatan				x		strong
9. Monthly Data						
Watts	x					
Mizoguchi				x		moderate
Shinohara-Mizoguchi	x					
10. Group Income Profiles						
Watts				x		weak
Ramanathan				x		strong
11. Temporarily Low Incomes						
Stafford				x		strong
Barten, Theil, Leender	x					
12. Instrumental Variables						
Liviatan (1)	x					
Liviatan (2)		x				moderate
13. Errors in Variables						
Saffran		x				strong
Simon-Aigner				x		strong
14. Other 2-or 3-Year Data						
Liviatan	x					
Taubman (1)				x		moderate

Study					Strength
Taubman (2)					moderate
Friend and Crockett			x	x	weak
Holbrook			x	x	strong
Holbrook-Stafford	x				
Reid			x		weak
Reid-Dunsing			x		strong
15. Occupation and Measured Incomes					
Mack	x	x	x		weak
16. Effect of Assets					
Various Authors	x			x	weak
Crockett-Friend				x	weak
Projector				x	moderate
Ramanathan					
Landsberger	x				
17. Distribution of Net Worth					
Crockett-Friend	x				weak
Projector-Weiss	x				weak
Projector	x				
Waters	x				
18. Relative Income					
Modigliani-Brumberg		x			weak
19. Age and Consumption					
Modigliani-Brumberg	x			x	moderate
Fisher	x			x	moderate
Farrell	x				
Clower and Johnson					
Kelley and Williamson				x	moderate
Projector	x			x	strong
Thore	x				
Landsberger					
Thurow	x			x	weak
20. Hypothetical Questions					
Simon-Barnes	x[e]				

Table 15 (*Continued*)

Test	(1) No Usable Evidence	(2) Results Disconfirm Full Permanent Income Theory	(3) Relative Income Theory	(4) Standard Income Theory	(5) Other Wealth Theories	(6) Strength of Evidence
				Results Consistent with Predictions of Full Permanent Income Theory and		
21. Miscellaneous Tests						
Farrell	x					
Modigliani-Ando	x					
Zellner	x					
Eicher	x					
Mincer	x					
Klein	x					
Liviatan (1)	x					
Liviatan (2)	x					
Modigliani-Brumberg	x					
Perrot	x					

NOTE: For an explanation of the evaluation of tests see the notes to Table 15.

[a] Not so for geographic groupings, but see Chapter 12.

[b] Deals only with detailed specification of permanent income theory.

[c] See footnote *b*, Table 14.

[d] See footnote *d*, Table 14.

consumption function and the higher propensity to consume out of measured than out of transitory income. *In other words, the evidence from all these tests is consistent with the standard income theory. This theory is able to reconcile what at first seems like a great deal of mutually conflicting evidence.* At the same time, two other wealth theories, the life cycle hypothesis and the normal income theory, have performed rather badly in these tests. Thus, the evidence of these tests strongly favors the standard income theory.[139]

139. Note added in proof: Since I wrote the above, some new material has appeared. Roger Betancourt published a group means test for Chile. His test, which used nondurable consumption, rejects the proportionality hypothesis, but shows that the propensity to consume is greater for permanent than for measured income. However, since his measured income is the income for only one month, this does not really disconfirm the measured income theories. (Roger Betancourt, "The Normal Income Hypothesis in Chile," *Journal of the American Statistical Association,* Vol. 66, June 1971, pp. 258–63.) F. Thomas Juster and Paul Wachtel found that, in quarterly data, the marginal propensity to consume nondurables was considerably lower for transitory than for permanent income. However, for durables and nondurables combined there was only a small difference between the two propensities to consume. (F. Thomas Juster and Paul Wachtel, "Inflation and the Consumer," *Brookings Papers on Economic Activity,* 1972:1, pp. 100–102.) On the other hand, A. S. Deaton and K. J. Wigley found that transitory income is largely saved. However, since they used quarterly data, this does not disconfirm the measured income theories. These theories do not really claim that income is consumed in the quarter of receipt. (A. S. Deaton and K. J. Wigley, "Econometric Models for the Personal Sector," Oxford University, Institute of Economics and Statistics, *Bulletin,* Vol. 33, May 1971, pp. 81–91.) Thus none of these studies change the unfavorable conclusions reached above for the full permanent income theory. Turning to the life cycle hypothesis, Keizo Nagatani has presented an important modification which takes account of uncertainty. In his model, households modify their expectations of future income on the basis of their current income receipts. As a result, a different pattern of lifetime consumption emerges. (In addition, Nagatani presents a criticism of Thurow's test discussed above.) As shown in this chapter, the life cycle hypothesis is supported in its general approach, but not in its detailed specifications by various tests. It would be extremely useful to see if Nagatani's modification allows it to pass the various tests of its detailed specification. (Keizo Nagatani, "Life Cycle Saving: Theory and Fact," *American Economic Review,* Vol. LXII, June 1972, pp. 344–53.)

Six

INTERNATIONAL TESTS

Some tests of the wealth theories have combined data from various countries, and in addition a number of studies not specifically concerned with the permanent income theory have dealt with differences in the saving-income ratios of countries at various stages of development. These studies, it may seem, should provide important evidence on the proportionality hypothesis. In this chapter I will first discuss whether differences in the saving ratios of rich and poor countries can be used to test the proportionality hypothesis, and then I will discuss various studies which have dealt specifically with the wealth theories.[1]

At first glance it may seem that a comparison of the saving-income ratios of rich and poor countries furnishes an obvious test of the proportionality hypothesis since the income difference between, say the United States and India, surely represents a difference in permanent income. But actually the matter is more complex.

Assume first that the data show no correlation between the per capita incomes of countries and their average propensities to consume. This would certainly be in agreement with the proportionality hypothesis, but it would not support this hypothesis against the measured income theories. This is so because the main rival to the permanent income theory is surely not the absolute income theory but the relative income theory, and it is not clear whether the relative income theory really predicts a significant difference in the average propensities to consume of rich and poor countries. With regard to the proportionality hypothesis, the relative income theory differs from the permanent income theory only because it assumes that a demonstration effect raises the average propensity to consume of low income households and lowers the average propensity to consume of high income households. Although there have been discussions of an international demonstration effect in the development literature, it is by no means clear that such an international demonstration

1. I am not discussing a relevant paper by Lydall in this chapter because I am taking it up in Chapter 8.

effect is really of significant magnitude. Hence, if the data show that the average propensity to consume is the same in rich and in poor countries, this could be interpreted not as a disconfirmation of the measured income theories per se but merely as a disconfirmation of an *international* demonstration effect. Since the existence of an international demonstration effect is something grafted onto the relative income theory, rather than a necessary implication of it, its disconfirmation does not really damage the relative income theory.

On the other hand, consider the possibility that the average propensity to consume is greater in poor than in rich countries. Would this upset the proportionality hypothesis? While it would certainly provide an argument against this hypothesis, it is only a weak argument.[2] The permanent income theory does *not* imply that the average propensity to consume is the same in rich and poor countries; all it implies is that the higher income of a country does not, in and of itself, cause its average propensity to consume to be low. The permanent income theory does not deny that many factors which cause a country's income to be low, may, at the same time, cause its average propensity to consume to be high. For example, it has been argued that in underdeveloped countries a dearth of entrepreneurial ability reduces investment, and hence saving.[3] If so, a high average propensity to consume in underdeveloped countries does not contradict the proportionality hypothesis. Thus, differences in the saving ratios of rich and poor countries tells us little about the proportionality hypothesis.

Fortunately, there are a number of studies which use differences in the saving ratios of various countries specifically to test the wealth theories. One of these is a study of the normal income theory by Irwin Friend and Paul Taubman.[4] In their model the desired stock of wealth is a function of normal income, and personal saving is explained by the discrepancy between this desired stock and the actual stock of wealth. They pooled cross-section and time-series data for twenty-two countries in the period 1953–1960.[5] They obtained normal income in two ways,

2. It would, however, invalidate some implications for economic development theory which Friedman drew from his theory. *A Theory of the Consumption Function* (Princeton, Princeton University Press, 1957), pp. 233–34.

3. See Albert Hirschman, *The Strategy of Economic Development* (New Haven, Yale University Press, 1958), p. 36.

4. "The Aggregate Propensity to Save: Some Concepts and Their Application to International Data," *Review of Economics and Statistics,* Vol. XLVIII, May 1966, pp. 113–23.

5. Such pooling may, however, be questionable. See Subramanian Swamy, "A Dynamic Personal Savings Function and Its Long-Run Implications," paper read at the Econometric Society Meetings, 1967. This paper also contains a test of the looser version of the life cycle hypothesis.

once as a simple average of three-year income and once by fitting a time trend. They ran regressions both for levels and for first differences, using in some regressions a taste variable. For the levels they concluded that:

The estimates of the marginal propensity to save out of transitory income . . . are extremely variable, depending on the definition of normal income adopted. They are, nevertheless, generally higher than the much more stable estimates of the marginal propensity to save out of normal income (but uniformly closer to the latter than to one). . . . The regressions with the highest correlations . . . point to an estimated marginal propensity to save out of transitory income of between .17 and .36. If tastes are not held constant, the range is even larger.[6]

The first difference regressions which Friend and Taubman ran were, on the whole, unsuccessful though they suggest that there is a significant negative asset effect on saving with a coefficient of around -0.07 to -0.10. Friend and Taubman concluded that, all in all:

Our empirical results have not been very impressive. . . . The estimated relation of the marginal propensity to save out of transitory income to the marginal propensity to save out of normal income is quite different depending on whether a level or a change regression is used, and on the precise form of the level or change regression, but the transitory propensity is always well under one. Both theoretical considerations and our belief that the level regressions are better . . . suggest to us that the propensity to save out of transitory income is greater than out of normal income, but again we do not know by how much, and we suspect that the difference has been exaggerated.[7]

While these results are of course consistent with the standard income theory, they are too vague to give it convincing support.[8]

Johnson and Chiu tested the permanent income theory in a specific way by using it to estimate saving, and then comparing their estimated saving to actual saving.[9] They first calculated permanent income by fitting a time trend to income, and then used this permanent income to

6. Friend and Taubman, *op. cit.*, p. 120.

7. *Ibid.*, p. 122.

8. In the equation for levels of the data the constant term of the *savings* regression has a *positive* sign, when the taste variable is included in the regression. Friend and Taubman attributed this disturbing result to nonlinearities and to errors in their taste variable. But it is not really so surprising. As far as the intercountry differences in income are concerned, their taste variable, the previous year's saving-income ratio, presumably picks up some of the effect of income differences. And for the inter-temporal income differences included in their pooled time-series and cross-section data, neither the permanent income theory nor the relative income theory predict that the intercept must be negative.

9. "The Saving-Income Relation in Underdeveloped and Developed Countries," *Economic Journal,* Vol. LXXVIII, June 1968, pp. 321–33.

estimate consumption. By subtracting estimated consumption from measured income, they obtained a permanent income theory prediction of saving. However, their method assumes that Friedman's k is constant, an assumption which, as they pointed out, does not really form part of the permanent income theory. They then correlated actual and estimated saving, and compared their correlation coefficients in these regressions with the correlation coefficients obtained by using the absolute income theory approach—that is, simply regressing saving against current income. They did this for forty countries and in half the cases obtained an R greater than 0.5. Moreover, for ten of them the permanent income theory approach had the higher correlation coefficient. This, they concluded, "lends added weight to the explanatory value of the permanent income hypothesis, since it is a much more complicated one than performed in the simple regressions of current saving on current income." [10] But this is not convincing. To be sure, their test of the permanent income theory not only assumes that k is constant but is also so indirect that considerable accuracy is probably lost. But is this sufficient to account for the fact that the simple absolute income theory had the higher correlation coefficient in thirty out of forty cases? Perhaps it is, perhaps it isn't. But it would surely be better to treat this test as showing an inconclusive result rather than to claim that it supports the permanent income theory.

Jeffrey Williamson applied several models to personal savings of Asian countries, pooling cross-section and time series data. [11] The first of these, a simple Keynesian model, shows the expected negative intercept for each country. The second is a model of Houthakker's. Using disposable personal income, the between-country marginal propensity to save (which Williamson interpreted as the long-run marginal propensity to save) is 0.16, while the within-country inter-temporal marginal propensity to save (which Williamson took to be the short-run marginal propensity to save) is 0.28. [12] Houthakker's distinction between labor income and property income turned out to be very important.

The third model used by Williamson is the Friend-Taubman model. [13] It shows a larger marginal propensity to save for transitory income than

10. *Ibid.*, p. 331.

11. "Personal Saving in Developing Nations: An Intertemporal Cross-Section from Asia," *Economic Record*, Vol. 44, June 1968, pp. 194–209. Again, such a pooling may not be legitimate. Williamson's analysis with respect to India has been criticized by K. L. Gupta, "Personal Savings in Developing Nations: Further Evidence," *Economic Record*, Vol. 46, June 1970, pp. 243–49.

12. Williamson used not the actual value of the variables but their deviations from the mean.

13. Williamson used a three-year moving average to measure normal income.

Table 16

Summary of Results—International Tests

Test	Results
1. Normal Income Model	Overall results not encouraging.[a] Greater marginal propensity to save transitory than permanent income
2. Johnson-Chiu Comparison of Actual and Estimated Saving	Inconclusive
3. General Lag Model	Good fit
4. Ball-Drake Model	Good fit
5. Singh-Drost	Good fits, but surprising variations by countries

[a] This is so for the Friend-Taubman test. In Williamson's test of the model the standard errors are large since only a small number of observations are available for each country.

for normal income. Unfortunately, the standard errors are often very large relative to coefficients so that it would probably be unwise to attach much importance to the precise ratio of the two propensities. In a final model Williamson introduced the price level, price expectations, and interest rates, and in this model, too, the marginal propensity to save is greater for transitory than for permanent income.

In a subsequent paper Williamson tested other consumption functions for Japan, Taiwan, Burma.[14] He also pooled the data for the three countries and, in addition, ran pooled regressions for these countries plus South Korea and the Philippines. He obtained very good results for a distributed lag model.

Williamson also tested the Ball-Drake model, and this, too, gave an extremely good fit. As pointed out in Chapter 2, this model requires that the sum of the current income coefficient and the lagged consumption coefficient are unity. Except in the case of Burma, Williamson's coefficients do just that, the difference between the sum of the coefficients and unity being *much* less than one standard error of either coefficient. Even in the case of Burma, the divergence of the sum of the coefficients from unity is slightly less (though only slightly so) than one standard deviation of either coefficient. However, the divergencies from unity are all in the downward direction. This is an important finding and will be discussed further in Chapter 13.

Finally, there is a paper by Balvir Singh and Helmar Drost in which they fitted permanent income regressions using a nonlinear iterative

14. Jeffrey Williamson, "Income Growth and Saving," *Philippine Economic Journal*, Vol. III, 1969, pp. 66–71.

least squares procedure for eleven countries.[15] They obtained good fits with their coefficient for the lag term always significant at the 5 percent or better level. However, it did show very great variation from country to country which does introduce an implausible element.

Table 16 summarizes the upshot of these international tests. It shows that a general lag model gives a good fit as does the Ball-Drake theory. But the normal income theory, once again, performs rather badly.

15. "An Alternative Econometric Approach to the Permanent Income Hypothesis: An International Comparison," *Review of Economics and Statistics,* Vol. LIII, November 1971, pp. 326–34. In addition to the material discussed here they also criticise the Friedman-Cagan lagged regression technique.

Part Three

TIME SERIES REGRESSIONS

INTRODUCTION

One of the standard ways of testing consumption function theories is to see how well they perform in a time series regression of aggregate consumption on aggregate income and other variables. Moreover, one can use such time series regressions not only to test a theory but also to determine the lag structure by allowing the regression to select the lags. Clearly, such time series regressions provide an important way of both specifying and testing the permanent income theory. In fact, it may seem that regressing aggregate data is *the* way of getting at the validity of the wealth theories.

However, aggregate regressions, while a useful way of testing the permanent income theory, do not necessarily represent the *best* way of testing it. This is so for several reasons. First, there is the well-known problem of single equation bias. In principle it would, of course, be possible to use a completely specified model. I have not done this for two reasons. One is that in the process of avoiding single equation bias one often increases the multicollinearity problem. The other and more compelling reason is the following. Fitting a regression to aggregate time series represents just one of the things one has to do to test the wealth theories. Since it is only part of my task, I cannot spend enough time on it to build an elaborate econometric model. On the other hand, any result obtained from a very simple model would be subject to the criticism that a more detailed model would yield different results. I have therefore followed both Friedman and Modigliani and Ando in using single equation tests.

Single equation bias is not the only problem one encounters when trying to investigate the lag in the consumption function by regressing time series. Perhaps a more serious problem is that the available lagged regression techniques have serious weaknesses. Not only can serial correlation create spurious lags, but there is the problem that the same reduced form of lagged regressions can be obtained from quite different economic structures.[1] Moreover, as Zvi Griliches has remarked, one should not "expect the data to give a clear-cut answer about the exact form of the lag. The world is not that benevolent. One should try to get more implications from the theory about the correct form of the lag and impose it on the data. . . . Not all is hopeless, but to get better answers to such complicated questions we shall need better data and much larger samples." [2]

While Griliches is undoubtedly right that one should not use the data both to specify the lag and to test the hypothesis embodying it, in this case it is the counsel of perfection. The permanent income *theory* does not itself specify the lag. Friedman treats the length of the lag and the weights to be assigned to each year entirely as an empirical issue to be determined by the data. The life cycle hypothesis is more helpful in this respect, for on the micro level it does give a theoretical specification of the lag: a household spreads out consumption of its assets at an even rate over its lifetime. But on the macro level it is less easy to work with. Here it specifies consumption as a function of labor income, nonhuman wealth, and the employment ratio. While this eliminates the problem of lagged regression it creates a serious specification problem. This is that it cannot be readily distinguished from another theory, such as Tobin's theory, which includes a wealth term in the consumption function but does not derive this wealth term from the life cycle hypothesis.

Griliches' statement that to test lag hypotheses we need "better data and larger samples" applies with great force to any attempt to test consumption function theories. National income data—particularly for the years prior to 1929—contain large errors, a fact brought home by the frequent revisions of recent data as well as by some work of Taubman discussed in Chapter 4. What is worse is that the errors in these data need not be random, but could lead to serious biases. Suppose that the income estimate is obtained from the product account side, or that initial estimates from the income flows side are adjusted to reduce the discrepancy with the products side. In this case current income and consumption share a common error term and the resulting bias leads to an underestimate of the lag. On the other hand, suppose that some components of income and consumption are estimated by fitting a trend to benchmark dates. This *may* create an upward bias in the length of the lag.

Another serious problem is created by capital gains. The data exclude them from income. While some capital gains should clearly be excluded, there are others, such as capital gains resulting from the accumulation of

1. See Zvi Griliches, "Distributed Lags: A Survey," *Econometrica*, Vol. 35, January 1967, p. 46.
2. *Ibid.*, p. 46.

retained corporate earnings, which should surely be included. This is particularly so when one is testing the wealth theories.[3] Capital gains are substantial. Bhatia has estimated capital gains, both accrued and realized, on four types of assets: corporate stock, residential and farm real estate, and livestock. For the period 1948–1964 they amounted to almost 12 percent of income, or more than twice as much as personal saving.[4] The rather cavalier exclusion of all capital gains from income therefore may create a serious bias.

Apart from the quality of the data, the quantity of the data also creates a problem when one tries to use regressions embodying long lags. There are less than 70 peacetime years for which national income data are available. It is often possible to compensate, at least in part, for the limited supply of annual data by using quarterly data, but given the long lag implied by the permanent income theory, quarterly data—available only for the postwar years—are not very helpful. Another possibility would be to add to the number of available observations by using national income data for several countries. Unfortunately, for most countries for which national income data are available for the prewar years, these data give only approximations of the trend of income and do not give adequate estimates of cyclical movements. And estimates of cyclical movements are, of course, needed to test consumption function theories.

In addition to the data problems, there is another serious problem with time series regressions. It arises when time series regressions are used to tell us something about the way households behave rather than just for forcasting. It is by no means clear that the lag produced by aggregate time series regressions shows how individual households react to income changes. The life cycle hypothesis argues very plausibly that the aggregate savings ratio depends largely upon the growth of population and income. Hence, the lag of consumption behind income shown by the aggregate

3. This point was made by Farrell, who attributed it to a suggestion by Kaldor. "The New Theories of the Consumption Function," *Economic Journal,* Vol. LXIX, December 1959, p. 693.

4. Kul B. Bhatia, "Accrued Capital Gains, Personal Income and Saving in the United States, 1948–64," *Review of Income and Wealth,* Series 16, December 1970, pp. 363–78. More recently, Michael McElroy has estimated capital gains in three areas, corporate business, unincorporated business (including farms), and residential real estate. In the period 1946–1968 gross capital gains were nearly twice as large as personal saving, and even if one eliminates those capital gains which merely reflect inflation, capital gains still exceeded personal saving. "Capital Gains and the Concept and Measurement of Purchasing Power," American Statistical Association, Business and Economic Statistics Section, *1970 Proceedings* (Washington, D.C., American Statistical Association, 1971), p. 135. See also John Arena, "Postwar Stock Market Changes and Consumer Spending," *Review of Economics and Statistics,* Vol. XLVII, November 1965, pp. 379–91.

data may reflect changes in population and income growth rather than the way individual households react when their income changes.[5]

I do not mean to give the impression that time series tests of the permanent income theory are useless. All the available data, cross-section as well as time series, are really not adequate for a fully reliable test. What one has to do is to use all the available data and hope that there are differences among the biases and errors in the data, so that the truth will emerge from a multitude of tests.[6]

There are two steps in testing the permanent income theory with time series data. One is to take a particular consumption function containing lagged income terms and let the regression choose the lags. The second step is to compare the predictive power of this consumption function with that of other consumption functions. This second step is necessary because it may well be the case that a particular consumption function generates long lags when the computer is allowed to choose the lags, but that another, quite different, consumption function with only short lags *predicts* better. Another reason for comparing various consumption functions is that there exist several different wealth theories and they should be tested against each other.

Friedman is well aware of the fact that it is necessary to test various hypotheses against each other and he did just that in his book, using as rivals to the permanent income theory the relative income theory and the absolute income theory. But since then many more consumption functions have been published, and all of these should, in principle, be tested against the permanent income theory. Unfortunately, this turned out to be too big a task, and I have had to limit, in the way described below, the number of rival theories I tested. But even these limitations left a large number of consumption functions and so I adopted a two-step procedure. I first tested various consumption functions by projecting them for three years and comparing the accuracy of their prediction with that of naïve models. I then allowed the survivors (surprisingly few) to compete against each other in a projection test. Accordingly, Chapters 7 and 8 compare various consumption functions with naïve models. (These chapters necessarily present many details and the reader interested only in the overall results may wish to skip to the summary tables at the end of each chapter.) Chapter 9 then does two things. One is to

5. I am indebted for this point to Malcolm Fisher.
6. It may be worth mentioning that in the preparation of this book, while doing the cross-section chapters, I was appalled by the inaccuracies of the data and felt that the time series data would really provide the better test. But while preparing the time series chapters I felt that the cross-section data were better.

use various methods of lagged regression to estimate the consumption function lag. The second is to compare the predictive power of different consumption functions by requiring them to estimate consumption beyond the period over which they have been fitted.

Seven

TIME SERIES CONSUMPTION FUNCTIONS NOT STRESSING WEALTH

The most obvious screening test for consumption functions is to see how well they forecast for some years beyond the period over which they were fitted. The projection test I used is to predict for three years ahead by means of the particular function and to compare the mean absolute error of the prediction with that of two naïve models.[1] One model, the "no change" model, assumes that consumption is equal to that of the previous period; the other naïve model (the "3 percent growth model") assumes that aggregate consumption is growing at a 3 percent annual rate. In some cases the function being tested predicts not the level of consumption (or saving) but its change. In these cases I used a naïve model which assumes that the change in consumption (or saving) is equal to the change experienced in the previous year.

This way of testing consumption functions is fairly crude, but this is justified by the fact that its only purpose is to select functions for the more elaborate test of Chapter 9. One weakness of it is that I am testing various functions over different periods rather than over the same span of years. Since the difficulty of predicting consumption varies from year to year, the different functions are not being graded by equally difficult tests. For example, in some years the naïve model predicts very well, so that functions being tested over these years have to perform much better than do other functions in order to pass this test.

A second problem is created by the frequent revisions of the basic series. A consumption function is fitted by its author over a certain number of years, and by the time the data for the next three years are available, the data for many of the years over which the function was originally fitted have been revised. Had the author of the function used the revised data, his coefficients might have been somewhat different. I have tried to minimize this problem by using the unrevised data where

1. My use of a single criterion, the mean absolute error is justified by the fact that I am using it merely as a preliminary screening device, not as a way of selecting the "best" function.

possible, and have not used the years following the major data revision of 1965 for functions fitted to the earlier data. Nonetheless, some part of this problem remains.

I have not looked at all the consumption functions available, but have limited the work involved by certain exclusions. First, I excluded all functions published prior to 1955 and after mid-1970. Second, I excluded functions fitted to foreign data. This is not chauvinism but reflects my need to cut down on the immense amount of work which would be involved in looking at functions fitted for foreign countries.[2] Third, I have not dealt with functions which relate only to nondurable consumption rather than to total consumption. Fourth, I have eliminated consumption functions which break total consumption into more than two parts and fit separate functions for each part (for example, durables, nondurables, and services). One of the issues here is the length of the lag in the total consumption function, and such disaggregated consumption functions do not furnish a good indication of this.[3] Fifth, for obvious reasons, my coverage of unpublished consumption functions is far from complete, and in fact is rather casual.[4] Sixth, I have not tested some functions which I want to run in Chapter 9 in any case. Seventh, I have not dealt with those studies which fit a consumption function only as an incidental by-product of some other work, such as estimating the interest elasticity of consumption or the real balance effect. Eighth, I have not dealt with functions fitted by spectral analysis, since these functions have generally dealt with a simple lag only rather than with a distributed lag.[5] While the best fit may be obtained for a very short lag by spectral analysis, the mean lag calculated from a distributed lag may be much longer.

Finally, there have been a number of studies dealing not with consumption but with saving. I have not taken up all these functions; this decision, to be candid, is justified more by my wish to save labor than by profound methodological considerations.[6]

2. This may seem an inadequate reason since one could argue that instead of omitting the foreign consumption functions, I could have used another equally rational criterion, such as omitting all functions published in odd years, or picking authors with names starting with consonants. But this is not so. Since I am unfamiliar with foreign data sources, the opportunity cost of evaluating consumption functions is much greater for a function fitted to foreign data than to U.S. data.

3. In a model discussed below, Goldfeld fitted an aggregate consumption function and disaggregated ones. The implied lags were sharply different.

4. Thus I missed William Totten's dissertation, "The Effect of Wealth on Consumption: Empirical Tests for Significance and Lags," University of Southern California, 1970.

5. The only exceptions to this are the studies discussed in Chapter 9 (see note 8).

6. Moreover, I excluded the consumption function fitted by Valavanis-

The questions which time series tests try to answer are similar to those discussed in the previous chapters, though the emphasis is different. As before, there is a problem of lags. However, in time series tests the orientation of this question is somewhat different from what it is in cross-section tests. In most cross-section tests, the question discussed is whether consumption depends on long-run income rather than only on current income. In time series tests the emphasis is not so much on the question of whether long-run income is relevant, but is more specific: it is the proper weight for each of the years.

Second, there is the proportionality hypothesis. Although this hypothesis has received a great deal of attention in cross-section tests, it has received much less discussion in time series tests. This is so because time series tests are less useful in evaluating it. It is a well-known fact that the saving-income ratio has not risen over time as the absolute income theory predicts. But this fact is consistent with the relative income theory as well as the permanent income theory. The relevant issue for the proportionality hypothesis is the behavior of different income groups at the same time, not the secular behavior of the saving ratio. Hence, time series data are much less applicable here than are cross-section data.

Third, there is the question of the relative magnitudes of the propensities to consume permanent and transitory income. A number of time series tests do try to answer this question. I have already taken up many of these studies in Chapter 4.

Despite the above-mentioned limitations, there are many consumption functions to be considered. This chapter deals with those which stress income or related variables; the next chapter deals with consumption functions stressing nonhuman wealth. Unfortunately, this division of labor does not lead to a clear-cut line of demarcation. A model which stresses wealth may include permanent income, and a permanent income model may include a wealth term. What I have done is to place in the

---

Vail ("An Econometric Model of Growth: U.S.A. 1869–1953," American Economic Association, *Papers and Proceedings,* Vol. XLV, May 1955, pp. 280–21). This model deals not with yearly data but with overlapping decades and this creates problems in projecting it. In addition, I have not tested some consumption functions fitted by Arnold Zellner ("The Short-Run Consumption Function," *Econometrica,* Vol. 25, October 1957, pp. 552–67). The two consumption functions Zellner found to be best rely critically on the use of quarterly data. For the purpose of testing the permanent income theory, rather than for forecasting, such functions are not very useful. I have not taken up a very sophisticated permanent income-type consumption function fitted by David Lindsey ("Expectations and the Consumption Function," unpublished manuscript). To use this function, which includes the velocity of money, it would be necessary to fit an Allais-type demand for money function first. I have excluded it on the rather questionable grounds that to do otherwise would involve a great deal of work.

wealth chapter only those consumption functions which specifically stress wealth, not those which merely include a term for wealth in the regression.

The next section of this chapter deals with consumption functions which are part of an econometric model in contrast to the separately fitted consumption function discussed in the following section. The last section then summarizes the results.

Econometric Models

In 1955 Klein and Goldberger published their classic model.[7] Its consumption function uses lagged consumption, income broken down into labor income, property income and agricultural income, liquid assets, and population. Klein and Goldberger fitted their consumption function twice, once up to 1950 and a second time up to 1952. I have only projected the first of these, and then only for two years, because this allows me to use the data they provide. Since they use the same consumption function for both periods, it does not really matter which period one uses for a projection test.[8] And it turns out that both of the naïve models had smaller mean absolute errors than did the Klein-Goldberger function.[9]

In a subsequent paper dealing with the charge by Milton Friedman and Gary Becker that the consumption function forecasts worse than a naïve model, Klein fitted another consumption function, using population, income, and net worth.[10] This function, when projected, is superior to a naïve model.[11]

7. *An Econometric Model of the United States* (Amsterdam, North Holland Publishing Co., 1955).

8. It could be argued that it would be fairer to use in the test the coefficients obtained by fitting the function to the longer period, particularly since the shorter function contains relatively few postwar years. But the criterion that the function predict better than two naïve models is a very modest one, and even a function fitted to the period 1929–1950 should be able to meet it. In any case, due to substantial revisions of the National Income Accounts in 1954, one could not really use a projection test on the 1929–1952 variant of the function without rerunning the regression.

9. Recently Ronald Cooper has compared the fit over the period covered, as well as the predictive success, of the Klein-Goldberger consumption function with that of an autoregressive model. In both tests the autoregressive model was superior. Ronald Cooper, "The Predictive Performance of Quarterly Econometric Models of the United States," in Conference on Research in Income and Wealth, *Conference on Business Cycles,* forthcoming.

10. "The Friedman-Becker Illusion," *Journal of Political Economy,* Vol. LXVI, December 1958, pp. 539–45. Klein also gave another model in this paper, which used lagged income in place of wealth. I have not projected this model because it is so similar to several others I have projected.

11. In his test of various consumption functions, Michael Evans reran the Klein regression using a different period. Again, when I projected it, the

The next econometric model which does not disaggregate consumption into more than two components is the Duesenberry-Eckstein-Fromm model.[12] Its consumption function has a past peak income term as well as a lagged consumption term. I have not tested this model because of the availability of the later Fromm model discussed below.

The Gallaway and Smith model published in the following year predicted the change in consumption from the change in income and the money stock.[13] This consumption function does worse on a projection test (fitted for the period 1958 I to 1960 III) than does a naïve model.[14]

In a model published in the following year Gary Fromm used a complex consumption function. This function has been tested by H. O. Stekler. He found that it predicts consumption as accurately beyond the sample period as it does during the sample period, but that even during the sample period its prediction is slightly inferior to that of his naïve model.[15]

The next model, one by Miroshima and Saito, used current income, the money stock, and the capital stock lagged one year.[16] I could not project this consumption function since I could not extend the capital stock figure they used. What I did was to evaluate the fit of the function over the period for which it was fitted. Since this gives an undue advantage to the function, I used as a foil two naïve models which are stronger than the naïve models I used for the projection tests. One model consisted of regressing consumption on time alone, and the other of regressing consumption on time and on income. The latter naïve model performed just about as well as the Miroshima-Saito model, with

---

results were better than those of the naïve models despite the fact that I used revised data to test a function fitted to the unrevised data. (Evans gave both quarterly and yearly regressions. I tested only the yearly one.) See Michael Evans, "The Importance of Wealth in the Consumption Function," *Journal of Political Economy,* Vol. 75, August 1967, Part I, pp. 335–51.

12. "A Simulation of the United States Economy in Recession," *Econometrica,* Vol. 28, October 1960, pp. 749–819.

13. "A Quarterly Econometric Model of the United States," *Journal of the American Statistical Association,* Vol. 56, June 1961, pp. 379–83.

14. However, I am not certain that I projected their regressions correctly. Their paper does not give enough detail to let one know exactly what they did and this information is no longer available. In particular, the money series I used probably does not correspond exactly to the one they used.

15. H. O. Stekler, "Forecasting with Econometric Models: An Evaluation," *Econometrica,* Vol. 36, July–October 1968, pp. 449–50. Ronald Cooper's test (*loc. cit.*) also rejects this consumption function by showing that it fits, and predicts, worse than an autoregressive model.

16. "A Dynamic Analysis of the American Economy," reprinted in Arnold Zellner, *Readings in Economic Statistics and Econometrics* (Boston, Little Brown & Co., 1968), p. 684.

R^2 being respectively, 0.981 and 0.982. I will assume that such a trivial difference does not provide any evidence that the money stock and the capital stock belong in a consumption function, and that this consumption function therefore fails the test.

Paul Smith used a two-stage least-square technique to test the permanent income theory.[17] He fitted separate functions to quarterly data for durables and nondurables for the years 1946–1960. Although he used Friedman's weight for the individual years, his method of determining permanent income differs slightly from Friedman's, since for the peacetime years he did not use a 2 percent growth factor. Moreover, he used the conventional definition of consumption. His results gave strong support to the permanent income theory. For nondurable consumption, permanent income was highly significant while transitory income had the wrong sign and was not significant. For durable consumption, on the other hand, permanent income, though significant, had a much smaller regression coefficient than transitory income (0.86 versus 1.002). Although Smith got a good fit over the period he covered, his model fails to pass a projection test.[18]

Irwin Friend and Paul Taubman have published a very small econometric model, but since they themselves have expressed dissatisfaction with its consumption function, I have not tested it.[19] In any case, their consumption function performed worse on Cooper's test than did his autoregressive model.[20]

Another small model was fitted by Gregory Chow.[21] This model cannot be used in a prediction test because it was fitted up to the date of a

17. "The Demand for Durable Goods: Permanent or Transitory Income?" *Journal of Political Economy*, Vol. LXX, October 1962, pp. 500–04.

18. In projecting Smith's model, I departed from his formulation in two minor ways. First, unlike Smith, I did not use a 2 percent trend to get permanent income for the war years, but used the Friedman weights instead. But since for the years used in my projection the war years had a maximum weight of 4 percent, this difference is trivial. Second, while Smith deflated his system of equations by using the GNP deflator, I used the deflator for the consumption component of GNP.

19. "A Short-Term Forecasting Model," *Review of Economics and Statistics*, Vol. XLVI, August 1964, pp. 229–36. Since this model represents a revised version of an earlier model by Friend and Jones ("Short Run Forecasting Models Incorporating Anticipatory Data," Conference on Research in Income and Wealth, *Studies in Income and Wealth*, Vol. 28, *Models of Income Determination* (Princeton, Princeton University Press, 1964), I did not test the earlier model.

20. *Loc. cit.*

21. "Multiplier, Accelerator and Liquidity Preference in the Determination of National Income in the United States," *Review of Economics and Statistics*, Vol. XLIX, February 1967, pp. 1–15.

big data revision. I have therefore tested it in another way. For the postwar years he covered, 1948–1963, I ran a logarithmic regression of consumption on time. This is, of course, similar to predicting by a logarithmic trend, and hence is really a percentage growth naïve model. This trend model for the postwar period had a somewhat higher correlation coefficient than did Chow's regression for the longer period. (Admittedly such a comparison of correlation coefficients is not really proper since the two regressions do not have the same dependent variable due to the difference in the periods covered. In this chapter I am using only a rough preliminary screening test for consumption functions.)

Lawrence Klein fitted an econometric model using ordinary least-square, two-stage least-squares and limited information methods.[22] Due to the revision of the national income data I again could not project this model for three years and therefore had to look at its performance for the period over which it was fitted. Its mean errors in predicting consumption were greater than those of a rival naïve model which used income and time as independent variables.[23] And a more recent model which Klein fitted, and which also could not be projected beyond the period of fit, performed worse than even a 3 percent growth model fitted to the same period.[24]

In a model oriented specifically to the monetary sector Stephen Goldfeld used a lagged consumption function which indicated a short lag for total consumption.[25] I projected this model not for the usual three-year period, but only for six quarters to avoid the bias resulting from the major 1965 data revision. For this period it predicts seasonally unadjusted consumption better than the two naïve models. But this is hardly a fair test. Anyone predicting consumption from a naïve model —that is, without any real theory—would surely allow for the existence of seasonality, and would use a 3 percent growth trend to predict

22. "Problems in the Estimating of Interdependent Systems," in Herman Wold (ed.), *Model Building in the Social Sciences* (Monaco, Union Européenne d'Edition, 1967).

23. However, it did perform better than a 3 percent growth model over the period of fit. But when evaluating the performance of a function over the years for which it has been fitted, a 3 percent growth model is too naïve a naïve model. For those years a more rigorous test is called for. This failure to predict consumption well does not mean that Klein's model is bad as an overall model. In fact, in using this model to predict total consumption, I am placing it at a comparative disadvantage. Klein predicted not total consumption, but consumption of durables and nondurables separately, thus providing more information than my naïve model.

24. "Estimation of Interdependent Systems in Macroeconometrics," *Econometrica,* Vol. 37, April 1969, pp. 171–92.

25. *Commercial Bank Behavior and Economic Activity* (Amsterdam, North Holland Publishing Co., 1966).

seasonally *adjusted* consumption rather than unadjusted consumption. And both naïve models predict seasonally adjusted consumption (both deflated and undeflated) better than does Goldfeld's equation.[26]

Albert Ando and E. Cary Brown in a recent study fitted two consumption functions, one using only income and lagged consumption apart from seasonal dummies, the other adding net worth to these variables.[27] They did this twice, once using as their income concept seasonally unadjusted disposable income as defined in the National Income Accounts (that is, personal income minus income tax *payments*), and the other time using a different measure of disposable income, namely seasonally adjusted personal income minus income tax *liabilities*. Ando and Brown themselves projected their regressions for three years and the results for all the regressions are better—in all but one case substantially so—than either of the two naïve models I am using. The regression which predicts best is the one using seasonally adjusted personal income minus income tax *liabilities* as the income variable and including net worth. The companion equation without the net worth variable is the second best. Among the two equations using the conventional definition of disposable income, and seasonal dummies in place of seasonally adjusted data, the equation without the net worth term does best. One disheartening fact appears when one compares the regression coefficients. They differ sharply between the two types of regressions.[28] That treatment of seasonality and of income taxes can make such a big difference to the results is disconcerting.

One important issue raised by this study is obviously the proper definition of disposable income. Unfortunately, the results do not unequivocally show that it is tax liabilities rather than tax payments which should be used to derive disposable income for fitting a consumption function. This is so because the equations using tax liabilities and tax payments also differ in their treatment of seasonals, and the superiority of one set of regressions over the other *may* be due to this factor. Unfortunately, the

26. A similar conclusion was reached by Ronald Cooper, *loc. cit.*

27. "Personal Income Taxes and Consumption Following the 1964 Tax Reduction," in Albert Ando, E. C. Brown and A. Friedlaender (eds.), *Studies in Economic Stabilization* (Washington, D.C., Brookings Institution, 1968), pp. 127–33. They also used the same equations in a previous study, "Lags in Fiscal and Monetary Policy," in Commission on Money and Credit, *Stabilization Policies* (Englewood Cliffs, N.J., 1963), p. 119ff.

28. In the regressions with a net worth term, the income coefficient is .636 in one equation and .144 in the other, while the net worth coefficients are .031 and .008. The lagged consumption terms, too, differ radically. In the regressions without net worth term, the differences are also great, the income coefficients being .764 and .194, "Personal Income Taxes and Consumption Following the 1964 Tax Reduction," *op. cit.*, pp. 127, 132.

data which I have available to compare the various consumption functions in Chapter 9 do not allow me to experiment with income adjusted for tax liabilities.

In another study Ando and Goldfeld fitted separate consumption functions for durables and nondurables, the latter being similar to the Ando-Brown equation for total consumption just discussed.[29] For durables Ando and Goldfeld got a *negative* coefficient for net worth. They, therefore, used the money stock in place of net worth, and this variable had the right sign. Ando and Goldfeld were uncertain whether the money stock is important on its own account or serves merely as a proxy for wealth. I have not tested the predictive accuracy of this consumption function because it uses a hard-to-obtain series, seasonally unadjusted disposable income. Instead, I will use a modified form of their consumption function, one which does not require hard-to-get data, in Chapter 9.

This completes the evaluation of consumption functions used in econometric models. Many other econometric models exist, but they break down consumption into more than two parts.[30] The next section will therefore take up consumption functions fitted without a full scale model. Before leaving the econometric models, however, it might be worthwhile to emphasize that the rather discouraging results obtained relate only to their consumption function. Since these models are primarily concerned with predicting income rather than consumption, they may be useful even if their consumption function flunks a naïve model test. I now turn to consumption functions which are not part of full-scale econometric models.[31]

Tests Using Friedman's Permanent Income or the Koyck-Nerlove Transformation

In a notable article Zellner, Huang, and Chau compared the permanent income theory, a theory combining permanent income and con-

29. "An Econometric Model for Evaluating Stabilization Policies," in Albert Ando, E. C. Brown, A. Friedlaender (eds.), *Studies in Economic Stabilization, op. cit.*, pp. 219, 238.

30. This is done by the Federal Reserve-M.I.T. model, the Brookings model, the Wharton model, and the Department of Commerce model, among others. Since I wrote this chapter, an additional model has been published by Lester Thurow ("A Fiscal Policy Model of the U.S.," *Survey of Current Business*, June 1969, pp. 45–64). I have not tested his consumption function here, but have included it in the functions tested in Chapter 9.

31. I am excluding from this discussion a paper by Arnold Zellner and Martin Geisel ("Analysis of Undistributed Lag Models," *Econometrica*, Vol. 38, November 1970, pp. 865–89) since they are concerned primarily with evaluating different regression techniques for a Koyck function rather than with the consumption function per se. I am also not taking up the various

sumption inertia, and a habit persistence theory.[32] In addition, they introduced another variable, liquid assets. However, their regression equations perform worse than a naïve model.

In their detailed investigation of demand for individual commodities Houthakker and Taylor also discussed the consumption function briefly.[33] Their theoretical framework is a habit persistence theory combined with a stock effect. Accordingly, they fitted a consumption function to U.S. and Canadian data which included the lagged value of consumption. They were not satisfied with their results since the fit did not seem good, and in addition, their quartely and their yearly functions were inconsistent. They then fitted a permanent income function which measured the change in permanent income by assuming that it is proportional to the change in measured income, an assumption which they admitted "does not do justice to the permanent income hypothesis." [34] They obtained an unsatisfactory fit and concluded that "the permanent income theory is not the answer to the difficulties encountered in the preceding section." [35] However, as G. L. Perry pointed out, their derivation of the permanent income equation is invalid since it imposes a special and unwarranted restraint on the coefficient values.[36]

In the process of testing various consumption functions using wealth, Michael Evans fitted a consumption function which made the consumption-income ratio a function of the percentage increase in income and the

consumption functions fitted by Friedman and Becker ("A Statistical Illusion in Judging Keynesian Models," *Journal of Political Economy*, Vol. LXV, February 1957, pp. 64–75). Some of these consumption functions are very similar to permanent income functions which I am testing in Chapter 9 in any case, and others are too simple to be taken as representative of modern consumption functions. Similarly, I did not test some functions fitted by Daniel Suits ("The Determinants of Consumer Expenditures: A Review of Present Knowledge," in Commission on Money and Credit, *Impacts of Monetary Policy*, Englewood Cliffs, N.J., 1963, p. 38). Those of his equations which use income are similar to one I am using in Chapter 9.

32. "Further Analysis of the Short-Run Consumption Function with Emphasis on the Role of Liquid Assets," *Econometrica*, Vol. 33, July 1965, pp. 571–81.

33. *Consumer Demand in the United States, 1929–1970* (Cambridge, Mass., Harvard University Press, 1966).

34. *Ibid.*, p. 180.

35. *Ibid.*, p. 182.

36. "Consumer Demand in the United States (A Review Article)," *American Economic Review*, Vol. LVII, September 1967, p. 838. Perry also reran the Houthakker-Taylor regression for saving using the revised National Income Accounts. This equation predicts better than my naïve models, but since it is a savings function rather than a consumption function, I am not using it in Chapter 9.

consumption-income ratio of the previous period.[37] This function predicts better than a naïve model even though I used a function fitted to unrevised data to predict the consumption total shown in the revised Commerce data.

In an outstanding but unfortunately unpublished dissertation, the late Richard Halfyard fitted a Koyck-Nerlove transformation of the permanent income theory to annual data for the period 1929–1958.[38] This work is not well known, and so I will describe it in greater detail than the more readily accessible material. Unlike Friedman, Halfyard obtained a significant intercept, and even more importantly, his weights indicate a much shorter consumption lag than do Friedman's weights; 80 percent of the weight falls on the current year. This is not so surprising since, as discussed in Chapter 3, Friedman's fit appears to be very sensitive to the exact specification used. But it should be pointed out that Halfyard used the conventional definition of consumption, and departed from Friedman's technique in some ways.[39]

Halfyard went on to develop his own version of a permanent income theory. His version uses more of a general equilibrium framework than do others. He looked upon consumption as derived from the demand for a stock of consumption goods, and hence as a function of the previous period's stocks of consumption goods, production assets (including human capital), and claims assets (liquid assets) as well as on the relative prices of these items. This leads to a rather complex equation which he simplified to a function using the previous period's consumption expenditures, changes in the lagged stock of claims assets, the change in the price of production asset (both lagged and current), the change in the price of consumption assets, and time. Most of the weight in this equation is carried by the lagged consumption term and the time trend term. Since income does not enter directly, it is not really a conventional consumption function.

Halfyard tested his hypothesis employing the usual criteria (R^2, Durbin-Watson statistic, and Chow statistic). In addition he looked at the forecasting error by using a prediction test. He projected consumption one year beyond the period covered by his regression for sixteen postwar

37. "The Importance of Wealth in the Consumption Function," *Journal of Political Economy*, Vol. 75, August 1967, Pt. 1, pp. 335–52.

38. "The Determinants of Aggregate Consumption Expenditures in the United States, 1929–1961," unpublished Ph.D. dissertation, University of California at Los Angeles, 1964, pp. 94–96.

39. Halfyard fitted his function over a different (and shorter) period, and his Koyck-Nerlove transformation does not include Friedman's allowance for a secular 2 percent growth in permanent income. In fact, Halfyard criticized Friedman's use of a time trend as arbitrary.

Table 17

Evaluation of Consumption Functions

	Results of Tests	
Consumption Function Fitted by	*Passed*	*Failed*
1. Klein-Goldberger		x
2. Klein (*Journal of Political Economy*)	x	
3. Gallaway and Smith		x
4. Fromm		x[a]
5. Miroshima and Saito		x[b]
6. Klein (Wold book)		x[b]
7. Klein (*Econometrica*)		x
8. Friend and Taubman		x[c]
9. Smith		x
10. Chow		x
11. Goldfeld		x
12. Ando and Brown	x	
13. Ando and Goldfeld[d]		
14. Zellner, Huang, and Chau		x
15. Evans	x	
16. Halfyard		x[e]

[a] Tested by H. O. Stekler and by R. Cooper, not tested here.

[b] Fit is not better than that of a consumption function using only income and time.

[c] Tested by R. Cooper, not tested here.

[d] Not tested here.

[e] Halfyard's consumption function passes a three-year prediction test, but does badly in subsequent years.

years, 1946–1961. One of his variables, the price of production assets, had the wrong sign, though fortunately it was not significant. Halfyard attributed this to collinearity. He therefore modified his regression equation by eliminating the prices of production assets and consumption assets.

Halfyard's hypothesis passed the test extremely well. In the previous chapters of his dissertation he had tested many other consumption functions; the simple Keynesian theory in several variants, the relative income theory, and a Koyck-Nerlove version of the permanent income theory. The last of these consumption functions had performed best, and so Halfyard used it as a basis of comparison with his own hypothesis. In doing so he added a time variable to it to obtain a fair comparison with his own equation, which also has a time variable. Halfyard's hypothesis did well in this comparison.

Halfyard's model passes the prediction test since it does better than either naïve model. However, I will not carry his consumption function forward into Chapter 9 for another reason. I happened to project it up to 1967 and found that its prediction errors grew very rapidly.[40] To be sure, in doing this projection to 1967 I used the National Income Accounts after the major 1965 revision, whereas he had fitted his function to the unrevised data. If he had used revised data he would presumably have obtained different coefficients.[41] However, the error grows so rapidly that it is hard to believe that it is all due to the revision of the data.

Conclusion

Table 17 shows the results of the above tests. All but three of the functions tested performed worse than the naïve models, or failed another test, which is hardly encouraging. The performance of these consumption functions, many of which come from econometric models, raises a serious question about the usefulness of such models. But it is worth noting that my evaluation of these consumption functions is based on a rather arbitrary test.

Such an evaluation of consumption functions is certainly not new. George Craig recently dealt not with consumption functions but with the complements of consumption functions, savings functions.[42] He tested a large number of savings functions against naïve models by fitting the single-stage least-squares regression equations for each function to the same set of data and then used them to project saving. While the absolute income theory performed badly on these tests, the wealth theories generally performed well, but so did the relative income theories and some other habit persistence theories.

40. The prediction errors for the years 1962–1967 (inclusive) are, in billions of 1954 dollars: 2.8, 2.9, 5.5, 18.1, 20.1, 23.5.

41. It is worth remembering that the revisions were in part due to conceptual changes in the accounts. But in addition the Flow of Funds data I used had also been revised.

42. George Craig, "Predictive Accuracy of Quarterly and Annual Savings Functions," *Journal of the American Statistical Association*, Vol. 65, September 1970, pp. 1131–145. Many of the functions fitted at an earlier time were tested in two studies by Robert Ferber, *A Study of Aggregate Consumption Functions* (New York, National Bureau of Economic Research, 1953), and "The Accuracy of Aggregate Savings Functions in the Postwar Years," *Review of Economics and Statistics*, Vol. XXXVII, May 1955, pp. 134–48.

Eight

TIME SERIES CONSUMPTION FUNCTIONS STRESSING WEALTH

The previous chapter discussed a large number of consumption functions which did not use nonhuman wealth at all or did not place much stress on it. This chapter completes the evaluation of consumption functions by taking up those functions which emphasize nonhuman wealth. Since there are fewer of them, I can take them up in greater detail.

A very early example of using wealth in a formally fitted consumption function is the work of William Hamburger discussed in Chapter 2.[1] Hamburger started out from a framework where consumption is determined by total resources, with human resources measured as a function of the current wage rate, more specifically as a function of the *annual* wage rate. He made his own estimate of wealth because he wanted to use a measure of the market value of wealth including "goodwill," a factor which changes noticeably between prosperity and depression periods. He employed the "use" definition of consumption. His fit for the period 1929–1941 and 1947–1950 was good, and he got a significant coefficient for wealth.[2] But when he used the conventional definition of consumption, his function did not do much better than the

1. See William Hamburger, "Consumption and Wealth," unpublished Ph.D. dissertation, University of Chicago, 1951; "The Determinants of Aggregate Consumption," *Review of Economic Studies,* Vol. XXII, 1954–55, pp. 23–34; and "The Relation of Consumption to Wealth and the Wage Rate," *Econometrica,* Vol. 23, January 1955, pp. 1–17.

Earlier James Tobin had suggested that the secular stability of the consumption function may be due to a rise in the ratio of wealth to income, but he did not fit a consumption function. See his "Relative Income, Absolute Income, and Saving," in *Money, Trade and Economic Growth* (New York, Macmillan, 1951), pp. 152–56.

2. However, when extended beyond the period covered, the function predicted badly for 1951–52, a fact which Hamburger was concerned about. ("The Relation of Consumption to Wealth and the Wage Rate," *op. cit.,* p. 8.) But it is certainly possible that the Korean war was at least in part responsible for this.

Modigliani and Duesenberry functions, whereas with the "use" definition of consumption it had done very much better.[3]

This study was criticized by Richard Brumberg for its method of estimating the current wage rate in times of substantial unemployment.[4] What Hamburger had done was to estimate labor income on the basis of the average annual wage rate, a procedure which implies that as real wages rose in the depression, the expected income of the unemployed rose proportionately. I have not projected the Hamburger function because his measure of wealth is not available for years subsequent to his study; for this reason, I have not used it in Chapter 9 either.

In another early article published several years before the use of wealth in consumption functions became popular, L. G. Melville made the consumption-income ratio a function of the wealth-income ratio plus the same ratio squared.[5] He used the square of wealth because he saw no reason to assume linearity in the wealth-consumption relation, and because the inclusion of the squared term gave a good fit. He got a very high correlation for the period 1929–1940. The function also "predicted" consumption in the previous years 1921–1928 well, but, not surprisingly, it did less well for the period 1941–1952.

Compared to my two naïve models, Melville's function does worse than either of them for the abnormal period, 1941–1947, but it does better than either one for the more relevant period 1948–1950, or for that matter, even for the longer period 1948–1952. For the latter, his mean error is only 61 percent of that of the better of the two naïve models. Considering that by 1948 eight years had passed since the last year included in his regression, and that there had been so many changes in the economy, the fact that his function can beat the two naïve models is really amazing. Many much more sophisticated consumption functions fail to predict as well as a naïve model even for the three years following right on the period over which they were fitted.[6]

A more widely known consumption function using wealth is that of Alan Spiro discussed in Chapter 2.[7] His consumption function, which

3. "Consumption and Wealth," *op. cit.*, p. 19.

4. "Utility Analysis and Aggregate Consumption," unpublished Ph.D. dissertation, Johns Hopkins University, 1953, pp. 29n–30n. Brumberg mentioned this criticism as originating with Franco Modigliani and Arnold Harberger, but he did not give any source.

5. L. G. Melville, "Consumption, Income, and Wealth," *Review of Economics and Statistics,* Vol. XXXVI, May 1954, pp. 220–25.

6. The fact that Melville's function does not predict well for the disturbed period 1941–1947 is not, I think, serious. Consumption was affected by so many extraneous factors in this period that had the function given a good fit for this period this would be grounds for suspicion rather than congratulation.

7. Alan Spiro, "Wealth and the Consumption Function," *Journal of Political Economy,* Vol. LXX, August 1962, pp. 339–54.

involves regressing consumption on current and past income, employs the "use" definition of consumption and includes undistributed corporate earnings in income. Spiro's regression gave a good fit, explaining 70 percent of the variation in consumption left unexplained by the trend. The coefficient of determination, .98, "is as high as those generally obtained by other investigators" but uses up one less degree of freedom.[8] Moreover, using this function which was fitted for the period 1905–1949 to predict for the years 1950–1956 shows an average difference between actual and predicted consumption of slightly less than 3 percent, which Spiro considered a successful prediction. However, his forecast does not predict the inflection points in actual consumption. Although Spiro found a 3 percent error satisfactory, it is greater than that of the naïve models so that a projection test actually rejects this model.[9] In a follow-up article, Spiro deduced from this theory the implication that during a depression consumption will fall only if saving is negative.[10] The data confirm this implication.

Spiro's results have been challenged by Michael Evans.[11] Spiro had deflated income by a GNP deflator. This, Evans argued, is wrong: personal disposable income should be deflated by an index which measures its purchasing power over those items actually bought directly with it, that is, consumer goods and services. Moreover, the use of a consumers price index is implied in the usual neoclassical analysis, which takes the household's consumption as zero degree homogenous in consumer prices and incomes. Evans showed that the use of a national income deflator in place of a consumer's price deflator makes a substantial difference to the results and biases the sum of current and past year mpc's towards unity, the value hypothesized by Spiro's theory. When he reran the test using the consumer's price deflator the sum of the two coefficients differs significantly from unity in most of the regressions.[12]

8. *Ibid.*, p. 345.

9. When projected for just three years his function also does worse than my naïve models.

10. "The Direction of Change of Consumption During Business-Cycle Contractions," *Journal of Political Economy*, Vol. LXXI, October 1963, pp. 470–80.

11. Michael Evans, "The Importance of Wealth in the Consumption Function," *Journal of Political Economy*, Vol. 75, August 1967, Part I, pp. 335–51.

12. Richard Halfyard tested the Spiro function using the conventional definition of consumption and disposable income in place of Spiro's definitions. With these definitions the function did not perform well. See Richard Halfyard, "Determination of Aggregate Consumption Expenditures in the United States, 1929–1961," unpublished Ph.D. dissertation, University of California at Los Angeles, 1964, pp. 51–52.

Evans' criticism is important. Spiro's consumption function started out with a wealth term, but before fitting it to the data he transformed it into a function containing only current and past income. It is, therefore, similar to the permanent income theory's consumption function and differs from this function only in the particular set of weights used, the absence of an income trend, and in the fact that its origin as a wealth function imposes the requirement that the sum of the coefficients for current and past income is unity. There is nothing in the traditional version of the permanent income theory which denies that the sum of the coefficients is *close* to unity; hence to establish Spiro's conclusion, it is necessary to measure the sum of the coefficients very precisely. By throwing doubt on the precision of Spiro's estimates Evans has successfully challenged it. In addition, Evans argued, the marginal propensity to consume implied by the Spiro model is too low to be realistic. In any case, quite apart from Evans' criticisms, the Spiro model, as pointed out above, failed the projection test.

Another consumption function using wealth, which is similar in some ways to the Spiro function, is the Ball-Drake model discussed in Chapter 2.[13] Ball and Drake transformed their wealth function into one using current income and lagged consumption with the constraint that the sum of income and consumption coefficients should be unity. They fitted separate regressions for the United States for 1929–1941, 1946–1960 and 1929–1960 excluding the war years, and for Britain, 1950–1960. In each case they used single-stage as well as two-stage least-square regressions, thus obtaining eight different equations. I have projected their U.S. regression equations for three years, and for those regressions which included the postwar years their results are superior to those of the two naïve models.[14]

Their analysis, too, has been criticized by Michael Evans. One of his criticisms is the point just discussed; Ball and Drake, like Spiro, used a GNP deflator instead of a consumer price deflator. In addition, Evans introduced a growth variable into their function, and it turns out that their function, when combined with a realistic growth rate, implies an unrealistic value for the marginal propensity to consume, a value quite far removed from the one they actually found.[15] Evans also

13. R. J. Ball and Pamela Drake, "The Relationship Between Aggregate Consumption and Wealth," *International Economic Review,* Vol. 5, January 1964, pp. 63–81.

14. The same is true for the Ball and Drake type regressions fitted to somewhat different years by Michael Evans (*loc. cit.*) despite the fact that I tested the regressions which were fitted to the unrevised data by using revised data.

15. Michael Evans, *op. cit.,* p. 337. Ball and Drake also fitted another function using only the wealth of the personal sector. This test is too subject to the above criticism that they used the wrong deflector.

criticizes Ball and Drake because when one introduces growth into their model, it implies that the marginal propensity to consume durables is less than the average propensity.

The best-known consumption function using wealth is the Modigliani-Brumberg-Ando function. In their time series test of this theory, Ando and Modigliani used two different consumption functions.[16] One (called hypothesis I) makes consumption a function of current labor income, and start of period assets. The second function (hypothesis II) adds another variable to this function, namely labor income multiplied by the ratio of the labor force to employment. Both functions were fitted for the period 1929–1959 (excluding 1941–1946) using the following three specifications: (1) levels of the data, (2) first differences, and (3) variables expressed as a ratio of labor income. Finding that the constant term, though significant, is small and could be accounted for by simultaneous equation bias and measurement error, they decided to stick with their homogeneity assumption, and accordingly they reran the regressions suppressing the constant term. Since they were unable to avoid least-square bias they relied on the fact that in two of their estimating methods (the regressions of the levels and of first differences), least square bias tends to lower the coefficient of the asset term, and in their third method (the regression of the variables expressed as ratios to labor income) least square bias is in the opposite direction. Hence, they were able to bracket the true value of the asset coefficient. They got good results for the period covered by their regressions. They also reported on some tests they undertook for the years 1900–1928 (a period for which the data are bad) and their results were in rough agreement with their model.[17]

This paper has been criticized by Michael Evans, who pointed out that although this consumption function gives a good overall fit, it does extremely badly when fitted to quarterly data for the postwar years, the coefficient of the wealth-income ratio being only one eighth of its own standard error. Since the prewar years included cover the Great De-

16. Albert Ando and Franco Modigliani, "The 'Life Cycle' Hypothesis of Saving: Aggregate Implications and Tests," *American Economic Review*, Vol. LIII, March 1963, pp. 55–84, and "The 'Life Cycle' Hypothesis of Saving: A Correction," *American Economic Review*, Vol. LIV, March 1964, pp. 111–113. The same consumption function was also used in Albert Ando, E. C. Brown, R. M. Solow, and J. Kareken, "Lags in Fiscal and Monetary Policy," in Commission on Money and Credit, *Stabilization Policies* (Englewood Cliffs, N.J., Prentice-Hall, 1963), pp. 111–16.

17. However, for this period the coefficients were "on the low side" a fact which they explained by the possibility of an estate motive which "probably plays a non-negligible role at least for the high-income and/or self-employed groups." "The 'Life Cycle' Hypothesis of Saving: Aggregate Implications and Tests," *op. cit.*, p. 73.

pression, Evans suggested that wealth may be important in years of severe depression but not in years of relatively full employment.[18] The poor performance of the Ando-Modigliani model in the postwar period is corroborated in an unpublished study by G. S. Maddala.[19] On George Craig's prediction tests the performance of the two Ando-Modigliani regressions was mixed. In predicting levels of saving both of them were superior to the naïve model for the conventional definition of consumption and saving, but for the "use" concept of consumption and saving the naïve model was superior to one of them. In predicting first differences of saving, the naïve models did better than the Ando-Modigliani equations for the conventional definition and worse for the "use" definition.[20]

But quite apart from questions of fit and predictive power, the Ando-Modigliani study suffers from another weakness. This is that it does not really establish a *firm* case for the inclusion of wealth in the consumption function. Their analysis has a term for labor income, but no explicit term for property income. The effect of property income is picked up by the asset coefficient. This raises the question whether their coefficient for assets is not merely a disguised property income coefficient.

Ando and Modigliani discussed this question and raised two points. One is that when they ran a regression using property income in place of assets, the property income term did much worse than the assets term had done in the previous regressions; in fact the coefficient for property income was not significant. Hence, they argued, one can reject the hypothesis that assets serve merely as a proxy for property income. But this is doubtful. Consumption may depend upon *permanent* property income rather than upon current property income, and permanent property income may be measured better by the stock of assets than by current property income.[21]

Their second argument is that the rate of return on assets is less than their coefficient for the asset term. Hence, this coefficient must represent something else besides consumption out of property income. And even if one adjusts Ando and Modigliani's implausibly low estimate of in-

18. Michael Evans, *op. cit.*, pp. 346–49.

19. "Some Notes on Aggregate Savings Function," Stanford University Research Center in Economic Growth, *Memorandum No. 42*, pp. 44–51.

20. "The Predictive Accuracy of Quarterly and Annual Aggregate Saving Function," *Journal of the American Statistical Association*, Vol. 65, September 1970, p. 1138.

21. Ando and Modigliani regressed not levels of income and consumption but first differences instead. Hence, in their regression transitory income got an undue emphasis. It is therefore not surprising that the property income term did not do well.

come from property to take account of a bias, their asset term still seems bigger than consumption out of property income.[22]

But this whole analysis was changed very substantially by the work of Branson and Klevorick. They took the Ando-Modigliani model and tested it for a money illusion by adding a price term.[23] They found strong evidence for a money illusion, and the inclusion of a price level term reduced the asset coefficient from Ando and Modigliani's 0.06 to 0.024.[24] This figure is less than the yield on assets, and may therefore represent merely consumption out of property income rather than consumption of assets per se.

They then fitted another regression in which they used disposable personal income in place of labor income. The (logarithmic) assets term is still significant in this regression, with its value being 0.082.[25] It is by no means clear that such a coefficient for the wealth term actually represents consumption out of wealth. First, as mentioned above, assets may operate as a proxy for *permanent* property income. Second, since Branson and Klevorick used disposable personal income, they did not really include all property income in their income measure because corporate saving is excluded from disposable personal income, as is the imputed yield of a household's stock of durables.[26] If households treat corporate savings as part of their income, which is what is called for by the rationality assumption, then consumption of this imputed income may well account for what looks at first glance like consumption out of wealth per se.[27] Thus, it turns out that once one allows for a money

22. Ando and Modigliani estimated the (after tax) rate of return on assets as 0.04 percent or less (*ibid.*, p. 75). But this is a bad estimate because they omitted corporate saving and the imputed income from the consumer's stock of durables from the return on assets, although they included consumer durables in the stock of assets.

23. W. H. Branson and A. K. Klevorick, "Money Illusion and the Aggregate Consumption Function," *American Economic Review*, Vol. LIX, December 1969, pp. 832–50. Branson and Klevorick used the Ando-Modigliani model without the employment term.

24. *Ibid.*, p. 841.

25. *Ibid.*, p. 842, and private communication.

26. Since Branson and Klevorick followed Ando and Modigliani in employing the "use" definition of consumption, they included the imputed yield from durables in consumption. It should therefore be included in income, too.

27. A "back of envelope" calculation suggests that exclusion of corporate saving and imputed income from durables might well account for the asset term. The 0.082 elasticity coefficient implies a marginal propensity to consume wealth of about 0.014. Corporate saving equaled 0.011 percent of wealth in the terminal year of the study. Imputed income from consumer durables equaled about 0.004 or so of wealth, so that property income is understated by about 0.015. Consumption of 0.014 out of 0.015 is not un-

illusion, the Ando-Modigliani function does not really provide any evidence for consumption out of assets per se. (I have not run the Branson-Klevorick model against my naïve models, but have tested it in the following chapter.)

In a paper which was unfortunately completed too late for me to treat adequately, Balvir Singh and Ramesh Kumar fitted a modified Ando-Modigliani function in which expected income is treated as not necessarily proportional to actual income.[28] Instead Singh and Kumar allowed for a more complex expectations formation mechanism wherein expected labor income depends on the growth rate and on the rate of change of income from the previous period. Due to data problems they substituted private disposable income for Ando and Modigliani's labor income. Hence measured property income is included in their income term so that their wealth term is less suspect than is Ando and Modigliani's. And their wealth coefficient, approximately 0.06, is highly significant. It is large enough to make it hard to argue that it picks up permanent as opposed to measured property income. There is, however, another difficulty with their analysis. When consumer durables are included in consumption (but not when they are excluded), their fit is trivially worse than that of Ando and Modigliani. Since the difference is trivial this would be relatively harmless except for the fact that Singh and Kumar selected their expectations function from among several alternatives on the basis of its fit. One would, therefore, expect their chosen function to fit better than the Ando-Modigliani function. Hence Singh and Kumar have not really established a firm case for the significance of the wealth coefficient if one uses the conventional definition of consumption.

Starting with a model similar to the Modigliani-Brumberg-Ando model, Arena made consumption depend on current income, net worth, capital gains, age of the population, and the distribution of these variables.[29] His results support a wealth model. The coefficients of net worth are strongly positive and significant, ranging from .03 to .05.

I have not projected Arena's regressions because at the time I could not locate data for one of his independent variables, household net worth, for subsequent years.[30] Instead, I compared the fit of his function

---

reasonable when one considers the standard error of the elasticity. This suggests that had income not been understated in these two ways, then the asset term of 0.082 could well have been zero.

28. "On the Ando-Modigliani Consumption Function," unpublished manuscript.

29. "The Wealth Effect and Consumption: A Statistical Inquiry," *Yale Economic Essays,* Vol. 3, No. 2, 1963, pp. 251–303.

30. Only after doing the work described above did I find out that such data are available from the Federal Reserve-M.I.T.-Penn Model.

with that of the 3 percent growth model for the last three years over which he fitted his function.[31] The naïve model was superior. However, this superiority could reflect merely the peculiarity of the particular years chosen; in these years, the naïve model was extraordinarily accurate. I therefore extended the comparison to all the available postwar years, which (since the naïve model loses a year) means 1947–1958. Evaluating the fit of a regression by looking at the errors during the period over which it was originally fitted, does, of course, create a favorable bias for the regression. Even so, the Arena model was not clearly superior to the 3 percent growth model. For the whole period 1947–1958 it was superior to the naïve model, but if one excludes the year 1947 (which the naïve model had to forecast on the basis of the abnormal year 1946) the naïve model is somewhat superior.[32] Since one can expect of a sophisticated model that it does *clearly* better than a naïve model, I conclude, somewhat arbitrarily, that Arena's model failed the test.

Harold Lydall fitted a saving function using wealth for the U.S. 1920–1941, Great Britain 1948–1960, and Australia 1948–1949 to 1961–1962.[33] In these periods the saving ratio shows no trend in the United States, an upward trend in Britain, and a downward trend in Australia. Hence he asked the wealth model to explain a wide variety of different patterns. His function was a very simple one expressing the percent of income saved (including durable goods purchases) as a function of only the wealth-income ratio. His R^2 was very high in all three cases and the wealth coefficient was highly significant, being $-.0656$ for the U.S., $-.0368$ for Britain, and $-.2407$ for Australia. But according to Michael Evans this study suffers from a serious weakness. As in the case of the Ball-Drake study, the actual rate of growth is not consistent with the saving-income ratio implied by the model.[34]

It is not reasonable to test this model by the usual projection test of extrapolating its prediction for three additional years for the U.S. since these were war years. I have therefore projected it backwards covering the three years preceding the period over which it was fitted, 1914–1916. It performed better than my naïve models.[35]

31. Arena fitted many regressions. I used only one of them, the one which fits best into his theory.

32. Since Arena did not give a table showing his predicted consumption for each year, I had to read the predicted values off his chart. While this creates some inaccuracy, I do not believe that it affects the result.

33. H. F. Lydall, "Saving and Wealth," *Australian Economic Papers*, Vol. 2, December 1963, pp. 228–50.

34. Private communication.

35. Since the Lydall model predicts not the level of saving but the saving-income ratio, I had to modify the two naïve models. One of them implies

Wealth is also used in G. S. Maddala's consumption function.[36] Maddala first regressed personal saving as a percent of disposable income on net private wealth as a proportion of disposable income, on employee compensation as a proportion of personal income as well as on the employment rate. While the last two variables did badly, wealth did very well, except in the postwar period when (in the regression omitting the two badly performing variables) its coefficient was less than its standard error. Maddala explained this bad result for the postwar period as follows:

The reason for the failure of this function to perform well in the postwar period is not hard to see. During the postwar period the share of consumer expenditures on durable goods (and housing) has risen as compared with the earlier period. Now, if wealth is a proxy for permanent income the effect of wealth on consumer expenditures on durable goods is ambiguous in the short run. . . . The higher the value of Yp or W the higher will be [the desired stock of durables] and hence, the larger will be the desired change. However . . . transitory income . . . affects savings part of which will take the form of a change in the stock of durable goods. The higher the level of permanent income, *relative to current income,* the lower will be this (unanticipated) change, in the stock. Thus . . . the effect of permanent income or wealth is ambiguous: it is a combination of the positive effect on desired stock . . . and a negative effect through transitory income.[37]

Thus Maddala appears to treat wealth as relevant, not for its own sake, but merely because it is a proxy for permanent income. Note, however, that even if wealth is relevant per se, the rise in consumer durables may account for the function doing badly since the data discussed above exclude consumer durables from wealth.

Maddala therefore redefined saving to include consumer durable expenditures minus depreciation on durables. This gives a better fit for the postwar period. Maddala concluded that "if we are to single out any single variable in terms of which the personal savings ratio is a stable function, it is the [wealth/disposable personal income ratio]. . . . This simple equation, however, is quite useless for predicting the postwar savings ratio—if we define savings as disposable personal income minus total consumer expenditures." [38] Since Maddala's model does not give a good fit for consumption defined to include the purchase of durables (the concept stressed in this book), I have rejected it without using a projection test.

---

that the current saving-income ratio is equal to last year's, and the other implies that it is equal to the average ratio of the previous five years.

36. *Op. cit.,* pp. 8–22.
37. *Ibid.,* pp. 19–21. Italics added.
38. *Ibid.,* pp. 21–22.

Another test of wealth models was undertaken by Richard Halfyard. He tested several functions not only by looking at their fit but also by seeing how well they predict for years beyond the time span covered by the regressions. He found that:

Total private nonhuman wealth and consumer nonhuman wealth add little to the predictive power or stability of the traditional consumption function. The inclusion of liquid assets gives mixed results: improvements of the fit, but poorer predictions. Expected income with its implicit inclusion of the return from human wealth as well as from nonhuman wealth seems to contribute to both prediction and fit.[39]

Although permanent income did perform better than nonhuman wealth, this conclusion, as Halfyard pointed out, is subject to one qualification; he used the conventional definition of consumption and defined income as disposable personal income. It is possible that had he used the definitions favored by Ando and Modigliani he would have obtained better results from the wealth model. Nonetheless, this test is an important rejection of the wealth hypothesis for my purposes, since I too am using the conventional definition of consumption.

To conclude this discussion, Table 18 summarizes the results of the projection tests. It shows that three of the six consumption functions tested pass this test. The fact that three wealth-type consumption functions predict better than a naïve model suggests that wealth may well have an effect on consumption.

But this favorable conclusion for the wealth models is subject to two qualifications. First, several wealth models did fail the projection test.[40] Second, the wealth-type consumption functions tested by Halfyard performed badly.[41] Third, the fact that a wealth function does better than simple naïve models is a necessary, but not a sufficient, condition for the validity of these wealth models. In addition to facing competition from naïve models, wealth-type consumption functions also face compe-

39. Richard Halfyard, *op. cit.,* p. 62.
40. The fact that some wealth functions do better than the naïve models and some do worse raises a nasty problem of interpretation. On the one hand, one could argue that the failure of some functions is due to their bad specification, and that this fact should not be taken as a reflection on the other wealth functions. But this is too easy a way out. If one tries enough specifications purely at random, it is likely that a few of them will outperform the naïve models regardless of the validity of wealth approach. It is incorrect to argue that the number of failures shown in Table 18 is not sufficient for this to be a real danger. It is quite possible that many other consumption functions using wealth have been fitted, and that they have not been published because they gave bad fits.
41. Halfyard tested different wealth models than I did because he did not focus on specific models presented in the literature, but instead added wealth variables to the usual consumption function variables.

Table 18

Evaluation of Wealth Functions

Consumption or Saving Function Fitted by	Results of Tests		
	Passed	Failed	Not Tested
1. Hamburger			x^a
2. Melville	x		
3. Spiro		x	
4. Ball and Drake	x		
5. Ando and Modigliani		x^b	
6. Arena		x^c	
7. Lydall	x		
8. Maddala			x^d

[a] Not tested because its wealth measure is not available.

[b] Mixed performance on Craig's test. Also bad fits for postwar period.

[c] This function was tested, not by projecting it, but by comparing its fit for part of the period over which it was fitted with naïve models. To say that it failed the test is somewhat arbitrary, it is a marginal case.

[d] Not tested since for the postwar period the coefficient of wealth is less than its standard error for the conventional definition of consumption.

tition from other consumption functions, such as functions using liquid assets, or permanent income, instead of wealth. It is instructive at this point to look at recent work on the demand for money. This work has shown that wealth explains the demand for money better than *measured* income. But this, in and of itself, does not confirm a wealth theory of the demand for money because permanent income also does better than measured income and *may* be superior to wealth; this issue is still unsettled. The real test for a wealth function, therefore, is not whether it is significant and performs better than a naïve model, but whether it performs better than some of the other consumption functions which have been fitted. This is the problem to be taken up in the next chapter.[42]

42. Note added in proof: Since the above was written, Franco Modigliani has presented additional evidence on the importance of wealth. Since the wealth coefficient was significant in his regression despite the fact that he used disposable personal income in place of disposable labor income, the wealth term cannot be treated as just a proxy for current property income. However, it could still be a proxy for permanent property income, though this may not be very plausible. (See Franco Modigliani, "Monetary Policy and Consumption," Federal Reserve Bank of Boston, *Consumer Spending and Monetary Policy: The Linkages* [Boston, Federal Reserve Bank of Boston, n. d.] p. 14.)

Nine

AGGREGATE TIME SERIES REGRESSIONS

This chapter has two purposes. The first is to test the standard income theory by regressing consumption on current and lagged income. The second is to complete the work of the two previous chapters by letting the surviving consumption functions, as well as certain other functions, compete against each other in a prediction test.

In fitting the regressions I did not use the Goldsmith data which Friedman used because more recent income and consumption figures have now become available. For the first part of the chapter, where my data go back to 1897, I have combined for the earlier years various estimates into consistent series.[1] In the second part of the chapter, dealing only with the postwar years, I used the standard, Department of Commerce, data.

Estimating the Lag

Any attempt to estimate the consumption function lag by regressing time series runs into the problem that we do not really have a good method of estimating lags in series which are as highly autocorrelated

1. The most recent secular income series is the NNP series published by John Kendrick. Unfortunately, a corresponding disposable personal income series is not available. To get disposable personal income for 1897–1920 I combined the Kendrick and the Goldsmith series by using Kendrick's estimate of NNP and the Goldsmith estimates of the difference between NNP and disposable personal income. For the period 1920–1928 I used Barger's estimate of disposable personal income and for subsequent years the Department of Commerce figures. I deflated both income and consumption prior to 1929 by Kendrick's GNP deflator, and from 1929 on, by the Department of Commerce deflator for the personal consumption component of GNP. (See John Kendrick, *Productivity Trends in the United States,* Princeton, Princeton University Press, 1961, pp. 296–97; Raymond Goldsmith, *A Study of Saving in the United States* [Princeton, Princeton University Press, 1955], Vol. 3, p. 429.) The Barger data are unpublished and I am grateful to Professor Barger and the National Bureau of Economic Research for making them available.

as are income and consumption. As Griliches has pointed out, instead of letting the data select the lag, one should obtain the lag a priori and then use the data, not to *estimate* the lag, but to *test* it.[2] But unfortunately, the standard income theory provides no way of estimating the lag a priori. To be sure, one can estimate the lag as I have done in Chapter 13 from household budgets and then see if this lag is confirmed by time series data. But even so, it is tempting to allow the time series regression to choose its own lag. This is the case because just about any lag pattern one uses will give a good fit in the sense of a high correlation coefficient and high *t* values. The question clearly is not whether these measures are significant at the 1 percent level, but whether they indicate that the lag pattern tested is better than alternative lag patterns.

There exist many techniques of lagged regressions, but there is little agreement about which is the best. This leaves two choices. One is to undertake basic research in econometrics to determine the best method of lagged regressions; the other is to try several techniques. Since my lack of the requisite abilities precludes the first of these, I have opted for the use of several methods. The three I chose are Fisher's method (ordinary least squares), the Cagan-Friedman exponentially declining weights technique, and finally, the polynomial lag technique developed by Dale Jorgenson.

Table 19 shows the results of regressing consumption on the incomes of the current and previous years.[3] Since the data prior to 1929 are much less reliable than the subsequent data, Table 19 shows the results separately for the whole period and for 1929–1968. In both cases there is only a short lag. The first year has about three quarters of the weight. In these regressions the coefficients are unconstrained, and unfortunately, they take advantage of this liberty. Some of the coefficients are (insignificantly) negative, a fact which makes little economic sense. Moreover, in a number of regressions the coefficients at first fall and then rise again; and this, too, is hard to accept.

The obvious answer to this difficulty is to constrain the coefficients. But eliminating the seemingly unreasonable behavior of some coefficients cannot be done, of course, without cost; by constraining the coefficients one may cover up some of the true behavior of consumption.

Table 20 shows the results of constraining the coefficients by imposing

2. Zvi Griliches, "Distributed Lags: A Survey," *Econometrica*, Vol. 35, January 1967, p. 46.
3. The work of actually fitting all the regressions was done by Mr. Hal Varian, using the University of California, Berkeley, computer and the T.S.P. and P.D.L. programs. In adition to the methods listed above, a nonlinear regression method, using a Gaussian approximation to the Cagan-Friedman regression was tried, but it was not successful.

Table 19

Results of Ordinary Least-Square Regressions*

Regression	Coefficients of Income with Lag of (Years)						t Value of Coefficients						R^2	Durbin-Watson Stat.	Percent Distribution of Coefficients					
	0	1	2	3	4	5	0	1	2	3	4	5			0	1	2	3	4	5
1897–1968																				
Current Year	.891						99.5						.9952	1.1	100					
1 Year Lag	.697	.204					11.0	3.1					.9960	.9	77	23				
2 Years Lag	.701	.118	.086				11.1	1.2	1.3				.9961	1.0	78	13	10			
3 Years Lag	.701	.120	.035	.050			11.0	1.3	.4	.8			.9962	1.0	77	13	4	6		
4 Years Lag	.689	.120	.040	−.054	.118		11.1	1.3	.4	−.7	2.0		.9965	.8	75	13	4	−6	13	
5 Years Lag	.692	.111	.049	−.058	.080	.039	11.2	1.2	.5	−.7	1.2	1.1	.9966	.9	76	12	5	−6	9	4
1929–1968																				
Current Year	.876						80.2						.9966	1.1	100					
1 Year Lag	.668	.210					7.9	2.5					.9974	1.1	76	24				
2 Years Lag	.689	.081	.111				8.0	.6	1.2				.9975	1.1	78	9	13			
3 Years Lag	.680	.132	−.035	.110			8.1	.9	−.3	1.4			.9978	1.0	77	15	−4	12		
4 Years Lag	.690	.130	−.057	.160	−.040		7.8	.9	−.4	1.2	−.5		.9978	1.1	78	15	−6	18	−5	
5 Years Lag	.682	.139	−.055	.170	−.093	.043	7.4	.9	−.4	1.2	−.7	.5	.9978	1.2	77	16	−6	19	−10	5

* Excluding 1917, 1918, 1942–1947.

Table 20

Results of Friedman-Cagan Regression Technique*

	I. WITH CONSTANT						II. WITHOUT CONSTANT			
Beta	R^2	Sum of Squared Residual	Coefficient of Income	Constant[b]	t Value of Constants	Durbin-Watson Statistic	R^2	Sum of Squared Residual	Coefficient of Income	Durbin-Watson Statistic
.10	.9796		.997	−12.1	−.5	.4	.9795		.988	.4
.15	.9829		.989	−10.5	−.5	.4	.9829		.981	.4
.20	.9852		.980	−7.5	−.4	.5	.9851		.975	.5
.25	.9866		.971	−3.9	−.2	.5	.9866		.968	.5
.30	.9876		.963	−.3	0	.6	.9876		.963	.6
.35	.9882		.956	3.3	.2	.6	.9882		.958	.6
.40	.9887		.949	6.5	.4	.6	.9887		.954	.6
.45	.9891		.944	9.5	.6	.6	.9890		.950	.6
.50	.9893		.939	12.3	.7	.7	.9892		.947	.7
.55	.9895		.934	14.7	.9	.7	.9894		.944	.7
.60	.9896		.931	17.1	1.1	.7	.9895		.943	.7
.65	.9898		.927	19.1	1.2	.7	.9895		.940	.7
.70	.9898		.924	20.9	1.3	.7	.9896	124132[a]	.939	.7
.75	.9899	120296	.921	22.7	1.4	.8	.9896	124156	.937	.8
.80	.9899	120009	.919	24.3	1.5	.8	.9895		.936	.8
.85	.9899	120034	.917	25.7	1.6	.8	.9895		.934	.8
.90	.9899	119960[a]	.915	27.0	1.7	.9	.9894		.933	.8
.95	.9899	120182	.913	28.2	1.8	.9	.9894		.932	.8
1.00	.9899	120310	.911	29.2	1.8	.9	.9893		.931	.8

* Years covered: 1898–1968, with 1917–1918 and 1942–1946 excluded.
[a] Best fit.
[b] In 1958 dollars per capita.

on the data exponentially declining weights as well as a 2 percent trend —in other words, using the Cagan-Friedman lagged regression method but treating the war years differently as described in Chapter 3. The table shows the goodness of fits obtained for various values of beta running from 0.10 to 1.00 in steps of 0.05. For the regressions including a constant, the coefficients of determination reach a peak of 0.9899, which is shared by all beta values from 0.75 to 1.00. However, it is possible to distinguish between these fits by looking at the sum of the squared residuals, which show that the best fit is obtained for a beta of 0.9. If one follows Friedman and excludes the constant from the regression, then the best fit is obtained for a beta value of 0.7. By contrast, Friedman estimated beta as 0.4. But as pointed out in Chapter 3, this value depends upon the treatment of the war years. An alternative treatment to Friedman's yields a beta value of 0.75 or 0.8 if a constant is included in the regression and 0.5 if there is no constant.

Since he estimated beta as 0.4, Friedman's regression implied a mean lag of two and one-half years. By contrast, the best fitting beta values of Table 20 imply a mean lag of only 1.1 years, if a constant is included in the regression and 1.4 years if the constant is excluded. The proportion of the total weight going to the first year in the best regression is 59 percent if a constant is included in the regression and 50 percent if the constant is excluded. In addition, the constant term is significant at the 10 percent level (two-tailed test).[4] Even so, the constant term is quite small and of little *economic* significance. It is certainly much smaller than the constant term one obtains from the absolute income theory. All of these results are, of course, subject to an important proviso; my treatment of the war years, like Friedman's, is essentially arbitrary. Hence it is not really possible to choose between these two divergent results.

The final regression technique I used is Jorgenson's polynomial lag method with a second degree lag.[5] Here, as in the case of the ordinary least-square regressions, the coefficients are unrestrained. Hence, the results shown in Table 21 contain two implausible elements. Some of the coefficients are negative (a few of them significantly so), and in addition the last year's coefficient always exceeds the previous year's

4. When Friedman included a constant term in his regression, it turned out to be negative and only one quarter of its standard error (*A Theory of the Consumption Function,* Princeton, Princeton University Press, 1957), p. 147n.

5. This is the technique used by Jorgenson in his studies of investment. See for instance, his "Anticipations and Investment Behavior," in J. Duesenberry, G. Fromm, L. Klein, and E. Kuh, *The Brookings Quarterly Econometric Model* (Chicago, Rand McNally, 1965), pp. 33–92.

Table 21

Results of Polynomial Distributed
Lag Regressions*

Function	Coefficient of Income	t Value of Coefficient	Percent Weight of Coefficient	R^2	Durbin-Watson Statistic
3 Year Function				.9953	.7
Current Year	.763	8.5	82		
1 Year Lag	−.055	0.4	−6		
2 Year Lag	.221	2.4	24		
5 Year Function				.9958	.7
Current Year	.639	14.3	68		
1 Year Lag	.206	8.9	22		
2 Year Lag	−.019	−.5	−2		
3 Year Lag	−.038	−1.7	−4		
4 Year Lag	.150	3.2	16		
7 Year Function				.9973	1.2
Current Year	.519	18.5	67		
1 Year Lag	.266	26.7	34		
2 Year Lag	.083	5.1	11		
3 Year Lag	−.030	−1.5	−4		
4 Year Lag	−.072	−4.3	−9		
5 Year Lag	−.044	−3.1	−6		
6 Year Lag	.055	1.7	7		
9 Year Function				.9968	1.2
Current Year	.461	18.5	56		
1 Year Lag	.272	25.3	33		
2 Year Lag	.124	12.0	15		
3 Year Lag	.018	1.2	2		
4 Year Lag	−.047	−2.7	−6		
5 Year Lag	−.070	−4.5	−9		
6 Year Lag	−.052	−4.3	−6		
7 Year Lag	.007	.4	1		
8 Year Lag	.108	3.3	13		

* Function fitted is second degree function; 1917–1918, 1942–1947 excluded.

coefficients. Neither of these peculiarities have economic meaning. Leaving these problems aside, the polynomial regressions show that a substantial proportion of the weight goes to the current year's income. This weight varies from 82 percent for the three year regression to 56 percent in the nine year regression. The fact that the first year's weight declines consistently as one lengthens the number of years included in the regression may seem to support the permanent income theory, since regressions fitted to still longer periods might reduce the first year's weight to 33 percent. But this support is deceptive. If one adds the weights of the first two years, it turns out that in all of the regressions the first *two* years account for most of the weight. Moreover, the proportion of the total weight accounted for by the first two years does not decline as one adds more years to the regression.[6]

To summarize these results, the ordinary least-square regressions as well as some of polynomial regressions attribute about three-quarters of the weight to the current year, while the Cagan-Friedman regression as well as the longer polynomial regressions attribute around 60 percent of the weight to the current year. These results are roughly in agreement with those obtained for the Swiss data in Chapter 13, and they support the standard income theory rather than the strict permanent income theory.

But while these results are favorable for the standard income theory, one cannot really say that time series regressions in general confirm the standard income theory and reject the strict permanent income theory. This is so because some other time series regressions support the strict permanent income theory. In an unpublished study Paul Mu fitted a Cagan-Friedman type regression with an additional term to catch autocorrelation and obtained results which are very similar to Friedman's.[7] Second, as discussed in Chapter 3, Friedman's treatment of the war years, which is just as legitimate as the one I used, yields his results. On the other hand, George Fishman, Gregory Chow, and Richard Levitan, and Philip Howrey, using spectral analysis, found a short lag.[8] Thus, various time series regressions give different results, and in the present state of the art, it is not really possible to choose between them.[9]

6. The sum of the weights for the first two years in the various regressions starting with the two year regressions are: 76 percent, 90 percent, 101 percent, and 89 percent.

7. "A Study of the Long Run Consumption Lag," unpublished Ph.D. dissertation, University of California, Davis, 1971, p. 131. In Mu's regression, when made comparable to Friedman's, the first three years obtain the following weights: 37 percent, 23 percent and 15 percent. Friedman's weights are 33 percent, 22 percent and 15 percent.

8. George Fishman, *Spectral Methods in Econometrics* (Cambridge, Harvard University Press, 1969), chap. 5; Gregory Chow and Richard Levitan, "Nature of Business Cycles Implicit in a Linear Economic Model," *Quarterly Journal of Economics*, Vol. LXXXIII, August 1969, p. 515; E. Phillip Howrey, "Stochastic Properties of the Klein-Goldberger Model," *Econometrica*, Vol. 39, January 1971, p. 82.

9. I would like to propose the following research project: Take a half dozen leading methods of estimating lagged relationships and use them to determine the mean lag of a dozen economic time series picked at random. Then compare the variance of the lags found when the identical time series is analyzed by the six methods with the variance of the lags found by each method when it is applied to the dozen different time series. I venture the guess that the variance will be greater for the different methods applied to the same data than for the same method applied to different time series. If

But if, as a result of this, the time series evidence does not firmly support the standard income theory against the permanent income theory, it certainly does not support the permanent income theory against the standard income theory either.

Prediction Test

To regress consumption on current and past income does not suffice to establish the standard income theory. To do so it is necessary to compare it with the consumption functions which survived the naïve model tests of the two previous chapters, and with various other wealth theories. Such a comparison should not be confined simply to contrasting correlation coefficients. This is so for two reasons. First, theories should not be tested against the same data which were used to formulate them, and second, the correlation coefficients obtained from time series tests of consumption functions are generally so high that there usually is little meaningful difference between them. Instead, the proper test is to fit the various consumption functions to the same set of data, and then have them predict consumption in years not included in the period of fit.

The specific prediction test I used covered only the years 1954–1968. I decided to use only the postwar years because the prewar data are less reliable and because the 1930s were clearly very unusual years.[10] Unfortunately, I could not obtain a consistent wealth series for the whole postwar period and had to drop the years prior to 1954.[11] The way I used the fifteen years of available data was to fit the consumption functions for various combinations of twelve years, and then to let the regressions fitted to these twelve data points predict consumption in all the available consecutive three year periods which could be obtained by varying the twelve years included in the regression. This generated "eleven" runs of three year predictions.[12] Unfortunately, for the life cycle hypothesis I had only twelve years of data since labor income after tax is not available for 1966–1968. Here the regressions covered only nine years, and I obtained only eight prediction runs. The life cycle

---

this guess turns out to be correct it would suggest that the lag one finds is more a matter of ones estimating technique than of what the data actually show.

10. For example, bank failures reduced wealth in the early 1930s. However, unless one knows to what extent the public believed that deposits in closed banks were permanently lost, one cannot determine the change in perceived wealth. And the stock market decline creates a similar problem.

11. I am indebted to the Federal Reserve System for providing the wealth figures used in FRB-MIT-Penn model.

12. The regressions were fitted by Hal Varian and Roozbeh Chubak using the T.S.P. program on the University of California, Berkeley, computer.

hypothesis is clearly formulated in terms of "use" consumption. I therefore used in this consumption concept these regressions and projections.

This procedure is, of course, subject to several qualifications. First, I used only a single equation approach, and hence the results are subject to bias. In particular, those regressions which stress current income are given an unfair advantage. My only defense is the rather inadequate one that to build complete econometric models for all the consumption functions would have been an insuperable task. The second weakness is that the regressions are fitted to so few years. My use of twelve years (and nine years for the life cycle hypothesis) is somewhat arbitrary. Alternatively, I could have used more years in the regressions by letting the regressions predict only one year's consumption. However, the ability to predict just one year would not have provided a very good test of the theories. Admittedly, the choice between predicting for too few years on the one hand, and on the other hand fitting the regressions to too few years, is not an easy one, and there is no obvious way of deciding between them.

A third problem is that I used the standard consumption and income data given in the National Income Accounts. As discussed in Chapter 4, Taubman has shown that other equally defensible consumption and income data yield different results. Since there is only a relatively small difference in the predictive accuracy of the various consumption functions I am testing, it is quite possible that had I used different consumption and income data, I would have obtained a different ranking of various consumption functions.

A fourth weakness is that I could not test various consumption functions in exactly the same form as their proponents did. I had to use the same set of data for all the functions I tested. But to do this I had to transform many of the functions, since their forms differed. Some were in aggregate terms, some in per capita terms, and some in ratio form. Moreover, while several had been fitted to yearly data, others had been fitted to quarterly data. In addition, while most functions had been fitted in natural numbers and constant dollars, one function had originally been fitted in logarithms and another had been fitted in current dollars. And the deflators used were not always the same. I fitted all the functions to yearly data in per capita real terms (using the GNP consumption deflator). In addition, I used the same measure of wealth for all functions, rather than the particular wealth measure relevant for each theory. Thus the poor results obtained for some consumption functions *may* not reflect a weakness of that theory, but may merely be the result of my transformation.[13] This is unfortunate, but the only alterna-

13. This is particularly the case for the Branson-Klevorick function, which is in logarithmic form and quarterly. In using annual data I had to approx-

tive—fitting all the functions to various specifications—would have been much too time-consuming.

Tables 22 and 23 show the results of this test. For each of the consumption functions, they show whether the signs of the coefficients are as predicted and give the coefficient of determination (corrected for degrees of freedom), the mean absolute error, the root mean square error, and the relative ranking of these functions by the two error measures.[14] Finally, they show, *for the functions with the correct signs,* their ranking by a combination of the two measures of forecasting error.[15] Since the error measures are more informative than the coefficients of determination, this combined error measure provides the best overall guide to how well the various consumption functions perform.

The first consumption function shown in Table 22 is a naïve model one, using just two variables, income and time, apart from a constant. It may seem inappropriate to call a consumption function using income a naïve model function. But in the present context it can serve as a naïve model. The various other consumption functions considered here include income as well as other terms, terms which are supposed to explain consumption, and hence to yield a better prediction of consumption than does a reliance merely on income and time.

The next two consumption functions (B and C) are ones which survived the tests of the previous two chapters and do not embody the wealth approach. Functions D and E can be interpreted as permanent income functions, though they can also be interpreted in other ways— for example, as habit persistence theories. Then there are two functions

---

imate their sophisticated quarterly lag structure in a very crude way. In addition, I employed the conventional definition of consumption rather than the use definition they worked with. Moreover, while they ran separate regressions using income and labor income, I used only the former. I modified the Crockett regression by using wealth in place of liquid assets. Two other members of the Pennsylvania school, Friend and Taubman, used wealth rather than liquid assets. (They also included a transitory income term and predicted saving rather than consumption.) What I called the Crockett equation is therefore really a mixture of the two Pennsylvania equations. Lydall had fitted his function to saving rather than consumption and omitted the constant. I modified his approach by using consumption as the dependent variable and adding a constant. This made it the same as the regression fitted by Klein and Ando-Brown.

14. In calculating the means of the root mean square errors, I added the squared errors for each of the three years being predicted, divided by three, took the square root, and then averaged the square roots for each of the eleven "runs."

15. Since the rankings of the two error measures are very similar, it was possible in all but one case to combine them into a single ranking consistent with a separate ranking on each of the two error measures. The one exception produced a tied rank.

Table 22

Performance of Various Consumption Functions

Function[a]	Independent Variables[b]	"Wrong" Signs	Mean R^2	Means of Absolute Errors[c]	Means of Root Mean Square Errors[c]	Ranking[d] Absolute Errors	Ranking[d] Root Mean Square Errors	Ranking[d] Combined Error Measures
A	C, Y, T		.998	$9.6	11.2	3	2	2
B	$C, Y, \Delta Y, M$	x	.996	12.5	15.3	6	8	—
C	$C, Y, \Delta Y, Y\left(\dfrac{Con}{Y}\right)_{-1}$	e	.996	16.2	18.3	11	11	8
D	C, Y, C_{-1}	x	.997	15.6	17.7	9	10	—
E	$C, Y_{-1}, \Delta Y, Con_{-1}$		.996	12.9	15.2	7	7	5[g]
F	C, Y, W		.998	8.3	9.5	1	1	1
G	$C, Y, W, \dfrac{W^2}{Y}$	f	.997	11.8	14.4	4[g]	5	4
H	$C, Y_L W, P_{-1}$	x	.977	50.3	51.9	13	13	—
I	Y, Con_{-1}		.994	15.8	17.2	10	9	7
J	$C, Y, Y_T W'$		.998	9.5	11.3	2	3	—
K	C, Y, W	x	.992	19.2	21.0	12	12	9
L	C, Y_s, W		.995	13.2	15.1	8	6	5[g]
M	C, Y_s, W, i		.996	11.8	13.1	4[g]	4	3

[a] Functions:

A. (naive model)
B. Ando-Goldfeld
C. Evans
D. Ando-Brown
E. Thurow
F. Ando-Brown, Klein, Lydall
G. Melville
H. Branson-Klevorick
I. Ball-Drake
J. Crockett
K. Mayer
L. Mayer
M. Mayer

[b]
$C.$ Constant
$Y.$ Income
$T.$ Time
$M.$ Money
$Con.$ Consumption
$W.$ Wealth
$Y_L.$ Labor income lagged
$P.$ Prices
$Y.$ Transitory inc.
$W'.$ Diff. between actual and desired wealth
$Y_s.$ Standard income
$i.$ Interest rate

[c] Per capita 1958 dollars.

[d] In ascending order.

[e] Sign of (Con/Y) wrong in 2 of 11 regressions.

[f] Sign of W negative and sign of W^2/Y positive; in Melville's article the opposite occurred, but the signs obtained here are not inconsistent with his theory.

[g] Two-way tie.

Table 23

Performance of Ando-Modigliani Functions and Naïve Model

Function[a]	Independent Variables[b]	"Wrong" Signs	Mean R^2	Means of Absolute Errors[c]	Means of Root Mean Square Errors[c]	Ranking[d] Absolute Errors	Ranking[d] Root Mean Square Errors	Ranking[d] Combined Error Measures
N	C, Y, T		.999	$ 5.8	$ 6.5	1	1	1
O	Y, W		.831	52.7	56.1	4	4	3
P	C, Y_L, W		.995	11.6	13.5	2	2	2
Q	$Y, W \frac{L}{E} Y_L$	[e]	.851	54.8	61.0	5	5	—
R	$C, Y_L, W, \frac{L}{E} Y_L$	[f]	.994	12.1	14.4	3	3	—

[a] Function N is a naïve model; all other functions were fitted by Ando and Modigliani.

[b] Y_L is labor income after taxes; $\frac{L}{E}$ is ratio of labor force to employment; for definition of other variables see note b, Table 22.

[c] Per capita 1958 dollars.

[d] Ranked in ascending order.

[e] Coefficient of $\frac{L}{E}Y$ negative in 7 out of 8 runs.

[f] Coefficient of $\frac{L}{E}Y$ negative in 3 out of 8 runs.

(F and G) using wealth. Again, while these functions fit into the wealth approach to the consumption function, they can also be treated as a modified absolute income theory, since Tobin many years ago suggested the inclusion of a wealth term in the consumption function. Moreover, one of the originators of Function F is Lawrence Klein, who is not a supporter of the wealth approach as I have defined the term.

The next three functions (H, I, and J) represent specific variants of the wealth approach. The first of them consists of the life cycle hypothesis with an allowance for a money illusion. The next one is the Ball-Drake model, and the last one represents the normal income theory.

The last three functions (K, L, and M) are modified standard income theory equations. What I did was use the income of only two years in place of the income of three or four years. Instead of allowing the regression to choose the weights for the incomes of each of these years, I combined the two year incomes, giving two-thirds of the weight to current income, in rough approximation to the income weightings shown by the Swiss data in Chapter 13.[16] The first of these three functions is a simple version containing no variable other than standard income. The next one adds a wealth term, and the third one adds an interest rate term (the Aaa bond rate) as well. Function N in Table 23 is again a naïve model, and the other functions in this table are Ando and Modigliani functions. My failure to test Friedman's permanent income function may at first glance seem surprising, but obviously I could hardly include the income of seventeen years in a regression fitted to only twelve years.

The results shown in Tables 22 and 23 are rather discouraging. *Only one of the seventeen consumption functions performed better than the naïve model,* and its superiority is not significant at the 10 percent level.[17] This suggests that consumption function theories really give us little ability to forecast consumption. With only one of so many consumption functions predicting better than the naïve model, it is tempting to say that it is probably a coincidence; that all of these consumption functions are really inferior to a naïve model. If this is the case, then perhaps consumption functions should be judged on some criterion other than their predictive performance. Perhaps a theory can give a great deal of insight and still be inferior to a naïve model as a prediction tool.[18]

16. The use of only two years' income means that these functions are similar to the Mack function discussed in Chapter 3 and hence can be thought of as absolute income theory functions instead of standard income theory functions. This is unfortunate, but using three years' income would have meant losing one more scarce degree of freedom for all the regressions.

17. To be sure, the lack of significance may reflect merely the small size of the sample, eleven observations.

18. Even if one argues that economic theories should be judged purely

This pessimistic conclusion, however, is subject to several qualifications. One is that the naïve model already predicts consumption very well so that it is hard to improve upon it. The second, as pointed out above, is that I fitted the regressions using the single equation technique. Had I used more highly regarded techniques I might have obtained better predictions. Third, all the regressions were fitted to only a few observations, and, particularly for some of the regressions using many variables, there were too few degrees of freedom. Fourth, as pointed out above, I had to transform many of the consumption functions from the way they had originally been fitted. Finally, there is the possibility that my naïve model was not so naïve after all. If there has been a steady secular change in tastes then this could be picked up by the time trend of the naïve model. But if changes in tastes are important, then this suggests that the various consumption function theories do not have much predictive power. This does not prevent them from providing important insights as well as predictions of specific effects such as policy actions, but it does suggest that a prediction test such as the one I am using is not a very useful test.

Turning to the relative performance of the consumption functions, the picture is clear. The function that uses just income and wealth does best.[19] This fact supports, of course, a general version of the wealth approach, but as pointed out above, it is also consistent with a modified absolute income theory.

The standard income theory, even in its best version, the version using wealth and the interest rate, is not outstanding. On the combined error measure it ranks third in a field of eight, behind both the simple wealth function and the naïve model. Its failure to perform better than the simple wealth model is surprising and disappointing. This is brought out most forcefully if one compares the standard income theory regression using wealth, but not the interest rate, with the simple wealth function. The only difference between the two regressions is that the standard income regressions use the income of two years with predetermined weights while the simple wealth equation uses only current income.[20]

---

by their predictive power, it does not follow that predicting the future value of a variable, as I am doing here, is the proper test. The term "prediction" as used in the statement "the function of theory is to predict" is used in a much broader sense than that.

19. Its superiority over the naïve model, however, is not significant (t value of less than one) which is hardly surprising since I have only eleven observations. Ironically, the Crockett regression does as well as the naïve model but the coefficient of the difference between actual and desired wealth has the wrong sign.

20. I also experimented with another set of regressions for the standard income theory in which I simply used the current year's and the previous

The superiority of the simple wealth regression, therefore, suggests that the previous year's income does not affect consumption, and that only the current year's income belongs in the consumption function. But this is contrary to much of the evidence presented in previous chapters; something must be wrong somewhere. One obvious culprit is single equation bias. This bias is naturally more serious in a regression which uses only current income than in one which uses an income measure part of which is predetermined. And similar reasoning can explain why the standard income theory does worse than the naïve model. This explanation may suffice to rescue the standard income theory, but I must admit that I found these results most disappointing.

Before concluding this discussion, it may be worth considering prediction tests which have been used by other economists. In his dissertation discussed in Chapter 7, Halfyard used a prediction test to evaluate the absolute income theory, the wealth theory, the Spiro model, and the Friedman function (in a Koyck-Nerlove version) as well as his own theory.[21] Using one year predictions, his own theory and Friedman's model did best. However, in his version of Friedman's model—based on a Koyck-Nerlove transformation—the current year received 80 percent of the weight, the previous year 16 percent, and year before that 4 percent. In the terminology I have used here, this is not really a strict permanent income theory, but is much closer to the standard income theory.

As discussed in Chapter 7, George Craig used a prediction test not on consumption per se but on saving.[22] He used a wide variety of functions and different forms of various functions—levels, first differences, yearly, and quarterly. He found that a permanent income type model, that is, a model using current income, lagged consumption, and assets and time performed best in forecasting the annual level of saving while liquid assets equations forecast annual differences in saving best (if one excludes a net worth model not grounded in theory).[23]

---

year's income and let the computer choose the best weight for each. In nearly every case, the previous year's income had a *negative* coefficient. I also ran these regressions employing the "use" concept of consumption and here the previous year's income had positive coefficients. I have no explanation for this discrepancy.

21. Richard Halfyard, "Determination of Aggregate Consumption Expenditures in the United States, 1929–1961," unpublished Ph.D. dissertation, UCLA, 1964.

22. George Craig, "Predictive Accuracy of Aggregate, Quarterly and Annual Savings Functions," *Journal of the American Statistical Association*, Vol. 65, September 1970, pp. 1131–45

23. This is so for conventionally defined saving. Craig also ran regressions on "use" saving.

Part Four

PERMANENT INCOME PROXIES

INTRODUCTION

The previous chapter dealt with time series regressions, and it showed that time series regression is a highly precarious way of evaluating the wealth theories. Despite its popularity, it does not permit a conclusive test. Fortunately, there are other ways of testing these theories. One is to use cross-section data and to classify households by some observable characteristic correlated with permanent income. It is possible to do this because households whose permanent incomes differ generally differ in observable characteristics, such as occupation.

One can treat the mean *measured* incomes of groups which differ in permanent incomes as representing differences in the mean permanent incomes of the households in these groups. In doing this there are three dangers. One is that groups with different permanent incomes may also have different transitory incomes. For example, suppose one compares white collar employees and unskilled laborers. In a recession year laborers probably have a greater negative transitory income component than do white collar workers. Fortunately, it is easy to guard against this danger. If one looks at the mean income of various groups, not in any single year but in many different years, then differences in transitory income cancel out, and one can treat differences in the mean measured incomes of various groups as differences in permanent incomes. A second safeguard I have used is that I have not simply looked at the mean income of several groups and taken their measured income ranking as indicating their permanent income ranking. In each case I have made an a priori judgment of their permanent income ranking before looking at the data, and have used the data only if they conform to this a priori ranking. This avoids the danger of ranking groups by their transitory income receipts in any one year.

The second danger is that households may shift between groups, so that the mean income of a group does not represent the long-run income of households in that group. Fortunately, this problem can be greatly reduced by using such broadly defined groups that households do little shifting between them; this is what I have done. The third danger is one discussed in Chapter 1, namely that differences in permanent income may be correlated with other factors which in turn affect the propensity to consume, so that there is a spurious correlation between the mean income of groups and their propensity to consume. As pointed out, this difficulty cannot be eliminated entirely. However, to a very considerable extent, it is possible to guard against it by seeing whether the groups being compared do differ in extraneous variables which could create a spurious correlation.

In deciding what groupings of households to use, one is essentially a prisoner of available data. These data allow one to classify households by the following characteristics: occupation, race, location, and education. I have used all but the last of these groupings. I did not use education because it is so highly correlated with occupation that to classify households by education as well as by occupation involves a great deal of duplication.[1] And if one is to use only one of these two variables, occupation is the better one because there are more budget studies which classify households by occupation than by education. Moreover, the variable by which one groups households should be one which *itself* has little effect on the propensity to consume. While occupation may not meet this criterion fully, it probably has less direct effect on the propensity to consume than education does. In any case, the work I *have* done with households classified by education rejects the proportionality hypothesis and hence supports the results one obtains from the other ways of classifying households.

The proportionality hypothesis can be tested by seeing whether the propensity to consume is, in fact, no greater in high permanent income groups (for example, households headed by professionals) than in low income groups (such as households headed by unskilled workers). But it is possible to go beyond such a simple test of the proportionality hypothesis; one can also test the measured income theories and the standard income theory. According to the measured income theory, the propensity to consume is the same for permanent income as for measured income. One can test this hypothesis by calculating the marginal propensity to consume twice—once the usual way from households grouped by measured income, and once from households grouped not by measured income but by, say, occupation. If the marginal propensity to consume is greater when households are classified by permanent income group than when they are classified by measured income, then the measured income theories are disconfirmed.

Moreover, one can use this technique not only to test but also to

1. I am indebted at this point to a suggestion by Jacob Mincer.

quantify the standard income theory. One can do this by comparing the marginal propensities to consume *of the same households* calculated in the two ways. To do this it is convenient to have anchor points. One obvious anchor point is provided by the permanent income theory; it is that the marginal propensity to consume permanent income is equal to the average propensity to consume. The other anchor point is the prediction of the measured income theories, that is, that the marginal propensity to consume is equal for permanent and for measured income. I have combined these two predictions into a measure called the "prediction coefficient," which is defined as $P = \dfrac{MPCP - APC}{MPCM - APC}$ where $MPCP$ is the marginal propensity to consume permanent income, APC is the average propensity to consume, and $MPCM$ is the marginal propensity to consume measured income. If the permanent income theory is valid, this expression takes a value of zero, while if the measured income theories are completely correct, it has a value of unity.

The prediction coefficient can be interpreted in the following way: The denominator measures the gap between the marginal and average propensities to consume when this gap is calculated conventionally—that is, when measured income is used. The numerator, on the other hand, measures the gap between the marginal and average propensities which remains even if one uses permanent income instead of measured income. The whole expression, therefore, shows the remaining gap as a proportion of the conventionally computed one.

I have called this the "prediction coefficient" because it shows the extent to which the measured income theories predict correctly. One can look upon the permanent income theory as a naïve model which asserts that the percentage of income consumed is independent of the level of permanent income, while the measured income theories represent attempts to go beyond such a naïve model and to predict the percentage of income consumed from a knowledge of the level of income. Traditionally, computations of the average and marginal propensities to consume based on *measured* incomes have suggested that the conventional theories are superior to a naïve model; but they involve a possible bias, which according to the permanent income theory accounts fully for their apparent superiority. The prediction coefficient is a device which measures the extent to which the superiority of the prediction survives the elimination of this bias.

While such a prediction coefficient is useful in many ways, it does suffer from two weaknesses. One is that in those cases in which it exceeds unity, or is negative, it has no ready economic interpretation. The prediction coefficient is defined as the percentage of the gap between the average propensity and the marginal propensity to consume which re-

mains if one uses permanent income in place of measured income. But
no such meaning is attached to the prediction coefficient in those cases
where the marginal propensity to consume measured income appears to
exceed the marginal propensity to consume permanent income, and the
prediction coefficient exceeds unity.[2] In these cases the prediction coefficient is merely a statistical artifact without a useful economic interpretation.[3] Hence, in averaging prediction coefficients, some of which lie
outside the zero to unity range, one should use not the arithmetic mean
but the median or a positional mean.

The other weakness of the prediction coefficient is that it is not a
robust statistic. Since the difference between the marginal and the
average propensity to consume is small, minor differences in one's estimate of the marginal propensity to consume can change the prediction
coefficient substantially. It is therefore unwise to focus on the value of
any single prediction coefficient; instead one should look at the average
of a set of these coefficients. I have therefore not calculated confidence
limits for the individual prediction coefficients, but have used significance tests only for all the prediction coefficients jointly.

In computing the marginal propensity to consume, I have used very
simple consumption functions, primarily because the data were insufficient to fit more complex ones. Most budget studies do not give information about the many variables usually included in elaborate multivariate functions. Moreover, even when such information is available
there are too few groups (and hence, too few degrees of freedom) to
fit elaborate functions. Fortunately, the use of a simple consumption
function does not do violence to the theories being tested.[4]

2. These cases probably result either from errors in the basic data, sampling
fluctuations, or, perhaps more likely, from differences in transitory income
receipts by various groups. While these transitory elements should cancel out
for all studies jointly, one would expect them to dominate the result in a few
cases.

3. Moreover, outside the zero to unity range, the prediction coefficient is
not symmetrical. It should be negative if the marginal propensity to consume
measured income is greater than the average propensity to consume. But as
pointed out below, I have excluded such cases from my sample. This reduced
the number of negative prediction coefficients without any offsetting reduction in the number of prediction coefficients greater than unity.

4. Friedman himself used a simple function, explicitly rejecting the more
ponderous consumption functions fitted by others. And the same holds true
on the other side of the debate. In the relative income theory, Duesenberry
used as independent variables only income and mean income of the community (or else previous peak income), and since the last two variables are
not relevant for an occupational test, a simple consumption function is a
fair test. Similarly, the absolute income theory, while it may use several

However, I have, when feasible, included household size as an additional independent variable. The number of persons per household is clearly one of the important determinants of consumption. Moreover, this variable becomes particularly significant when comparing the marginal propensity to consume of households as computed from an occupational grouping with the same propensity calculated from an income class grouping. When households are grouped by measured income, there is a positive relation between income level and family size. But if households are grouped by occupation, there exists, in many of the data used here, no such positive correlation. Hence, a bias may be created if family size is ignored. However, if the family size variable had the "wrong" (i.e., negative) sign, I excluded family size from the regression.

I computed the marginal propensity to consume permanent income in two different ways. In those cases where I had three or more groups I used regressions. But in those cases where I had only two groups I calculated the marginal propensity to consume permanent income by subtracting the mean consumption of one group from that of the other, and dividing by the difference in mean income.[5] For the marginal propensity to consume measured income I used regression analysis throughout. In calculating these regressions I weighted the various groups and income classes by the number of households.[6] I treated each budget study as a separate unit and calculated a prediction coefficient for it. An alternative procedure would have been to pool all the data. I did not do this because there are substantial differences in methods, and in the definitions used, among the various budget studies, so that the data are not homogeneous. Moreover, to pool the data would have required purchasing power parity exchange rates, and for many of the years covered these are not available.

---

independent variables, is basically an assertion that the higher the level of income, the lower the percentage consumed even if other variables are left out of consideration.

5. What I did is essentially equivalent to an instrumental variable approach developed many years earlier by Abraham Wald ("The Fitting of Straight Lines if Both Variables Are Subject to Error," *Annals of Mathematical Statistics,* Vol. 11, 1940, pp. 284–300). I was made aware of this point only after I had completed most of this work by an unpublished paper by Richard Peterson ("Professor Mayer's Instrumental Variable: A Test of the Permanent Income Hypothesis"). In this paper Peterson developed a much more sophisticated and subtle method than the one I am using.

6. I used the number of households and not the square root of the number of households because I wanted each household to have exactly the same weight in the permanent income regression as it has in the measured income regression.

Chapters 10, 11, and 12 apply the methods discussed above to households classified by occupation, race, and location. Of the various ways of grouping households by permanent income proxies, occupation is the most useful for testing the permanent income theory. This is so, in part, because of the large number of available budget studies which classify households by occupation. In addition, an occupational grouping does not suffer from some of the weaknesses of the other two available groupings. As I shall point out in Chapter 11, when one compares the propensities to consume of black and white households, there are so many other factors involved, apart from income differences, that the prediction coefficients may well be biased. And if one classifies households by location, one can obtain only a limited number of prediction coefficients.

As a final point, a warning may be in order. Household income and consumption data are subject to very large errors, and in many budget studies the quality of these data is exceedingly poor.[7] But, as in the case of time series data, one must make do with what one has.

7. In the Introduction to Part III, I mentioned the problem created by the exclusion of capital gains from income. This is also a problem for cross-section data. However, since the high income groups are often only very thinly represented in the household surveys, this problem is probably not so severe for cross-section tests as it is for time-series tests.

Ten

OCCUPATION AND CONSUMPTION

One advantage of using the average propensities to consume of various occupations to test the permanent income theory is that this is a very simple and straightforward test. As pointed out earlier, however, there are three dangers. One is the possibility of households shifting between occupations so that the mean income of an occupation does not tell us much about the household's permanent income. I have guarded against this danger by using broadly defined groups such as manual workers versus white collar workers. Movement between such broadly defined classes is quite infrequent.[1] A second danger is that the relative incomes of various occupations may fluctuate over time so that in the year covered by a particular budget study one occupation may be receiving more transitory income than another. I have avoided this problem by using thirty-four budget studies spread over the period 1912–1963 and over a dozen countries. Given such a large sample, differences in the receipt of transitory income among various occupations should cancel out, so that the difference in the mean incomes of various occupations reflects *on the average,* though not necessarily in any single case, differences in permanent rather than transitory income. The third danger is that occupation may be correlated with some variable other than permanent income, and that this variable may have a significant effect on the propensity to consume. This problem is discussed in the last section of this chapter.

Using the mean incomes of various occupations as a measure of permanent income is not new. As pointed out in Chapter 4, it was done by Friend and Kravis in one of the earliest tests of the permanent income theory as well as by many other investigators such as Modigliani and Ando. I have tried to go beyond these earlier studies in three ways. One is to use, for the reason just given, many budget studies in place of

1. See Seymour Lipset and R. Bendix, *Social Mobility in an Industrial Society* (Berkeley, University of California Press, 1959), chaps. 2, 5; and C. Anderson, "Lifetime Inter-Occupational Mobility Patterns in Sweden," *Acta Sociologica,* Vol. 1, pp. 168–202.

just a single one. Another is to test not only the full permanent income theory but also the measured income theories and the standard income theory. The third difference is that I am dealing with the possibility of spurious correlation by looking for variables correlated with occupation which may have an independent effect on the average propensity to consume.

The Sample

I have attempted, though not with complete success, to include all budget studies since 1900 which provide usable data, with certain exceptions described in Appendix IV. Since only a relatively small proportion of the numerous budget studies undertaken in this period give data on occupations, this turned out to be a feasible task.

The use of early budget studies may need justification since we are primarily concerned with what occurs at the present time. First, as mentioned above, the assumption that the measured income of an occupation equals, on the average, its permanent income can be justified only if one uses a large number of studies over a long period of time. Over the short run, it is quite possible for one group of occupations to have consistently positive transitory income while another group has consistently negative transitory income; only by taking a long span of time can one ensure that differences in income represent permanent rather than transitory differences. Second, the permanent income theory is supposed to be a general theory of consumption behavior. As such it should fit the earlier data as well as contemporary data. Third, while as a general rule, current data are substantially more reliable than earlier data, for consumption function studies the earlier data may be as reliable, or even more reliable, than many current ones.[2] The data given in many of these

---

2. With respect to sampling procedure and clarity of definitions, current studies are greatly superior to earlier ones. On the other hand, income and expenditure were probably recorded much more accurately in earlier studies than in many current ones. At one time one of the major disputes among budget investigators was whether to use account books kept by the household during the survey period, and checked periodically by the investigator, or whether to use an ex post survey relying on the household's recall of income and expenditures. The former method has the advantage of increased accuracy but has two disadvantages. First, it limits the sample to families willing to undertake a substantial task, and consequently to families who may not be representative of the population at large. Second, the very process of keeping account books may cause the household to change its expenditure habits. Hence, although the account book technique is still used in some European budget studies, American and British studies rely on the ex post method. It may very well be the case that for most consumption items the household can recall its expenditures accurately enough (or with randomly distributed errors) so that the ex post technique is best. But for determining the

budget studies needed some processing to provide usable income and consumption figures. These procedures are described in Appendix IV.

The Results

Table 24 shows the budget studies used, the coefficient of ranked correlation between the mean income of the occupation and the average propensity to consume, and for those cases where it could be computed, the prediction coefficients.

The results shown in Table 24 strongly reject the proportionality hypothesis.[3] The signs of the ranked correlation coefficients show that in only 2 of the 31 unequivocal cases (Zurich 1919 and Czechoslovakia 1925–1926) does the higher-paid occupation consume a larger percentage of its income than the lower-paid occupation. And in the former case the result can be explained by the fact that those in the higher-paid occupations were largely government employees. Since there had been a substantial inflation in previous years, the measured real income of this group was presumably below its real permanent income. In two additional cases (Great Britain 1955–1956 and Norway 1958) there is considerable doubt about the results. But even if one gives these two doubtful cases to the permanent income theory, there are only 4 cases out of 34 in which the measured theories predict incorrectly. The probability of getting so many "successes" merely by "chance" is less than 1 percent.[4]

---

propensity to consume,—the account book technique may well be superior, because in an ex post survey, at least one important source of errors is not random—income is generally underestimated. While there is no easy way of choosing between these two methods, there is a good possibility that the older surveys are better for fitting consumption functions than the contemporary American ones; a budget study could certainly have many weaknesses and yet provide more accurate saving figures than the 1950 Bureau of Labor Statistics study.

3. The reason why the ranked correlation coefficient is so frequently (minus) one, is that in many studies there were only two usable occupational groups, so that the coefficient has to be (plus, or else minus) unity.

4. The significance test I used throughout this chapter is a simple binomial test. I have treated each individual study as a unit and not applied significance tests to the difference of the two marginal propensities to consume within each study. Significance tests applied to any single budget study taken in isolation would understate the import of the results. Assume, for example, that in each of, say, six budget studies the difference between the marginal propensities to consume computed from occupational and from income class groupings is significant only at the 20 percent level. If the differences are all in the same direction, then the differences for all studies taken together are clearly significant, in spite of the fact that none of the individual studies has significant results at a respectable significance level. Moreover, within a single study, a significance test would have little meaning. One of the disturbances,

Table 24

Ranked Correlation Coefficients and Prediction Coefficients

Locality	Date of Study[a]	RHO[b]	Prediction Coefficient[c]	Occupations Covered and Number of Households[d]	Source Number[e]
Switzerland	1912	−0.8[f]	.1[f]	U = 26, SK = 515, E = 201[g], = 49	26
Zurich	1919	+1.0	—		36
Finland	1920–21	−1.0		[h]	12
Sweden	1923	−1.0	.4	W = 437, E = 117	23
Amsterdam	1923–24	−1.0[j]	.2[j]	W = 747, E = 445[i], MC = 208	7
Czechoslovakia	1925–26	+1.0	Negative	WC = 81, MC = 64	8
Minnesota	1926–27	.7	—	W = 51, E = 115	6
Denmark	1931	−1.0	3.6	U = 41, SE = 46, SK = 41, C + M = 78, P = 44	9
Sweden	1933	−1.0	.9	W = 140, O = 31	24
Netherlands	1935–36	−1.0	.9	W = 526, MC = 195, E[l] = 524	15
Switzerland	1936–37	−1.0	.5	W = 278, E = 206	25
Switzerland	1937–38	−1.0	.9	W = 741, E + O = 713	25
United States	1948	.4	.6	W = 321, E + O = 269	34
United States	1949	.4		P = 216, C = 275, SK + SE = 758, U = 303[k]	30, 31
Switzerland	1949	−1.0	1.4	[i]	27
Urban United States	1950	.7	.5	W = 274, E = 244	35
Switzerland	1951	−1.0	.7	[m]	28
Great Britain	1951–52	−1.0		W = 160, E = 102	4
Switzerland	1952	−1.0	.7	C + S = 330, SK = 807, U = 388, M = 259[n]	29
Great Britain	1952–53	.4		W = 151, E = 100	2
Coimbra (Portugal)	1953–54	−1.0	.7	C + S = 292, SK = 730, U = 358, M = 154[n,o]	18
Great Britain	1953–54	.8	.6	W = 1183, O = 857	17
Denmark	1955	.8[j]		C + S = 336, SK = 809, U = 248, M = 417	10, 11
Sweden	1955	−1.0		[p] W = 526, E = 236	21
Great Britain	1955–56	+.5[q]		[r]	3
Evora-Viseau (Portugal)	1955–56	−0.7[s]	.5	W = 87, O + E = 88	19, 20
Sweden	1957	−0.9[s]		[t]	22
Israel	1957–58	−0.6		M + P = 270, C = 599, SK = 707, U = 534	13
Norway	1958	−1.0[u]		W = 2401, O = 1035	16
United States	1958–59	−1.0		W = 1068, E = 2127	1

Japan	1960	−1.0	.2		5, 14
Urban United States	1960	−0.9	.6	W = 1095, E = 1501	32
Urban United States	1961	−1.0	.6		32
Urban United States	1963	−.5[w]	.6	P + O = 198, C + S = 133, SK = 152, S.E. = 125, U = 123	33

[a] In some cases no date was given for the study and had to be surmised from the date of publication.

[b] Coefficient of ranked correlation between mean income of occupation and its average propensity to consume. Coefficient is *not* weighted by number of households in occupation.

[c] For U.S. in 1960 and 1961, .6 is a single figure for both years.

[d] Occupational code: C, clerical workers. E, white collar employees. M, managerial. MC, middle class. O, officials. P, professionals. S, sales. SK, skilled manual workers. SE, semiskilled manual workers. U, unskilled manual workers. W, manual workers. WC, working class.

[e] For sources, see Appendix IV.

[f] Insurance premiums treated as consumption.

[g] Middle rank officials and teachers only.

[h] I regrouped data into two classes: (a) teachers, middle rank government officials, government white collar employees, and officials of private enterprises (44 households); (b) lower ranking white collar employees of private enterprise and manual workers (41 households).

[i] Lower ranking white collar employees only.

[j] The data understate saving and income, and since this understatement is greater for the lower income group than for the upper income group, there is a bias in favor of the permanent income theory.

[k] Clerical occupation includes other (nonprofessional) white collar employees, and unskilled occupation includes service workers.

[l] The actual number of spending units in each occupation is not given, and due to oversampling of the high income groups, it differs somewhat from the proportion of the total population in each occupational group. The proportion of the total population in each of the groups covered is: professional and semiprofessional, 7 percent; clerical and sales, 13 percent; skilled and semiskilled, 27 percent; unskilled and service, 12 percent. The total number of households covered is slightly over 3,000.

[m] The exact number of cases in each occupation is not given. The total sample covered more than 12,000 households.

[n] Includes technical employees.

[o] Number of cases in each group is approximate only.

[p] 548 higher officials and employees, 1,132 lower officials and employees, 515 skilled workers, 745 unskilled workers.

[q] Rho is positive if company directors are included in the sample, and negative if they are excluded. The study states that the saving of company directors is understated. Moreover, even if one includes company directors, Rho is −1.0 if receipts from inheritances are included in income.

[r] 32 company directors, 77 doctors, and 45 dentists.

[s] Since the relative income position of two of the occupations covered, lower officials and lower business managers, is unclear, I computed Rho twice—once excluding lower officials and once excluding lower business managers. Rho is −0.9 in the former case and −0.7 in the latter case.

[t] 23 higher business managers, 34 lower business managers, 70 academically trained employees exclusive of farmers and business managers, 47 higher officials, 185 lower officials, 22 foremen, and 499 workers.

[u] The marginal propensities to consume of the two occupations are very similar, so that it is possible, though perhaps not very likely, that the difference between them is merely the result of differences in household size.

[v] Occupations used are the same as for 1950. The number of cases in each occupation in the sample is not given. The total sample (including the self-employed and unemployed) amounted to 4,463 households in 1960 and 4,879 households in 1961.

[w] Median coefficient for the 5 cities covered. The mean is −0.4. For two of the five cities, Rho is positive.

It is worthwhile to look not only at all cases jointly, but also at their components. First, one may look at prewar and postwar studies separately. There are twelve prewar studies, and in all but two of them the measured income theories predict correctly. This is significant at the 3 percent level. For the postwar period there are 22 studies and, even if one gives the two doubtful cases to the permanent income theory, the measured income theories predict correctly in 20 of these 22 cases, a result significant at the 1 percent level. The fact that the results are significant for each period taken separately is useful because it shows that the outcome is really based on a long period of time, and cannot be explained away by the higher-paid occupation having more positive transitory income for a brief span of years.

Another way of separating the data is to select the most reliable ones. There are 19 studies which have a sample of more than 500 households and seem reliable and relevant in every way.[5] These 19 cases do not include the two in which the average propensity to consume is clearly less for the lower income group than for the upper income group, though they do include the two doubtful cases. But even if one gives these two doubtful cases to the permanent income theory, the measured income theories predict correctly at the 1 percent significance level.

But the "success" of the measured income theories is a severely qualified one, since the marginal propensity to consume *permanent* income is greater than the marginal propensity to consume *measured* income. As previously pointed out, in such a case the prediction coefficient is less than unity. And this is true for 16 out of the 19 coefficients shown in Table 24, a result which is significant at the 1 percent level.[6]

---

perhaps the main one, is the existence of positive (or negative) transitory income. There is no reason at all for assuming that *within* any one single budget study transitory income is randomly distributed.

These problems disappear if one takes as the unit of observation not the individual household but the whole budget study, treating the propensity to consume of an occupation or income class as though it were the propensity to consume of a single representative household in this group. If one assumes that budget studies occurred in years which were chosen randomly with respect to the distribution of transitory income, one can then apply significance tests to the results. Calling each case where the average propensity to consume of the lower-paid occupation exceeds that of the higher-paid occupation a "success" for the measured income theories, one can see if the resulting number of successes could be due to chance.

5. I excluded the Japanese study from this set because it covers less than a full year.

6. Some of the prediction coefficients shown in Table 24 differ from those given in a previous version of this test ("The Propensity to Consume Permanent Income," *American Economic Review*, Vol. LXI, December 1966, pp. 1164–66). This is due to the fact that here I calculated the marginal

Thus the data reject both the permanent income theory and the measured income theories and show that the truth lies in between. The prediction cofficients allow one to see where it lies between the two theories. Table 25 shows the medians and the positional means for the data from Table 24. These medians and positional means are more meaningful than the arithmetic means, because the arithmetic means are too heavily influenced by a few extremely large cases. And, as pointed out in the Introduction to Part III, these extreme cases have little economic meaning.

The medians and positional means of Table 25 show that in predicting the proportion of income consumed, the measured income theories are at least as close to the truth as is the full permanent income theory. The medians and positional means suggest that if one uses permanent income in place of measured income, only about one-half to one-third of the difference between the average propensity and marginal propensity to consume disappears.[7]

Table 25 also shows some breakdowns of the overall results. There is virtually no difference between the results for postwar and prewar studies. In addition, the results for selected studies (that is, the most applicable and reliable ones) are very similar to those for all studies together, thus suggesting that the results are not merely the consequence of errors in the data.

These results are in agreement with those obtained from Indian data by Firouz Vakil, who obtained the following prediction coefficients for India: rural 1962–0.7, urban 1960–0.6, all India 1964–0.7, Delhi 1959– 0.2.[8] The median of these four prediction coefficients is the same as the median for all studies shown in Table 25.

Other Variables

Table 24 shows that there is a negative correlation between permanent income and the propensity to consume. But this, in and of itself, does

---

propensity to consume measured income (needed to estimate the prediction coefficient) by regression analysis, whereas in the previous paper I had used for a number of the coefficients the "median break" method (described therein). Although there really is no way of settling the matter unequivocally I feel now that the way I calculated the prediction coefficient here is better than my previous method. Fortunately, it does not make much difference which method one chooses. Although some of the individual coefficients change substantially, the overall results are virtually unaffected.

7. To be sure, due to the small size of the sample, one cannot reject the *possibility* that it is quite a bit greater than this.

8. "The Propensity to Consume Permanent Income in India," *Economic Development and Cultural Change,* forthcoming. Vakil also fitted log regressions and compared the permanent and measured income elasticities. The ratio of the former to the latter ranged between 1.01 and 1.17.

Table 25

Medians and Positional Means of Prediction Coefficients

Studies	Median	Positional Mean-Mid 50 Percent	Number of Studies
All Studies	0.6	0.6	19
Prewar	0.5	0.6	9
Postwar	0.6	0.6	10
Selected Studies[a]	0.6	0.7	8

SOURCE: Table 24.

[a] Sweden 1923 and 1933, Switzerland 1936–1937, 1937–1938 and 1949, U.S. 1948, Great Britain 1953–1954, U.S. 1960–1961.

not suffice to show that higher income *causes* a lower propensity to consume. The observed result could be due to another variable correlated with permanent income. To check whether or not this is actually the case one has to go through the tedious process of looking for such a variable.

In his well-known text, Gardner Ackley mentioned the following variables as affecting the consumption function: the interest rate, consumer credit terms, sales effort, relative prices, deferred demand, stocks of consumer durables, price and income expectations, income distribution, demographic factors, wealth, liquid assets, the money stock, capital gains, and subjective and cultural factors. When dealing with cross-section data, the following three other variables should be added to Ackley's list: frequency of home ownership, contractual saving commitments, and pension arrangements. Friedman suggested that the main variables determining the average propensity to consume are "the rate of interest, the relative dispersion of transitory components of income and of consumption, the ratio of wealth to income, and the age and composition of consumer units." [9] Fortunately, nine of these eighteen variables can be dismissed quickly. The interest rate should (since I am excluding the self-employed) be roughly similar for all occupations. Relative to income, consumer credit may be more readily available for high income, than for low income, households. But even if this is the case, it can hardly account for the results shown in Table 24, since consumer credit was less important in prewar Europe, the source of some of the data. Nor can the third variable, sales effort, fairly account for the lower average propensity to consume of the higher occupations, since high income households are presumably exposed to at least as much sales effort as

9. Gardner Ackley, *Macroeconomics,* New York, 1961, chap. 12; Milton Friedman, *A Theory of the Consumption Function* (Princeton, Princeton University Press, 1957), p. 232.

low income households. Relative prices can also be dismissed quickly; their effects should cancel out over the many studies used here.

The fifth variable, deferred demand, is relevant only during war and in the immediate postwar period. Since I excluded such years, this variable does not matter here. The stock of consumer durables, too, is a variable less important for cross-section than for time series data. One can assume that on the average, over the studies covered, households held the equilibrium amount of durables. Similarly, price and income expectations are not relevant, since for the whole range of studies considered, favorable and unfavorable expectations should cancel out. The eighth variable, income distribution, is clearly not applicable.

Finally, there is the proportion of saving which is contractually committed. This factor may well be important in time series studies, since it limits the amount by which saving can easily be reduced, but it is not likely to be significant for a cross-section study. One can assume that over the whole range of studies considered, households are saving their equilibrium amount so that the existence of contractual saving does not serve as a major restraint on their consumption.

The other nine variables cannot be dismissed so easily. First, there is the demographic variable. One aspect of this, family size, has already been taken into account by including household size in many of the regressions. The other relevant demographic variable is age. But apart from variations introduced by differences in the school-leaving age one would expect households in different occupational groups to have roughly the same mean age, and this belief is borne out by the few available data.[10]

Unfortunately, for the next variable, nonhuman wealth, little information is available, but the limited information which covers Sweden, Denmark, and Britain does show a positive relationship between mean income of an occupation and net worth as a percent of income.[11]

10. The 1950 Bureau of Labor Statistics survey showed the following average ages: salaried professional and managerial, 42 years; clerical and sales, 42 years, skilled wage earners, 43 years; semi-skilled wage earners, 41 years; unskilled wage earners, 48 years. (Irving Kravis, *The Structure of Incomes,* Philadelphia, University of Pennsylvania Press, 1962, p. 81.) The fact that the average age of salaried and professional employees is no higher than the average age of wage earners may seem surprising. Apparently the later entry into the labor force of managerial and technical employees is offset by the fact that this type of employment has expanded more than others in recent years, so that there has been a relatively large number of young recruits into these occupations. I have tabulated the mean ages of various occupations from two other studies, U.S. 1948 and Britain 1953–1954, and neither of them showed much relation between occupation and age.

11. Sweden, Konjunkturinstitutet, *Hushållens Sparande år 1955* (Stockholm, 1963), pp. 71, 179; Denmark, Statistiske Department, *Statistiske Un-*

As pointed out in Chapter 5, the effect which wealth has on the consumption function is uncertain. While in the orthodox view wealth has a positive effect on consumption, there is some evidence suggesting that the opposite might be the case. If the orthodox view is correct, then the positive correlation of mean occupational income with the wealth-income ratio creates a bias in favor of the proportionality hypothesis and so is clearly unable to account for the unfavorable results reached above. However, if wealth has a negative effect on consumption, the coefficients of ranked correlation are biased against the proportionality hypothesis. But a negative effect of wealth on consumption itself contradicts the wealth theories.

The few available data suggest that the next variable, the ratio of liquid assets to income is positively correlated with the mean income of occupations.[12] Hence, if as is frequently asserted, liquid assets *do* have a positive effect on consumption, this factor would tend to raise the consumption of the higher occupations relative to the consumption of the other occupations and thus would not be able to account for the results reached above.

The next variable, the stock of money, is one about which almost no information is available since budget surveys do not ask questions about currency holdings. But money holdings excluding currency are included in liquid assets, and if one assumes that a dollar of money has the same effect on consumption as a dollar of nonmoney liquid assets, then one does not have to treat this variable separately.

Home ownership is an important variable for two reasons: first, home ownership may stimulate saving, and second, our method of measuring saving treats homeowners differently from tenants. On the one hand, by not counting depreciation of the house as consumption, the surveys understate consumption, but on the other hand, the fact that many surveys do not count minor maintenance and repair expenditures as saving creates a partially offsetting overstatement of consumption. Moreover, the fact that imputed rent is usually not treated as income and consumption does give a small downward bias to the propensity to consume. Finally, in many of the earlier budget studies used it is likely that investment in homes was counted as consumption.

The data on the relative frequency of home ownership show a confusing picture. But in any case a positive relationship between occupa-

---

dersøgelser No. 3 Osparing i lønmodtagerhusstandene 1955 (Copenhagen, Statistiske Department, 1960), pp. 24, 63. The British data are unpublished data for 1953–1954. For U.S. data see Chapter 15.

12. The available data are ones I tabulated from the U.S. 1948 study and the British 1953–1954 survey. Unfortunately, both of these surveys exclude currency.

tional incomes and home ownership cannot be invoked to discount the positive correlation between occupational income and the saving ratio. If high income households are more prone to be homeowners than low income households, and if home ownership raises the saving-income ratio, the resulting correlation of income and the saving ratio is not spurious, but measures the *indirect* effect of income differences on the saving ratio.

The one variable mentioned by Friedman which is not included in Ackley's list is the relative dispersion of transitory income and consumption. A greater dispersion leads to greater saving since households guard against risk by accumulating wealth. The relative dispersion of transitory consumption can be ignored—there is no reason to assume that it varies among occupations. The relative dispersion of income is probably greater for the lower-paid occupations than for the higher-paid ones, since unemployment is greater for these occupations.[13] Hence, this factor, too, is not able to explain the results shown above.

The next variable is capital gains. The fact that I am excluding the self-employed, who presumably account for a large proportion of capital gains, alleviates this problem. In particular, for those studies which compare white collar employees and manual workers, capital gains are presumably quite unimportant. Insofar as capital gains do occur among the groups covered in the above studies, capital gains (as a proportion of income) are probably positively correlated with permanent income. Hence, by excluding capital gains from income, but including consumption out of capital gains in the consumption figure, the data probably raise the propensity to consume more for households with high permanent income than for households with a low permanent income. The direction of this bias is in favor of the proportionality hypothesis, and so this factor, too, cannot be held responsible for the poor showing of the hypothesis.

The type of pension system is a variable which is frequently omitted from the consumption function; yet it could be important when comparing the propensities to consume of different occupations, since they may have different pension arrangements. There are two aspects to this problem. First, since budget studies generally do not count the employers' or government's pension contribution as saving, total saving is under-

13. For data on unemployment rates of various occupations in the postwar United States, see R. A. Gordon, "Has Structural Unemployment Worsened?" *Industrial Relations Review,* Vol. 3, May 1964, p. 62. These data show substantially greater unemployment rates for manual workers than for white collar employees. However, the (negative) correlation of occupational income and unemployment rates is not perfect due to the fact that clerical and sales employees both have a lower incidence of unemployment than do "craftsmen, foremen, etc."

stated. Moreover, it is highly probable that many of the budget studies did not even count the employee's contribution as saving. The understatement of pension savings is a general problem with cross-section data, and it also applies to other cross-section data cited both for and against the permanent income theory. But as pointed out in Chapter 5, at least in the United States there is little evidence that coverage by private pension systems reduces the rate of saving apart from pension contributions. Hence, if one is interested in saving other than saving via pension funds, one does not have to attach much importance to variations in the pension fund coverage of different occupations. In addition, until recently, pension coverage, at least in the U.S., was quite minor. Moreover, for one of the above-cited studies (U.S. 1958–1959), separate data for covered and noncovered households are available and they both reject the permanent income theory.

The final variable, subjective and cultural factors, is vague, and thus hard to analyze. Yet it should at least be mentioned because it *may* account for some of the differences in the propensities to consume of various occupations. Thus, it is possible that households with relatively high permanent incomes save a relatively large percent of their income, in part because they are better educated, and hence have more foresight, and perhaps also because they are more influenced by the "puritan ethic" than are poorer households.

To summarize: Of the eighteen variables, seven (consumer credit terms, relative prices, deferred demand, stocks of consumer durables, home ownership, expectations, and income distribution) are not relevant, and three others (age, interest rates, and sales effort) can be ignored since there are probably no serious differences among occupations, at least in the postwar United States. Three others (liquid assets, capital gains, and the dispersion of transitory income) create a bias in favor of the permanent income theory. Two variables, the money stock and contractual saving commitments, are distributed in an unknown way, but as I have pointed out, this does not present a serious problem.

This leaves only two variables, wealth on the one hand, and cultural and psychological factors on the other, which could be used to explain away the failure of the proportionality hypothesis on this occupational test. But the wealth variable can be used to defend the proportionality hypothesis only if one takes the unorthodox position that wealth has a negative effect on consumption, a position which is contrary to the wealth theories. This leaves only the psychological and cultural variable, and this variable was dealt with in Chapter 1.

Conclusion

When one uses the mean income of various occupations as a measure of permanent income, the results are unfavorable for the proportionality hypothesis. There are only two ways one can escape this conclusion: take refuge in an empirically untestable separation of psychological and cultural effects from the effects of income, or argue—contrary to the spirit of the wealth theories—that wealth has a negative effect on consumption.

But this test not only refutes the proportionality hypothesis, it also challenges the measured income theories, and hence it supports the standard income theory.[14] Moreover, it goes further than this; it quantifies the standard income theory by showing that the prediction coefficient is approximately one-half to two-thirds. This quantification is, of course, subject to one weakness: I have not been able to adjust the prediction coefficient for the effects of the variables discussed in the previous section.[15]

14. To be sure, one could defend the measured income theories by invoking the three variables mentioned above which create a bias in favor of the proportionality hypothesis. However, none of these factors seem very important.

15. The prediction coefficient depends upon the difference in the marginal propensities to consume permanent and measured income. Hence, what is relevant here is the relative size of the biases these variables create in the estimates of these two propensities to consume. This relative size of the biases is hard to get at, but in many cases it is presumably fairly small.

Eleven

CONSUMPTION AND RACE

There are some "standardized facts" which any theory of the consumption function should be able to explain. One of them is the difference in the propensities to consume of black and white households, so let us see whether the measured income theories, the full permanent income theory, or the standard income theory can explain it best.[1] There are two things to be explained. One is that at each income level black households have a smaller propensity to consume than do white households. The second is that when one combines households in all income groups, black households have a higher propensity to consume than do white households. The second of these observations is easily explained by the absolute income theory, but the smaller propensity to consume of black households at each income level is much more puzzling, and it has received a great deal of attention. Indeed, just because it is so puzzling, the explanation of this fact has become an important task for any consumption function theory.

Previous Explanations

One explanation, advanced by Dorothy Brady and Rose Friedman, and used as important evidence by Duesenberry, is the relative income

---

1. The use of this difference in testing consumption function theories has been challenged by Broadus Sawyer, who argued that race per se is not a factor influencing the propensity to consume, but that it merely masks the effect of other variables. ("An Examination of Race as a Factor in Negro-White Consumption Patterns," *Review of Economics and Statistics*, Vol. XLIV, May 1962, pp. 217–20). But this comment misses the point. The reason why the black-white savings difference has attracted attention is precisely because it can be treated as showing the effect of other variables, such as relative income, or permanent income, rather than because of any effects specific to race. Anyone who assumes that the difference in the average propensity to consume of black and white households is due to a racial factor per se could not use this difference as demonstrating the significance of

theory explanation.[2] Insofar as the emulation effect operates within each racial group, a black household with an income of, say, $7,000 has less "contact with superior goods" than does a white household with the same income, and hence it is under less pressure to consume as much as a white household. As a result, at the same income level, black households save more than white households. Not surprisingly, when households are classified not by measured income but by their relative position in the income distribution of their own race, most of this difference in saving disappears. Moreover, as Brady and Friedman pointed out, since blacks do have *some* contact with the goods consumed by whites, the relative income theory as well as the absolute income theory can explain the greater average propensity to consume for blacks when households in all income groups are combined.[3]

Another explanation which does not invoke the relative income theory and which is consistent with the absolute income theory is the availability of consumer credit. Richard Sterner, Gunnar Myrdal, Faith Williams, and Alice Hanson, as well as James Tobin, have pointed out that limitations on the availability of consumer credit inhibits dissaving by black households and hence reduces their consumption.[4] As Tobin has shown, the main difference in the saving of black and white households is not a difference in positive saving but turns out to be a difference in *dissaving*. Since the relative income theory implies a difference in positive saving as well as in dissaving, Tobin argued that it fails this test. In addition to credit availability, Tobin also used the lower stock of

---

permanent income, relative income, liquid assets, and so on. What the various consumption function theories do in using the difference between black and white households is to *reject* a racial interpretation of this difference by showing that it can be explained without invoking a racial difference.

2. Dorothy Brady and Rose Friedman, "Savings and the Income Distribution," in Conference on Research in Income and Wealth, *Studies in Income and Wealth*, Vol. 10 (New York, National Bureau of Economic Research, 1947), pp. 262–65; James Duesenberry, *Income, Saving and the Theory of Consumer Behavior* (Cambridge, Harvard University Press, 1952), pp. 50–52.

3. Dorothy Brady and Rose Friedman, *op. cit.*, p. 265.

4. Richard Sterner, *The Negro's Share* (New York, Harper & Brothers, 1943), p. 93; Gunnar Myrdal, *An American Dilemma* (New York, Harper & Brothers, 1962), p. 368; Faith Williams and Alice Hanson, *Money Disbursements of Wage Earners and Clerical Workers 1934–36, Summary Volume* (U.S. Bureau of Labor Statistics, Bulletin 638, 1941), p. 32; James Tobin, "Relative Income, Absolute Income, and Saving," in *Money, Trade and Economic Growth, Essays in Honor of John H. Williams* (New York, Macmillan, 1956), pp. 143–49.

wealth of black households to account for in their lower level of dissaving.[5]

As discussed in Chapter 3, Friedman explained the lower average propensity to consume of black households at each income level by invoking the permanent income theory. And in fact a similar explanation had been offered many years earlier by Richard Sterner and Gunnar Myrdal.[6] The permanent income theory explanation has been buttressed by Robert Brown and Franklin Fisher, who showed that it can account for the greater dissaving of black households.[7] This is so because the representative white household with negative transitory income in a low income group has experienced a proportionately much larger reduction in income than is true for black households, and hence dissaves more.[8]

Apart from these explanations using the permanent income theory, the relative income theory, wealth, and consumer credit, some economists have invoked a number of other factors. Sterner and Myrdal argued that due to the lesser chances for advancement there is a greater reservoir of ability at low income levels among black than among white households.[9] Faith Williams and Alice Hanson stressed that black households face greater insecurity, have fewer liquid assets, and also tend to carry life insurance more frequently than white households.[10] Leo Fish-

5. James Tobin, *op. cit.*, p. 144.

6. "There may be quite a number of other factors, either operating independently or influencing the credit rating of families. In any given income group White families are more likely than Negro families to have seen 'better days.' Such families may have savings to draw upon or they may not have become adjusted to their more limited incomes. In any given income group, also, White families probably include a large proportion which have reason to anticipate higher earnings in the future and hence find it easier than Negro families to obtain credit and less necessary to keep their expenditures within their current incomes." Richard Sterner, *op. cit.*, p. 93. For a similar statement by Gunnar Myrdal, see *An American Dilemma, op. cit.*, p. 368.

7. "Negro-White Savings Differentials and the Modigliani-Brumberg Hypothesis," *Review of Economics and Statistics*, Vol. XL, February 1958, Part 1, pp. 79–81. While this article is written in terms of the life cycle hypothesis, it can readily be applied to the permanent income theory too.

8. To be sure, in the upper income classes black households are more likely than white households to have positive transitory income, but since there are relatively more white households with permanently low incomes than there are black households with permanently high incomes, one would expect the permanent income theory effect to show up more for dissaving than for saving.

9. Richard Sterner, *op. cit.*, p. 93; Myrdal, *op. cit.*, pp. 368–69.

10. *Op. cit.*, p. 32.

man pointed to greater insecurity,[11] while Friend and Schor have suggested that the observed phenomenon may in part simply reflect errors in the data.[12] Lawrence Klein and H. W. Mooney concluded that neither relative income nor consumer credit availability nor wealth gives an adequate explanation of the difference in the average propensity to consume, and that a valid explanation has to introduce such variables as job security and demographic factors.[13]

The Standard Income Theory Explanation

In addition to these various theories, the standard income theory, too, can account for the difference in the average propensity to consume of black and white households. It accounts for the lower average propensity to consume of black households at each measured income level by using the explanations invoked by both the relative income theory and the permanent income theory. It explains the greater average propensity to consume for all black households taken together, not as Friedman did by pointing to special factors (the frequency of entrepreneurs and the peculiarities of the sample), but quite simply by the lower average income of Blacks—that is, by the failure of the proportionality hypothesis.

The standard income theory can be applied to this problem in a specific way by calculating prediction coefficients using the difference in the mean measured incomes of the two races as a measure of the

11. "Consumer Expectations and the Consumption Function," *Southern Economic Journal,* Vol. 20, January 1954, pp. 243–51.

12. "Who Saves?" *Review of Economics and Statistics,* Vol. XLI, May 1959, Part 2, p. 234. Friend and Schor adjusted the savings estimates of the 1950 BLS expenditure survey for the understatement of cash and deposits. Since white households held proportionately more deposits than black households, this reduced the gap between the two saving rates. The adjusted data showed no difference in the savings ratios of white and black households with incomes of over $3500. However, this adjustment is very much open to debate. In making up for the underreporting of cash and deposits, Friend and Schor raised all reported holdings proportionally. But this implies that the greater the holdings reported by a household, the greater the amount by which it is underreporting its holdings. There seems to be little justification for this assumption; the opposite assumption seems, if anything, more plausible.

13. "Negro-White Savings Differentials and the Consumption Function Problem," *Econometrica,* Vol. 21, July 1953, pp. 425–56. See also James Stafford, Keith Cox and James Higginbotham, "Some Consumption Pattern Differences between Urban Whites and Negroes," *Social Science Quarterly,* Vol. 49, December 1968, p. 629. This paper argues that because of psychological deprivation, black households have a greater urge for "compensatory consumption."

difference in their permanent incomes. Unfortunately, relatively few budget studies are available for this, since obviously foreign budget studies are not applicable. Hence, I have used some budget studies in this chapter which I would not have used if I had as many of them available as I did for occupational groups. Moreover, the fact that there are a number of special factors, such as job insecurity, which may well play an important role in explaining the difference in the average propensity to consume of black and white households means that these prediction coefficients may be biased. In addition, as Friend and Schor pointed out, there are serious problems about the accuracy of the data.

The first available budget study is for 1916, and covers manual and clerical employees in the District of Columbia.[14] Unfortunately, it excludes salaried workers earning more than $1,800, thus presumably excluding a number of households with positive transitory income. This creates potentially serious biases, though the direction of the net bias is not clear.

The next budget study classifying households by race covers 1934–1936.[15] Unfortunately, it used highly restrictive eligibility requirements. Looking at all income classes jointly, it showed black households as having a slightly *smaller* average propensity to consume than white households, thus reversing the usual findings. However, as Friedman pointed out, the smaller average propensity to consume for black households shown by this study is probably due to its restrictive eligibility requirements.[16] Then there is the 1935–1936 budget study used by Friedman, and discussed in Chapter 3. I have not undertaken separate calculations for this budget study, but have used Friedman's data instead.[17]

The next set of data come from the postwar Survey of Consumer Finances. In his dissertation Horace Mooney pooled data from annual surveys for 1947–1950.[18] He excluded entrepreneurial households and

14. "Cost of Living in the District of Columbia," *Monthly Labor Review*, Vol. 5, October 1917, pp. 1–17.

15. Faith Williams and Alice Hanson, *op. cit.*

16. *A Theory of the Consumption Function* (Princeton, Princeton University Press, 1957), p. 84n.

17. For six of the eight cities for which Friedman gave data, it is possible to calculate the prediction coefficients with little additional work. To calculate these coefficients, I needed the number of families in each group. I used the number of families providing expenditures as given in BLS *Miscellaneous Publication* 648, Vol. 8, pp. 22–23, 30–33, 38; and U.S. Department of Agriculture, *Changes in Assets and Liabilities of Families, Miscellaneous Publication 464* (1941), pp. 93–96.

18. "Some Factors Associated with Negro-White Savings Differentials," unpublished Ph.D. dissertation, University of Michigan, 1953, pp. 215–16.

presented his data separately for the North and the South. This separation is important because the Keynesian consumption function does not
seem to apply even to the *measured* income of southern black households.[19] I have therefore used only his data for the North.[20] In his
study there are no entrepreneurial households to bias the results, but
unfortunately, there is again a bias resulting from the eligibility requirement. The data exclude relief families as well as nonrelief families with
very low incomes and broken families. This probably ensures that a
larger proportion of black than white families were excluded. Since the
excluded families are very likely to have negative transitory income
and hence a high average propensity to consume, the average propensity
to consume of black households is presumably biased downwards more
than is the case for white households.

The unpublished data from the Survey of Consumer Finances for
1948 which I used in Chapter 10 also provide information on the
respondent's race. Since there is no serious eligibility requirements
problem, and further since I excluded entrepreneurial households, this
figure is not subject to the criticisms which can be made of all the
previously discussed coefficients.

19. For the South his data show the following:

Income Class	Number of Spending Units	Saving-Income Ratio
$0–999	121	0.8%
1000–1999	159	2.0
2000–2999	71	−0.3
3000–3999	21	0.1
4000 and over	10	−4.4

SOURCE: *Ibid.*, pp. 214–15.

As Mooney pointed out (pp. 12–13) a similar thing showed up in the
1935–1936 *Study of Consumer Purchases*. However, in the 1960–1961 BLS
expenditure survey, southern black households had a normal consumption
function. This failure of the usual consumption function in two budget studies
is very puzzling, and I know of no explanation for it.

20. The permanent income theory attempts to reconcile a cross-section
marginal propensity to consume measured income which is less than the
average propensity with the contradictory results shown by time series data.
A cross-section study in which the marginal propensity to consume is greater
than the average propensity can tell us little about the permanent income
theory. Admittedly, this may seem unfair to the permanent income theory,
for these results can be read as a rejection of the measured income theories
and the standard income theory. But since the saving behavior of southern
Negro households as shown in these two studies differs so sharply from that
shown in other studies, it must be ascribed to some special factor.

The next budget study is the 1950 Bureau of Labor Statistics survey,[21] a study which is bad for testing consumption function theories because of data defects.[22] Eligibility requirements pose no serious problem here, but self-employed households are included in the data. The Bureau of Labor Statistics 1960–1961 consumer expenditure study provides data by race within each occupation so that it is possible to exclude the self-employed.[23] And this is what I did.

The final study which is available is a Bureau of Labor Statistics survey for five cities in 1963. I used only two of these cities (Houston and Kansas City) since the others each have less than twenty black households in their sample.[24]

Results

As Table 26 shows, with one exception (the 1934–1936 budget study) the data reject the proportionality hypothesis. And this exception is a budget study, which as Friedman pointed out is very seriously biased by its eligibility requirements.[25] But since most of the other budget studies also suffer from biases, it would be unfair to the permanent income theory to throw out this particular study. Even if the deviant case is not eliminated, the proportionality hypothesis is rejected by seven out of eight cases. The probability of this being merely due to sampling fluctuations in a universe where the marginal propensity to consume is the same for black and white households is less than 5 percent.

But there is a nasty complication. The reason I am using several budget studies and not a single one is that in any one year one group may be receiving more transitory income than the other. But here the years covered by some of the budget studies overlap. The deviant study covers two years, 1934–1936, and one of these years (1935–1936) is also a year covered by one of the other studies.[26] Similarly, the Mooney

21. Wharton School of Finance and Commerce, *Study of Consumer Expenditures, Incomes and Saving* (Philadelphia, University of Pennsylvania Press, 1957), Vol. 18, p. 50.

22. See Franco Modigliani and Albert Ando, "The 'Permanent Income' and the 'Life Cycle' Hypothesis of Saving Behavior: Comparison and Test," in Irwin Friend and Robert Jones, *Consumption and Saving* (Philadelphia, University of Pennsylvania Press, 1960), Vol. 2, pp. 51–73.

23. U.S. Bureau of Labor Statistics, *Consumer Expenditures and Income, Cross Classification of Family Characteristics* (*BLS Report 237–38, Supplement 2, Part A*, July 1964), pp. 50–52.

24. Bureau of Labor Statistics, *Consumer Expenditure and Income, BLS Reports,* 237–79, 237–82, p. 7, 1965.

25. *Op. cit.*, pp. 84n.

26. The 1935–1936 study actually covers only a twelve months period, and I am therefore considering it as a one-year study. Similarly, since the

Table 26

Prediction Coefficients—Race

Budget Study	Rejects Proportionality Hypothesis	Prediction Coefficient	Biased Due to	
			Eligibility Requirements	Differences in Frequency of Entrepreneurship
1916	x	.5	x	
1934–36		−.1	x	
1935–36	x	.3	x	x
1947–50	x	.5	x	
1948	x	.7		
1950	x	.3		x
1960–61	x	.3		
1963	x	.1		x

study covers three years, 1947–1950, and two of my other studies cover two of these years, 1948 and 1950. To make matters worse, the 1948 study used the same set of basic data—though with differences due to eligibility requirements, which Mooney used as a part of his three-year pooled data. Hence, it is not really correct to apply a significance test as though all the eight cases represent independent observations.

Table 27 shows what happens if allowance is made for this fact by excluding certain budget studies. If one excludes all the one-year budget studies covering a year also covered by a longer budget study, the proportionality hypothesis is rejected at the 20 percent level. In all other cases, it is rejected at the 10 percent level. I do not know of any criterion for selecting the best among these sample adjustments. I therefore conclude from this that the comparison of the average propensities to consume of white and black households tends to reject the proportionality hypothesis, but that it *may* not do this at a significance level which makes this evidence conclusive.

Table 26 shows the prediction coefficients for the various budget studies. In calculating them for several of these budget studies I ran into a surprising difficulty. It is hard to calculate the marginal propensity to consume measured income. When I regressed consumption on both income and on family size, I obtained a negative constant term in five of the regressions, and a negative family size term in another regression. In these cases I reran the regression omitting the family size term.[27] But

1934–1936 study covers only a twenty-four-month period, I am treating it as a two-year budget study.

27. In still another regression, the one for the 1948 budget study, I also obtained a negative coefficient for family size. However, its value is so trivial

Table 27

Probability Levels if Sample Is Adjusted in Various Ways

Budget Studies to Be Excluded	Number of Budget Studies	Percent Probability Observed Results Due to Chance[a]
None	8	3.5
Longer Period	6	1.6
Shorter Period	5	18.8
Excluding Shorter Period Study Only if Based on Same Data	7	6.2

SOURCE: Table 26.
[a] Using single tailed binomial test.

this raises a serious question about the accuracy of the coefficient of the income term even in those regressions in which I did not obtain wrong signs for the intercept or for family size. If the family size term can distort the signs in some regression, it may also be distorting the size of the income coefficient in those regressions in which the signs are correct. This is a serious problem. A small error in estimating the marginal propensity to consume can have a big effect on the prediction coefficient since it is calculated as a residual.

The median of the prediction coefficients shown in Table 26 is 0.3.[28] As I pointed out above, most of the budget studies I used in this chapter are ill-suited for this purpose. It is therefore advisable to look not only at the median of all studies but also at the two budget studies which are best for this test, the 1948 and 1960–1961 studies. Their prediction coefficients are 0.7 and 0.3, respectively.

All in all, these data suggest a lower prediction coefficient than that which emerged in the occupational test of the previous chapter. But for the reasons discussed above, as well as because of the small size of the sample, I consider the mean prediction coefficient obtained on this test less reliable than the one obtained in the previous chapter.

Other Variables

As before, there is always the possibility that the effect I am attributing to differences in permanent income could be due to other factors. Of the eighteen variables discussed in connection with previous

---

(0.02) that it does not really create a problem and I did not recalculate the regression. In one other regression I did not use a family size variable because I had only four income classes.

28. Adjusting the sample for duplication of years along the lines of Table 26 makes no difference to the median value of the prediction coefficients.

tests, there are five which *may* reduce the propensity to consume of black households. One is that black households hold a lower ratio of liquid assets to income than do white households.[29] And the same is true for wealth. Second, consumer credit is less available to black households, and third, the interest rate paid on consumer credit is probably higher for black households.

Fourth, there is the fact that white households probably receive more capital gains relative to income than do black households. Since these budget studies do not treat capital gains as income, but do include consumption out of capital gains in consumption, the average propensity to consume of white households is biased upward relative to that of black households.

Then there is the dispersion of transitory income—in other words, insecurity. As I pointed out above, some authors have explained the high savings of black households at each income level as a defense against greater economic insecurity. However, there are two problems with this explanation. One is that while greater insecurity raises the demand for wealth, once the wealth-income ratio has been raised to its equilibrium level the extra incentive to save disappears.

The other difficulty is that it is not certain that black households really do face greater income variability than white households. To be sure, they experience more unemployment. But given the fact that our unemployment compensation system has a fixed dollar ceiling on benefits, unemployment—insofar as it does not exceed the maximum compensation period—results in a smaller percentage cut in the incomes of blacks than of whites. However, since black workers tend to stay unemployed longer than whites, they are more likely to exhaust their unemployment benefits, which tends to make their income more variable again. But, there is still another countervailing factor. If forced onto relief, it probably means a smaller percentage reduction in income for black than for white households.[30] It is therefore not certain that income is really more variable for black than for white households. Klein and Mooney found that anticipated temporary income changes did not differ very much for the two groups.[31] However, as pointed out in Chapter 4, responses to questions about income expectations are a very poor indicator of actual income changes.

29. L. Klein and H. W. Mooney, *op. cit.*, p. 434, and Henry Terrell, "Wealth Accumulation of Black and White Families: The Empirical Evidence," *Journal of Finance*, Vol. XXVI, May 1971, pp. 363–78.

30. The frequency of relief is higher among black households and this may raise their average propensity to consume. Since households have to use up assets prior to being given relief, a household likely to be seeking relief in the future has less of an incentive to save.

31. Lawrence Klein and H. W. Mooney, *op. cit.*, pp. 444–45.

Offsetting, at least in part, these six factors which may lower the average propensity to consume of black households relative to white households, is the fact that a given family income means a smaller per capita real income for black than for white households.[32] The other variables discussed in Chapter 10 are ones which are not relevant, such as relative prices, or ones for which no information is available, such as attitudes toward saving.[33]

Conclusion

The evidence from this chapter is not as strong as that from the comparison of occupations. But this should not obscure the fact that the standard income theory can explain the difference in the black-white saving ratios better than either the full permanent income theory or the relative income theory. In order to explain the higher propensity to consume of black households at all income levels combined, Friedman had to invoke the lower frequency of entrepreneurship among black households and the eligibility requirements imposed in the budget studies. The standard income theory does not need to invoke these special factors. And, it should be noted, these factors are not applicable to two budget studies (1948 and 1960–1961), both of which, all the same, show for all income levels combined a higher propensity to consume for black than for white households and therefore disconfirm the proportionality hypothesis. Similarly, the standard income theory is superior to the relative income theory because it can explain why the main difference between black and white households shows up among dissavers by invoking the Brown-Fisher argument discussed above.[34]

32. See Henry Terrell, "The Data on Relative White-Nonwhite Income and Earnings Reexamined: A Comment on the Papers by Guthrie and Ashenfelter," *Journal of Human Resources,* Vol. VI, Summer 1971, pp. 386–91.

33. Home ownership is more frequent among whites, but the proportion of households repaying mortgage debts is about the same in both groups. (Mooney, *op. cit.,* p. 158.) Insofar as home ownership affects the propensity to consume through the repayment of mortgage debt, the frequency of home ownership is not relevant.

34. Unfortunately, it is not possible to evaluate the standard income theory's explanation vis-à-vis the absolute income theory's explanation (availability of consumer credit and assets).

Twelve

LOCATION AND CONSUMPTION

In the foregoing chapters I classified households by occupation and race; this leaves one other feasible permanent income proxy, geography. Comparing the propensities to consume of households in different locations is not new. For example, Rose Friedman and Dorothy Brady, as well as James Duesenberry, used such a geographic test as support for the relative income theory, a test which was criticized by Tobin, who was in turn criticized by Friedman.[1]

In this chapter I am using a classification of households by location to test the (1) absolute income theory, (2) the relative income theory, (3) the full permanent income theory, (4) the standard income theory, and (5) these theories combined with the further hypothesis, stated by Kuznets, that urbanization, in and of itself, raises the average propensity to consume.[2] (I am not testing the other wealth theories since they are

1. Rose Friedman and Dorothy Brady, "Savings and the Income Distribution," in Conference on Research in Income and Wealth, *Studies in Income and Wealth*, Vol. 10 (New York, National Bureau of Economic Research, 1947), pp. 250–65; James Duesenberry, *Income, Saving and the Theory of Consumer Behavior* (Cambridge, Harvard University Press, 1952), pp. 52–54; James Tobin, "Relative Income, Absolute Income and Saving," in *Money, Trade and Economic Growth, Essays in Honor of John H. Williams* (New York, Macmillan, 1951), pp. 149–52. Milton Friedman, *A Theory of the Consumption Function* (Princeton, Princeton University Press, 1957), pp. 173–81.

2. "Proportion of Capital Formation to National Product," American Economic Association, *Papers and Proceedings*, Vol. XLII, May 1952, p. 521. Harold Watts, too, has suggested such an urbanization effect for young households. ("Long Run Income Expectations and Consumer Saving," in Thomas Dernburg, Richard Rosett, and Harold Watts, *Studies in Household Economic Behavior*, New Haven, Yale University Press, 1958, p. 129.) James Morgan's data show that, on the whole, the saving-income ratio decreases with increasing population. ("An Analysis of Expenditure and Saving," in Richard Kosobud and James Morgan, *Consumer Behavior of Individual Families over Two and Three Years*, Ann Arbor, Survey Research Center, University of Michigan, 1964, p. 123.)

not directly applicable here in any way which differs from the full permanent income theory.) The data available for this are groupings of households by (1) farm, rural nonfarm, and urban status, (2) regions, (3) city type, and (4) city income. The last of these tests is the most important one since it deals specifically with the permanent income theory and with the standard income theory. As will be shown below, other tests do not distinguish between the permanent income theory and the relative income theory.

Geographic tests of the permanent income theory face several difficulties. One is the problem of determining permanent income. Even the determination of the *relative* level of permanent money income is not always as easy as it was for the groups discussed in the preceding chapters. Second, there is the price index problem. The same money income denotes different real incomes in various parts of the country, and price indexes to adjust for this are available only for selected cities. Both of these difficulties mean that the analysis must be limited to ranking tests comparing households generally in two or three localities at a time. When taking two or three localities at a time, permanent income *ranking* can be determined, even though it is not possible to determine permanent incomes in dollar terms. Differences in price levels are much less dangerous for a ranking test than for a test which tries to quantify permanent income differences more precisely. One can assume that price level differences are positively correlated with income differences, but are not sufficient to reverse these differences.

A third difficulty is that differences in the mean incomes in various localities are usually fairly small, so that it is relatively easy for other variables to swamp the effect of income differences. Finally, there is the fact that the relative income theory does not provide an unambiguous testable prediction for geographic tests since its definition of "peer group" is so vague.

Given these difficulties, I have confined the analysis to U.S. data; but the foreign data I have come across do not contradict my conclusion.[3] I have calculated prediction coefficients only for the comparison of cities with different incomes, the one case where geographic price indexes are available.

Before starting on the various tests, it is necessary to review the implications of the consumption function theories for geographic differences in the average propensities to consume. These implications are

3. Among U.S. data, I did not use the 1950 BLS survey since these data are bad. See Franco Modigliani and Albert Ando, "The 'Permanent Income' and the 'Life Cycle' Hypothesis of Saving Behavior: Comparison and Tests," in Irwin Friend and Robert Jones, *Consumption and Saving* (Philadelphia, University of Pennsylvania Press, 1960), Vol. 2, pp. 51–73.

obvious for both the absolute income theory and the permanent income theory. The absolute income theory predicts that the average propensity to consume is negatively correlated with the income level, while the permanent income theory, through its proportionality hypothesis, implies that this correlation is zero.

The implication of the relative income theory is harder to determine. On Duesenberry's own interpretation, its prediction is the same as that of the permanent income theory. This is so because households are affected by the consumption of other households in their own locality rather than by consumption of households all across the nation.[4] As pointed out in Chapter 2, the relative income theory rejects the proportionality hypothesis only because of the emulation effect; hence if there is no interregional emulation effect, then the two theories share a common implication as far as a geographic test is concerned.[5] But it is by no means clear that the emulation effect is, in fact, locally confined. Due to national advertising, as well as travel, households do have contact with superior goods consumed in other places. Hence, if the proportionality hypothesis is disconfirmed by a geographic test, this would require only a minor modification in the relative income theory rather than its abandonment. The situation of the relative income theory with regard to a geographic test is quite different from that for tests using occupation or race. In most geographic tests the relative income theory (with a local emulation effect) has the same implication as the permanent income theory, and a quite different implication from the absolute income theory.

As far as the standard income theory is concerned, since it combines elements of the permanent income theory and the relative income theory, its prediction depends upon whether the relative income theory's emulation effect is entirely local or not.

Comparison of Urban, Rural Nonfarm, and Farm Households

Table 28 shows the average propensities to consume of farm, rural nonfarm, and urban households for 1961. Looking at households outside standard metropolitan areas first, the relative money incomes of these three types of households corresponds to a priori expectations—incomes are lowest for farmers and highest for urban households. Ac-

4. "Our basic theory shows that the saving ratio for an individual family is a function of its position in the income distribution. *This result is produced by social factors which are local in character.*" James Duesenberry, *op. cit.*, p. 52, italics added.

5. This, of course, relates only to the proportionality hypothesis. The lag hypothesis cannot be tested with geographic data. Differences in the marginal propensities to consume permanent and transitory income can be tested here only in the city income test.

Table 28

Mean Income and Average Propensity to Consume: Urban, Rural
Nonfarm, and Farm Households, 1961

Income and Propensity to Consume	Outside Standard Metropolitan Areas			Inside Standard Metropolitan Areas		
	Urban	Rural Nonfarm	Farm	Urban	Rural Nonfarm	Farm
Mean Income[a]	$4594	$3806	$3509	$5585	$5637	$4409
Average Propensity to Consume[b]	.942	.936	.862	.926	.926	.881
Family Size	3.1	3.6	3.7	3.0	3.4	3.8
Age of Head	48	46	52	50	51	51
Percent with Persons 65 Years and Over	22	19	25	28	30	25
Percent Homeowners	52	71	70	60	65	71

SOURCE: Based on U.S. Bureau of Labor Statistics, *Consumer Expenditures and Income*, BLS Report #237–93, Supplement 1, p. 11.
[a] Money income after taxes plus value of items received without expense minus "account balancing difference."
[b] Gifts and contribution included in consumption.

cordingly, unless this ranking by money incomes fails to carry over into
real incomes, the measured income theories predict that farmers have
the highest average propensity to consume and urban households the
lowest. This is exactly the opposite of what the data show, and this
fact tends to support the proportionality hypothesis and to reject the
absolute income theory. To be sure, the difference in the average propensities to consume of urban and rural nonfarm households outside
metropolitan areas is trivial, but since the difference in money income
is fairly substantial (21 percent) the absolute income theory implies
that the propensity to consume should be noticeably greater for rural
nonfarm households, and hence it is contradicted by these data. However, the 21 percent income difference does not carry over fully into
real income, and to this extent this difference in the average propensities
to consume of urban and rural nonfarm households is not strong evidence against the absolute income theory.

For households inside standard metropolitan areas, the picture is
complicated by a discordant fact; contrary to my expectations, the
money income of rural nonfarm households slightly exceeds that of
urban households. Since this *may* represent a difference in transitory
income rather than in permanent income, it is probably best to forgo
a comparison of urban and rural nonfarm families. But for farm households the average propensity to consume is substantially less than it is
for urban and for rural nonfarm households, so that these data, too,

Table 29

Mean Income and Average Propensity to Consume
Urban, Rural Nonfarm, Farm Households, 1935–1936

	Type of Household[a]		
Income and Propensity to Consume	Urban	Rural Nonfarm	Farm
Mean Income[b]	$2064	$1607	$1259
Average Propensity to Consume[c]	.892	.877	.875

SOURCE: Based on U.S. National Resources Planning Board, *Family Expenditures in the United States, Statistical Tables and Appendixes*, pp. 127 and 130.

[a] Nonrelief families only.
[b] Income before personal taxes.
[c] Personal taxes and gifts are included in consumption.

reject the absolute income theory. And as Table 29 shows, this rejection of the absolute income theory is confirmed by data for 1935–1936, and here the difference in the average propensity to consume of urban and rural nonfarm households, while still fairly small, is larger than in Table 28.

But before one can take this rejection of the absolute income theory seriously, one should ask whether these results may not be due to the influence of extraneous variables offsetting the effect of income differences on the average propensities to consume. Accordingly, Table 28 shows several variables which affect consumption. The first of them, family size, can hardly be responsible for the lower average propensity to consume of the groups with lower income, since it points in the wrong direction. The age variable, too, cannot account for the observed differences in the average propensities to consume since it shows little systematic relation to income. And the same is true, outside standard metropolitan areas, for the next variable, the percent of households containing an older person. However, the proportion of households who own their own home is negatively related to income in these data. If, as has often been claimed, home ownership lowers the recorded average propensity to consume, it could account for the observed results. When discussing occupational groups, I dismissed differences in homeownership, because such differences are not an independent factor, but at least in part merely reflect income differences. But here this treatment is less justified, not only because differences in home ownership may reflect differences in costs and benefits of home ownership, but also because here the correlation between income and home ownership is negative. However, differences in home ownership cannot explain the difference in the average propensities to consume of farm and rural nonfarm households outside standard metropolitan areas, and so the

Table 30

Mean Income and Average Propensity to Consume by Location and Employment Status, 1961*

Income and Propensity to Consume	Self-employed Households			Other Households		
	Urban	Rural Nonfarm	Farm	Urban	Rural Nonfarm	Farm
Mean Income	$8477	$6181	$4579	$5730	$4125	$4083
Average Propensity to Consume	.920	.899	.861	.973	.970	.931

SOURCE: Based on Kathryn Murphy, "Spending and Saving in Urban and Rural Areas," *Monthly Labor Review*, Vol. 88, October 1965, p. 1175.

NOTE: For definition of income and consumption, see notes to Table 28.

* All data are only approximate since they were derived as residuals from rounded data.

absolute income theory cannot be saved by invoking differences in home ownership.

One other variable which may be relevant is the frequency of entrepreneurship. Accordingly, Table 30 shows the average propensities to consume of households classified by employment status, and it supports the results shown in Tables 28 and 29.

But there is another variable which may be called upon to save the absolute income theory. This is the taste variable, or more specifically, an urbanization effect.[6] If, as may well be the case, farmers place the most stress, and urban households the least stress, on the traditional virtue of thriftiness, the above results can be reconciled with the absolute income theory.

Thus, the absolute income theory, in its simple form, is rejected by these data. But if one modified the theory by introducing an urbanization effect, then this theory can be saved. This is not to say that these data then support it as against the permanent income theory and the relative income theory, but at least they do not reject it. The relative income theory with a local emulation effect, or with an urbanization effect, is consistent with these data, as is the standard income theory. And the full permanent income theory is, of course, not contradicted either.

Regional Differences

The 1960–1961 Survey of Consumer Expenditures provides data for urban areas classified into four regions, and they can be used for another test. Unfortunately, no comparable data are available for other years so

6. Actually, this term is a misnomer because farm households and rural nonfarm households do not really differ in the degree of "urbanization."

that it is not possible to classify the urban areas of these four regions by permanent income.[7] However, it is a well-known fact that incomes are lower in the South than in other regions, and hence one can contrast the average propensity to consume in the South with that in other regions.

Table 31 shows the average propensities to consume for urban places in the four regions. Comparing the South to the West and the Northeast, the absolute income theory's prediction is wrong, and it is correct only if the South is compared to the North Central region. And since the data relate only to urban areas, the urbanization variable cannot be invoked to support the absolute income theory.[8] To be sure, the differences in the average propensities to consume, particularly those between the South and the West, are fairly small. But since the income difference between the South and the West are substantial (22 percent), the absolute income theory predicts that the average propensity to consume is smaller in the West, and this prediction is falsified.

Thus the absolute income theory, with or without an urbanization effect, fails this regional test. The relative income theory with only a local emulation effect makes no prediction about the correlation of regional incomes and propensities to consume. It is, therefore, not contradicted by these data. But if the emulation effect is not local, then it is contradicted. And the same is true for the standard income theory. The full permanent income theory is, of course, in no way contradicted.

City Size

A third way of testing the absolute income theory is to classify cities by size. Since it has been established that *within* standard metropolitan areas mean incomes and city size are negatively correlated,[9] one can use this fact to classify city types by permanent income. Table 32 shows the average propensities to consume for three city types within standard metropolitan areas. The results are mixed. The smallest city type has the highest income, and in accordance with the absolute income theory, the lowest average propensity to consume. But the central cities have a lower income and also a *lower* average propensity to

7. Many data for regions as a whole exist, but since low income regions are generally less urbanized than richer regions there is a danger of confusing the effects of income and urbanization.

8. It is doubtful that the *degree* of urbanization can save the situation for the absolute income theory since the standard metropolitan areas included in the sample are, on the average, larger in the Northeast (though not the West) than in the South.

9. See Edward Mansfield, "City Size and Income," in Conference on Research in Income and Wealth, *Regional Income, Studies in Income and Wealth,* Vol. 21 (Princeton, Princeton University Press, 1957), pp. 285–86.

Table 31

Mean Income, Average Propensity to Consume, and Selected Variables,
Urban Families of Two or More Persons, by Regions, 1960–1961

Income and Propensity to Consume	South	West	North-east	North Central
Mean Income After Taxes	$6111	$7485	$6946	$6560
Average Propensity to Consume	.933	.941	.944	.908
Family Size	3.5	3.6	3.4	3.6
Age of Head	46	44	47	45
Percent Homeowners	57	59	52	62

SOURCE: Based on U.S. Bureau of Labor Statistics, *Consumer Expenditures and Income, Urban Places in the Southern Region, 1960–61, Urban Places in the Western Region,* BLS Report 237–37, Suppl. 2, Pt. A, p. 4. BLS Report 237–36, Suppl. 2, Pt. A, p. 4; *Urban Places in the Northeastern Region,* BLS Report 237–34, Suppl. 2, Pt. A, p. 4; *Urban Places in the North Central Region,* BLS Report 237–35, Suppl. 2, Pt. A, p. 4.

NOTE: For definition of income and consumption, see notes to Table 28.

consume than do "other cities 50,000 and over." Hence the absolute income theory predicts correctly for two comparisons and incorrectly for the third. The latter result could *perhaps* be explained as due to differences in family size, but differences in the proportion of homeowners and in the proportion of households with old members may be responsible for an offsetting bias. Obviously, in this case one cannot appeal to an urbanization variable to save the absolute income theory.

However, once again, the difference in the average propensities to consume of central cities and "other cities" is small, and in this case, the income difference is fairly small, too (12 percent in 1960 and 13 percent in 1961). And, insofar as living costs are higher in central cities, these figures overstate the difference in real income. When one takes account of this, as well as of the difference in family size, and considers the fact that the absolute income theory does predict correctly in two of the three cases, it would be unwise to treat this city size test as disconfirming the absolute income theory. It is probably better to treat it as inconclusive. If one were to treat it as otherwise, it would be very hard to explain the results of the following test.

City Incomes

The available data permit one more geographic test, a test specifically oriented to the permanent income theory and the standard income theory. This is a test using the real permanent income of cities. If there is a negative correlation between the average propensity to consume and the permanent incomes of cities, this would disconfirm the full permanent income theory. And if this correlation is less pronounced for

Table 32

Mean Income, Average Propensity to Consume, and Selected Characteristics,
by City Size Inside Metropolitan Areas, 1960 and 1961

Income, Propensity to Consume	1960			1961		
	Central City	Other Cities 50,000 and Over	Places Under 50,000 in Urban Areas	Central City	Other Cities 50,000 and Over	Places Under 50,000 in Urban Areas
Income	$5958	$6666	$7768	$5856	$6597	$7723
Average Propensity to Consume	.946	.950	.928	.938	.950	.909
Family Size	2.8	3.0	3.5	2.9	3.1	3.4
Age of Head	48	47	44	49	47	45
Percent Homeowners	43	47	69	40	48	69
Percent with Person 65 and Over	23	22	17	26	22	16

SOURCE: Based on U.S. Bureau of Labor Statistics, *Consumer Expenditures and Income, Urban United States, 1960–61*, BLS Report 237–38, Pt. A. Suppl. 1, pp. 11 and 16.
NOTE: For definition of income and consumption, see notes to Table 28.

permanent incomes than for the measured incomes *within* each city, this would support both the standard income theory and the relative income theory in versions which do not confine the emulation effect entirely to the particular locality in which the household resides.

The ranking of cities by their income which one obtains by looking at the Bureau of Labor Statistics data is, of course, a ranking by *measured* income only; but using other data it is possible to see whether this ranking corresponds to a ranking by permanent income. Department of Commerce data give per capita income for standard metropolitan areas for certain postwar years, six of them at the time of writing— (1950, 1959, 1962, 1965, 1966, and 1967).[10] For each of these six years I ranked a sample of cities by their measured income. I then considered a difference in measured income to indicate a difference in permanent income only if this differential persisted for these six years, and if it also showed up in the Bureau of Labor Statistics surveys for both 1960 and 1961.

10. "Metropolitan Area Incomes in 1967," *Survey of Current Business,* Vol. 49, May 1969, pp. 26–30. This source also gives prewar income figures but since these years are too far in the past, I did not use them. These data relate to the whole standard metropolitan area while the BLS data refer only to a narrower area.

The city income data are, of course, in money terms, while the proper comparison requires real income. Fortunately, for selected cities the Bureau of Labor Statistics provides a series of standard budget costs for a moderate living standard.[11] I used this index in conjunction with the city CPI index to deflate the income data.[12] The necessary data are available for only eighteen cities.

Although the ranking of cities in the Commerce data varies little from year to year, there is *some* variability, and, probably in part because of sampling fluctuations, there is some difference between the ranking of these cities in the Bureau of Labor Statistics surveys on the one hand and the Commerce income data on the other. These differences are too great to permit one to test the proportionality hypothesis in the most obvious way, that is, by a ranked correlation of city permanent income and city saving-income ratios. Instead, I had to use another technique, one which does not require such a great consistency of rankings. What I did was to consider cities two at a time, selecting the "city pairs" by a reproducible procedure which I decided upon before looking at the average propensities to consume of these cities.[13]

Table 33 shows the average propensities to consume, as well as the prediction coefficients for each of the city pairs.[14] In seven out of eight cases the higher income city had the lower propensity to consume. This

11. U.S. Bureau of Labor Statistics, *City Worker's Family Budgets for a Moderate Living Standard, Autumn, 1966, Bulletin No. 1570–1,* Washington, D.C., 1968.

12. Bureau of the Census, 1968, *Statistical Abstract* (Washington, D.C., 1968), p. 348. Combining these two indexes actually resulted in a hybrid index since they use different weights.

13. I used the following procedure to select city pairs: First, I ranked the cities by family real income in the BLS surveys (separately for 1960 and 1961) and divided the list at the median. I then tried to "marry" the highest ranking city above the median to the highest ranking city below the median, the second highest city above the median to the second highest city below the median, and so on. This "marriage" had to be validated by my permanent income criterion; in each of the years for which I had data, the real income of the higher city had to exceed that of the lower city. In addition, the income differential had to exceed 5 percent in the BLS survey I used. This provided three city pairs for 1960, and one for 1961. I then took the remaining cities and tried to "marry" the highest city above the median to a city below the median starting with the highest ranking city. I did this until I had used up all the cities I could pair in this way. This provided two additional city pairs each year.

14. To calculate the prediction coefficients I needed the marginal propensity to consume measured income. I calculated this by regresssing for (the two cities combined) consumption on income and family size. Unfortunately, I ran into the same problem as in the previous chapter. In half the cases either the constant term or the family size coefficient was negative. In these cases I again omitted the family size variable.

result is significant at a 5 percent level on a binomial test. Thus, once again, the proportionality hypothesis fails a test. This failure is impressive because the income differences between the cities being compared are fairly small, so that it should be relatively easy for other variables to swamp the effect of income differences on the propensity to consume.

Since the prediction coefficient is greater than unity in five out of eight cases, these data do not reject the measured income theory's prediction. But while these data do not support the standard income theory vis-à-vis the measured income theories neither do they reject the standard income theory at any meaningful level of significance.[15]

The median prediction coefficient is 1.5, though for the reason explained on page 284, this is hardly a very reliable figure. While it is, of course, much higher than is predicted by the standard income theory, this difference is not significant; on a binomial test the probability that the true value of the prediction coefficient is as low as 0.4 can be rejected only at the 15 percent significance level.

Table 33 shows that usually the higher income city is larger when measured by the population of the standard metropolitan area. Thus, insofar as city size has a positive effect on the propensity to consume, the prediction coefficients are downward biased.[16] On the other hand, not surprisingly, education is positively related to city income, and this *may* create a bias in the opposite direction. Three other variables, average family size, percent of home ownership and average age of head, show little if any systematic relation to the relative income of cities within each city couple. Thus there are no obvious extraneous variables which can explain the failure of the proportionality hypothesis on this test.

Conclusion

As Table 34 shows, this set of tests rejects the absolute income theory, with and without an urbanization effect, as well as the full permanent income theory. The situation is more complex for the relative income

15. I calculated the prediction coefficients not only by using regression to obtain the marginal propensity to consume measured income, but also by breaking the data for each city at the median income class and comparing mean income and consumption above and below the median. All but one of the prediction coefficients calculated in this manner were above unity, thus rejecting at the 5 percent level the standard income theory's prediction that this coefficient is less than unity. However, there is little reason to think that this method of calculating the prediction coefficients is superior to the regression method described in the previous footnote.

16. But Mizoguchi has shown that at least for Japan, city size does not have a significant effect on saving. *Personal Savings and Consumption in Postwar Japan* (Tokyo, Kinokuniya Bookstore Co., 1970), p. 169.

Table 33

Average Propensity to Consume, Prediction Coefficients, and Selected Characteristics of City Pairs

Cities	Average Propensity to Consume		Prediction Coefficient	Real Income of 1st City as Percent of 2nd City's	Population of 1st SMA as Percent 2nd SMA's Population 1960	Education of Head		Average Family Size		Percent Owning Own Home		Age of Head	
	1st City	2nd City				1st City	2nd City	1st City	2nd City	1st City	2nd City	1st City	2nd City
1960													
Washington-Pittsburgh	86.9	94.7	1.83	112.9	83	12	10	3.1	3.7	43	56	45	50
Chicago-Philadelphia	89.7	98.1	3.84	108.4	143	11	10	3.2	3.1	46	64	46	47
Los Angeles-Atlanta	93.9	94.7	0.49	109.4	594	11	10	3.1	3.1	49	49	53	46
Cleveland-Baltimore	85.5	94.4	1.47	127.2	111	11	10	3.5	3.2	64	58	47	45
Detroit-St. Louis	93.0	91.9	−1.52	109.0	179	10	10	3.3	3.4	65	62	48	47
1961													
Chicago-Pittsburgh	94.2	96.7	.95	114.3	259	11	10	3.3	3.1	47	59	47	49
Washington-Baltimore	88.4	94.3	1.80	117.6	116	12	9	3.1	3.0	42	57	46	47
Cleveland-St. Louis	89.5	92.9	1.60	123.2	91	11	10	3.2	3.2	61	56	48	47

sources: Based on B.L.S. Reports 237 (series for individual cities). Deflated as described in text, U.S. Census Bureau, *Statistical Abstract 1966*, pp. 18–19.

Table 34

Performance of Various Theories on Geographic Tests

Comparison of	Absolute Income Theory	Absolute Inc. Theory Plus Urbanization Variable	Relative Income Theory	Full Perm. Income Theory	Standard Income Theory
Farm, Rural Nonfarm, Urban Households	F	P	P[a]	P	P[a]
Regions	F	F	P[b]	P	P[b]
City Size[e]					
City Income	P	P	P[d]	F	P[d]

NOTE: P, passes; F, fails.

[a] With local emulation effect only or urbanization variable.

[b] With local emulation effect only.

[e] Performance of all theories inconclusive.

[d] With emulation effect *not* locally confined.

theory and the standard income theory. They pass the regional test only if the emulation effect is entirely local, and they pass the city income test only if the emulation effect is *not* entirely local. Thus, unless one is willing to argue—and it is a rather artificial argument—that the emulation effect operates between cities but not between regions, both of these theories are rejected too. Thus this set of geographic tests appears to disconfirm *all* the usual consumption function theories.

While it is certainly possible that all of these consumption function theories are invalid, it is rather unlikely. This raises the question whether one of the tests is invalid instead. The most likely candidate is the regional test. This test is based entirely on the comparison of the South with other regions, and the low average propensity to consume in the South, in spite of its low income, may be due to cultural factors. Harold Watts, who also got disparate results when comparing saving behavior in the South and North, suggested: "The explanation of the differences by region may lie well outside the field of economics. Differences in cultural values between the north and south, particularly those which concern family relationships, may affect saving behavior." [17]

It is therefore possible to argue that it is the regional test which is to be rejected, rather than all our usual consumption function theories. If so, then the absolute income theory, the relative income theory, and the standard income theory all with an urbanization variable pass this remaining set of geographic tests. Only the full permanent income theory

17. "Long-Run Income Expectations and Consumer Saving," in Thomas Dernburg, Richard Rosett, and Harold Watts, *Studies in Household Economic Behavior* (New Haven, Yale University Press, 1958), p. 129.

fails. (Admittedly, as discussed in footnote 15, if one treats the data a different way the standard income theory fails, too.)

However, there are two points to be made against dropping the regional test. One is that to drop a test previously decided upon just because it rejects all the theories considered is a questionable method. The second is that the regional test used here is reinforced by some Japanese results. A comparison of the saving ratios of Japanese prefectures does not show a lower propensity to consume for the high income ones.[18] Moreover, when Lott regressed the log of the APC on various characteristics of households he obtained an insignificant coefficient for the rural-urban variable.[19]

Another possibility is to reject the city income test. If so, these geographic tests would still eliminate the absolute income theory (with and without an urbanization variable) but not the relative, standard, and full permanent income theories. However, it is hard to see why this test should be eliminated. All in all, the results of these geographic tests are by no means as clearcut as the results of the previous tests.

18. Mizoguchi, *op. cit.*, pp. 122–25.
19. William Lott, "The Effect of Demographic Characteristics and the Interest Rate on the Consumption Function of an Economy over Time," (unpublished Ph.D. dissertation, North Carolina State University, 1969) p. 32.

INTRODUCTION

The material presented in Part IV does not exhaust the various tests one can undertake with household data. Another way of testing the permanent income theory is to use budgets covering the same household for several years. Since the essence of the permanent income and life cycle theories is that a single year is too short a period over which to compare income and consumption, using household budgets which cover several years is really the most straightforward way of testing these theories. The fact that this method has not been used much in the past reflects the scarcity of such data rather than any dissatisfaction with the method. However, I have obtained some small samples of household budgets covering several years, and have used them in the following two chapters. Chapter 13 deals with two samples of five-year budgets and Chapter 14 deals with a small group of budgets covering anywhere from five to thirty-four years. Chapter 15 uses the net worth of households in still another test of the proportionality hypothesis.[1]

1. In addition, as explained in Appendix I, I tried to use another source of data, the Consumer Expenditure Panel data of Consumers Union.

Thirteen

SOME TESTS
WITH FIVE-YEAR BUDGETS

A major difficulty in testing the wealth theories of the consumption function has been the absence of data giving the household's income over many years. But fortunately, two small samples of continuous five-year budgets have recently become available, and in this chapter I am using these data in a battery of tests. Since these data do not give the household's wealth, they cannot be used to test the life cycle hypothesis and some of the other variants of the wealth theory. However, they can be used to test the standard income theory, the permanent income theory, and the Ball-Drake hypothesis. Two things are particularly valuable about these data. One is that they provide a direct way of estimating the lag in the consumption function from household data, and second, they provide a good opportunity for discriminating between the standard income theory on the one hand and the permanent income theory on the other.

The Data

In the postwar period the Swiss and the German governments have both undertaken annual budget surveys, and a small number of households have been carried forward from one survey to the next. Through the courtesy of Dr. L. Heiniger of the Bundesamt für Industrie, Gewerbe und Arbeit, I have obtained usable annual budgets for 124 Swiss households covering a five-year period (1962–1966).[1] In addition, through the courtesy of Mrs. Reddies and Dr. Martin of the Statistisches Bundesamt, I obtained data which allowed me to reconstruct five-year budgets for fifty-four West German households (1959–1963). The German data are not as suitable for testing the permanent income theory as are the Swiss data because they exclude households whose consumption moved outside certain set limits. Thus, the German households

1. For thirty-four of these households, data are available for a full ten years. However, due to the small size of this subsample, I did not use the full ten-year data.

included in the survey for five years are ones whose consumption is fairly stable. The permanent income theory is less relevant for households whose measured income is close to their permanent income. Since there is less of a "permanent income effect" for these households, one would expect that random elements and "reverse causation" may swamp it. And as will be shown below, the permanent income theory and the standard income theory do, in fact, perform much worse for these German data than for the Swiss data.[2]

Appendix V provides a brief discussion of the data as well as of the definitions of income and consumption which I used. Before proceeding it may be worthwhile to consider the reliability of the data. One problem is that this sample can hardly be considered a representative one. Households willing to stay with successive budget studies for five years or more must surely be unusual. And if they are not so to start with, participation in these surveys might make them so. Since they are likely to be particularly careful and rational, one might expect that they are just those households most likely to behave in accordance with the permanent income theory. However, it is by no means clear that this is actually the case to any significant extent. The saving-income ratio of the Swiss households is 7 percent, which is somewhat lower than the 10 percent saving-income ratio of all households in the one-year budget studies. Hence, they are perhaps *not* more cautious and forward looking than other households. Even if there is a bias in these data, there is an offsetting advantage. Households willing to stick with a budget study for five or more years probably record their incomes and consumption more accurately than other households.[3]

In any case, if one were to reject these tests because households who participate in continuous budget surveys differ from other households, one would also have to reject important evidence used to support the permanent income theory. As discussed in Chapter 3, Friedman used samples of households participating in budget surveys for three years in two of his tests. And he referred to the results of one of these tests

2. In addition, the correlation coefficients are much lower for the German data than for the Swiss data. The less the income variability in the sample, the smaller is the proportion of the consumption variance which can be explained by income variance.

I am reporting the results obtained from the German data despite their limited suitability for testing the permanent and standard income theories because it is important to report negative evidence as well as confirming evidence.

3. Robert Ferber, "Does a Panel Operation Increase the Reliability of Survey Data: The Case of Consumer Savings," American Statistical Association, *Proceedings of the Social Statistics Section,* 1964 (Washington, D.C., 1964), pp. 10–16.

(presented at the end of his survey of the budget study evidence) as "in some ways the most striking bit of evidence for our hypothesis that has so far been adduced." [4]

Another problem is that, as pointed out by Daniel Suits,[5] cross-section data are also subject to a simultaneous equation bias. Insofar as households meet a temporary increase in "needs" by increasing their labor input, causation runs from transitory consumption to transitory income, rather than from income to consumption. This is a weakness of all cross-section data.[6]

One bothersome problem in using household data to test the permanent income theory is that such data are often derived from saving surveys and that consumption is then estimated by subtracting saving from income. As pointed out earlier, this creates a common error term in income and consumption and thereby biases the test against the permanent income theory. Fortunately, the Swiss data do not suffer from this problem. They are direct estimates of consumption, and hence they allow one to redo one of Nissan Liviatan's tests discussed in Chapter 5 in a way which meets Friedman's criticism. The German survey included both consumption and saving questions, and it is possible that in some cases households "adjusted" their consumption data to make them consistent with their reported income and saving.

4. *A Theory of the Consumption Function* (Princeton, Princeton University Press, 1957), p. 109. This test is the "effect of change in income" test. The other test using a three-year panel is the one comparing the income elasticity of consumption with the correlation of incomes in different years.

5. "The Determinants of Consumer Expenditure: A Review of Present Knowledge," in Commission on Money and Credit, *Impacts of Monetary Policy* (Englewood Cliffs, New Jersey, Prentice-Hall, 1963), p. 2.

6. How important is it in this case? Unfortunately, it is not possible to answer this question fully, but for the Swiss data some information about it is available. Households increasing their labor input can do so in two ways. One is to work overtime, the other to put additional family members into the labor force. No information is available on the first of these, but there is some information on additional earners, since the data give the head's income as well as total family income. In 22 percent of the cases the head's income accounted for less than 80 percent of family income. However, in a number of cases the earnings of other family members represent, not transitory income but permanent income, since these family members are in the labor force for a relatively long time. If one eliminates all those cases where the head's earnings were less than 80 percent of family income for three out of four consecutive years, the remaining households account for only 15 percent of the Swiss sample. And presumably, in a number of these cases causation does not really run from consumption "needs" to income either. On the other hand, even in households where the head's income accounts for more than 80 percent of family income, causation may still run from consumption to income, particularly since consumption "needs" may make the head work overtime.

One difficulty which bedevils many consumption function studies is the difficulty of measuring income and saving for the self-employed, and also for homeowners. But here all families are headed by employees, and in the Swiss survey only eight are homeowners. To be sure, the exclusion of the self-employed, and essentially of homeowners, means that the results may not be applicable to the whole population. It is certainly conceivable that the permanent income theory applies much better to the self-employed than to employees.[7]

There is relatively little difference in the incomes of the households covered. On the one hand, this makes it more difficult to distinguish the permanent income theory from its rivals, but on the other it reduces heteroscedasticity.

The Tests

I have used these data in eight tests of the permanent income theory and in one test of the Ball-Drake hypothesis. The following matrix shows the various tests, in their order of appearance, together with the particular hypothesis which they test.

| | *Hypothesis Tested* | | | |
Test	*Lag*	*Proportionality*	*Definition of permanent Income*	*Ball-Drake*
1. Length of accounting period	x	x		
2. Weight of years	x			
3. Koyck function	x			
4. Max. likelihood function	x			
5. Errors in variables		x		
6. Instrumental variables		x		
7. Comparison of income elasticities		x		
8. Past vs. Future Income			x	
9. Ball-Drake Test				x

The use of several tests of the same hypothesis may seem superfluous; after all, if a hypothesis fails just one of the tests, this shows that these data reject it. Nonetheless, I have used several tests to reinforce my results, and to show that they are not due merely to the peculiarity of a test. I did not use the German data in all of these tests because of the

---

7. See Michael Farrell, "The New Theories of the Consumption Function," *Economic Journal*, Vol. LXIX, December 1959, p. 692.

small size of the samples, and their exclusion of households with substantially fluctuating consumption.

Lengthening the Accounting Period

The basic "message" of the permanent income theory approach is
that a single year is too short a period for a meaningful comparison of
income and consumption, and that one has to look at these variables
over a longer period.[8] The obvious way to test this hypothesis is therefore to lengthen the accounting period and to see what happens if one
averages the household's income and consumption over several years.
Lengthening the accounting period is itself not a new technique. As
shown in Chapter 5, such a test has been used before, but never with
data for as many as five years, and not with valid results.

The rationale of this test can be seen by considering what happens
to the proportion of the measured income variance accounted for by
transitory elements as one lengthens the span of time covered by the
income and consumption data. It is the hallmark of transitory income
that it is positive in one period and negative in the other. The longer the
period one covers the greater is the extent to which positive and negative transitory elements cancel out. Differences in permanent income,
however, are not reduced in this way as one lengthens the accounting
period. As a result the proportion of the measured income variance accounted for by transitory elements decreases as one lengthens the period
covered. Now the permanent income theory asserts that the permanent
income elasticity of consumption is unity, hence, as one lengthens the
accounting period (and thus increases the relative importance of the
permanent element in the measured income variance) one should get a
measured income elasticity of consumption which comes closer and
closer to unity. Moreover, since according to the permanent income
theory consumption is a function of permanent rather than of transitory
income, the correlation coefficient should rise as one lengthens the accounting period.

8. Thus Friedman wrote: The central theme of this monograph can be
illustrated by a simple hypothetical example. Consider a large number of
men. . . . Let them receive their pay once a week, the pay days being
staggered, so that one-seventh are paid on Sunday, one-seventh on Monday
and so on. Suppose we collected budget data . . . for one day chosen at
random. . . . We would record the one seventh with an income . . . as
having positive savings, the other six-sevenths as having negative savings.
Consumption might appear to rise with income, but, if so, not as much as
income. These results tell us nothing meaningful about consumption behavior;
they simply reflect the use of inappropriate concepts of income and consumption. . . . *It is the central theme of this monograph that the use of a
period as long as a year does not render the error in actual data negligible,
let alone eliminate it entirely* (*op. cit.*, p. 220, italics added).

Accordingly, I did the following. I first regressed consumption on income and family size (measured by "quets") in each year separately to provide estimates of the marginal propensity to consume and the income elasticity for measured income. I then added up, for each household, consumption in two years and regressed this on the income of the two years and on family size. I then redid this regression using consumption, income, and average family size for three years, and then for four years and five years.

Table 35 shows the results of such a test. To start with the Swiss data, the outcome of this test is unfavorable for the permanent income theory. To be sure, lengthening the accounting period raises the correlation between income and consumption, but as columns 5 and 10 show, the marginal propensity to consume and the income elasticity change very little.[9] Taken at face value, these data show that using a single-year accounting period imparts a downward bias of only 2 percent to the marginal propensity to consume and to the income elasticity. Moreover, a two-year accounting period is all that is needed to eliminate this bias.[10]

To be sure, these results are based on a small sample. It would therefore be highly desirable to establish confidence limits. Unfortunately, it is not possible to do this rigorously. If one adjusts the multi-year marginal propensity to consume for sampling error, one should also adjust

9. Standing by themselves, the marginal propensities to consume and the income elasticities show an erratic pattern. Fortunately, this can easily be accounted for. It is not really proper to compare marginal propensities to consume (or income elasticities) calculated for different periods. Suppose that, for some reason, the marginal propensity to consume falls in the third year of a three-year period. If one calculates the marginal propensity to consume for three years, one averages a lower marginal propensity to consume of the third year with the higher marginal propensities to consume of the other two years. The results may well be a three-year marginal propensity to consume which is less than the two-year marginal propensity to consume. But this fact could hardly be cited as showing that lengthening the accounting period to three years reduced the marginal propensity to consume. One should compare the marginal propensities to consume of a three-year accounting period with the mean of the marginal propensities to consume for each of the three years and not with the marginal propensity to consume measured income over a two-year period.

10. It is true that the correlation improves as one adds more years, but as Friedman has pointed out ("Reply to Comments on 'A Theory of the Consumption Function,' " in Lincoln Clark, ed., *Consumer Behavior,* New York, Harper and Brothers, 1958, Vol. 3, p. 468) this is not really relevant. The purpose of the permanent income theory is not to explain the behavior of the individual household, but to explain the behavior of groups of households by providing estimates of the relevant parameters. And for this the relevant thing is not R^2, but what happens to the income elasticity, and so forth.

Table 35

Effect of Lengthening Accounting Period

Length of Accounting Period	(1) R²ᵃ	(2) Natural Numbers Regressions R²ᵃ as Percent of Mean R² for Individual Years in Accounting Period	(3) MPC	(4) Standard Error	(5) MPC as Percent of Mean MPC for Individual Years in Accounting Period	(6) R²ᵃ	(7) Logarithmic Regressions R² as Percent of Mean R² for Individual Years in Accounting Period	(8) Income Elasticity	(9) Standard Error	(10) Elasticity as Percent of Mean Elasticity for Individual Years in Accounting Period
Swiss Sample										
1 Year	.833	100	.830	.035	100	.829	100	.893	.038	100
2 Years	.867	107	.836	.031	102	.856	106	.901	.035	102
3 Years	.872	109	.814	.030	102	.867	109	.886	.033	102
4 Years	.876	111	.825	.030	102	.873	109	.896	.032	102
5 Years	.889	111	.832	.028	102	.887	110	.905	.031	102
German Sample										
1 Year	.734	100	.873	.073	100	.755	100	.903	.071	100
2 Years	.820	112	.839	.055	99	.854	109	.918	.053	101
3 Years	.903	120	.888	.040	101	.899	114	.934	.043	103
4 Years	.881	120	.848	.043	100	.869	116	.896	.048	103
5 Years	.862	123	.821	.046	99	.854	118	.874	.050	102

EQUATION USED: $C_N = a + bY_N + cF$ where N denotes the number of years, F is family size, and C and Y have their usual meaning.

ᵃ Not corrected for degrees of freedom.

the marginal propensity to consume for the individual years in the same direction. This is so, because a sampling error which affects income or consumption for the five-year totals must necessarily also affect income and consumption in at least one of the five years. Unfortunately, there is no way of knowing by how much to change the individual year figures as one adds, say, two standard errors to the five-year coefficient. Thus it is not really possible to calculate accurately the confidence limits for the ratio of the multi-year to single-year income elasticities. But fortunately, the direction of the error is known; not adjusting the individual year coefficients as one adds two standard errors to the five-year coefficients biases the ratio upwards, and hence one can presumably get an upper limit to the confidence intervals. And if one does add two standard errors to the five-year income elasticity, the ratio of this five-year elasticity to the mean of the five individual year elasticities rises to 1.09. (And this ratio is the same for the marginal propensities to consume.) Such a 1.09 ratio is inconsistent with the permanent income theory. If the variance of the permanent component accounts for, say 85 percent of total variance of measured income, then the permanent income theory implies that this ratio should be 1.18.[11]

Moreover, Table 35 provides significant evidence against the permanent income theory in another way. The income elasticity of consumption computed from the five-year data differs from unity, and this difference is significant at the one percent level (one tailed test).

The German data shown in the lower half of Table 35 do not support the permanent income theory either. Again, as columns 1 and 6 show, lengthening the accounting period to three years raises the coefficient of determination. However, the marginal propensity to consume does *not* rise as the accounting period is lengthened, and the income elasticity rises only moderately. The income elasticity is well below unity, significantly so at the five percent level (one tailed test) in two out of the four cases (years 4 and 5).

One can use these data to calculate the prediction coefficient. It turns out to be 0.8 for the Swiss data, but for the German data it is essentially unity. But as pointed out above, the German data are biased against the permanent income theory.

Weights of the Years

Another obvious test is to follow Friedman and search for the optimal lag by applying different weights to the incomes of each household in

11. Table IV-B in Appendix IV suggests that the variance of the permanent component does, in fact, account for less than 85 percent of the variance in measured income, since the correlation coefficients of incomes in various years are less than 0.85.

various years.[12] The weighting pattern I used is a very simple one. I took the integers from 1 to 10, divided them by ten and raised them to the power corresponding to one plus the particular year. For example, for the weighting pattern corresponding to 0.5, the current year got a weight of 0.25, the previous year a weight of 0.125 and so on.[13]

Table 36 shows coefficients of determination, and the *t* values of the income term for all the weights I tried. I ran regressions for all five years combined, for four years and for three years. Looking at the Swiss data first, the coefficients of determination rise monotonically and smoothly to a peak at the 0.4^n weights and then decline. To be sure, this test is not conclusive because the differences in the R^2's are rather small.

The German data show virtually no lag since the coefficients reach their maximum value for the shortest lag pattern tried. Given the fact that the German sample tends to exclude households with fluctuating consumption, this difference between the Swiss and German regressions is not surprising.

But in any case, both sets of data show lags substantially shorter than Friedman's lag. This is shown in Table 37, which gives the percentage weights for various years as well as the mean lags implied by the 0.4^n and 0.1^n weights.

Fitting Lagged Regressions

Most of the extant methods of fitting lagged regressions require data for many more years than the five years available here. However, the Koyck-Nerlove method of regressing consumption on current income and the previous year's consumption can be used on these cross-section data. I therefore regressed each household's consumption on its current income and on its consumption of the previous year.

The results, shown in Table 38, reject the hypothesis of a long lag. The estimate of the mean lag implied by the four Swiss regressions varies from half a year to about three-quarters of a year. And in three out of four cases the upper confidence limit is no greater than a one-year lag. These results agree with those of the previous test. The Swiss sample showed a mean lag of 0.6 years, exactly the same as the average of the mean lags for the four years on this test. The German data, once again,

12. This test is essentially similar to Friedman's test of fitting a lagged regression to income. The only differences are, first, that I used my test in a cross-section context rather than regressing time series directly. Second, unlike Friedman, I did not use a trend of income, and, third, I used five-years' income in place of Friedman's seventeen years' income. Fourth, Friedman tried more (and different weights) than I did.

13. To be sure, the use of geometrically declining weights is arbitrary, but since I could not use all feasible types of weights, I decided to follow Friedman and use geometrically declining weights.

Table 36

Effect of Different Weights

	5-Year Horizon		4-Year Horizon		3-Year Horizon	
Weights[a]	R^{2}[b]	t Value of Income Coefficient	R^{2}[b]	t Value of Income Coefficient	R^{2}[b]	t Value of Income Coefficient
Swiss Sample						
1.0^{n}	.812	22.1	.818	22.6	.828	23.3
$.9^{n}$	.822	22.8	.825	23.1	.832	23.7
$.8^{n}$	.831	23.5	.832	23.6	.836	24.0
$.7^{n}$	.838	24.2	.838	24.1	.839	24.3
$.6^{n}$	.844	24.7	.842	24.6	.842	24.6
$.5^{n}$	.847	25.0	.846	24.9	.845	24.8
$.4^{n}$	.848	25.1	.847	25.0	.846	24.9
$.3^{n}$	.847	25.0	.846	24.9	.845	24.9
$.2^{n}$	.844	24.7	.844	24.7	.844	24.2
$.1^{n}$	.839	24.3	.839	24.3	.839	24.3
German Sample						
1.0^{n}	.395	5.8	.406	6.0	.435	6.3
$.9^{n}$	.412	6.0	.421	6.1	.446	6.5
$.8^{n}$	.430	6.3	.437	6.4	.458	6.6
$.7^{n}$	.450	6.5	.455	6.6	.470	6.8
$.6^{n}$	.470	6.8	.473	6.8	.484	7.0
$.5^{n}$	.490	7.1	.492	7.1	.499	7.2
$.4^{n}$	.509	7.3	.509	7.3	.513	7.4
$.3^{n}$	.530	7.6	.530	7.7	.531	7.7
$.2^{n}$	.540	7.8	.540	7.8	.540	7.8
$.1^{n}$	.552	8.0	.552	8.0	.552	8.0

EQUATION USED: $C = a + bY' + cF$ where Y' is a weighted average of current and past incomes.

a Letter n denotes the year, with the current year taken as 2.

b Not corrected for degrees of freedoms.

are less favorable for the permanent income theory since they show a lower mean lag. However, due to the small size of the sample the confidence intervals are very large.

Another lagged regression technique which can be used here is a maximum likelihood technique developed by Leon Wegge.[14] I first fitted this technique to the Swiss data for all five years and in the next two runs used only four years and three years of data, respectively. In an additional regression, instead of using the fifth year's consumption, I

14. "A Family of Function Iterations and the Solution of Maximum Likelihood Estimating Equations," *Econometrica*, Vol. 37, January 1969, pp. 122–30. I am indebted to Leon Wegge for providing a computer program and other help.

Table 37

Percentage Weights for Various Years Implied by the Weighting Patterns

	Weighting Pattern		Friedman Weights		Weighting Pattern		Friedman Weights	
	$.4^n$	$.1^n$	Actual	Trun-cated	$.4^n$	$.1^n$	Actual	Trun-cated
Year	Percent Weight in Each Year				Cumulative Percent Weights			
T	61	91	33.0	38	61	91	33.0	38
T-1	24	9	22.1	26	85	100	55.1	64
T-2	10	0	14.8	17	95		69.9	81
T-3	4	0	9.9	11	99		79.8	92
T-4	2	0	6.7	8	100		86.5	100
Total	100	100	86.5	100				
Mean Lag[a] (Years)	.6	.1	2.0[b]	1.2				

SOURCE: For Columns 3 and 4, Milton Friedman, *A Theory of the Consumption Function*, p. 147.

[a] Mean lag counting current year as zero lag and multiplying each subsequent year by its weight.

[b] Obtained as described in previous note. If the lag is derived from a continuous rather than a discrete function by using the beta coefficient it is 2-1/2 vears.

used as the dependent variable the fourth year's consumption. The results are shown in Table 39. The last four columns of this table show the implied weights. The weights for the first year are significantly larger (5 percent level, one tailed test) than Friedman's estimate of 0.33.[15] The average of the mean lags for all four runs is 0.6 year, which is of course the same as that obtained in the previous two tests. However, the run using the fourth year's consumption as the dependent variable has an unpleasant peculiarity—it implies a marginal propensity to consume in excess of unity. Similarly, the first run is suspicious because the coefficients for the second- and third-year lags are insignificantly negative while the fourth year lag is significantly positive. This "tail" problem also

15. To calculate the significance level I subtracted 1.66 standard errors from the first year's coefficient and then expressed it as a percent of the total weight. This procedure assumes that a sampling error which raises the first year's coefficient is just offset by a sampling error which lowers the weights of other years. However, if one assumes instead that the sampling error responsible for overstating the first year's coefficient did not result also in an understatement of the coefficients of other years, my conclusion is reinforced.

Table 38

Results of Koyck-Nerlove Regressions

Independent Variable, Consumption of Year	Lagged Consumption Term		R^{2a}	Implied Mean Lag (Years)	Confidence Limits of Mean Lag[b]	
	Coefficient	Standard Error			Lower	Upper
Swiss Sample						
2	.425	.077	.816	.7	.4	1.4
3	.330	.067	.808	.5	.2	.9
4	.366	.067	.830	.6	.3	1.0
5	.371	.065	.867	.6	.3	1.0
German Sample						
2	.054	.113	.731	.1	c	.4
3	−.117	.129	.797	c	c	.2
4	.176	.119	.692	.2	c	.7
5	.083	.136	.562	.1	c	.6

EQUATION USED: $C_1 = a + bY_1 + cC_0 + dF_1$.
[a] Not corrected for degrees of freedom.
[b] 2 standard errors.
[c] Negative.

exists, though in a much less pronounced fashion, for the next run. The most plausible pattern is that shown for the three-year horizon case where the mean lag is 0.5, which is very similar to the previously obtained results.

In addition to comparing the mean lags one can compare the weights for the various years shown by this test and by the weights of the year's test (Table 37). The first-year weights given there for the preferred weighting pattern corresponds fairly closely to the current year weights obtained in this maximum likelihood test. For the previous year the weights are also fairly similar.

All in all, these three tests of the lag—the weight of the year's test, the Koyck-Nerlove test, and the maximum likelihood test—show strong agreement among each other. The fact that they all show a short lag does not mean, of course, that long run income expectations play no role at all in the consumption function. It would be most surprising if this were the case. All the above results show is that for *year to year* changes in income, such as experienced by a sample of "settled" households, there is only a short lag in consumption.

Errors in Variables Model

In Chapter 5 (p. 155), I discussed Bernard Saffran's errors in variables test of the proportionality hypothesis. I applied his model to the

Table 39

Results of Maximum Likelihood Regressions, Swiss Sample

Income with	5th Year Consumption as Dependent Variable									4th Year Consumption as Dependent Variable			Percent of Sum of Coefficients (Dep. Var. is Consumption of Year)			
	5-Year Horizon			4-Year Horizon			3-Year Horizon			4-Year Horizon			5 / 5-Year Horizon	5 / 4-Year Horizon	3 / 3-Year Horizon	4 / 4-Year Horizon
	Coefficient	Stand. Error	t Value	Coefficient	Stand. Error	t Value	Coefficient	Stand. Error	t Value	Coefficient	Stand. Error	t Value				
No Lag	.592	.080	7.4[a]	.590	.082	7.2[a]	.593	.082	7.2[a]	.700	.095	7.3[a]	62.0	62.7	63.7	67.2
1 Year Lag	.178	.102	1.8[b]	.189	.104	1.8[b]	.210	.104	2.0[b]	.321	.126	2.5[a]	18.7	20.1	22.6	30.8
2 Year Lag	−.024	.115	−0.2	.005	.118	0.0	.128	.093	1.4	.030	.132	0.2	−2.5	0.6	13.7	2.8
3 Year Lag	−.030	.117	−0.3	.157	.093	1.7[b]	—	—	—	−.009	.105	−0.1	−3.1	16.7	—	−0.9
4 Year Lag	.238	.093	2.6[a]	—	—	—	—	—	—	—	—	—	24.9	—	—	—
Mean Lag (Years)													1.0	.7	.5	.3

[a] Significant at 1 percent level.
[b] Significant at 5 percent level.

Swiss data taking the horizon as five years. This yielded a permanent income elasticity of consumption well below unity (0.93), just barely significantly so at the 5 percent level.

Instrumental Variables

In one of his tests of the permanent income theory described in Chapter 5, Nissan Liviatan used income and consumption of another year as instrumental variables. As I pointed out in Chapter 5, this test was criticized by Friedman because Liviatan had obtained his consumption figures by subtracting saving from income, and also because Liviatan used a two-year horizon. Since my data give direct estimates of consumption, and cover a span of five years, they are not subject to these criticisms. I therefore repeated Liviatan's test using as the instrumental variables consumption or income of all other years.[16]

Table 40 shows the results. The regressions using income as the instrumental variable provide no support for the permanent income theory. To be sure, both in natural numbers regressions and in the log regressions the instrumental variable coefficient always exceeds the ordinary least-square coefficient. But, as in Liviatan's regressions, the differences are small.[17] More particularly, in the log regressions the instrumental variable coefficient is, contrary to the prediction of the permanent income theory, less than unity in every case. And in two cases this difference from unity is significant at the 5 percent level.

However, the story is different when the instrumental variable is consumption. Here the instrumental variable coefficients are much higher than the ordinary least square coefficients. Moreover, four of the five log coefficients are insignificantly above unity, thus supporting the permanent income theory. But this support is deceptive. The use of consumption as an instrumental variable provides a biased estimate of the permanent income elasticity of consumption. Consider, for example, two households, one thrifty and the other spendthrift. The thrifty household will *caeteris paribus*—have lower consumption than the spendthrift household in all the years covered, thus creating a positive correlation between consumption in various years.[18]

16. In this test I did not use the family size variable.
17. The magnitude of this difference can be put into perspective by taking the log regression and seeing to what extent the instrumental variable coefficient is closer to unity (the value predicted for it by the permanent income theory) than is the ordinary least square coefficient. It turns out that, on the average, the use of the instrumental variable coefficient in place of the ordinary least-square coefficient reduces the gap by only 23 percent.
18. Liviatan used another factor to show the probability of serial correlation for two-year data. This is that unusual consumption resulting, for example, from illness, is likely to spill over into a second year. Friedman,

Table 40

Results of Instrumental Variables Test, Swiss Sample

	Natural Numbers						Logs					
	Ordinary Least Square		Instrumental Variable				Ordinary Least Square		Instrumental Variable			
			Income		Consumption				Income		Consumption	
Dependent Variable Consumption of Year	Regression Coefficient	Standard Errors	Regression Coefficient	Standard Errors	Regression Coefficient	Standard Errors	Regression Coefficient	Standard Errors	Regression Coefficient	Standard Errors	Regression Coefficient	Standard Errors
1	.871	.037	.881	.040	.958	.044	.939	.038	.942	.041	1.025	.044
2	.856	.044	.879	.046	.983	.050	.913	.043	.937	.045	1.039	.049
3	.782	.040	.786	.042	.872	.045	.866	.042	.878[a]	.044	.973	.049
4	.818	.039	.853	.042	.931	.045	.889	.042	.916[b]	.045	1.010	.049
5	.844	.035	.894	.039	.973	.044	.907	.038	.953	.042	1.056	.048

EQUATION USED: $C = a + bI$ where I is the instrumental variable.
[a] Elasticity significantly different from unity at 1 percent level.
[b] Elasticity significantly different from unity at 5 percent level.

Predicted and Actual Income Elasticities

As discussed in Chapter 3, Friedman has shown that if the permanent income theory is correct, the correlation between the incomes of two years spanning the horizon on the one hand,[19] and the income elasticity of consumption on the other, are really measures of the same thing, the proportion of the income variance accounted for by the permanent element. He then presented the results of an unpublished test by Miss Reid who had tested the permanent income theory by comparing these two measures.[20] I decided to repeat the test with the Swiss data.

I divided the Swiss sample into nine arbitrary groups of thirteen budgets each and calculated the correlation of incomes within each of these groups between (1) years one and three, (2) years one and four and (3) year one and year five, thus using three-year, four-year and five-year horizons.[21] My next step was to calculate the income elasticity of consumption within each of these groups. If the permanent income theory is correct, both of these are measures of the *same* thing, the proportion of income differences accounted for by the permanent element. Hence a regression of one of these measures on the other one should

---

however, argued that high consumption in one year may lead to low consumption in the next year, particularly if durables are included in consumption. I therefore reran two of the instrumental variable regressions used as the instrumental variable consumption three years earlier. This did not change the results noticeably; one of the regression coefficients went up and one went down. See Nissan Liviatan, "Tests of the Permanent Income Hypothesis Based on a Reinterview Savings Survey," in Carl Christ (ed.), *Measurement in Economics: Studies in Mathematical Economics and Econometrics in Honor of Yehuda Grunfeld* (Stanford University Press, 1963), p. 51; and Milton Friedman, "Note on Nissan Liviatan's Paper," *ibid.*, pp. 62–63.

19. I am using the term "horizon" as did Friedman in this connection to denote a planning period rather than as the reciprocal of the discount rate.

20. *A Theory of the Consumption Function, op. cit.*, pp. 184–95. Modigliani and Brumberg also used Miss Reid's test as support for the life cycle hypothesis. "Utilities Analysis and the Consumption Function: An Interpretation of Cross-Section Data," in Kenneth Kurihara, *Post-Keynesian Economics* (London, George Allen and Unwin, 1955), pp. 184–95.

21. I correlated the natural numbers only. This is in accordance with the arithmetic variant of the permanent income theory. In view of the results obtained, I did not consider it worthwhile to test the variability version, too, by using logarithmic regressions. I did not include a family size variable in the regressions shown in Table 41 since it is not clear that family size is a determinant of the income elasticity. However, I also ran regressions including family size and the results of these regressions are somewhat more unfavorable for the permanent income theory than the results shown in the table.

yield a regression coefficient of unity and a correlation coefficient which departs from unity only insofar as there are errors in the data. To be sure, since I have only nine observations (one for each group of thirteen households) one must expect a substantial erratic element and large standard errors.

Table 41 shows the results of such a regression, and these results refute the permanent income theory. The coefficients of determination are quite low, only a single one being above 0.4. Conceivably this could be explained by the large errors in my estimates of both variables. (Since both the variables are derived from very small samples, large errors are not implausible.) But what is much more serious for the permanent income theory are the regression coefficients. They are all far from their expected value of unity, all but one being below 0.6. In two-

Table 41

Relation Between Two Measures of the
Income Elasticities of Consumption, Swiss Sample

Year	R^{2a}	Regression Coefficient	Standard Error	t Value
5-Year Horizon				
1	.058	.187[b]	.285	.7
2	.128	.310[b]	.305	1.0
3	.488	.592[c]	.229	2.6
4	.082	.194[b]	.245	.8
5	.146	.288[b]	.263	1.1
4-Year Horizon				
1	.001	.038[b]	.384	1.0
2	.137	.322[b]	.306	1.1
3	.133	.080[b]	.261	.3
4	0	−.007[b]	.293	.0
5	−.052	−.220[b]	.358	−.6
3-Year Horizon				
1	.022	.192[c]	.486	.4
2	.092	.609	.722	.8
3	−.132	−.421[b]	.407	−1.0
4	.248	.569	.374	1.5
5	.135	.336[b]	.321	1.0

NOTE: Number of cases in each of the yearly regressions is 9.

EQUATION USED: $E = a + b\overline{R}$ where E is the income elasticity of consumption and $\overline{R}$ is the correlation coefficient of incomes in different years corrected for degrees of freedom.

[a] Not corrected for degrees of freedom.
[b] Difference between coefficient and unity significant at 5 percent level.
[c] Difference between coefficient and unity significant at 10 percent level.

thirds of the cases their divergence from unity is significant at the 5 percent level.

The measured income theories, on the other hand, predict no correlation at all between the income elasticities and the income correlations. But in the majority of cases shown in Table 41, there is a positive, though low, correlation between the two. Although the regression coefficients are usually far from significant, they generally have the right sign. Thus these results are entirely consistent with the standard income theory.

This is in sharp conflict with the results reported by Friedman. Presenting Miss Reid's unpublished results, he gave a scatter-diagram of the income elasticity of consumption and the correlation of incomes over a three-year period. In this scatter-diagram, the coefficient of ranked correlation of the two variables is about 0.8.[22]

Past versus Future Income

Much of the evidence for the permanent income theory can also be interpreted as supporting a habit persistence theory. What is needed to distinguish conveniently between the two is information on expected future income rather than on past incomes only. The habit persistence theory asserts that past income affects current consumption; the permanent income theory asserts that future, as well as past, income does so. The obvious way to distinguish between the two theories is to include separate terms for past and for future income in a regression and see if the future income term is significant.

One should distinguish between two types of income expectations here. One is a long-run prediction of income where the horizon may extend over much, or all, of the household's life-span. Then there is a short-run prediction of income, extending no more than a few years into the future.

The role of short-run income expectations can be investigated with these Swiss budgets. Table 42 shows the outcome of stepwise regressions.

22. When one obtains results which differ sharply from those reached by others, it is a good idea to check the accuracy of one's data. I, therefore, checked the income elasticities and the income correlations using different computer programs. In addition, I checked the data used to construct my income and consumption totals. I found a few errors in the transcription or keypunching stages, but they were quite minor. For one household the family size variable (quets) was misstated by 10 percent in one year, for another household income in one year was off 2.4 percent, and in a number of other cases there were errors amounting to less than half a percent of income. Such errors are well within the range of reporting errors one generally finds in consumption and income data.

Table 42

Significance of Current, Past, and Future Incomes, Swiss Sample, Levels

Incomes	R^2 [a]	t Values of Income Coefficients					Beta Coefficients					Regression Coefficients				
		Year					*Year*					*Year*				
		T	T−1	T−2	T+1	T+2	T	T−1	T−2	T+1	T+2	T	T−1	T−2	T+1	T+2
A. Third Year Consumption Starting with Previous Years																
Current Year	.769	18.8										.760				
Current Year Plus Two Previous Years	.773	6.5	1.5	−.7			.721	.208	−.075			.646	.196	−.069		
Plus one following year	.774	5.5	1.5	−.6	−.7		.783	.216	−.071	−.079		.702	.204	−.066	−.067	
Plus two following years	.774	5.3	1.5	−.6	−.6	0	.783	.216	−.071	−.080	.002	.702	.204	−.066	−.068	.002
B. Third Year Consumption Starting with Following Years																
Current Year Plus Two Following Years	.770	7.6			−.4	0	.902			−.059	0	.809			−.050	0
Plus One Previous Year	.774	5.3	1.4		−.6	0	.775	.161		−.083	.001	.695	.152		−.071	.001
Plus Two Previous Years	.774	5.3	1.5	−.6	−.6	0	.783	.216	−.071	−.080	.002	.702	.204	−.066	−.068	.002
C. Second Year Consumption																
Current Year	.770	18.8					.846					.831				
Current Year Plus One Previous Year	.773	6.3	1.4				.707	.154				.694	.149			
Current Year Plus Following Year	.771	7.0			.8		.770			.083		.756			.078	
Current Year, Past Year Plus Following Year	.774	4.7	1.2		.6		.659	.144		.062		.647	.139		.058	

[a] Not corrected for degrees of freedom.

Part A gives the results of regressing consumption first on current income alone, then on current income and previous incomes, and finally on current income, previous income, and on the incomes of subsequent years. Part B repeats some of these regressions, this time introducing the incomes of future years ahead of the incomes of the previous years. In all of these regressions the independent variable is consumption in year three. Part C of Table 42 uses consumption of year two in place of year three consumption to confirm these results with a few additional regressions.

The results are dramatic and unequivocal. The effect of adding the immediately preceding year's income is in sharp contrast to the effect of adding the following years' income. While the income of the immediately preceding year is generally significant at the 10 percent level (one tailed test) the following year's income has a t value always less than one, and its coefficient frequently has the wrong sign. And income two years ahead also plays no role; its regression coefficient is trivial. This unimportance of income two years in the future does not, however, contrast with the role played by income two years into the past. Here, too, the coefficients are always insignificant and always have the wrong sign.

Since a household's incomes in various years are highly correlated, it is possible that the coefficient of the current year's income picks up effects which should really be attributed to incomes in the other years. I therefore supplemented this table by regressing the first differences of incomes for several of the regressions shown in Table 42. The results, given in Table 43, corroborate those of Table 42.[23]

What do these results imply? Obviously they do not imply that households completely disregard the following year's income in their decisions about current consumption. A household knowing that its income next year will be, say three times its current income, would presumably let this knowledge affect current consumption, and a similar thing holds for a household expecting its income in the next year to dwindle to zero. But such households do not constitute my sample. What these data do show is that moderate income changes, such as those actually experienced by these households, do not have much effect on consumption in the previous year. This conclusion can be interpreted in several ways.

23. For the immediately preceding year the coefficient is negative. This is as it should be. The difference in income between two adjacent years is inversely related to the proportion of the income variance which is accounted for by differences in permanent income. If the marginal propensity to consume is greater for permanent income than for transitory income, then the greater the income difference, the lower should be the marginal propensity to consume. Hence, in Table 43 the previous year's income, though not significant at the 10 percent level, has the correct sign, while the coefficient for the future year's income has the wrong sign.

Table 43

Significance of Current, Past, and Future Incomes
Swiss Sample, First Differences

Income	R^{2a}	t Values of Coefficients of					Regression of Coefficients				
		Income	D1	D2	D3	D4	Income	D1	D2	D3	D4
Current Year Income Plus	.769	18.8					.760				
D1 + D2	.773	17.9	−1.5	.7			.773	−.196	.069		
D1 + D2 + D3	.774	17.9	−1.5	.6	.7		.773	−.204	.066	.067	
D1 + D2 + D3 + D4	.774	17.8	−1.5	.6	.6	0	.773	−.204	.066	.068	−.002
D3 + D4	.770	18.5			.4	0	.758			.050	0
D1 + D3 + D4	.774	18.2	−1.5		.6	0	.777	−.152		.071	−.001

NOTE: D1 is difference in incomes between Year T and Year T − 1; D2 is difference in incomes between Year T and Year T − 2; D3 is difference in incomes between Year T and Year T + 1; D4 is difference in incomes between Year T and Year T + 2.

ᵃ Not corrected for degrees of freedom.

One is to say that households do take the *expected* income of the following year into account in determining their consumption, but that their expected income is not adequately approximated by the incomes they actually receive in those future years. This interpretation is questionable, however, because it implies irrationability. If households are so poor at forecasting future incomes, then it is irrational for them to try to do so; they should simply use current incomes as a naïve model guide.

A second possibility is that households do govern their consumption in accordance with permanent income, but that this permanent income is a long-run concept not closely related to income of the next two years. Third, there is the possibility that the permanent income theory is, in fact, invalid—that due to habit persistence, past income as well as current income affects current consumption, but future income does not.

Test of the Ball-Drake Hypothesis

In Chapter 2 I described the consumption function theory developed by Ball and Drake. Their theory requires that the income and wealth coefficients sum to unity. I have tested this theory with the results shown in Table 44. At first glance this table seems to confirm the theory since the sums of the income and consumption coefficients *are* fairly close to unity. However, the divergence is not random. In every single case, the sum of the coefficients falls short of unity. The probability of such a result being due to chance is less than one percent. (To be sure, since my samples consist of the same households in various years, this state-

Table 44

Test of Ball-Drake Hypothesis

Dependent Variable Is Consumption of Year	Coefficient of		Sum of Two Coefficients	Standard Errors	
	Income	Previous Year's Consumption		Income	Previous Year's Consumption
	Swiss Sample				
2	.516	.422	.938	.066	.077
3	.550	.343	.893	.059	.068
4	.553	.360	.913	.056	.064
5	.553	.370	.923	.054	.064
	German Sample				
2	.859	.110	.969	.099	.111
3	1.050	−.090	.960	.105	.119
4	.734	.227	.961	.115	.125
5	.787	.183	.970	.114	.125

EQUATION USED: $C_1 = aY_1 + bC_0 + dF_1$.

ment implies that the behavior of the same household in various years furnishes independent observations.) [24] Thus their theory fails this test.

Conclusion

To summarize the results obtained in this chapter succinctly, it is convenient to adopt the following linguistic convention. I will use the term "suggest" for results which are *not* significant at the 5 percent level, and the term "show" to denote results which are significant at the 5 percent level.

To start with the proportionality hypothesis, three of the tests *show* that this proposition is invalid, that the proportion of income consumed does fall with rising income.[25] And one of these tests (lengthening the accounting period) goes further than this; it *suggests* that the difference between the permanent and measured income elasticities of consumption is not very great. It *suggests* a difference of only 2 or 3 percent.

Turning the length of the lag, two tests *show,* and two other tests *suggest,* that the mean lag is not as long as Friedman claimed.[26] In fact, one of the tests *shows* that it is a year or less. In addition, another test *suggests* that the actual income of the following year has much less effect on current consumption than does the income of the previous year, and that it may very well have virtually no effect at all.

Clearly, these results are highly unfavorable for the full permanent income theory. At the same time they provide no support for the measured income theories. The standard income theory, on the other hand, survives this set of tests with flying colors.

24. Moreover, my regressions are not, strictly speaking, independent of each other since consumption of one year is a dependent variable in one regression and independent variable in the other. However, I do not see why this should create a systematic bias. The sum of the coefficients is also less than unity in all but one of the time series regressions Ball and Drake used to support their theory. And when Jeffrey Williamson fitted the Ball-Drake model to Japan, Taiwan, and Burma as well as to a number of Asian countries combined, the sum of the coefficients was below unity, too. (Jeffrey Williamson, "Income Growth and Saving," *Philippine Economic Journal,* Vol. VIII, September 1969, p. 69)

25. The tests *showing* this are the lengthening of the accounting period test, the errors in variables test, and the instrumental variables test using income. In addition, the correlation of actual and estimates income elasticities *shows* that either the proportionality hypothesis, or the hypothesis that the transitory income elasticity of consumption is zero, is invalid.

26. They are the Koyck-Nerlove test, the maximum likelihood test, the weights of the years test, and the lengthening of the accounting period test.

Fourteen

LONG-RUN BUDGETS

In the previous chapter I dealt with a fairly small number of budgets covering a relatively long span of time. In this chapter I am going further in this direction by introducing a very small number of budgets which follow households for an even longer period. Relying on such a small number of budgets is unusual for consumption function studies. However, small samples have been used in another branch of economics, the empirical study of business firms.

In addition to the Swiss budgets used in the previous chapter, thirty-four of which cover ten years, I obtained twenty-four budgets which follow households for a period ranging from six to thirty-one years. The latter are not the product of a statistical survey but are based on account books kept by households for their own use. They cover several countries and various dates. I have not combined these budgets but have analyzed each one as a separate entity, for two reasons. First, the definitions and accounting methods used by these households probably differ, and second, I do not have purchasing power parity exchange rates which would allow me to combine the budgets for various countries.

As in the previous chapter there is a problem of the representativeness of the households. Households keeping account books are presumably more rational and cautious than other households, and hence, they are more likely to act in accordance with the wealth theories than are other households. Another problem is that the nature of these data prevents the use of correlation analysis because consumption is extremely variable.

The Data

In addition to the Swiss budgets described in Appendix V I have used twenty-four budgets gathered from various sources. One source consists of eleven unpublished French middle-class budgets gathered by Mme. Perrot and kindly made available to me. They cover varying years from

1866 to 1953. Then, I collected a number of Swiss and German budgets published in various journals mostly in the late nineteenth and early twentieth century.[1] Finally, there are four American budgets, two from a Ph.D thesis and two from an article in a popular journal. These budgets are described in Appendix VI.

I used after-tax income, except for the French data, and where feasible, adjusted consumption for expenditures which represented the cost of earning an income,[2] such as expense accounts. I also subtracted old age insurance and life insurance premiums from consumption if they were given in the data, and where possible subtracted receipts from boarders and lodgers from income and from consumption.[3] The French data, as well as some of the others, gave the number of consumption units or persons in the household, and in these cases I used income and consumption per consumption unit or person. I used real rather than nominal values. For the German data I used the Hoffmann deflator and for the Swiss data the Notz deflator.[4] Unfortunately, the latter has a gap and for the earlier years of some of the budgets (and in one case for all of the years covered) I could not deflate.[5] The French data were in some

1. For the sake of uniformity, I limited the sample to budgets after 1850 in developed countries. I had to discard many budgets because they included in income items of capital consumption.

2. I did not adjust the French data for taxes since this would have been time-consuming. Since the taxes *may* represent property taxes rather than income taxes, their subtraction from income and consumption might, in any case, have been unwarranted.

3. This amounts to assuming that the household has no net income from boarders and lodgers; the other alternative of including income from boarders and lodgers in consumption adds a spurious common element to both.

4. Walther Hoffmann, *Das Wachstum der Deutschen Wirtschaft* (Berlin, Springer, 1965), pp. 598–601; Emil Notz, *Die Säkulare Entwicklung der Kaufkraft des Geldes* (Jena, Gustav Fisher, 1925), p. 99. One of my German budgets was for the postwar period. This I deflated by the price index for a four person employee household with a middling income given in the 1964 *Statistisches Jahrbuch*.

5. Fortunately, the limited information available on price movements shows that price movements were moderate during this period. The one budget which could not be deflated at all by the Notz index covers the years 1866–1885. A price index covering every fifth year shows a value of 62 for 1865 and of 69 for 1885. (See Jürg Siegenthaler, "Zum Lebensstandard Schweizerischer Arbeiter im 19 Jahrhundert," *Schweizerische Zeitschrift für Volkswirtschaft und Statistik,* Vol. 101, December 1965, p. 426.) Two other Swiss budgets have some years which are not covered by the Notz index since they started in 1883 and 1885 while the Notz index is not available until 1892. The Siegenthaler index gives values of 67 for 1880, 69 for 1885, 73 for 1890, and 79 for 1895, thus suggesting that the failure to adjust for price changes prior to 1892 does not do *very* much damage.

cases already deflated and in the others I used the Singer-Kerel deflator.[6] For the U.S. data I used the BLS index and the Reese index.[7]

Tests

I have used these data in three quite simple tests. One consists of charting them, and, without using a formal statistical test, just seeing to what extent they support the permanent income theory. The second test is to classify income changes into sustained changes and temporary changes, and to compare the income elasticity of consumption in these two cases. The third test consists of using a moving average of income as a measure of permanent income, and comparing the income elasticities of consumption for permanent income thus defined and for measured income.

Originally, I had intended to use lagged regression on these data to search for the optimal weights. However, the great variability of consumption prevents such a test. Essentially, the problem results from the occurence of transitory consumption. The question is sometimes asked, what happens to transitory consumption in the permanent income theory? The answer is that when one combines the budgets of many households, transitory elements in consumption normally average out. But when dealing with individual budgets, one cannot rely on this convenient property of transitory consumption, and as the charts below show, transitory consumption is a substantial element of total consumption.[8]

Another test which may seem tempting at first is to calculate permanent income for each household and then to test the proportionality hypothesis by comparing households with different permanent incomes. But such a test would be of questionable value because of the peculiar way, self-selection, in which the sample was chosen. Suppose that high (permanent) income households are much more prone to keep household accounts than are low income households. If so, the low income households included in the sample are likely to belong to a very special type of household. More precisely, assume that there are two determinants of whether a household keeps accounts, its permanent income and its thriftiness. If so, the low income households included in the

6. Jean Singer-Kerel, *Le Coût de la Vie à Paris de 1840 à 1954* (Paris, Librairie Armand Colin, 1961), pp. 534–35. I used the "Indice general" given in this source. The fact that the index relates to Paris whereas my budgets come from various parts of France obviously creates some inaccuracy.

7. Albert Rees, *Real Wages in Manufacturing 1890–1914* (Princeton, Princeton University Press, 1961), p. 117.

8. I experimented with excluding durable purchases (furniture and clothes) from consumption for some budgets, but even this did not eliminate the transitory element sufficiently.

sample are more likely to have a tendency to be thrifty. Of course, the converse is possible, too, and the bias may be the other way round, but since there is this danger of a substantial bias, I have not undertaken this test.

Visual Test

The charts in Appendix VI show income and consumption of those households for whom I have at least fifteen year's data. These graphs can be used to answer two questions. First, is there any evidence of lifetime averaging, and second, do changes in consumption lag behind changes in income in the sense that the main effect of an income change is delayed, say a year?

Lifetime averaging relates to the question of the length of time needed to isolate "permanent" income. The formal theory of household behavior suggests that one *may* have to take the household's whole lifetime with due allowance for the estate motive. But on a priori grounds one cannot say how long the horizon is. In principle, unless uncertainty is absolute (so that households are unable to forecast at all beyond a certain interval) one would expect that income in *all* future years has *some* effect on the household's current consumption, but the optimal trade-off between accuracy and simplicity *may* require one to look at expected income for only a limited number of future years. The empirical issue here is how much is lost by confining attention to only a few years. Friedman adopted an agnostic view on the length of the horizon. As pointed out in Chapter 2, he interpreted the relevant coefficient of his regression equation as showing the implicit rate of interest rather than the length of the horizon. Modigliani, Brumberg, and Ando, on the other hand, explicitly assumed that the household's horizon includes its whole future life span. However, as pointed out in Chapter 5, empirical tests do not provide strong support for their hypothesis. In view of this uncertainty about the length of the horizon, even a small number of long-run budgets may provide useful information. Of my long-run budgets, seventeen cover fifteen years or more and should therefore tell us something about lifetime averaging.

In all but three of them (budgets I, Q, and S) consumption is closely aligned with income over a relatively short span of years—that is, fourteen out of the seventeen cases reject the hypothesis of lifetime averaging.[9] Admittedly, seventeen cases constitute a very small sample, but the fact that all but three of the cases agree in rejecting the hy-

9. Even budget Q need not be interpreted as supporting lifetime averaging. Since this budget shows little trend in income, it cannot tell us much about lifetime averaging.

pothesis offsets this disadvantage to some extent. Another problem is created by the fact that there is some trend correlation between income and "needs." Generally, the income of these households is growing over time, and so is the size of their families and the ages of their children. Hence, some of the correlation of current income and consumption may be spurious. But note that this problem does not exist for some of the budgets (K, O, Q, S, T), either because they are expressed in consumption units, or else, as in one case, because the household is childless. Moreover, we find a close relationship between income and consumption even in those cases in which income declines, a fact which can hardly be explained away by a correlation of incomes and "need." All in all, these budgets provide *some* evidence against the notion of lifetime averaging.

The results of this test of lifetime averaging appear to differ from the results of one of Friedman's tests, the relation of age and saving, discussed in Chapter 3. Friedman did find evidence for this hypothesis, but as pointed out his test does not necessarily support the notion of full lifetime averaging; it is also consistent with partial lifetime averaging. It is tempting to argue that the gap between the results of these two tests may be reduced by saying that there is a tendency toward lifetime averaging, but that it is not strong enough to show up in the long-run budgets. But this explanation is weakened by the fact that most of these long-run budgets do not even show a tendency towards lifetime averaging.

The second question to be asked of these graphs is the nature of the consumption lag. In a number of economic time series there appears to be an easily visible lag, in the sense that turning points in one series are followed by clear turning points in the other. Here such a lag would correspond to a consumption function which makes consumption a function of income in a single previous year. The wealth theories, by contrast, use the average income of many years. Here the data give a clear answer—the turning points of consumption do not show any particular consistent lag behind income. While one-year lags do show up occasionally, so do leads. In this respect they support the permanent income theory.

Finally, one rather disturbing characteristic of these data should be noted. This is the difference among households. Some of the budgets show a very strong and consistent tendency to consume transitory income while others show very little if any consumption of transitory income. This suggests that there are some households who do behave as the permanent income theory predicts, while others behave quite differently.

Table 45

Classification of Income Changes

Type of Change	Previous Year	Income Changes Following Years		
		1	2	3
Permanent Increase	− or 0	+	+	+
Transitory Increase	+ or 0	+	−	−
Permanent Decrease	+ or 0	−	−	−
Transitory Decrease	− or 0	−	+	+

NOTE: − denotes income lower than the base year; 0 denotes income equal to that of the base year; + denotes income higher than in the base year.

Permanent and Transitory Income Changes

Long-run budgets allow one to test the wealth theories by comparing the effects of permanent and transitory income changes. One can separate permanent from transitory income changes by looking mainly at future income rather than, as Friedman did, at previous income. In this way one can distinguish between the permanent income approach and the habit persistence theory.

I classified income changes into permanent and transitory ones in the following way: I calculated the year-to-year changes in income, and (1) if income was not lower in the base year than in the previous year, and (2) was maintained at a higher level than in the base year for the following three years, I called the increase *from the base year* to the *following year* a permanent increase. On the other hand, if income was higher than in the base year for only the first year, and was less than it was in the base year in the two following years, I called this a transitory income increase. I applied similar rules to distinguish between permanent and transitory income *decreases*. These criteria are summarized in Table 45. Many income changes did not fit into any of these categories and so I did not use them. I also excluded cases in which the income change was less than 3 percent, or in which the family had moved to a different locality.

I then calculated the (arc) income elasticity of consumption between the base year and the following year for all my long-run budgets as well as for all the Swiss budgets discussed in the previous chapter.[10] I have not presented the simple mean of these elasticities in Table 46 because of a statistical problem. This is the interpretation of negative

10. I did not include the German five-year data used in the previous chapter since they provide almost only cases of income increases and these are already heavily represented in my sample.

income elasticities. In one sense, negative income elasticities are easy to interpret because they show that there are some income changes in which a simple consumption function does not work—a fact which is hardly surprising when one is dealing with particular income changes in individual budgets where other factors such as "needs" cannot be treated as constant. A much more puzzling problem arises when one looks at the *magnitude* of a negative elasticity. A simple interpretation of the magnitude of these negative coefficients would run as follows: negative income elasticities show that the mean income elasticity which one obtains when one looks only at the "correct" (that is, positive) income elasticities is too great. To get a true average one must subtract the negative coefficients from the positive coefficients. Thus, if it would turn out to be the case that the positive income elasticities are the same for permanent and transitory income changes, but that the negative income elasticities are much greater (algebraically) for transitory income changes, it would follow that the *average* income elasticity is less for transitory income than for permanent income. In other words, algebraically large negative coefficients reject the hypothesis of a large positive income elasticity more than do algebraically small negative elasticities.

Table 46

Income Elasticities by Type of Income Change

Measure	Income Increase		Income Decrease	
	Permanent	Transitory	Permanent	Transitory
Median	.7	.9	.8	.8
Mean of Upper 50% of Coefficients	2.1	a	1.7	1.9
Mean of Nonnegative Coefficients	1.4	a	1.2	1.3
Percent of Coefficients Negative	15	50	22	19
Frequency Distribution[b]				
Negative	16	7	5	4
0 and under 0.2	11	0	0	0
0.2 and under 0.4	8	1	1	4
0.4 and under 0.6	7	0	4	1
0.6 and under 0.8	13	0	1	1
0.8 and under 1.0	12	1	1	2
1.0 and over	38	5	11	9
Total	105	14	23	21

[a] Too few cases for meaningful average.
[b] Represents number of income changes, not number of households.

But this is misleading. Consider the two cases which can lead to large negative income elasticities. In the first case, there is a small change in income and a large change in consumption *in the opposite direction*. In this case there is no problem. The fact that the perverse change in consumption is large does more to disconfirm the hypothesis that the income elasticity is positive and large than would have been true for a smaller change in consumption.

But now consider the other case, in which the income elasticity of consumption is negative and large, not because the absolute change in consumption is large but because the change in income has been very small. Consider this large elasticity in terms of the hypothesis that the *mean* income elasticity of consumption is positive and large. We observe a decrease in consumption and an increase in income. If consumption declines in face of only a small rise in income, this does little to destroy the plausibility of the hypothesis that the average income elasticity of consumption is large and positive. After all, many factors could swamp a small change in income. On the other hand, if consumption declines despite a *large* increase in income, this does make the hypothesis of a large positive income elasticity less plausible. Hence, if the income elasticity is negative, then an algebraically *large* elasticity disconfirms the hypothesis *less* than does a small income elasticity in one case (small income change), and more in the other case (large change in consumption). Thus in the domain of the "wrong" sign the magnitude of elasticities has no simple, unique interpretation in terms of the hypothesis.[11]

Since the magnitude of the negative elasticities is meaningless, I have not used the arithmetic mean or any measure involving the magnitude of the negative elasticities. Instead, Table 46 shows the median, the arithmetic mean of the upper half of the distribution, the mean of the nonnegative coefficients, and the percent of the coefficients which are negative as well as their frequency distribution.

Looking first at income increases, Table 46 shows a substantially greater income elasticity for permanent than for temporary income in-

11. Using a weighted mean would ameliorate but not solve this problem. Consider, for example, the following two cases; in both consumption declines by 20 percent, while income rises by 10 percent in one case and by only 1 percent in the other. Multiplying the income elasticity by the percentage change in income yields the same weighted income elasticity in both cases. But surely the fact that consumption declined by 20 percent in the face of a 10 percent income increase should count more against the hypothesis that the income elasticity is positive and large, than should the case where the same decline in consumption is associated with only a 1 percent increase in income.

creases;[12] in fact, the median income elasticity for temporary increases is zero. Although at first glance this zero income elasticity seems to give dramatic support to the permanent income theory, it does not really confirm this theory because the difference between the two medians, while in the right direction, is not significant at the 10 percent level.[13] However, the percent of cases with negative coefficients *is* significantly greater (at the 1 percent level) for transitory than for permanent income increases. Hence this comparison of permanent and transitory income increases *does* reject the measured income theories.[14]

Turning to income decreases, the picture looks much less satisfactory for the permanent income theory—the data show virtually no difference in the income elasticity of permanent and transitory income. However, given the small size of the sample, one cannot treat this as a firm rejection of the full permanent income.

In addition to testing the permanent income theory, the data of Table 46 also throw some light on the habit persistence theory. This theory is sometimes presented as saying that households adapt very much faster to income increases than to income decreases. Table 46 does not support this with regard to permanent income changes. To be sure, the small size of the sample results in such high confidence intervals that one cannot reject the hypothesis that for permanent income, the income elasticity of consumption is *substantially* greater for income increases than for decreases, but at least one can say that the data of Table 46 show nothing of the sort. The theory had a chance to show what it can do and failed it. Even if it cannot be rejected because of high standard errors, it does lose at least *some* credibility by its poor performance on this test. For transitory income changes the situation is even worse; the income elasticity is *greater* for income decreases than for income increases, though the difference is not significant.

12. The frequency distribution in the lower part of Table 46 appears to be U shaped. However, this is merely the result of open-ended classes.

13. I used the significance test for medians given by Sidney Siegel (*Nonparametric Statistics for the Behavior Sciences,* New York, McGraw-Hill, 1958, pp. 111–15). I did not test the significance of the differences in the two means shown in Table 46, because since they are means of the truncated distribution, they are not nearly as meaningful as the median. A warning about my use of significance tests may be in order. I am treating as a separate observation each income change rather than each household. But since a single household may be responsible for several of the income changes, these income changes are not a randomly selected sample.

14. It is not possible to see whether or not these data also reject the standard income theory because to do so one would have to know the proportion of negative coefficients predicted by this theory, and there is no way of obtaining such a prediction.

These results are therefore contrary to the asymmetrical habit persistence theory as used for example, by Duesenberry, but they are by no means implausible. While a habit factor may operate with greater force against cutting consumption than against raising it, there is another factor working in the opposite direction. This is credit rationing, and possibly, a reluctance to draw down savings. A household experiencing an income increase is certainly in a position to decide whether or not to adjust its consumption accordingly. However, a household with an income decline may not be able to maintain its consumption, though it may want to.

To summarize, this test rejects the measured income theories since it shows that the marginal propensity to consume is greater for permanent than for transitory income *increases*. However, for income decreases no such tendency shows up in the data. While this is unfavorable for the permanent income theory, it does not really disconfirm it because of the small size of the sample. Finally, this test casts doubt on the asymmetrical habit persistence theory.

Moving Average

Another way of separating permanent from transitory income is to fit a moving average to income, and to treat the deviations of measured income from its moving average as transitory income. To be sure, as I pointed out in Chapter 4, there is little authority for treating *permanent income* as a moving average of measured income. In fact, Friedman has specifically rejected this interpretation.[15] However, members of the Pennsylvania School have measured *normal income* as a moving average. In any case, since it is an obvious test which can be done with my long-run budgets, I fitted a five-year moving average (centered in the middle year) to my long-run budgets as well as to the thirty-four ten-year Swiss budgets. The results are surprising. I had hoped that this test would support the results reached in the previous section, and as a glance at Table 47 will show, I was sorely disappointed. In the previous test for income increases the marginal propensity to consume was greater for permanent than for transitory income, but for income *decreases* no difference between the two showed up. The moving average test shows almost exactly the opposite. For income increases the marginal propensity to consume is greater for *measured* than for normal income.[16]

15. "Windfalls, the 'Horizon' and Related Concepts in the Permanent Income Hypothesis," in Carl Christ (ed.), *Measurement in Economics: Studies in Mathematical Economics and Econometrics in Memory of Yehuda Grunfeld* (Stanford, Stanford University Press, 1963), p. 5.

16. The difference between the two medians is not significant, but the difference in the proportion of negative coefficients is significant at the 1 percent level.

But for income decreases the opposite is true.[17] In fact, for normal income decreases the marginal propensity to consume exceed unity for all budgets combined, though not much significance can be attached to this; it could easily be the result of sampling fluctuation. If one eliminates as few as four cases from the 143-case sample, the median becomes 0.9. I do not know of any formal significance test which fits this type of problem, but I will assume that this difference is not significant.

This difference between the two results has an important implication. It shows how easily different ways of measuring "permanent" income can lead to different results. Since there is no obviously correct way of measuring permanent or normal income, this fact provides a persuasive reason for not relying on a single test, and for subjecting the wealth theories to many different tests.

The obvious question is now which test is to be preferred. For income *increases* I believe that my earlier test is superior to the moving average test. In using an unweighted moving average to estimate permanent income, the income of each previous and future year is given as much weight as is the current year's income. However, the tests of the preceding chapter show that this is inappropriate, and that the current year's income should be weighted much more heavily than the income of other years. Hence, it is not surprising that when permanent income is estimated from a moving average its coefficient frequently has the wrong sign and its median value is low. This explains why the marginal propensity to consume normal income increases, shown in Table 47, is so low. It does not, however, explain why this propensity is so high for *decreases* in "permanent income."

Actually, this disagreement between the two tests is not as great as may seem at first. The previous test found no difference in the two income elasticities, but this does not deny that in actuality one of the two *may* be greater. Due to the small size of the sample, the equality of the two medians does not provide convincing evidence against this proposition.

Conclusion

In this chapter I have tried to exploit the very limited supply of really long-run budgets. The small and scattered supply of these budgets allows only tentative conclusions. One of the questions left open in the previous chapter concerns the length of the horizon. It showed that income of the two or three immediately following years has relatively little effect on current consumption. But this did not settle the question whether the horizon is much longer than this. Thus in this chapter I tried to see if

17. The difference in the proportion of coefficients which are negative is significant at the 10 percent level (two-tailed test).

Table 47

Normal and Measured Income Elasticities
Estimated by Moving Average

Measure	All Budgets		10-Year Swiss Budgets		All Other Budgets	
	Normal Income	Measured Income	Normal Income	Measured Income	Normal Income	Measured Income
Income Increases						
Median	.43	.77	.40	.82	.43	.63
Percent Negative	43.6	25.2	46.0	14.0	42.0	34.0
Income Decreases						
Median	1.15	.64	2.22	1.00	.66	.33
Percent Negative	37.8	30.4	35.7	20.5	39.7	40.0
No. of Increases[a]	243	274	100	121	143	153
No. of Decreases[a]	143	168	70	83	73	85

[a] Represents number of income changes, not number of households.

households average their income over their life span. The data show
little evidence that they do. They also show that households do not simply
wait a specific period of time before adapting their consumption to income changes.

I then separated income changes into permanent and transitory ones
and found that the marginal propensity to consume was greater for
permanent than for transitory income *increases,* which disconfirms the
measured income theories. However, no such distinction between permanent and transitory income showed up for income decreases. While
this fact is unfavorable for the permanent income theory and the standard
income theory, due to the small size of the sample, it cannot be treated
as a convincing disconfirmation. In addition, these data give no support
to the asymmetrical habit persistence theory in its usual form.

Unfortunately, the moving average test does not support the above
results. This discrepancy can be explained by the fact that the moving
average technique provides a very poor measure of permanent income.

Fifteen

THE DISTRIBUTION OF
NET WORTH

In the previous two chapters I dealt with household budgets covering several years. Another way one can get away from using data relating to consumption or saving of a single year is to look at net worth (henceforth referred to simply as wealth) instead of at the flow of saving or consumption. There are two advantages of this. First, the data on the distribution of wealth give much more detail on the top income groups than do other data. Much of the economy's saving is done by high income groups, who in the published budget studies are all thrown into a single "$10,000 and over," or at best "$15,000 and over" income class. It is certainly possible that the full permanent income theory is correct for the top income classes and not for other income groups. If so, this fact would not be revealed by the generally used cross-section data. Second, for the upper income groups a considerable part of saving is presumably saving out of capital gains rather than out of ordinary income. And capital gains, which are very large compared to saving, are not included in income in the budget studies.

On the other hand, there are three disadvantages of looking at the stock of wealth instead of at saving or consumption. One is that it allows one to test only one part of the permanent income theory, the proportionality hypothesis. The second disadvantage of a wealth test is that one cannot calculate a prediction coefficient. Third, for reasons soon to be discussed, it presupposes a fairly short horizon so that it is a test of Friedman's permanent income theory but not of the Modigliani-Brumberg-Ando life cycle theory. However, the evidence of Chapter 13 suggests that a three-year horizon is all that is needed.

I am not the first to use the stock of wealth to test the proportionality hypothesis. It was done first in an informal manner by Milton Friedman (see p. 61) and in much more detail by Jean Crockett and Irwin Friend in a study discussed in Chapter 5.[1] What I have done is to

1. See also Robert Clower and Bruce Johnson, "Income, Wealth and the Theory of Consumption," in J. N. Wolfe (ed.), *Value Capital and Growth,*

present the data in a different way, and also to meet one of Tobin's objections to the Friend-Crockett study by excluding households whose wealth resulted from inheritances.[2]

Implications of the Theories

To test consumption function theories by the distribution of wealth, one must first develop the implications of these theories for the wealth distribution. The implication of the measured income theories is clear. Since high income households save a larger proportion of their income than low income households, holding age constant, their ratio of wealth to income must be higher.

However, the implication of the permanent income theory for the wealth-income ratios of different measured income classes is less obvious. For the moment, ignore transients and consider only households who are permanently in their income decile. If the saving ratio of these households is independent of their permanent income level, then for each age group the ratio of wealth to permanent income (which is here equal to measured income) should be the same at each income level.

Now introduce transients, that is, households with positive or negative transitory income. Ignore for the moment that such households will have been saving positive (and dissaving negative), transitory income, and assume that the ratio of wealth to *permanent* income is the same for these households as for other households. If so, for households with negative transitory incomes the ratio of wealth to *measured* income must exceed the ratio of wealth to *permanent* income, and hence they must have a higher ratio of wealth to measured income than households permanently in that income group. Conversely, in the income groups above the mean, transient households have a lower ratio of wealth to measured income than households permanently in that income group. Thus, in income groups below the mean transients raise the average wealth-income ratio, and in income groups above the mean they lower the wealth income ratio. Hence the permanent income theory implies that the ratio of wealth to measured income is greater in the lower measured income classes than in the high measured income classes.

Now we must remove the assumption that the ratio of wealth to

---

Papers in Honour of Sir John Hicks (Edinburgh, The University Press, 1968), p. 65. They pointed out that wealth is distributed like the cube of income, a fact which supports their theory as against the permanent income theory.

2. James Tobin, "Comments on Crockett-Friend and Jorgenson," in Robert Ferber (ed.), *Determinants of Investment Behavior* (New York, National Bureau of Economic Research, 1967), pp. 156–60.

permanent income is the same in every income class, and make allowance for the fact that households with negative transitory income may have been reducing their wealth while households with positive transitory income will have added to their wealth. To do this it is first necessary to consider the number of years over which a household treats a change in income as being only transitory. I will work with horizons of one, three and five years.

First, take a one-year horizon and consider households who had negative transitory income for the full year. They dissave their negative transitory income, thus reducing their wealth by $\frac{y}{W}$ (100) percent, where y is the *reduction* in income and W is the stock of wealth. Their measured income has declined by $\frac{y}{Y}$ (100) percent, where Y is the level of income. Hence if their stock of wealth is equal to one year's income, their wealth and income have declined in the same proportion, and their wealth-income ratio is constant. If, as is normally the case, the stock of wealth exceeds income, then the percentage decline in wealth is less than the percentage decline in income, and the ratio of wealth to measured income is greater for transients with negative transitory income than for other households.

Now extend the horizon to three years. Some of the households with negative transitory income will have had negative transitory income for the whole period which goes to make up the three-year horizon. They will have reduced their wealth by $\frac{3y}{W}$ (100) percent, while their measured income has fallen by only $\frac{y}{Y}$ (100) percent.[3] Hence if their stock of wealth is equal to three year's income, their ratio of wealth to measured income is the same as that of households permanently in that income class. But some households have had a lower income not for the full three-year period which goes to make up the horizon, but for only one year, and other households for only two years. If one assumes that households with negative transitory income are evenly distributed by the number of years encompassed in the horizon, the average household with negative transitory income has been reducing its wealth below what it otherwise would be by the equivalent of one-and-a-half years' reduction in income. Thus in this case, the ratio of wealth to measured income will be lower for the average household with negative transitory income

3. To simplify matters I am ignoring the trend in income and the yield on wealth.

than for households without transitory income only if the ratio of wealth to income is less than 1.5. Similarly, for a five-year horizon the critical wealth-income ratio is 2.5.

The Data

Having seen the different implications for the wealth-income ratio of the permanent income theory on the one hand, and the absolute and relative income theories on the other, let us turn to the data. They come from a special tabulation of the Federal Reserve's wealth survey.[4] To avoid a factor which interferes when one wants to argue from wealth data to saving and consumption behavior, my data exclude all households with inherited assets. In addition, they exclude all households who did not work full-time all year. The purpose of this exclusion is to eliminate a portion, presumably a substantial portion, of households with negative transitory income. But since by no means all households with transitory income were eliminated (nothing was done to eliminate households with positive transitory income, for example) the permanent income theory prediction is still the same as before.

Two other characteristics of the data should be noted. First, the survey found that households often had difficulty estimating their equities in life insurance policies, retirement funds, and annuities—"many participants could not even make approximate estimates."[5] Accordingly, I excluded these unreliably estimated items.[6] Second, equity in automobiles, but not in other consumer durables, is included in wealth.

Results

Table 48 shows the wealth-income ratios for all households jointly as well as for various age groups. I have shown the "under 35 years" age group separately but its wealth-income ratio is so low (105 percent) that, given a three-year horizon, it cannot be used to test the permanent income theory. The sample is extremely skimpy for the "over 65 years" age group so that this group does not provide a good test of the theory either. The other data in this table can, however, be used to reject the proportionality hypothesis. Contrary to the implication of this theory, but in accordance with the implications of the measured income theories,

4. I am grateful to the Board of Governors, Federal Reserve System, for providing the (unpublished) data. For a discussion of the survey see Dorothy Projector and Gertrude Weiss, *Survey of Financial Characteristics of Consumers* (Washington, D.C.: Board of Governors, Federal Reserve System, 1966).

5. *Ibid.*, p. 2.

6. I also computed the wealth-income ratios including these assets for Tables 48 and 49. This did not change the results.

the wealth-income ratio generally increases with rising measured income.[7]

But Table 48 is subject to the objection that it combines self-employed and employee households. It is certainly possible that the top income classes shown in Table 48 are largely populated by self-employed businessmen. If so, the high wealth-income ratios of these classes could be explained not as a contradiction of the permanent income theory but as one more manifestation of the well-known fact that self-employed businessmen have a high saving-income ratio. Moreover, for both self-employed businessmen and salaried businessmen, income as measured in household surveys may be a bad index of true income because of the importance of fringe benefits for senior executives. Thus a survey of the total compensation of the top three executives in twenty-five manufacturing corporations found that even if certain types of compensation are ignored, total compensation was somewhat more than 150 percent of current payments.[8]

To avoid this problem, Table 49 shows the wealth-income ratio for all households broken down into nonfarm self-employed business households, salaried business households and other households. Unfortunately, the sample is too small to allow one to subclassify all these occupational groups by age. However, the last two columns of the table do show nonbusiness households in two age groups.[9]

For the two types of business households the wealth-income ratio declines with rising income below the $10,000 level, but after that it increases with rising income. For nonbusiness households the wealth-income ratio is negatively correlated with income below the $7500 level

7. Admittedly, as Jacob Mincer has suggested (private communication) the exclusion from the data of households not working full-time all year creates a bias. In those years in which they do work full time all year they have, on the average, positive transitory income, and in other years negative transitory income. By including only households working full time all year, I am biasing the sample toward households whose transitory income is positive. Hence I am understating the ratio of their wealth to their permanent income. The famliy head not working full time all year is more common in the low income classes than in the middle and upper income classes, and hence the ratio of wealth to permanent income is understated more at the lower end of the income distribution than in the middle and upper end. But while this bias may be important when comparing low income households with middle and upper income households, it can hardly account for the results when one compares the wealth-income ratios of the middle and upper income groups shown in Table 48.

8. Leonard Burgess, *Topic Executive Pay Package* (New York, Free Press of Glencoe, 1963), p. 118.

9. I excluded the two younger age groups since their overall wealth-income ratios are low, and the "65 and over" age group because the sample is too small.

Table 48

Net Worth as Percent of Income, End of 1962

Net Worth as Percent of Income

1962 Income	All Households[a]	Age of Head — Under 35	35–44	45–54	55–64	62 and over
0–$2,999	421	293	381	497	316	749[b]
3,000–4,999	124	15	62	326	256	303[b]
5,000–7,499	137	51	125	149	306	191[b]
7,500–9,999	155	54	183	146	342	369[b]
10,000–14,999	188	73	154	232	244	433[b]
15,000–24,999	258	103[b]	208	210	429	636[b]
25,000–49,999	828	6260[b]	522	647	691	473
50,000–99,999	906	—	929	1508	637	718
100,000 and over	1648	—	2462[b]	1410[b]	2056	1454
Average[c]	222	105	177	264	378	489

Number of Consumer Units in Sample

1962 Income	All Households	Age of Head — Under 35	35–44	45–54	55–64	65 and over
0–$2,999	68	18	14	15	13	8
3,000–4,999	160	63	39	24	26	8
5,000–7,499	253	82	72	57	35	7
7,500–9,999	213	60	65	56	26	6
10,000–14,999	242	35	76	81	43	7
15,000–24,999	146	7	39	51	42	7
25,000–49,999	99	7	15	35	28	14
50,000–99,999	90	0	15	28	24	23
100,000 and over	39	0	2	6	18	13
Total	1310	272	337	353	255	93

SOURCE: Based on unpublished data provided through the courtesy of the Board of Governors, Federal Reserve System.

NOTE: Excludes households with inherited assets and households not working full time all year. Net worth as of end of year, income for whole year. Net worth excludes equities in life insurance policies, retirement funds, and annuities. Net worth as of end of year, income for whole year.

[a] Weights used to combine age groups are estimated number of consumer units in universe.

[b] Fewer than 10 cases in class.

[c] Computed by averaging wealth-income ratios of groups.

Table 49

Net Worth as Percent of Income by Selected Occupations, End of 1962

	All Age Groups						Nonbusiness Households[a]			
	Net Worth as Percent of Income			Number of Cases in Sample			Age of Head			
							Net Worth as Percent of Income		Number of Cases in Sample	
1962 Income	Self-Employed Businessmen	Salaried Businessmen	Non-Business Households[a]	Self-Employed Businessmen	Salaried Business Households	Non-Business Households[a]	45–54	55–64	45–54	55–64
0–$2,999	999	b	102	23	3	42	b	b	9	9
3,000–4,999	679	b	79	16	6	138	122	258	17	25
5,000–7,499	466	116	104	26	18	209	139	190	52	26
7,500–9,999	35	94	145	17	25	171	150	299	46	22
10,000–14,999	435	142	149	29	46	167	191	201	54	31
15,000–24,999	714	226	197	28	41	77	165	300	29	23
25,000–49,999	951	394	820	45	11	43	299	b	16	9
50,000–99,999	1054	1088	267	47	21	22	b	b	7	2
100,000 and over	1494	2135	b	14	18	7	b	b	1	3

SOURCE: Based on unpublished data provided through the courtesy of the Board of Governors, Federal Reserve System.

NOTE: Excludes households with inherited assets and households not working full-time all year; net worth excludes selected items listed in note to Table 48.

[a] Includes farmers.

[b] Not shown since fewer than 10 cases in class.

and positively above that level. For nonbusiness households in the 45–54 age group the wealth-income ratio rises with income. For the 55–64 age group no clear-cut pattern emerges, perhaps because the limited sample size prevented the derivation of the wealth-income ratio for several income classes. All in all, with the exception of nonbusiness households aged 55–64 where the pattern is erratic, Table 49 suggests that the wealth-income ratio falls with rising income in the lower part of the income distribution and increases with rising income in the upper part of income distribution. Thus, one part of the evidence rejects the implication of the measured income theories, and the other part rejects the implication of the permanent income theory. The combination of these two facts rejects both types of theories and is in accord with the standard income theory.

Both Tables 48 and 49 are open to the objection that they use a wealth-income ratio which is a hybrid. The wealth data include accumulated capital gains, but current capital gains are not included in the income data. I have tried to see if the exclusion of capital gains from income can account for the results shown in these tables by making some very crude estimates of capital gains. These are extremely crude and attempt to measure only the general order of magnitude of the change which results if one includes capital gains in income.[10] The survey year, 1962, was a year which saw a stock market decline and hence in that year the capital gains pattern was unusual. I have therefore supplemented this estimate with another one which assumed greater capital gains. Using two estimates allows one to see if the wealth-income ratio is sensitive to the capital gains estimate used to construct the income plus capital gains variable.

Table 50 shows the results.[11] Estimate I shown in this table is based

10. The Federal Reserve Survey gives the types of assets held by various income groups (Dorothy Projector and Gertrude Weiss, *op. cit.*, pp. 110–11, 118–19). I assumed that the households covered in my subsample (that is, households with a head employed all year and with no inherited assets) had the same relative distribution of assets. For own homes and other real estate owned I used a capital gains rate equal to the rise in the Boeck residential construction cost index, 1.9 percent. For publicly traded stock I used the 10 percent decline in Moody's composite index, and for marketable securities other than stock I used the unweighted mean of the change in various types of bond prices, 3.3 percent. (The data come from the U.S. Department of Commerce, *Business Statistics*, 1965, pp. 52, 72, 105.) I used an arbitrary 5 percent figure for directly owned interests in a business or profession. For all other assets (and for debts) I assumed no capital gains or losses. I must confess a minor slip in these calculations. I used a beginning-of-year instead of an end-of-year base to calculate the percentage change in asset values. But this has only a very minor effect on the results.

11. Table 50 does not show the wealth-income ratio for households below 35 years since their wealth-income ratio is relatively low. The "over 65

Table 50

Illustrative Estimates of Net Worth as Percent of
Income Adjusted for Capital Gains

	All Households		Households with Head Aged			
			35–54		55–64	
1962 Income	Estimate I	Estimate II	Estimate I	Estimate II	Estimate I	Estimate II
0–$2,999	396	348	379	328	310	271
3,000–4,999	121	116	150	143	248	228
5,000–7,499	136	128	133	127	299	266
7,500–9,999	155	145	160	152	339	294
10,000–14,999	188	172	189	176	244	220
15,000–24,999	257	228	206	189	448	354
25,000–49,999	879	559	566	428	777	496
50,000–99,999	882	564	1214	672	625	446
100,000 and over	5661	857	1651	a	b	947
Averageᶜ	185	166	180	166	262	266

SOURCES: Based on Dorothy Projector and Gertrude Weiss, *Survey of Financial Characteristics of Consumers;* unpublished data provided through the courtesy of the Board of Governors, Federal Reserve System; U.S. Department of Commerce, *Business Statistics,* 1965.

NOTE: For definitions of households included and assets covered, see the notes to Table 48. For number of households in each class, see Table 48.

ᵃ Not shown since fewer than 10 cases in class.

ᵇ Income adjusted for capital gains is negative due to capital losses resulting from stock market decline.

ᶜ Mean of the income classes weighted by the number of consumer units in the universe.

on an approximation of the capital gains actually received in the survey year, while Estimate II is based on a more generous and hence more normal volume of capital gains.[12] The data once again show the wealth-income ratio generally rising with income, thus suggesting that the failure to include capital gains in income cannot account for the fact that Tables 48 and 49 contradict the proportionality hypothesis.

But to say that these data contradict the proportionality hypothesis is only part of the story. The other part is that they also support the standard income theory against the measured income theories because

years" group is excluded because the sample is too small. The 35–44 and 44–45 years age groups had to be combined because no separate data on asset holdings were available for these two groups.

12. For Estimate II I used the following increase in asset values: own homes and other real estate 5 percent; publicly traded stock 5 percent; marketable securities other than stock 3.3 percent; directly owned interest in a busines or profession 10 percent; and miscellaneous assets 5 percent.

they do show *some* "permanent income effect." While the wealth-income ratio rises with income, it does not do so uniformly. In every case shown in the above tables, the lowest income class has a higher wealth-income ratio than does the next income class. As Table 49 shows for the self-employed and for salaried businessmen, the wealth-income ratio declines with rising income until one reaches an income level of over $10,000. Moreover, for nonbusiness households in the 55–64 years age bracket the wealth-income ratio really does not show a clearly rising pattern. The measured income theories are therefore able to explain only a part of the observed behavior of the wealth-income ratio; the other part can be explained better by the permanent income theory.

This conclusion is supported by Table 51. This table shows the wealth-income ratio for the whole Federal Reserve sample, and hence unlike Tables 48 and 50 it includes households not working full time all year.[13] In the full Federal Reserve sample the wealth-income ratio *falls* for incomes below $7500, a segment which included almost 70 percent of the survey population.[14] By contrast, in Table 48 the wealth-income ratio falls only for incomes below the $5000 level, that is, it falls only for one income class instead of two. Thus for the majority of the population the only way one can reject the proportionality hypothesis is to use the great insight of the permanent income theory, the importance of transients.

The results of this test are of course subject to some criticisms. In his discussion of a similar test by Jean Crockett and Irwin Friend, James Tobin raised several issues. One is the need to hold age constant, and the other is the fact that wealth results from capital gains as well as from saving.[15]

The first of these criticisms is hard to evaluate. Crockett and Friend, as well I, classified households into ten-year age groups, and hence adjusted, at least in part, for age. Tobin's view that this adjustment is insufficient is hard to test. There is, however, some evidence which *suggests* that it is invalid. To spell out Tobin's argument in detail, it amounts to saying that (1) income and age are positively correlated, and that (2) wealth and age are positively correlated to such an extent that the wealth-income ratio rises with income purely as a result of the age factor.

If one could find an age group within which age and income are not positively correlated, then any correlation between income and the wealth-income ratio could not be attributed to the age variable. Un-

13. Another difference between the two samples is that Table 51 includes households with inherited assets.

14. Dorothy Projector and Gertrude Weiss, *op. cit.,* p. 151.

15. *Op. cit.,* pp. 156–60. Tobin also raised the point that some assets may be the result of bequests rather than of saving. This point is not relevant for my test since I excluded such households.

Table 51

Net Worth as Percent of Income
Whole Federal Reserve Sample

1962 Income	Percent
0–$2,999	475
3,000–4,999	246
5,000–7,499	205
7,500–9,999	216
10,000–14,999	230
15,000–24,999	350
25,000–49,999	830
50,000–99,999	1061
100,000 and over	1071

SOURCE: Dorothy Projector and Gertrude Weiss, *Survey of Financial Characteristics of Consumers*, pp. 110, 130, 149.

NOTE: For definition of net worth, see note to Table 48.

fortunately, no data are available on age and income within each of the ten-year age groups. However, there is something one can use to infer this relationship. Consider nonbusiness households aged 45–54 in Table 49. The mean income of these households is $8482. This exceeds the income of the 35–44 age group ($7640) as well as that of the 55–64 age group ($7427). Thus, income and age are positively correlated when one compares this age group with a younger one, and negatively correlated when compared with the older one. This suggests that within this age group there is probably little, if any, positive correlation between age and income so that the data I used from this age group are immune to Tobin's criticism. Another piece of evidence is that Crockett and Friend did use age as an independent variable in some of their regressions and that it did not change their results. To be sure, Crockett and Friend did not make some of the adjustments I made in my test, and it is conceivable that if one were to make both their adjustment for age and my own adjustments, the data would no longer reject the proportionality hypothesis.

Tobin's second criticism, the fact that not only saving, but also capital gains go to build wealth is easier to counter. The rational household consumes a certain proportion of the yield on its stock of human plus nonhuman wealth regardless of whether this wealth represents accumulated saving or fortuitous capital gains.

Another weakness is that, as in many other cross-section tests, the effects attributed to income may be due some other variable correlated with income. In Chapter 10 I listed seventeen of these variables. Eleven of them are not relevant here or else bias this test in favor of the proportionality hypothesis, but the others do create a potential problem. One of these is the interest rate. If the rate of interest does have a positive effect on saving, and *if* higher income households do receive a higher return on their saving, then this might explain, at least in part, the higher wealth-income ratio of the higher income households. However, the bias would be in the opposite direction if saving is negatively related to the interest rate, or if the relevant interest rate (which is an average of the borrowing and lending rate) is greater for low income than for high income households. One of the demographic variables, age, has already been discussed, and no information is available on the other one, family size. Home ownership is positively correlated with measured income, so that if home ownership does raise the saving ratio it would bias this test against the permanent income theory. Insufficient information is available on the next two variables, contractual saving and pension fund coverage, to determine the direction of the bias. And the same is true for the final variable, subjective and cultural factors.

Then there is the fact that the wealth data I am using do not cover implicit equities in publicly sponsored saving programs such as Social Security.[16] To this extent, the wealth-income ratio is understated for all households, with the understatement being, of course, much greater for the low income than for the high income groups. Fortunately, this qualification is probably not very important for the very high income groups covered by my data.

A fourth weakness, discussed above, is that this analysis assumes that the horizon is relatively short and hence does not apply to the life cycle hypothesis approach with its much longer horizon. With these limitations, however, I believe that this test, once again, rejects the proportionality hypothesis.

16. I am indebted for this point to Miss Reid (private communication).

Sixteen

SUMMARY AND CONCLUSION

In this book I have dealt with many tests of the wealth theories, and the time has now come to pull the results together. I will first discuss the implications of these tests for some specific hypotheses. Then I will take up most of the wealth theories discussed in Chapter 2. The final part of the chapter discusses the extent to which these tests quantify the standard income theory.

The Proportionality Hypothesis

This hypothesis has been strongly disconfirmed by the above tests. Among the previous tests (discussed in Part II) it is disconfirmed by the six following tests:

(1) Group means
(2) Time series
(3) Instrumental Variables
(4) Errors in Variables
(5) Other tests with two- or three-year data
(6) Distribution of net worth

Besides the fact that six tests represent a relatively large number of disconfirmations, there is the fact that some of these tests are the result of studies undertaken by several investigators using different sets of data and different techniques. Five new tests presented above also disconfirm the proportionality hypothesis. They are:

(1) Occupation and Consumption
(2) Race and Consumption
(3) City income
(4) Tests with five year budgets
(5) Net worth of households.[1]

Thus there are many tests which disconfirm the proportionality hypothesis. What is even more persuasive, of all the many tests which have been undertaken by friends of the hypothesis, *not a single one sup-*

---

1. This is essentially the same test as the distribution of net worth test listed above. However, it is based on different data and different methods.

ports it. It is generally not possible in economics to obtain a "critical" test—that is, a test so immune from criticism that almost everyone *has* to accept it. Every test offered above in disconfirmation of the proportionality hypothesis is open to some objection. For example, one could argue that variables, such as "cultural factors," are correlated with permanent income and that this could account for the failure of the proportionality hypothesis on the occupation test. Similarly, one could reject the tests using the five-year data by arguing that households keeping account books differ from the general run of households. But even if one does this sort of thing for every disconfirming test, how could one account for the fact that *none* of the tests—including the ones undertaken by Friedman—document the proportionality hypothesis? Put in another way, to reconcile the above findings with the proportionality hypothesis one would have to accept a number of subsidiary hypotheses, such as the nonrepresentativeness of bookkeeping households. While any one of these propositions may seem plausible, it is a good deal harder to accept *all* the special hypotheses one would need to reconcile the results of the above tests with the proportionality hypothesis. On the other hand, to *reject* the proportionality hypothesis does not require one to accept any special hypotheses at all. I therefore conclude that the proportionality hypothesis is definitely invalidated.

The Income Elasticity of Transitory Income

The full permanent income theory asserts that the income elasticity of transitory income is zero. As pointed out in Chapter 2, there is some question whether this is, at present, a refutable hypothesis. This is so primarily because the full permanent income theory asserts that what is consumed is the yield received from transitory income, and we do not have an estimate of this yield. Moreover, for estimating the transitory income elasticity of consumption the definition of consumption presents a much more serious problem than it does for testing the proportionality hypothesis. Thus someone who insists on really rigorous confirmation or disconfirmation must accept the agnostic verdict that for now this hypothesis is neither confirmed nor disconfirmed. But if one is willing to work with the conventional definition of consumption, and to accept the assumption that the yield on transitory income is less than, say 40 percent—hardly a wild assumption—then there is evidence (shown in Table 52) that the transitory income elasticity of consumption *is* greater than zero.

The life cycle hypothesis does not claim that the income elasticity of transitory income is zero; rather it argues that assets are consumed over the household's life span so that the transitory income elasticity of consumption depends in a specific way on the household's age. Since the

Table 52

Relative Marginal Propensities to Consume Out of
Permanent or Normal and Transitory Income

Author	Reference	MPC out of Transitory Income as Percent of Permanent or Normal Income MPC	Permanent Income Measured by
Ramanathan	p. 116	87	Class means of education and age
Friend (India)	p. 116	73[a]	Class means of numerous groups
Parry U.S.	p. 118	66–72 ⎫	Class means of numerous groups
U.K.	p. 118	83–87 ⎬	
Israel	p. 118	82–85 ⎭	
Mincer (a)	p. 132	67–70	Employment equation
(b)		51–63	Trend of income
(c)		46	Friedman perm. income
(d)		44[b]	Past peak income
Taubman	p. 134	40–76	Regressions using normal income
Taubman	p. 159	62–79	Simple average of 2-year income, Fisher's method, Koyck method
Williamson[c]	pp. 199–200	86	Comparisons of incomes between countries

NOTE: Ratio of marginal propensity to consume transitory income relative to permanent income includes in *transitory income* consumption out of permanent income obtained by saving the transitory income.

[a] Equation preferred by Friend.

[b] This is actually a relative income equation rather than a permanent income equation, so the estimate does not really refer to permanent income.

[c] Williamson referred to the within-country marginal propensity to save not as the propensity to save transitory income, but as the short run propensity to save. In addition to the above, Williamson also ran regressions in which he measured normal income by an income trend. For all countries combined the marginal propensity to consume transitory income as 85 percent of the marginal propensity to consume normal income thus defined. If price expectations are included in the regression this falls to 77 percent.

life cycle hypothesis does not assume, as does the permanent income theory, that there is a high yield on transitory income, its implication for consumption out of transitory income is testable. And as we shall see, it is refuted. This leaves the lag hypothesis, which will be discussed below in connection with the standard income theory.

Transitory versus Permanent Income

At the other extreme from the hypotheses just discussed are the measured income theories, with their hypothesis that the income elasticity is the same for permanent and for transitory income.[2] Here, too, the tests speak as if with one voice, and they falsify this hypothesis. They provide numerous instances of observed phenomena which are not explicable by the measured income theories, but which are explained by the hypothesis that the income elasticity is greater for permanent than for transitory income. And this implies, of course, that there is *some* lag in the consumption function. Thus, while the more extreme ideas of the full permanent income theory and strict life cycle theory are invalidated, the basic *tendency* they describe passes these tests unscathed, and is, in fact, strongly confirmed. To see this interplay of the confirmation of the general tendency and disconfirmation of narrow specificity, let us look at each of the theories in turn.

The Life Cycle Hypothesis

The specific predictions of the narrow life cycle hypothesis have not performed well on these tests. Ando and Modigliani's regressions did very badly on the prediction test. In addition, a number of the tests have dealt with some specific predictions of the strict life cycle hypothesis and their results have not been very favorable to it. Holbrook's test shows that it performs worse than the absolute income theory on the root mean square criterion, but better on the absolute error criterion. Compared to the strict permanent income theory, it is again inferior on the root mean square criterion, while its relative performance on the absolute error criterion is mixed. In the Kelley-Williamson test with Indonesian data the performance of the life cycle hypothesis was mixed, too. A more precise evaluation of the hypothesis is possible using Mrs. Projector's test, and on this test it performed no better than a naïve model did.[3] Moreover, the handful of long-run budgets discussed in Chapter 14 give it little support.

On some of these tests the data have supported the life cycle hypothesis partially in the sense of showing an effect in the direction predicted by it, but the specific quantitative predictions of this theory have not stood up well. This is not really surprising, since quite aside from any sophisticated tests, there is a readily ascertainable fact which is hard to reconcile with the life cycle hypothesis. This is that retired households are, on the whole, net savers.[4] This strongly suggests that there is a bequest motive.

2. To be sure, these theories are not formulated in terms of permanent and transitory income. But by the very fact of combining permanent and transitory income into a single variable, they imply that there is no useful difference between the two.

3. Landsberger's test gives some limited support to the life cycle hypothesis, but as discussed above, it is not very strong support.

4. The 1960–1961 BLS survey shows among retired households net saving

All in all, the performance of the strict life cycle hypothesis has not been good. But this in no way invalidates the loose version of the theory discussed in Chapter 2. All the detailed disconfirmations of the theory have related to the implications of the strict version. For reasons given in Chapter 2 I have not tested the loose version. However, it is a theory which a priori I find highly plausible. Admittedly, it has to be somehow reconciled with the fact just mentioned, the positive saving rates of retired households. This might require considerable modification.

The Permanent Income Theory

Little additional need be said about the full permanent income theory. As shown above, one of its major hypotheses, the proportionality hypothesis, is thoroughly disconfirmed. Another hypothesis, the zero transitory income elasticity, is either not testable at present, or insofar as it is testable it, too, is disconfirmed. In addition, various tests suggest that it greatly overestimates the lag. However, as discussed in Chapter 2 nearly all the tests which have been performed relate to the conventional definition of consumption. One could, therefore, argue that the permanent income theory *as formulated rather than as tested by Friedman* has not really been disconfirmed. But as pointed out in Chapter 2 for the proportionality hypothesis, the treatment of durables is relatively unimportant, and in any case Saffran's test, which did employ the use definition of consumption, does disconfirm this hypothesis.

The Normal Income Theory

Although this is a highly plausible theory, it has, on the whole, performed indifferently on the various tests, including some of those presented by its proponents. The tests by Mrs. Crockett and Friend, by Mrs. Projector, and by Friend and Taubman give it but little support. In the prediction test it predicted well, but an important coefficient had the wrong sign. On the other hand, it performed well in tests on Indian data by Ramanathan and by Friend. Since this theory is a priori plausible, its mixed performance may be the result of its empirical specification rather than of a fault in its fundamental approach.

General Wealth Models

Lydall presented a model in which saving depends on wealth as well as income. This is similar to some consumption functions suggested many years ago by James Tobin, and to consumption functions subsequently fitted by Lawrence Klein and by Ando and Brown. While Lydall's derivation of his savings function makes it part of the wealth approach, the

in every income class above $3000. *Survey of Consumer Expenditures and Income, Urban U.S. 1960–61* BLS Report 237–38, Suppl. 2, Part A, p. 48.

work of Tobin, Klein and Ando-Brown is not really part of the wealth theories as I have defined them here. But leaving problems of taxonomy aside, the results of the prediction test of Chapter 9 support these theories. Unfortunately, they cannot be tested properly with budget study data, and hence I have not been able to test them, as I would like to have done, with several different types of data and methods. But the projection test allows at least a tentative conclusion in favor of the proposition that nonhuman wealth does play a role in the consumption function. The fact that I was not able to use this variable in my budget study tests, therefore, represents a weakness of these tests.

Other Theories

For the other variants of the wealth approach fewer tests are available. Spiro's model, as pointed out in Chapter 7, performs worse than a naïve model. Again, as in the case of the normal income theory, this may be the fault merely of its particular specification. The same is true for the Arena model. The Ball-Drake theory fails because the sum of the coefficients departs from unity in a systematic way.

The Standard Income Theory

The standard income theory is not really so much a theory as it is a convenient way of specifying the idea that the truth lies in between the measured income theories on the one hand and the full permanent income theory and the strict life cycle hypothesis on the other. To that extent, the standard income theory is confirmed—or at least not disconfirmed—by all the tests except for these: (1) Bonin's test, which for reasons discussed above I have rejected; (2) the regional test, the results of which could easily be due to the peculiarities of the South; and (3) the prediction test, where its disappointing performance may be due to single equation bias. Given the number of tests I took up, this represents a rather favorable outcome.[5]

Perhaps the more important "message" of this book, therefore, is not a substantive one but a methodological one. I believe I have shown that at least in the case of the wealth theories of the consumption function, it is not necessary to brush aside previous tests of a theory as hopelessly conflicting. At least in this case, it has been possible to reconcile the results of previous tests.

But the success of the standard income theory in reconciling conflicting results is a limited one if one cannot make the theory more specific than to formulate it merely as an in-between theory. Let us see whether the

5. To be sure, as pointed out above if one estimates the city income prediction coefficients in a different way, then this test supports the measured income theories and disconfirms the standard income theory.

various tests discussed above agree on more specific propositions. There are two critical parameters to the standard income theory. One is the marginal propensity to consume transitory income relative to permanent income or measured income. The other is the length of the lag.

A number of the tests discussed in Part II provide estimates of the marginal propensities to consume permanent and transitory income. The results of these tests are shown in Table 52.[6] Since my focus is on the conventional definition of consumption, I have used that in this table. Some of the tests provide several estimates because the authors fitted separate regressions for various groups and did not provide a regression for their whole sample, or because they used several different time series or different methods. This is why the ratios shown in Table 52 are frequently a range rather than a single value.

All the ratios shown in Table 52 are fairly substantial. The (unweighted) mean ratio is 69 percent and the median is 70 percent.[7] This figure has to be adjusted for consumption out of the yield of transitory income when it is saved. Unfortunately, this yield is not known, but some illustrative figures may suggest the order of magnitude involved. If one assumes that the yield from investing transitory income is 10–15 percent, and that the marginal propensity to consume permanent income is 0.9, then a ratio of .69 for the marginal propensity to consume transitory income to the marginal propensity to consume permanent income implies that around 57 percent of the transitory receipt is consumed and 43 percent invested.[8] A 33 percent yield implies that about 46 percent is

6. I excluded several studies from Table 52. One of these is the Watts study using monthly data, because monthly data involve an unusual definition of transitory income. Another is the Stafford-Holbrook test, which employs an unusual definition of consumption. I have also excluded one of Taubman's cross-section tests because his more plausible equation combines permanent income with past peak income and hence is not really comparable to the other results shown in Table 52. In addition, I have excluded Friend and Taubman's international test since the results were so different depending upon whether they used the levels or the first differences of the data. I also excluded Ramanathan's estimates based on income trends; he presented numerous estimates and they encompass an extremely wide range of values for the ratio of the marginal propensities to consume permanent and transitory income. Moreover, I excluded Bonin's test because of doubts about the validity of its results. Finally, I excluded Holmes' estimates because they relate to the use definition of consumption.

7. If Holmes' estimates for the U.S. based on the use definition of consumption are included the mean becomes 66 percent and the median 69 percent.

8. If 58 percent of transitory income is consumed and 42 percent is invested at a 10 percent yield, then permanent income increases by 4.2 percent. If the marginal propensity to consume is 0.9 then 3.8 percent is consumed out of this permanent yield so that the total increase in consumption

consumed and 54 percent is invested. Both of these figures, of course, are far removed from Friedman's hypothesis that none of the transitory income is consumed. However, it should be kept in mind that I have used the conventional definition of consumption and, in addition that many of the estimates used in Table 52 refer not really to Friedman's permanent income but to some related normal income concept.

In most of my own tests I did not estimate the marginal propensity to consume transitory income. Instead I calculated prediction coefficients. These prediction coefficients are summarized in Table 53 and have a mean of about two-thirds.[9] As this table shows, there is a substantial difference in the coefficients calculated by various tests. This is not surprising because the prediction coefficients for any single test also show much variability. This variability, both within a specific test and among tests is, of course, rather discouraging and reduces the reliance one can place on the average of these prediction coefficients.

On the other hand, it is encouraging that (for an assumed yield of 10-15 percent) the stories told by Table 52 and 53 are in close agreement. Both suggest that as far as the relative size of the marginal propensities to consume permanent and transitory income are concerned, the permanent income theory is about two-thirds "wrong" and one-third "right."[10]

Turning to the length of the lag, much less information is available. The usual way of analyzing this problem is to rely on time series regres-

---

attributable to the transitory income receipt is 61.8 percent. Given the marginal propensity to consume of 0.9 out of permanent income, this 61.8 percent represents 69 percent of the marginal propensity to consume permanent income.

9. My results are therefore in very close agreement with Vakil's prediction coefficients for India cited in Chapter 10. Simon and Aigner obtained prediction coefficients of about one third in their errors in variables test but this estimate is critically dependent upon the validity of Friedman's lag structure. Liviatan's tests, like mine, compare consumption out of measured and permanent income. They suggest that the measured income theories, while in error, are less in error than is the permanent income theory. However, all but one of these tests is subject to a common error term bias.

10. Table 52 deals with the marginal propensity to consume permanent and transitory incomes while Table 53 deals implicitly with the marginal propensity to consume measured income. To compare their results I assumed that 85 percent of the variance in measured income is due to the variance of permanent income, and that the marginal propensity to consume permanent income is 0.9. Combining the marginal propensities to consume permanent income (0.9) and the marginal propensity to consume measured income yields a marginal propensity to consume measured income of 0.84. The marginal propensity to consume transitory income (0.55) is 65 percent of this.

Table 53

Prediction Coefficients

Test	Median of Prediction Coefficients	Number of Prediction Coefficients
Occupation	.6	19
Black-White	.3	8
Geographic	1.6	8
5-Year Data	.8[a]	1
Median of Medians on Each Test	.7	—
Median of All Coefficients Combined	.6	36

[a] Swiss data only. German data, which are biased in favor of the measured income theories, have a prediction coefficient of about unity.

sions. However, as discussed in Chapter 9, I do not believe that regressions of aggregate time series yield reliable results. The mean lag obtained from regressing aggregate time series data seems to vary substantially depending upon the methods used.

I believe that the ideal data for estimating the lag are cross-section data giving household income and consumption for a series of years. But few such data are available. A common "make-do" procedure, using the Koyck-Nerlove technique on two years of data, is dangerous because of the high degree of autocorrelation in consumption and income data. The only previous study which used a different technique to determine the lag from cross-section data is one of Holbrook's tests and he found a short lag.

Among my own tests only the tests with the five-year Swiss data provide a reliable guide to the length of the lag. Fortunately, there are three of these tests, and they are in close agreement, showing a lag of around half a year. In addition, some information on the length of the lag can be obtained from the handful of long-run budgets charted in Chapter 14. While some of them suggest long-run consumption averaging, most do not.

But this is only part of the story. Some other tests, such as the tests undertaken by Watts and Stafford, suggest that consumption is affected by expected income many years in the future. Indeed, on a very simple level, there is an obvious piece of evidence for this. This is that households save much more during the peak earning years than they do in retirement. This conflict of the evidence suggests that the notion of *the lag* is too simple, and that a more complex construction is required. It appears that households do take long-run income expectations into account in deciding on current consumption, but that their consumption is influenced to only a limited degree by income in the two or three preceding years.

It seems that there are really two different kinds of lags. One kind deals with the household's view of its total life span. Here there may be a long lag. On the other hand, for year-to-year income fluctuations such as measured by most of my data, the lag is short. I am not sure how to reconcile these two lags, or for that matter how to measure the life span lag accurately, since so few data on really long-term income and consumption are available. This problem of the dual lag is the main loose end of this study.

In Defense of Vagueness

It is usual in economics to present very specific empirical results, often expressed as a percentage given to one place of decimals. My results, on the other hand, are far from that precise. One reason for this is that I have used many different tests, and since different tests yield different median prediction coefficients, it would hardly be right to present my results as a precise number. Another reason is the nature of the question I am asking. Instead of asking whether a certain theory is "right" or "wrong" I am asking to what *extent* the theory is right or wrong. On this type of question there is a much greater chance of obtaining divergent but interesting results from various tests than there is in asking the more simplistic question dealing with "right" or "wrong." In fact, this is precisely what happened. My tests are in agreement in rejecting the full permanent income theory at one extreme and the measured income theories at the other extreme. To the much more demanding question of quantifying the error of the two extreme positions my tests still give vague results. But it is to this demanding question rather than to extreme questions, such as the validity of the proportionality hypothesis, that future work should be addressed.

Appendix One

SOME ATTEMPTED TESTS WITH CONSUMERS
UNION PANEL DATA

There is something to be said for discussing tests which fail, as well as those which succeed. Accordingly I am describing in this Appendix a set of tests which did not provide acceptable results. The data for these tests come from an annual survey of its subscribers undertaken by Consumers Union, the publishers of *Consumer Reports*.[1] These surveys include some extremely interesting questions not usually covered in household surveys. In particular, the survey asked households to give their "normal income," [2] a piece of information of obvious interest to anyone testing the wealth theories.

To be sure, there are some disadvantages to using these data. One is that this sample is not representative of American households as a whole, since the subscribers to *Consumer Reports* have substantially above-average income and education,[3] and *may* be unusually careful and cautious in consumption and saving behavior. Two other factors which reduce the representativeness of my sample is that the particular data tape I worked with excluded all single-person households and households with a head less than 30 years old.

---

1. I am indebted to Albert Hart, Charlotte Boschan, Carl Jordan, F. T. Juster, Lewis Solmon, and the National Bureau of Economic Research for providing me with the data tape from the 1959 survey.

2. The specific question asked was "In planning your expenditures what level of income do you regard as normal for your household?" For good and sound reasons economists generally distrust people's statements of how, and why, they act, and prefer objective data instead. All the same, I believe that this question about normal income provides useful information. This is so because our objective measures of permanent income are rather poor too, and may well be inferior to such a subjective measure. However, in looking at the actual answers given to this question, one problem did appear. This is that the respondents frequently gave a figure essentially equal to their current income, rounded downwards to the nearest $1000.

3. For a description of the sample see F. Thomas Juster, *Anticipations and Purchases* (Princeton, Princeton University Press, 1964), Appendix C.

Another disadvantage of these data is that they do not give a direct estimate of consumption or saving, so that saving must be obtained as the change in asset holdings.[4] Since asset holdings can change as a result of gifts (given and received) and capital gains or losses, there is a danger that saving is measured very badly for some households. To guard against the more extreme over- and understatements of saving I excluded all households who appeared to save or dissave more than 50 percent of their income.[5]

My first, and most obvious, test was to regress saving first on measured income and then on "normal income." In both regressions I used a number of additional variables—family size, age of head, home ownership, and mortgage status. As Table I-A shows—in sharp contrast to the permanent income theory and the standard income theory—the marginal propensity to *save* turned out to be *greater* for "normal income" than for measured income.

These results were confirmed by my second test, which consisted of using both normal income and transitory income (that is, measured income minus normal income) in the same regression. And, as Table I-A shows, the marginal propensity to save was greater for normal income than for transitory income.

My third test dealt with the role played by the income of the previous two years, and the expected income of the following year. I did this regression twice, once using the income levels of various years, and once expressing the incomes of other years as a ratio to the current year's income. As Table I-B shows, the results of this test give no support to the permanent income theory. Only current income and income lagged one year have the right sign and neither are significant.[6] Income lagged two years is significant but has the wrong sign. In the ratio regression

---

4. I did not calculate savings totals from changes in asset levels myself but used the savings figures calculated by Phillip Cagan in connection with his use of these data in his *The Effect of Pension Plans on Aggregate Saving* (New York, National Bureau of Economic Research, Occasional Paper No. 95, 1965). These ratios were on the data tape.

5. In addition, I excluded self-employed households because of a printing error on the questionnaire, households not giving all the information needed for my regressions, and those whose responses contained obvious errors. After these exclusions my sample consisted of 2802 households.

6. A high previous income suggests a high permanent income. Hence, if the marginal propensity to save is, in fact, greater for transitory than for permanent income, then, holding current income constant, the greater is previous income, the lower should current saving be. Hence, the coefficient of previous income should be negative. And the same applies to the coefficient for expected income.

only expected income has the right sign, and it is not significant. However, the two past incomes are significant—with the wrong sign.[7]

But none of these results furnish acceptable evidence against the permanent or standard income theories. Instead, all of them have to be thrown out as unreliable. This is so because the *marginal* propensity to save measured income is slightly less than the *average* propensity to save.[8] Since the opposite is one of the most strongly confirmed propositions of consumption function research, these results are highly implausible. They certainly cannot be used to test the permanent and standard income theories. These theories try to explain the coexistence of a constant average propensity to consume in the time series data with the marginal propensity being less than the average propensity to consume in the cross-section data. Cross-section data which do not exhibit the usual relationship between the average and marginal propensities therefore provide no test of these theories. I have therefore discarded such data in the few cases where I came across them.

What explains the marginal propensity being less than the average propensity to consume in these data? I really do not know, but there are two obvious possibilities. One is that there is an error in the data. The original data tape I received had to be transformed in a rather complicated way to produce the data cards actually used in the regressions. Something may have gone wrong in this process.[9] The second possibility is suggested by the very low coefficients of determination. In cross-section regressions using individual households rather than groups of households, coefficients of determination tend to be quite low. The lowness of my coefficients is certainly not unique.[10] However, they do show that my regressions "explain" usually less than 10 percent of the observed saving. Obviously, important variables have been omitted. This is inevitable since many individual idiosyncrasies affect the savings of each household. But suppose that some of these omitted variables are correlated with income. If so, the marginal propensities to save have

7. In addition, I tried a regression using expected changes in income. It showed no meaningful pattern; both expected increases and expected decreases were associated with higher savings.

8. For measured income the average propensity to consume is 0.891 while the marginal propensity is 0.897; for normal income they are 0.882 and 0.885 respectively.

9. Since, at this point in my work, my research funds had become negative I could not check up to see what, if anything, had gone wrong.

10. Thus Malcolm Fisher, in his test of the wealth theories, got many coefficients of determination even lower than mine. "Explorations in Savings Behavior," Oxford University, Institute of Economics and Statistics, *Bulletin*, Vol. 18, August 1956, pp. 270–73.

Table I-A

Coefficients of Savings Regressions Using Different Income Measures

Variable	Measured Income			Normal Income			Transitory and Normal Income		
	Coefficient	Standard Error	t Value	Coefficient	Standard Error	t Value	Coefficient	Standard Error	t Value
Y	.103	.006	16.8	—	—	—	—	—	—
Y_T	—	—	—	—	—	—	.082	.013	6.3
Y_N	—	—	—	.115	.007	15.6	.111	.007	15.9
N	−50.285	20.351	−2.5	−60.835	20.561	−3.0	−54.193	20.447	−2.6
A	.231	3.666	.1	1.208	3.687	.3	.035	3.666	.1
H	−78.672	77.266	−1.0	−81.271	77.774	−1.0	−75.986	77.244	−1.0
M	128.770	80.794	1.6	156.697	81.397	1.9	137.642	80.895	1.7
Constant	318			292			285		
R^2	.098			.086			.099		

CODE:
  Y, Measured
  Y_T, Transitory Income
  Y_N, Normal Income
  N, Family Size
  A, Age of Head

  H, Homeowner Status
    (Dummy variables used:
    1 for ownership, 2 for renting)
  M, Mortgage on Home
  — Not Computed

Table I-B

Coefficients of Saving Regressions
Using Current, Expected, and Past Measured Incomes

Variable	Level Regression			Ratio Regression		
	Coeffi-cient	Standard Error	t Value	Coeffi-cient	Standard Error	t Value
Y	.022	.023	1.0	—	—	—
N	−52.488	20.373	−2.6	−.004	.002	−2.0
A	−.952	3.715	−.3	.000	.000	.7
H	−84.304	77.093	−1.1	−.013	.008	−1.8
M	127.102	80.756	1.6	.012	.008	1.6
Y'_{+1}	.015	.020	.8	—	—	—
Y_{-1}	−.006	.020	−.3	—	—	—
Y_{-2}	.081	.024	3.3	—	—	—
Y'_{+1}/Y	—			−.018	.020	−.9
Y_{-1}/Y	—			.079	.020	4.0
Y_{-2}/Y	—			.137	.026	5.4
Constant	326			.079		
R^2	.104			.015		

NOTE: Y' is Expected Income; — is Not Computed. For definition of other variables, see Table 1-A.

been estimated inaccurately. And since the omitted variables are so important, such a bias is not at all unlikely. In any case, while I have no way of knowing what caused it, it is clear that something is wrong with the data shown in Tables I-A and I-B.

FRIEDMAN'S PERMANENT INCOME ESTIMATE
by Hal R. Varian

This Appendix is intended as a disconfirmation of Wright's results, which indicate a numerical error in Friedman's regression. Unlike Wright I used the same procedure, and *exactly* the same data as Friedman used, and have found results that support those found by Friedman.[1]

Friedman estimates permanent income by the following formula:

$$y_p(T) = \beta \int_{-\infty}^{T} \exp\left[(\beta - \alpha)(t - T)\right] y(t)\, dt \qquad (1)$$

where $y(t)$ is observed income in period t, β is a coefficient of adjustment, and α is a trend variable. Friedman exogenously estimated α as being .02 and stated that: "This did not affect the fitting process but only the interpretation of the computed constants."[2] Ignoring α then, we have:

$$y_p(T) = \beta \int_{-\infty}^{T} \exp\left[\beta(t - T)\right] y(t)\, dt \qquad (2)$$

Friedman did not state exactly what discrete analogue of (2) he used; however, the following is natural, and yields intermediate results that agree with some quoted by Friedman (see below).

Let us assume that $y(t)$ is a step function, constant during the year, and changing only between years. We integrate (2) over a one-year period:

$$y(n) \int_{n-1}^{n} \beta \exp\left[\beta(t - T)\right] dt = y(n) \exp\left[\beta(t - T)\right]_{n-1}^{n}$$
$$= y(n) \exp\left[\beta(n - T)\right](1 - \exp\left[-\beta\right])$$

Friedman used a 17-year approximation to the integral, yielding:

$$y_p(T) = \sum_{t=T-16}^{T} y(t) \exp\left[-\beta(T - t)\right](1 - \exp\left[-\beta\right]) \qquad (3)$$

1. I am indebted to Milton Friedman and Colin Wright for making the data available.

2. *A Theory of the Consumption Function,* (Princeton, Princeton University Press, 1957), p. 146.

Table II-A

Weights for First Five Years

Beta	Income Lag (years)				
	0	1	2	3	4
.1	.116	.105	.095	.086	.078
.2	.188	.154	.126	.103	.084
.3	.261	.193	.143	.106	.079
.4	.330	.221	.148	.099	.067
.5	.394	.239	.145	.088	.053
.6	.451	.248	.136	.075	.041
.7	.503	.250	.124	.062	.031
.8	.551	.247	.111	.050	.022
.9	.593	.241	.098	.040	.016
1.0	.632	.233	.086	.031	.021
1.1	.667	.222	.074	.025	.008
1.2	.699	.210	.063	.019	.006
1.3	.727	.198	.054	.015	.004
1.4	.753	.186	.046	.011	.003
1.5	.777	.173	.039	.009	.002

The estimation procedure is a maximum likelihood method involving evaluating (3) for various values of β, regressing consumption on y_p, and choosing as the estimate of β the one that yields the highest R^2.

The weights generated from (3) are presented for the first five years in Table II-A. Notice that the weights for $\beta = .40$ agree completely with the weights Friedman cites. Presumably then, the other weights also agree.

The regressions were run on the years 1905–1951, omitting the war years, 1917, 1918, and 1942–45, as Friedman indicated. The regression equations were:

$$c(t) = k_1 y_p(t) \tag{4}$$
$$c(t) = k_2 y_p(t) + c \tag{5}$$

and the results were:

$$c(t) = .9188 y_p(t) \qquad \beta = .50$$
$$(.00637)$$

$$c(t) = .9584 y_p(t) - 189.02 \quad \beta = .40$$
$$(.03433) \qquad (204.89)$$

The R^2 statistics are summarized in Table 3 in the text.

As can be seen, the results are fairly similar to Friedman's. He estimated $\beta = .40$, $k_1 = .88$, $c = -4.0$, and $R_1^2 = .96$. Wright, on the other hand, in estimating the weight that current income has in determining permanent income, found this to be "in the range .7–.8." The values of this variable, B, in these regressions are: $B_1 = .394$ if there is no constant term in the regression, and $B_2 = .330$ if there is a constant term.

SOME NOTES ON CORPORATE SAVING

The usual approach to the consumption function makes consumption depend on disposable personal income. And in fitting their regressions to annual data, both Friedman on the one hand and Modigliani and Ando on the other, used disposable personal income.[1] However, the inherent logic of the permanent income theory and of the life cycle hypothesis implies that undistributed corporate profits should be included in income and in saving. Both personal saving and corporate saving enter the household's utility function, and whether it saves directly, or indirectly through retained corporate earnings, should have relatively little effect on its total saving. If a household exercises foresight and rationality one would expect it to be rational enough to count corporate saving as part of its income. To be sure, one could argue that observed corporate saving is not really the proper variable to add to income, and that one should use instead discounted expected capital gains, but this variable is not directly observable.

Since the great bulk of the tests of the permanent income theory—both cross section and time series—exclude corporate saving, they are, in this way, not really adequate tests of the theory, although they may be very useful in informing us about the highly important relationship of consumption to disposable personal income. This suggests that some disagreement between the theory and the results of the tests may occur without discrediting the theory. Unfortunately, it is not possible to eliminate this problem by adjusting the cross-section tests to take account of undistributed corporate earnings.[2] For one thing, stock ownership data are generally not available. On the level of testability one has, in most cases, no choice but to discard the logic of the theory and to use personal income in place of personal income plus undistributed corporate income.

1. More precisely, Modigliani and Ando use labor income rather than personal income in their regression analysis.
2. But in those cross section tests which deal only with employees corporate saving is likely to be unimportant.

But corporate saving should not be completely disregarded and so this Appendix will discuss it briefly.[3]

One of the hypotheses of the permanent income theory, the lag hypothesis, does fit corporate savings, and this explanation of dividend payments versus retained earnings has been used by John Lintner.[4] It follows from this that the marginal propensity to save differs for permanent and for transitory profits, and an analysis along these lines has been formally set out by M. R. Fisher.[5] We face a conflict between time series and cross section results, and, once again the permanent income theory is able to resolve this conflict. Fisher suggested that if one assumes that transitory elements cancel out, one can approximate the marginal propensity to save *permanent* profits by the ratio of mean corporate saving to mean corporate profits. On two tests, however, the correlation of the dividends—profits ratio with (1) mean profit increases and with (2) the relative dispersion of permanent profits, the permanent income theory was not successful. This Fisher attributed to the disturbing influence of other variables.[6]

Another issue discussed by Fisher is the proportionality hypothesis— that is, the question whether small and large companies distribute the same proportion of their earnings. Fisher rejected Dobrovolsky's finding that there is little difference between the propensities to save of small and large firms, and concluded that large firms have a higher saving ratio than small firms. He explained this by three factors: a greater dispersion of measured and permanent profits for small firms, a greater expectation of rising profits for large firms, and more pressure to distribute profits for small firms. P. Sargent Florence, too, found a positive correlation of firm size and saving ratios except for the brewing industry.[7] However, in a subsequent paper, P. E. Hart showed that the proportionality hypothesis fits that industry, too.[8] But this use of the proportionality hypothesis was criticized by Tony Lancaster, who argued that

3. Since corporate saving is a somewhat peripheral issue for the wealth theories, I have not tried to cover all the extensive literature on it.

4. "Distribution of Incomes of Corporations among Dividends, Retained Earnings and Taxes," American Economic Association, *Papers and Proceedings,* Vol. XLVI, May 1956, pp. 97–113.

5. "L'Epargne et les Profits des Enterprises dans L'Hypothese du 'Revenu Permanent,' " *Economie Applique,* Vol. 10, October 1957, p. 149.

6. But Fisher's test using the dispersion of profits is subject to the criticism that he ignored the growth rate of profits. See Tony Lancaster, "Business-Saving and Normal Income," *Review of Economic Studies,* Vol. XXX, October 1963, pp. 209–10.

7. "Size of Company and Other Factors in Dividend Policy," *Journal of the Royal Statistical Society,* Vol. 122, 1959, Part I, pp. 80–83.

8. "The Business Propensity to Save and Size of Firms," *Review of Economic Studies,* Vol. XIX, February 1962, pp. 147–50.

the proportionality hypothesis relates to permanent income and therefore cannot be tested by using measured profits.[9] In a subsequent paper Hart used a test of Theil's and also an instrumental variables test to reject Lancaster's criticism.[10]

In another study, using the permanent income theory explicitly, Michael Davenport criticized Lintner's analysis for giving implausible results for steady state earnings.[11] Davenport assumed that the marginal propensity to pay dividends is greater for permanent than for transitory earnings. By approximating normal earnings by a three-year average, he found that in nine out of ten cases the marginal propensity to pay dividends out of transitory earnings was not significantly different from zero at the 5 percent level.[12] In addition, he confirmed once again the lag hypothesis as applied to dividends. Finally, he tested a rival to the permanent income theory, the relative income theory, by seeing if a corporation's dividend payments could be explained by dividends paid by other corporations in the same industry—that is, by an emulation effect. This theory did not perform well.[13]

What do these findings about corporate saving imply for the permanent income theory? First, consider the lag in dividend distribution. Insofar as consumption depends upon income *receipts*, the existence of a long lag in the distribution of dividends would suggest that the lag in the consumption function is greater if one relates consumption to national income than to personal income. However, it is in the spirit of the permanent income theory to argue that consumption depends not upon income receipts, but upon changes in (human and nonhuman) wealth and the interest rate. If business saving shows up in an increase in wealth right away, the fact that some income is not distributed by corporations should not lengthen the lag of the consumption function. However, due to imperfections of the capital market, there may at times be a lag between business saving and the appreciation in the market value of the corporation. But market imperfections may create a lead as well as a lag in the revaluation of assets. Hence, one cannot be sure that there really *is* a net lag. Thus, the existence of corporate saving may, but need not, add an additional lag to the consumption function.

9. "Business Saving and Normal Income," *op. cit.,* pp. 203–216.
10. "Business Saving and Errors in Variables," *Review of Economic Studies,* Vol. XXXII, July 1965, pp. 225–32.
11. Michael Davenport, "Some Cross Section Tests of the 'Normal' Earnings Hypothesis of Corporate Savings," *Yorkshire Economic Bulletin,* Vol. 20, May 1968, pp. 3–14.
12. *Ibid.,* p. 11.
13. Another paper, R. Goffin, "La distribution des dividendes dans l'hypothese de revenu permanent," *Revue Economique,* Vol. 21, November 1970, pp. 929–91, reached me too late to be included here.

The fact that corporations adjust dividends with a lag, and behave in the way predicted by a permanent income theory may, at first glance, seem to support the permanent income theory. If we observe that a certain theory can explain the behavior of corporations, does this not suggest that the same theory should be able to explain the behavior of households? But this reasoning is questionable. If households already on their own account behave in the way described by the permanent income theory, why should they want corporations to even out the dividend stream for them, when they could simply save positive transitory dividends and dissave negative transitory dividends? If evening out dividends is desired by stockholders, and Lintner does suggest that this is so,[14] then this might mean that households experience some difficulty in evening out their consumption stream if income fluctuates. But the evening out of the dividend stream by corporations cannot really be cited as evidence against the permanent income theory since it might be due to other considerations. Thus it neither supports nor disconfirms the theory.

The proportionality hypothesis as applied to corporations of different size has little bearing on the permanent income theory, though, of course, it is an important consideration in a study of business finance. The permanent income theory was never applied by its originators to corporations. Nor can the proportionality hypothesis be extended to corporations as a corollary of the permanent income theory for households. The proportionality hypotheses enters the permanent income theory in the following way. The theory asserts that there is no reason to assume that the income elasticity of saving is greater than, or less than, unity, and the data suggest that it is approximately equal to unity. This reasoning cannot be carried over directly to corporations—here there are grounds for thinking that the income elasticity of corporate saving is greater than unity,[15] but this does not in any way cast doubt on the applicability of the proportionality hypothesis to households.[16]

To summarize, the study of corporate saving adds little to the evidence for or against the permanent income theory. The fact that corporate dividends adjust with a lag may, but need not, lengthen the lag between changes in national income and changes in consumption. Moreover, the existence of the dividend lag does not provide arguments either for or against the lag hypothesis as applied to households. Similarly, the ap-

14. John Lintner, *op. cit.*, p. 99.
15. See David Smith, "Corporate Saving Behavior," *Canadian Journal of Economics and Political Science,* Vol. 29, August 1963, pp. 303–04.
16. If the data were to show that the proportionality hypothesis is valid for corporations this would not support the permanent income theory against the relative income theory. An emulation effect for corporations is not part of the relative income theory.

plicability of the proportionality hypothesis to corporations throws no light on the validity of this hypothesis. The only conclusion which does emerge is a rather disheartening one; many tests of the theory are based on an income concept different from that called for by the logic of the theory.

Before leaving this topic entirely it is worthwhile to look at the relative magnitudes of corporate and personal saving. Table III-A shows the proportion of total private saving accounted for by corporate saving. There are several things worth noting in this table. First, there is the fact that corporate saving is a quite substantial proportion of total

Table III-A

Corporate Saving as Percent of Private Saving:
Goldsmith Estimate 1897–1949, and Commerce Estimate 1929–1967

Year	Goldsmith Estimate[a]	Year	Goldsmith Estimate[a]	Commerce Estimate	Year	Goldsmith Estimate[a]	Commerce Estimate
1897	40.9	1922	15.3		1947	26.0	52.1
98	23.8	23	23.3		48	32.0	50.2
99	21.6	24	17.7		49	39.6	58.3
1900	37.6	25	22.2		1950		45.8
01	35.7	26	31.2		51		40.7
02	21.2	27	14.1		52		39.8
03	46.2	28	32.1		53		36.4
04	24.6	29	18.1	44.2	54		40.0
05	17.8	1930	−10.2[b]	15.8	55		48.3
06	20.8	31	730.43[c]	−2379.2	56		39.1
07	31.1	32	77.3[c]	86.8	57		38.0
08	17.6	33	63.8[c]	80.4	58		32.0
09	13.7	34	63.0[c]	132.4	59		44.7
1910	27.9	35	−206.6[b]	−24.7	1960		44.1
11	24.2	36	−61.5[b]	−10.1	61		38.8
12	12.8	37	−11.2[b]	13.6	62		43.0
13	28.8	38	−19.4[b]	50.7	63		44.8
14	23.4	39	−1.6[b]	30.0	64		43.4
15	21.5	1940	20.2	43.5	65		46.7
16	39.7	41	13.2	22.6	66		45.5
17	20.6	42	7.6	14.5	67		37.4
18	3.4	43	10.1	14.9			
19	20.7	44	10.5	14.4			
1920	30.7	45	6.5	11.6			
21	56.3	46	11.1	23.4			

SOURCES: Raymond Goldsmith, A Study of Saving in the United States, Vol. I, pp. 345-349. *National Income and Product Accounts of the United States, 1929-1965*, pp. 78-79. *Survey of Current Business*, Vol. 48, July 1968, p. 34.

[a] Social accounting concept, excluding saving via consumer durables.

[b] Corporate saving negative, personal saving positive.

[c] Both corporate and personal saving negative.

saving. A theory which tries to explain the household's allocation of disposable income between consumption and saving by looking at the marginal utility of present versus future consumption should surely include corporate saving in its purview; it cannot be ignored as empirically minor.

Second, there does not seem to be a pronounced trend in the proportion of total saving accounted for by corporate saving, at least after the early years of the present century. Admittedly, it is hard to determine whether or not a trend does exist due to the discrepancy between the Department of Commerce data and the Goldsmith data, as well as to the special events of the 1930s and the war years.

As mentioned above, I have limited the sample by excluding certain budget studies. First, budget studies for underdeveloped countries and for communist countries are excluded to keep the sample fairly homogenous. Second, budget studies for the immediate post-World War II years—that is, the years before 1948 for the United States and 1949 for Europe—are also left out for the same reason. Third, I excluded, with one exception, budget studies covering less than a full year.[1] As explained in Chapter 5, budget studies covering less than a year do not provide a fair test of the measured income theories.

Fourth, in a few budget studies the average propensity to consume out of *measured* income was rising or stable instead of falling as one goes up the income scale. I excluded these cases as abnormal (or else as

1. Many of the studies covering less than a full year are Japanese. Japanese wage and salary earners receive a substantial part of their income in the form of bonuses. To avoid the complications this creates, one set of annual Japanese budget surveys excludes December. Using these studies would mean excluding an important part of household incomes, and this may bias the results. I therefore made a compromise between using questionable data and limiting the sample too much, by including only one of these studies. There exist another set of Japanese budget studies which cover a full year. However, there the problem is that the bonus is received in the last month covered by the survey. Hence, unless households anticipate their bonuses correctly, or spend most of the bonus in December, a good part of this year's income affects consumption mainly in the following year. (This does not mean that Japanese households behave in accordance with the permanent income theory, but rather that, for the purpose of testing the consumption function theories, the survey year should start in December.) To be sure, while this problem would be serious for the prediction coefficients it would not really matter for the ranked correlation coefficients. Had I known of the existence of these full year data earlier I would therefore have used them to derive ranked correlation coefficients. However, by the time I found out about them (through the courtesy of Professor Mizoguchi) I already had a sufficient number of ranked correlation coefficients.

subject to error).[2] The permanent income theory attempts to reconcile the falling average propensity to consume shown by cross-section data with the very roughly stable propensity shown by time series data. It is therefore not applicable in those cases in which the cross-section propensity is rising or stable instead of falling.

Fifth, I have not, with one exception, used budget studies for more than three consecutive years in the same country.[3] Since the distribution of transitory income among occupations in any one year may well be positively correlated with its distribution in the previous year, the inclusion of budget studies for many consecutive years for the same country would interfere with the representativeness of the sample, and hence with the significance test.

Sixth, I have excluded budget studies based on too few budgets, and seventh, I have excluded studies for which I did not have the original source but only a report in a statistical yearbook, since these yearbooks do not discuss the peculiarities of the data. Finally, to save time, I relied primarily on published data.[4]

2. This includes one budget study (Holland 1951) in which the propensity to consume for clerical workers does not fall with rising measured income when insurance is included in consumption. I had used this in an earlier version of this test (*American Economic Review*, December 1966) but upon reconsideration decided not to use it.

3. The one exception is Britain, but here one of the budget studies used deals with a quite different group of occupations than the other three studies.

4. Several budget studies had to be excluded because they are not readily available in any American library participating in the inter-library loan system, or because the citations I had to them was inadequate. There are probably a number of budget studies I missed inadvertently. My attempt to cover them all was made possible by the existence of a magnificent annotated bibliography, Faith Williams and Carle Zimmerman, *Studies of Family Living in the United States and Other Countries: An Analysis of Material and Methods* (U.S. Dept. of Agriculture, Miscellaneous Publication No. 233, Washington, D.C., 1935). For the postwar period I could not locate the source of several budget studies cited in the *International Labor Yearbook*. In addition, I dropped several budget studies for reasons specific to the particular study. A Norwegian study for 1918–1919 combined life and accident insurance. If both are treated as saving, the propensity to consume of the better-paid occupation is less than that of the lower-paid occupation, but if the whole insurance item is treated as consumption this result is reversed. In the absence of a more detailed breakdown of insurance expenditures this study, therefore, does not lead to any firm conclusion. For the mid-thirties, a Latvian study had to be left out because it contains calculating errors, and I omitted an Estonian study because the income difference between the two occupations was rather minor, and in addition, most of the households in one occupation were government employees whose (probably unrecorded) retirement saving may well differ substantially from that of other households. I excluded an Austrian budget study because the response rate

I was faced with the problem of deciding whether to treat as a separate unit of observation each budget study publication or the year, a problem raised by the fact that a Portuguese budget study is reported in two separate publications each covering one city, while on the other hand two of the budget studies, one Swiss and one American, give completely separate data for two years. I decided to treat the year as the unit of observation, thus combining the two Portuguese studies into one while counting the Swiss and American studies as two separate studies each.

Within each study I have not used all occupations given. As mentioned above I have limited the analysis to those occupations for which one would expect a clear-cut income difference. Thus, the most common distinction I used is between manual workers on the one hand and white collar employees or officials on the other.[5] I have excluded occupational

---

was only 7 percent, and two Israeli surveys, one which shows a substantial overall deficit which suggests that something is unusual and one which excluded contributions to a compulsory loan from saving. But the most obvious omission clearly is the 1935–1936 *Survey of Consumer Purchases* which was used by Friedman for his occupational test. I have not used these data because the occupational grouping is not independent of the household's measured income. The survey included in the tabulation by occupation only those households whose income fell within the following limits:

White	Wage Earners	Clerical	Salaried Business and Professionals	Salaried Professionals
New York	$500–3999	$750–3999	$1250–10,000 up	$1250–10,000 up
Columbus	500–3999	750–4999	1250– 7,500 up	1250– 7,500 up
Atlanta	500–2999	750–2999	1250– 7,500 up	1250– 7,500 up
Negro				
New York	500–2999	750–2999	750– 2,999	750– 3,000 up
Columbus	250–1749	750–2999	250– 2,999	500– 2,999
Atlanta	0–1499	250–2250 up	250– 2,250	250– 2,250 up

(Bureau of Labor Statistics, *Bulletin #648, Family Expenditures in Selected Cities· 1935–1936*, Vol. 8, p. 4).

Since for some of the occupations there are open-ended income classes at the top of the income distribution, households with large positive transitory income are included for these occupations—but they are excluded for other occupations. And conversely, occupations with low income classes at the bottom of the income distribution included more households with negative transitory income than do other occupations. Hence, a comparison of the propensities to consume of these occupations has little validity. Just to see what would happen, I *did* run such a comparison and it shows the usual negative correlation between the income level and the percent of income consumed. The coefficient of ranked correlation was −1.0 for New York, −0.8 for Columbus, and −0.8 for Atlanta.

5. I have translated the German term "Beamte" as "officials." While this is not really an accurate translation, it is the closest I can get to the

groups such as "retired and unoccupied" and "armed forces and protective services" because for many households these groupings do not represent their permanent status. One important exclusion is self-employed households. In addition to the fact that the data for such households are particularly unreliable, they must be excluded because both the permanent income theory and the measured income theories assert that entrepreneurial households save more than nonentrepreneurial households. Finally, I have, in all but one case, left out farm worker households because of the problems created by non-money income. So much for the exclusions. The budget studies I used are listed at the end of this Appendix. A brief duplicated description of each of these budget studies is available upon request.

Definitions of Income and Consumption

I have generally subtracted taxes from both income and consumption. Granted that the tax figure given in the budget studies may, at times, include property taxes (thus creating a discrepancy in the treatment of renters and homeowners), after-tax income is generally a better determinant of consumption than before-tax income. In any case, subtracting taxes from both income and consumption has only a minor effect on the ratio of consumption to income.[6] When figures were available, I frequently subtracted union and professional association dues from income and consumption, since they represent a cost of earning income.[7] When possible, I included non-money income (such as home produced foods)

---

meaning of the German term. Since the American and British social structure differs from the German one, the word has no exact counterpart in English. Basically it covers a wide variety of occupations ranging from lower white collar jobs to executive jobs. Similar terms occur in other European languages and I have translated them, too, as "officials." The German term "Angestellte" and similar terms in other languages I have translated as "white collar employees."

6. There is, however, a minor difficulty here. If income taxes are based, not on this year's income, but on last year's income, then subtracting currently paid taxes lowers income disproportionately for those households whose income was higher in the previous year than in the current year. The alternative procedure of using before-tax income and consumption would not improve matters.

7. Insofar as unions and associations provide sickness and unemployment benefits or recreational benefits, union dues should not really be subtracted. But there is no way of separating union dues into these components. In general, I have not tried to follow exactly the same procedure in all budget studies, so that any errors introduced by using one method rather than another would affect only a limited number of studies. In any case, differences in the data provided in various budget studies would make complete consistency impossible.

in income, but excluded (when given) the costs of producing such income.

The main problem in the definition of consumption is the treatment of insurance. The estate-building component of life insurance should be included in saving, while that part of the premium which covers administrative costs is an element of consumption. The pure insurance component of the premium creates a more complex problem. In principle there are two ways of treating it. One is to treat the premium on a pure insurance policy as saving, and to treat the benefits received from such a policy not as income (and hence, saving) but as a transfer of assets. The alternative method is to treat the pure insurance premium as consumption and the receipt from the policy as income and saving. While this is the preferable method for many cases, it will not do for a comparison of the propensities to consume of households in different occupations. Since insurance is most likely to cover the main earner of the household, the receipt from insurance is likely to occur at the time when the household has lost its previous occupational affiliation. If insurance is counted as saving at that time, saving via pure insurance is not attributed to the right occupation. Most commonly, it would be attributed to the "retired" group.

I have therefore treated life insurance premiums wholly as saving despite the fact that this involves some inaccuracy, since that part of the premium corresponding to the insurer's administrative costs is consumption.[8] This treatment implies that receipts from life insurance policies should be excluded from income. But unfortunately budget studies generally list all insurance receipts as a single item. However, since I have excluded retired and unoccupied households from the data,[9] these insurance receipts listed in the budget study presumably represent, in large part, receipts from health and property types of insurance rather than life insurance, and so I have not subtracted them.

Several budget studies do not give expenditures on life insurance premiums per se, but list only expenditures on all types of insurance together. In these cases I included the whole insurance item in consumption. Fortunately, in cases where I did the calculations both ways,

8. In many of the European budget studies used here the insurance system is, in part, a component of the social security system, and it would be hard to compute the administrative loading factor, if any, included in the insured person's premium.

9. This still leaves some households who receive life insurance benefits and have a member in the labor force. But it seems likely that in many of the European studies, households whose head died during the survey year were excluded from the survey. To be sure, households whose head died prior to the survey year may receive life insurance installments during the survey year. They are included if the current household head is employed.

the treatment of insurance as either consumption or as saving usually made little difference.

Sources of Data Used

1. P. Cagan, *The Effect of Pension Plans on Aggregate Saving*, National Bureau of Economic Research, Occasional Paper #95, New York, 1965.
2. L. Klein, "Patterns of Savings: The Surveys of 1953 and 1954," *Bulletin*, Oxford Institute of Economics and Statistics, Vol. 17, May 1955, pp. 173–214.
3. ———, K. Straw, and P. Vandome, "Savings and Finances of the Upper Income Classes," *Bulletin*, Oxford Institute of Economics and Statistics, Vol. 18, November 1956, pp. 293–319.
4. H. F. Lydall, *British Incomes and Savings*, Oxford, Oxford University Press, 1955.
5. K. Yoshihara (Chief General Affairs Section, Bureau of Statistics), letter, Tokyo, February 7, 1964.
6. C. Zimmerman, *Incomes and Expenditures of Village and Town Families in Minnesota*, Univ. Minnesota Agric. Experiment Station, Bulletin No. 253, St. Paul, 1929.
7. Amsterdam, Bureau van Statistiek der Gemeente Amsterdam, Statistiche Mededeelingen No. 80, *Huishoudrekenigen van 212 Gezinnen uit Verschillen de Kringen der Bevolking*, Amsterdam, 1927.
8. Czechoslovakia, Zprávy, *Státniho Úradu Statistického Republiky Ceskoslovenské*, vol. 7, No. 112–117, 1926.
9. Denmark, Denmarks Statistik, "Hushholdningsregnskaber 1931," in *Statistiske Meddelelser*, ser. 4, vol. 100 No. 1, Copenhagen 1937.
10. ———, *Opsparing i Lønmodtagerhusstandene, 1955*, Statistiske Undersøgelser No. 3, Copenhagen, 1960.
11. ———, "Udgifter og Opsparing i Lønmodtagerhusstande," *Statistiske Efterretninger*, Dec. 1957, vol. 49, pp. 1129–47.
12. Finland, Sosialiministeriet "Perhetalouksien elinkustannukset vousina 1920–1921," *Sosiaaline Aikakauskirja*, vol. 18, 1924, pp. 800–816.
13. Israel, "Survey of Family Savings 1957–58," *Bank of Israel Bull.*, No. 10, Oct. 1959, pp. 17–41.
14. Japan, Office of the Prime Minister, *Annual Report on the Family Income and Expenditure Survey, 1960*, Tokyo, n.d.
15. Netherlands, Centraal Bureau voor de Statistiek, *Huishoudrekeningen van 598 Gezinnen*, Gravenhage, 1937.
16. Norway, Statistisk Sentralbyra, Norges Offisielle Statistikk *Forbruksundersøkelsen* 1958, vols. 1 and 2, Oslo, 1961 (mimeo.).

17. Oxford University Institute of Statistics, Card deck and related information from 1953–54 Incomes and Savings Survey.

18. Portugal, Instituto Nacional de Estatística, Estudos No. 30, *Inquérito ás condicões de viva da populãcao da cidade de Coimbra, 1953–54,* Lisbon, 1958.

19. ————, Estudos No. 35, *Inquérito ás condicões de viva da populãcao da cidade de Evora, 1955–56.* Lisbon, 1960.

20. ————, Estudos No. 37, *Inquérito ás condicõ es de viva da populãcao da cidade de Viseau, 1955–56,* Lisbon, 1960.

21. Sweden, Konjunkturinstitutet, Meddelanden Ser. B: 25, *Hushållens Sparande år 1955,* vol. 1, Stockholm, 1959.

22. ————, Meddelanden Ser. B: 31, *Hushållens Sparande år 1957.* Stockholm, 1963.

23. Sweden, Sveriges Officiella Statistik, Socialstyrelsen, *Levnadskostnaderna i Städer och Industriorter omkring år, 1923,* Stockholm, 1929.

24. Sweden, Sveriges Officiella Statistik, K. Socialstyrelsen, *Levnadsvillkor och Hushållsvanor i Städer och Industriorter, omkring år 1933,* Stockholm, 1938.

25. Switzerland, Department Federal de l'Economie Publique, *Budgets Familiaux de la Population Salarié, 1936–37 et 1937–38.* Suppl. No. 42, *Vie Economique.* Berne, 1942.

26. Switzerland, Schweizerisches Arbeitersekretariat, *Die Lebenshaltung schweizerischer Arbeiter und Angestellter vor dem Krieg.* Zurich, 1922.

27. Switzerland, Volkswirtschafts Department, "Budgets Familiaux de la Population Salariée année 1949," *La Vie Economique,* Feb. 1951, vol. 24, 49–62.

28. ————, "Budgets Familiaux de la Population Salariée année 1951," *La Vie Economique,* Sept. 1952, vol. 25, 388–402.

29. ————, "Budgets Familiaux de la Population Salariée année 1952," *La Vie Economique,* Oct. 1953, vol. 26, 380–94.

30. U.S. Board of Governors of the Federal Reserve System, "1951 Survey of Consumer Finances, Pt. IV," *Fed. Res. Bull.,* Sept. 1951, vol. 37, 1061–78.

31. U.S. Board of Governors of the Fed. Res. System, "1952 Survey of Consumer Finances," *Fed. Res. Bull.* Sept. 1952, vol. 38, 974–1001.

32. U.S. Bureau of Labor Statistics, *Consumer Expenditures and Income, Urban United States 1960–61,* BLS Rept. No. 237–38, Washington, D.C., 1964 and 1965, and Suppl. 2, Part A to BLS Report 237–38.

33. ———, *Survey of Consumer Expenditures,* BLS Reports 237–79 through 237–83, Washington, D.C., 1965.

34. University of Michigan, Survey Research Center, Card Deck from 1949 Survey of Consumer Finances.

35. University of Pennsylvania, Wharton School of Finances and Commerce, *Study of Consumer Expenditures, Incomes and Savings,* Vols. 1, 18. Philadelphia, 1956 and 1957.

36. Zürich, Statistisches Amt der Stadt Zürich, *Statistik der Stadt Zürich,* No. 28, Haushaltsrechnungen aus dem Jahre 1919, Zürich, 1921.

NOTES ON THE TEST WITH 5 YEAR BUDGETS

Description of Data

The Swiss data were gathered by the account book method; that is, households were asked to list their incomes and expenditures throughout the year in account books provided for this purpose.[1] Such a method is superior in one way to the method used in American surveys (a retrospective inquiry about expenditures during the previous year). Account book records are much more accurate than a respondent's memory. There is, of course, a countervailing disadvantage, the lack of representativeness. Households volunteering to keep account books are likely to be more careful in their expenditures than other households, and they also tend to have an above average income. Thus, in these data white collar employees are overrepresented relative to manual workers, and government employees were probably overrepresented as well. The survey excluded the self-employed as well as farm employees. Households with initially unemployed, or only partially employed, heads were excluded too, but those who experienced temporary unemployment during the survey year were not excluded. The data include non-money income, such as imputed rent, in both income and consumption. In selecting households for the survey there was some attempt to obtain families with fairly similar incomes and family circumstances. Table V-A shows the income distribution of the households, while Table V-B shows the correlations of their incomes in various years. The degree of

1. For descriptions of these data see Switzerland, Bundesamt für Industrie, Gewerbe und Arbeit, "Haushaltungsrechnungen von Familien unselbstständiger Erwerbender mit Zehnjähriger Buchführung, 1957–1966," *Die Volkswirtschaft*, 1968, No. 5; Eidgenössisches Volkswirtschafts-department, *Haushaltungsrechnungen von Familien unselbstständig Erwerbender, 1936/37 und 1937/38*, Supplement 42 to *Die Volkswirtschaft* (Bern, Verlag des Schweizerischen Handelsamtsblattes, 1942). The latter relates to a previous survey, but the methods described therein are the same as those used to derive the data employed here.

Table V-A

Distribution of Households by Income

Swiss Sample		German Sample	
Income, Final Year (Thousands of 1963 F.S.)	Number of Households	Income, Final Year (Thousands of 1950 D.M.)	Number of Households
11 & under 13	8	6 & under 7	10
13 & under 15	24	7 & under 8	6
15 & under 17	33	8 & under 9	15
17 & under 19	25	9 & under 10	8
19 & under 21	20	10 & under 11	9
21 & under 23	6	11 & under 12	3
23 & under 25	5	12 & under 13	0
25 & over	3	13 & over	3
Total	124		54

Table V-B

Correlation of Incomes in Various Years

Year	Number of Years Between Years Correlated			
	0	1	2	3
Initial Year		R^2		
1	.849	.755	.666	.584
2	.836	.731	.644	
3	.838	.759		
4	.825			

NOTE: Correlations were run without a constant term and R^2 is not corrected for degrees of freedom.

income stability it shows is in line with that given by Friedman for U.S. nonfarm households.[2]

The German data, too, were obtained from account books.[3] The sample was limited to middle income employees living in cities of 20,000 and over. Only four-person families with at least one of the children under 15 years old were included. Families whose consumption ex-

2. *A Theory of the Consumption Function, op. cit.,* p. 187.

3. For a more detailed discussion see the following publication from where this summary is taken: Hannelore Reddies, "Das Verfahren der laufenden Wirtschaftsrechnungen von 1950 bis 1964 und ab 1965," *Wirtschaft und Statistik,* August 1965, pp. 496–500.

penditures moved outside certain limits for any length of time were excluded from the survey.[4] Both income and consumption include imputed items, but since the imputed rent from owner-occupied homes was combined in the data with withdrawals of capital, I could not include the imputed rent in income, although it is included in consumption. Since there were probably few homeowners in the sample, this disparity creates little trouble.[5]

The Variables

I obtained my income measure by subtracting, from total family income, personal taxes as well as receipts from insurance policies which the data include in income.[6] Insurance receipts (which the U.S. Bureau of Labor Statistics classifies as "other money receipts" rather than as income) should not be treated as income. Receipts from life insurance policies are mainly a repayment of capital, and receipts from property insurance are not *net* income either, because they represent a replacement for destroyed capital.

Receipts from medical insurance are more of a problem. Following a "human capital" approach, they should generally be excluded from *net* income. On a less formal basis, there is a persuasive reason for excluding both medical and property insurance receipts from both income and consumption. Since they are receipts obtained to cover specific expenditures, the marginal propensity to consume such receipts is presumably greater than the marginal propensity to consume ordinary income.

I deducted insurance receipts from consumption as well as from income. This is admittedly an unusual procedure. There would be no justification for it if the insurance receipts are receipts from life insurance. But the small size of these receipts suggests that they are receipts from property and medical insurance rather than from life insurance. And if such receipts are excluded from income, they should also be excluded from consumption.[7] Essentially, what I am doing amounts to

4. Letter from Mrs. Reddies of the Statistisches Bundesamt. The limits rose over time to take account of generally rising incomes. In 1960 they were 420 DM-620 DM per month. *Ibid.*, p. 497.

5. I have no direct information on the number of homeowners in my sample. But among all the families surveyed—most of whom did not provide data for five years, and hence are not included in my sample—only about 10 percent were homeowners.

6. Because of data problems, I included motor vehicle license fees in personal taxes.

7. Parenthetically, it might be worth noting that since U.S. budget studies do not include these insurance receipts in income, but do include the corresponding expenditures in consumption, they are really not quite suited for testing consumption functions.

treating the household as a conduit receiving medical and property insurance payments and passing them on to sellers of corresponding services and property. This is of course what happens automatically under those medical insurance plans which make their payments directly to the hospital or physician. It might be worth stating that I decided upon my definitions of income and consumption before I ran any of the regressions, and that I did not experiment with any regressions based on different definitions.[8]

In computing the marginal propensities to consume and the income elasticities, except when explicitly stated otherwise, I included a family size variable in all the regressions. This family size variable, called "quets," is a measure which makes allowance for the ages and sex of family members.

All of the above refers to the 124 Swiss budgets. The 54 German budgets required different treatment. It is not possible to separate insurance receipts from pension receipts and so I included insurance receipts in income and consumption.[9] For obvious reasons I deflated both the Swiss and German data.[10]

8. I would be glad to make the Swiss data available to anyone who would like to experiment with different definitions. (For the German data permission from the Bundesamt would be required.)

9. I also had to include gifts received in income since they could not be separated from public relief. Union dues and the like I included in consumption and did not subtract them from income. Contributions to government health insurance, unemployment insurance, and Social Security I included in taxes, which of course were subtracted from income. These data required extensive processing since the raw data consisted of daily figures.

10. For the German data I used the price index for middle-income employees.

Swiss Budgets

Budget A. (Source: E. Hofmann, "Zwei Haushaltungsbudgets über einen Zwanzigjährigen Zeitraum," *Archiev für Soziale Gesetzgebung und Statistik,* Vol. 6, 1893, pp. 49–113.) This family, which was very thrifty, received income both from the husband's salary as a white collar worker in a business establishment and from the earnings of a retail store operated by the wife. The household accounts were kept sharply separated from the store accounts. At least for some time actual income was less than *expected* permanent receipts since the household expected large profits from the store and also a large inheritance—neither of which materialized. The household tried to live on its earned income and to save its interest receipts but could not do this every year. Some years medical expenses were high, and there were capital losses in several years. At the start of the budget the husband was 26 years old. One child was born during the first year and other children followed until 1876. During half the period it was a six-person family.

Budget B. (Source: Max Duttweiler, "Eine Zürcher Wirtschaftsrechnung von 1883–1910. *Zeitschrift für die Gesamte Staatswissenschaft,* Vol. 71, 1915, pp. 84–127.) This budget follows a family of a white collar employee from its formation to its end. The family was well off; when they lived in the country, though not when they lived in the city, they were among the most prominent people of their locality. At the age of marriage when the budget started, the husband was 32 years old; one child was born in 1884, the other in 1886. In 1907 one of the children contributed some of his earnings as compensation for his board and lodging. The family lived in Zürich until 1887, then until 1898 they lived in a small hamlet, and from then on in Zürich again. Expenditures were abnormally high in 1879–1899 due to the return to Zürich, and again starting in 1904–1905, due to educational expenditures for the son. They declined in 1907–1908, when these educational expenditures stopped and the son became partially self-supporting.

There are some peculiarities of the data. First, income does not include interest receipts. But since the household had no inherited assets, its interest receipts were presumably fairly small, and so I used this budget nonetheless. Receipts from the sale of personal property were included in income and, unfortunately, cannot be subtracted. I subtracted the total insurance item although some of it was property insurance. In 1908 the son repaid to the family money spent on his studies. I did not count this as income.

Budget C. (Source: Ernst Ackermann, "Einnahme und Ausgabsbewegung einer westschweizerischen Lehrerfamilie," *Schriften des Verein für Sozialpolitik,* Vol. 146, Pt. 1, 1917, pp. 127–197.) This budget of a teacher starts a few years after his marriage. There were two children born in the second and third year of the budget period, and in addition, the mother-in-law was part of the household in the early years. The budget includes an imputed item for rent on the owned home and I excluded inheritances from income. In 1893 the family moved to Western Switzerland.

Budget D. (Source: Ernst Ackermann, "Einnahme und Ausgabsbewegung eines ostschweizerischen Textilarbeiterhaushalt in 21 Jahren," *Schriften des Verein für Sozialpolitik,* Vol. 146, Pt. 1, 1917, pp. 1–60.) At the beginning of the budget the husband was 27 years old and was in the third year of marriage. The first child was two years old at the start of the budget and the second was born in the initial year. Other children were born subsequently, but two of the four children died. In the second year of the budget the husband changed jobs and the family moved. The husband built his own home in 1901, and the fact that expenditures for this purpose were treated as consumption presumably explains the great peak in consumption in that year. I included gifts received in income, and did not adjust income and consumption for a lodger since the amount received was minor.

German Budgets

Budget E. (Source: Richard Ehrenberg, "Aus Beamten Haushaltungen," *Tühnen-Archiev,* Vol. 2, 1907, pp. 316–346.) This is the budget of a higher official, who in addition to his regular salary was able to earn some outside income. There were four children, born in 1876, 1884, 1885, and 1893. The family moved frequently. It lived from 1876 to 1885 in a small town with low rents, but high other costs. The period 1885–1889 was spent in a suburb of Berlin, the years 1889–90 in a cheap small town. Then the family lived from 1890 to 1896 in a larger city with average living costs, and from 1896 on in a very expensive locality. The budget appears to include for some years imputed rent on an owned home. Taxes are given only as averages for several years. The same is true for insurance premiums, and since the source states that the insurance premiums declined regularly for the years 1891–1906 I estimated the yearly figures for this period on the assumption of an arithmetically declining trend. Unfortunately, the insurance figures given do not include all saving via insurance so that consumption is over-stated, at least in some years, but the sum involved appears to be quite minor.

Budget F. (Source: Erna Meyer-Pollack, "Der Haushalt eines höheren Beamten in den Jahren 1880–1906," *Schriften des Verein für Sozialpolitik,* Vol. 145, Pt. 4, 1915, pp. 1–92.) This budget of a judge used fiscal years starting in October. At the outset the family had been married for five years and had three sons. In 1882 two other children were born. In addition, an adult relative lived with the family since 1892, and from an earlier period the wife's father had lived with the family. In August 1888 the family moved to Berlin, a fact which raised rents and other costs. Unfortunately, the income figures include an expense account. The budget was influenced by a special factor—the husband was sickly, a fact which required major vacation trips. In 1900 his sickness, as well as expenses for the son, accounted for unusually high expenditures.

Budget G. (Source: Karl von K (Keller) "Wirtschaftsrechnungen," *Zeitschrift für die Gesammte Staatswissenschaft,* Vol. 62, #4, 1906, pp. 701–738; Karl von Keller *Wirtschaftsrechnungen.* Leipzig, Lindenau, privately printed, 1908.) This budget started after one year of marriage when the husband was 46 years old. The only child was born in 1896 and the mother-in-law lived with the family from 1895 to 1899. The husband was sickly, a fact which strongly influenced his career. He had to give up his job on an agricultural estate in 1896 and moved to a rural community. He changed jobs in 1899 but had to give up the new job in 1901, receiving three months' extra salary. He moved to a large city, became an insurance agent, took up a business career and obtained additional income by writing. However, because of sickness, he had to give up his job; he became a tutor, obtained casual employment as a bookkeeper, and also sold insurance.

Budget H. (Source: Karl Bittmann, *Arbeiterhaushaltungen und Teuerung.* Jena, Gustav Fisher, 1914.) This is a budget of a wood-worker starting two years after marriage. There are no children or other relatives. The income figure given includes only earnings and does not mention interest. I do not know whether this is due to the fact that this family received no interest at all, or if the interest earnings are simply not listed; in any case, if so, they are not likely to have been large.

Budget I. (Source: W. Neuling, "Die Wirtschaftsführung einer mittelbürgerlichen Familie in den Jahren 1949–1965," *Jahrbücher für Nationalökonomie und Statistik,* Vol. 181, April 1968, pp. 404–467.) This is the budget of a higher government official. The family had lost all its possessions during World War II, and in the early years its budget is dominated by the need to restore its stock of consumer capital. I therefore excluded the years prior to 1951, though the replacement demand for clothing continued after that time. I deflated the data by the price index for four-person worker families with middle incomes (*Statistisches Jahrbuch* 1964 and 1967), but Neuling claimed that this index understates the price rise actually experienced by this type of family. I made the following adjustments to the data. When the household received a separation allowance due to the husband having to work in a different city and thus maintain two households, I subtracted it (as well as a moving allowance, if received) from income. I excluded a capital gain included in income in one year. I subtracted a tax refund received on account of a dowry given to the daughter the previous year from the income of the year in which it was received, and I also eliminated an equivalent amount from consumption of the previous year. I also excluded from income premiums received for a saving contract and for a building contract since these items should not be considered income earned in any one year.[1]

French Budgets

Budgets J-T. These unpublished budgets I obtained through the courtesy of Mme. Perrot, who had used them in her study of the consumption function.[2] They all relate to middle class (bourgeois) households. I have no information on the individual households. Taxes are included in income and consumption and all insurance premiums are treated as consumption. Mortgage repayments create no problem since these families did not have mortgages outstanding.

U.S. Budgets

Budgets U and V. (Source: John M. Oskison, "Three Family Budgets," *The Mother's Magazine,* Vol. XI, 1916.) These two budgets come from a popular article describing how families can save, and both of them are accounts of high saving families. Little information on the households is given. The first family was headed by a bookkeeper 45

1. Through inadvertence, I omitted this budget in the test comparing permanent and transitory income changes. I subsequently added to the results of this test the one case from this budget in which income decreased permanently. All the other usable cases are cases of permanent income increases, and given the fact that my sample of these cases is already large, I did not take the trouble to add them.

2. *Le Mode de Vie des Familles Bourgeoises 1873–1953* (Paris, Librairies Armand Colin, 1961).

years old at the time of the survey; the second was that of a 52-year-old professional man. Life insurance premiums are combined with other insurance premiums, and so I deducted all insurance premiums from consumption. I did not subtract the item called "taxes, etc." from both income and consumption, since it probably consisted more of property taxes than of income taxes.

Budgets W and X. (Source: Ruth Deacon, "A Study of Expenditures of Nine Farm Families over a Period of Years," unpublished Ph.D. dissertation, Cornell, 1954.) I have used only two budgets out of the nine given here because the other households either had some farm income throughout the period or their records did not cover enough years.[3] Budget W also included a moderate amount of farm income, but only in the postwar years. In both cases I excluded the war years as not relevant.

Both households received income from professional services. Budget W starts with the year of marriage, while budget X starts later in life when the family was preparing for retirement and the husband was forty years old. Household W had two dependents at the beginning of the period and five at the end, while household X started with four dependents and ended with two.

Unfortunately, the data include mortgage repayments in consumption, a fact which is relevant for budget W and for the postwar years of budget X. Another potential problem is created by the fact that income was defined to include long term loans—although Professor Deacon believes that there were no such cases of long term loans in budgets W and X.[4]

3. Farm budgets are not very useful for this analysis because of the difficulty of distinguishing consumption from business expenses.

4. Private communication.

BUDGET A

SWISS FRANKS

Note: Income and consumption are not deflated.

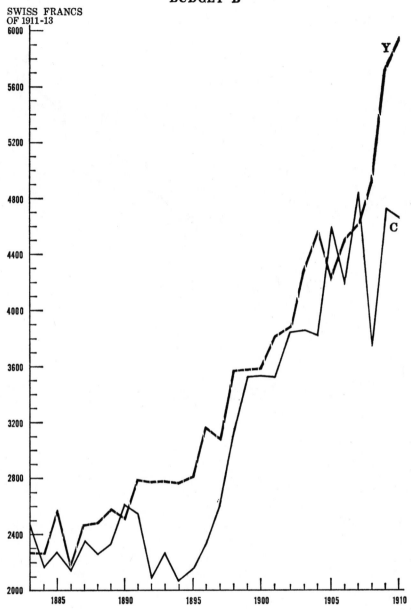

SWISS FRANCS
OF 1911-13

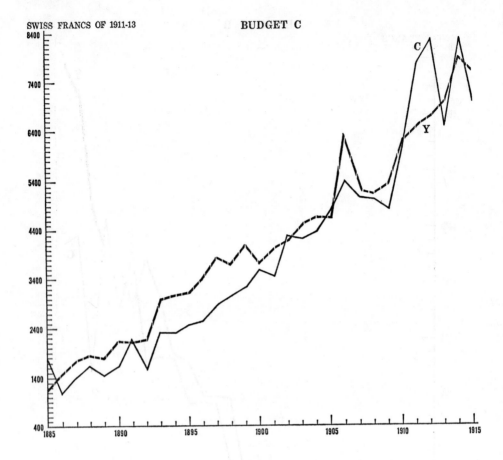

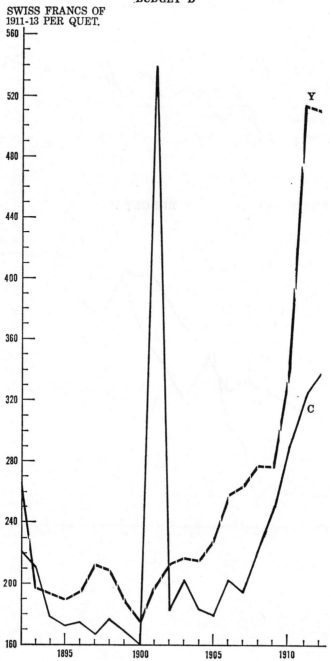

SWISS FRANCS OF
1911-13 PER QUET.

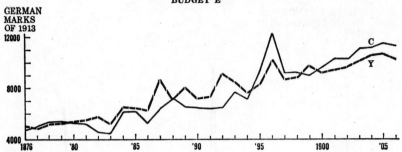

BUDGET E

GERMAN
MARKS
OF 1913

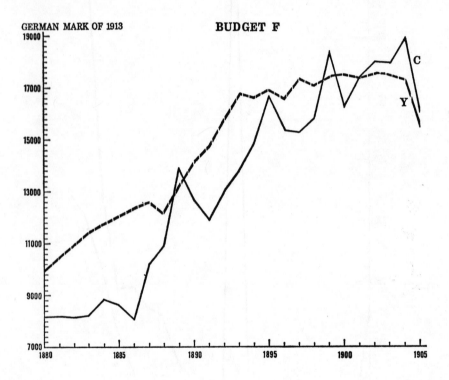

GERMAN MARK OF 1913

BUDGET F

BUDGET H

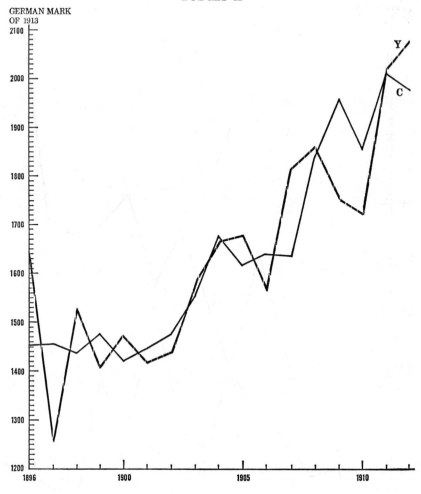

GERMAN MARK
OF 1913

BUDGET I

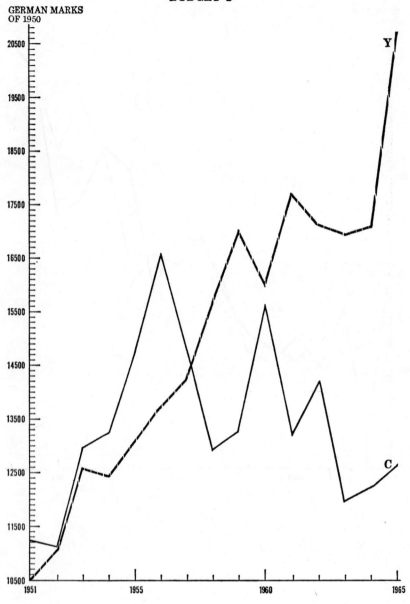

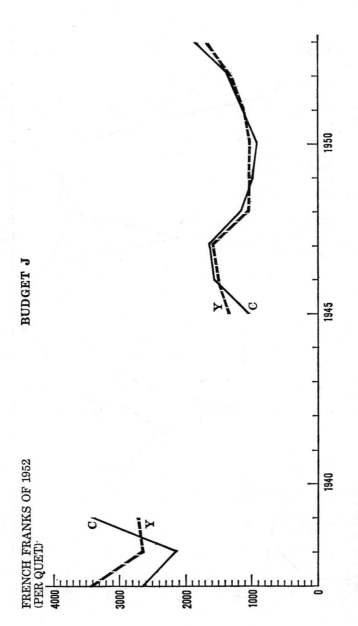

BUDGET J

FRENCH FRANKS OF 1952
(PER QUET):

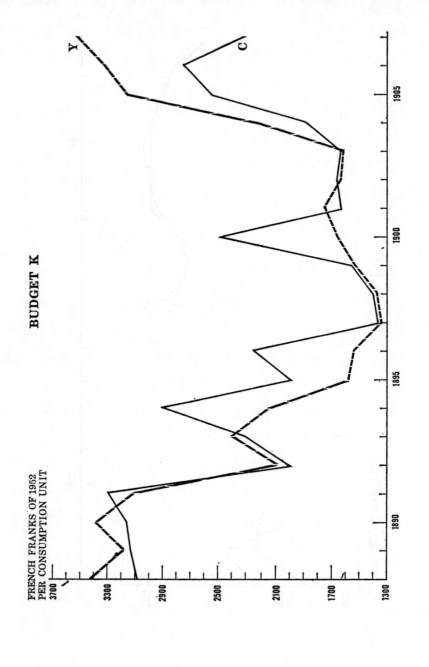

BUDGET K

FRENCH FRANKS OF 1952
PER CONSUMPTION UNIT

FRENCH FRANKS OF 1952
PER CONSUMPTION UNIT

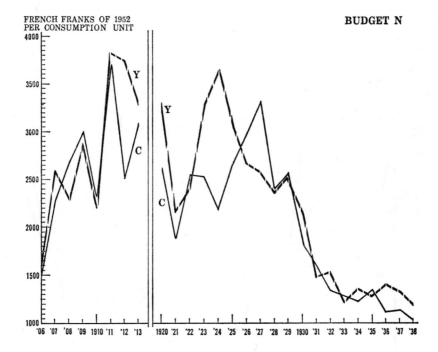

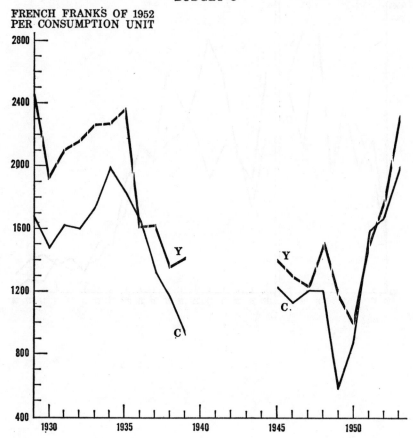

FRENCH FRANKS OF 1952
PER CONSUMPTION UNIT

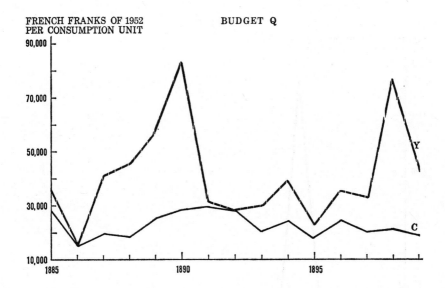

FRENCH FRANKS OF 1952
PER CONSUMPTION UNIT   BUDGET Q

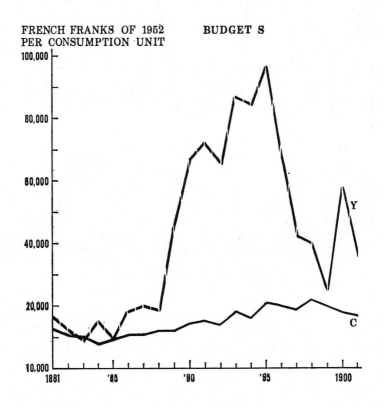

FRENCH FRANKS OF 1952   BUDGET S
PER CONSUMPTION UNIT

399

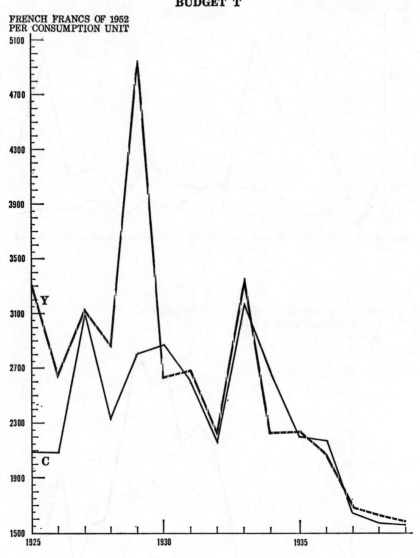

FRENCH FRANCS OF 1952
PER CONSUMPTION UNIT

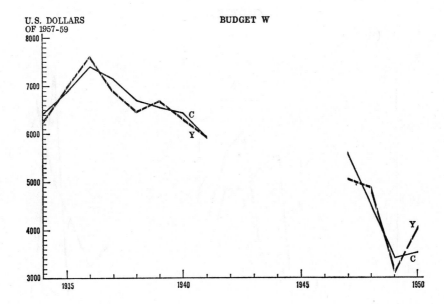

U.S. DOLLARS
OF 1957-59

BUDGET W

BUDGET X

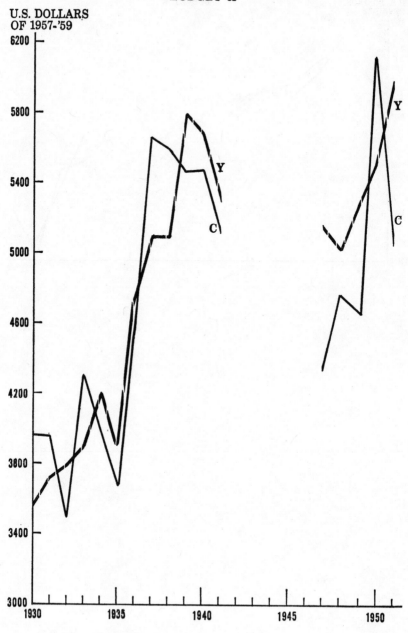

Index

Abnormal saving ratios, 154
Absolute Income Theory: defined, 19; and race, 69, 272–273; modified, 77; and NSLI dividend, 95; and Guthrie's test, 114; and mean income of groups, 118; and transitory income increase, 128; and Watt's test, 149; and Taubman's test, 158; and Holbrook's test, 161–163; and Liviatan's test, 184; and prediction tests, 222, 247, 248; and geographic tests, 285–286, 288–290, 293–296
Account books, 260n, 379
Accounting period, 184, 304–307
Ackley, G., 25, 266
Actual and estimated income elasticities, 81–87, 315–317
Adjustment period, 38, 170–171
Age: and consumption, 30–31, 174–179; and saving, 33, 52, 70, 176–177, 327; and Modigliani-Ando test, 110; as classification principle, 110, 114; Ramanathan's test, 115; as variable in regressions, 117, 160, 169, 173, 230; in distribution of net worth test, 172, 344–345; and income elasticity of consumption, 175; and equilibrium consumption, 179; and the occupational test, 267; and geographic test, 287, 290, 293
Aigner, D., 107n, 155–157, 184n, 354n
Albin, R., 98n
Anderson, C., 259n
Ando, A., 26, 27, 33, 96n, 109, 110, 111, 112, 113, 131n, 167n, 175, 185, 205, 217, 218, 227–230, 233, 244n, 245, 246, 259, 278n, 284n, 326, 335, 350, 351–352, 365
Annuities, 338
Arak, M. A., 36n, 132–133, 140
Arena, J., 33, 207n, 230–231, 352
Arithmetic variant, 37–38
Asia, 199, 322n

Asimakopulos, A., 113–114, 143
Aspiration effect, 169–170
Asset adjustment model, 173, 174n. *See also* Wealth
Assets, 167–174, 175–176, 227, 249. *See also* Wealth
Asymmetrical habit persistence theory, 331, 334
Atkinson, A. B., 51n
Austin, J., 112n
Australia, 231
Autocorrelation, 235–236, 241

Balanced growth path, 61
Ball, R., 43, 50, 200, 201, 226–227, 245, 320–321, 352
Bank failures, 242n
Barger, H., 235n
Barnes, C., 41n, 169, 179–180
Barten, A. P., 152
Becker, G., 213
Bendix, R., 259n
Bequest motive, 28, 29, 31, 32, 350
Bequests: and definitions of consumption, 14; in Modigliani-Ando model, 29; and windfalls test, 96; and non-income receipts, 153–154; and net worth tests, 173n, 338
Beta coefficient, 79–80, 238, 239, 363
Betancourt, R., 195n
Bhatia, K. B., 207
Bias in deriving consumption data, 124n, 153, 158, 185, 302
Binomial test, 261n, 293
Bird, R., 95, 102
Black households, 68–70, 272–282
Bodkin, R., 93, 94, 95, 96, 98, 99, 102n
Bonin, J., 139, 140, 352, 353n
Bonus, 148–149
Brady, D., 24, 48, 174, 272–273, 283
Brake effect, 108n, 167
Branson, W. H., 229–230, 243n, 245
Bristol, R., 67n